PARTIES
AND THE
GOVERNMENTAL
SYSTEM

A Book of Readings

PARTIES AND THE GOVERNMENTAL SYSTEM

A Book of Readings

GAROLD W. THUMM
Bates College

EDWARD G. JANOSIK
University of Pennsylvania

Prentice-Hall, Inc., Englewood Cliffs, New Jersey

PARTIES
AND THE
GOVERNMENTAL
SYSTEM

Printed in the United States of America

Library of Congress Catalog Card Number: 67-17409

PRENTICE-HALL INTERNATIONAL, INC., London
PRENTICE-HALL OF AUSTRALIA, PTY. LTD., Sydney
PRENTICE-HALL OF CANADA, LTD., Toronto
PRENTICE-HALL OF INDIA PRIVATE LTD., New Delhi
PRENTICE-HALL OF JAPAN, INC., Tokyo

To Our Parents

Preface

As editors of this book of readings, we designed it for use in our own courses in political parties. We included in it those articles in scholarly journals and excerpts from books that we should like our own students to read. We chose materials utilizing a variety of approaches to the study of political parties; each approach makes its own contribution.

We believe the goal of courses in political parties is to cultivate the student's understanding and appreciation of them as institutions of democratic government. In order to include materials which would aid the student in developing a conceptual framework, we were often forced to omit articles we found interesting and informative, but which contributed less to his theoretical development. Furthermore, we think the student can appreciate the nature of political parties only as he distinguishes their functions from those of other institutions of their environment. We have therefore devoted some space to considerations of aspects of democratic systems other than our own.

In order to include as many selections as possible, we have rigidly limited our own writing. We assume that those using the volume will, if possible, use it as it was intended to be used: in conjunction with a standard text or integrated set of extended readings, and accompanied by lectures providing explanation and continuity. We have therefore not attempted to present such materials in our introductory sections. As an additional space-saving device, footnotes have been omitted.

We appreciate the assistance of all those who helped with this effort. Our thanks go especially to Professor Frank J. Sorauf of the University of Minnesota, who gave us valuable advice on the organization and selection of materials, and to Dr. Joan Gotwals of the University of Pennsylvania Libraries, for providing facilities that greatly aided our work.

G. W. THUMM
E. G. JANOSIK

Contents

PART TWO

POLITICAL PARTIES: ORGANIZATION
AND COMPOSITION

American Political Parties: General

American Political Parties: State and Local

American Political Parties: National

Politicians

PART THREE

POLITICAL PARTIES AND THE ELECTORATE

The Electorate

Electoral Parties

Voting Behavior

PART FOUR

POLITICAL PARTIES AS ELECTORAL ORGANIZATIONS

PART FIVE

PARTY AND GOVERNMENTAL POWER

Party in the Legislative Process

Party and Ideology

PART SIX

THE FUTURE OF AMERICAN PARTIES

PARTIES
AND THE
GOVERNMENTAL
SYSTEM
A Book of Readings

PART ONE

Parties
and
Party Systems

What is a political party? In answering that question, the student might define "party" *descriptively*; he would speak in terms of organization and structure. More scientifically, he would probably define it *functionally*; he would speak rather of the role of the party in political society. A party is thus an organism that performs certain functions; conversely, whatever organism performs those functions is a party.

His question then becomes: What is it which warrants defining the agency which does it as a political party? While there are many ways of stating the answer to that question, there is broad agreement as to what the answer should include. In one way or another, parties do three things: 1) They provide the electorate with alternatives—alternatives in personnel for filling public offices, alternatives in programs of public policy. In doing this they consolidate and eliminate myriads of possible choices so that the voter's choice can be determinative. 2) They serve as agencies of restraint by providing opposition to and criticism of actions proposed or taken by government. 3) They organize controversy. They awaken the interest of the citizen in public affairs, educate him regarding the merits of candidates and issues, and generally contribute to his political socialization.

In their differing treatments of party functions, Sir Ernest Barker and Samuel J. Eldersveld demonstrate the similarity of democratic parties. Sigmund Neumann points out that in at least some respects even dictatorial parties perform functions identical to those of democratic ones. While Robert K. Merton stresses the role of the organization or its "boss," he speaks of *party* organization, and the function is still that of the party.

Probably no topic is more vital to a theory of political parties or to the incorporation of political parties into a systematic theory of politics than the ecology of political parties. What factors are conducive to the development of specific party systems? David B. Truman discusses the impact of federalism on a party system; by comparing the Canadian and Australian experience with that of the United States he found that, while federalism does produce a tendency to decentralized parties, other factors have played a major role in determining the character of American parties. James MacGregor Burns turns to the separation of powers that he found displayed in a "four-party system" requiring a president to engage in coalition politics rather than to rely on a disciplined majority party. Turning to the local level, J. Leiper Freeman sees local party systems interrelated with, rather than integrated into national and state systems.

To operate the American party system successfully, both major parties must be flexible and pragmatic in their programs and avoid sacrificing a chance for victory in order to maintain abstract principle. Voters move more readily from a group coalition supporting one party to the other when there are no ideological obstacles to their movement.

Political Parties:
Nature and
Functions

1. REFLECTIONS ON THE PARTY SYSTEM

Sir Ernest Barker

We may ... define a party as a social formation which has two distinct but complementary functions—first that of serving as a *social reservoir* for the collection of a set of connected political ideas from the area of society; and secondly that of serving as a *political conduit* by which the ideas so collected flow from their social reservoir into the system of the State and turn the wheels of political machinery in that system. So conceived, party per-

From Sir Ernest Barker, "Reflections on the Party System," *Political Parties and the Party System in Britain,* ed., Sydney D. Bailey (New York: Frederick A. Praeger, Inc., 1952), pp. 194-201, excerpts. By permission of The Hansard Society for Parliamentary Government.

forms the service of enabling society to run into the State, and thus of keeping the action of the State constantly and wholesomely responsive to the play of social thought. . . .

What has just been said may lead us to reflect that our system of government, as it stands today, is a system of four factors—party, the electorate, Parliament, and cabinet. What is the relative strength of these factors, and what balance, if we can properly speak of balance, should be expected among them? It has often seemed to the writer that this system of four factors involves the reconciliation of two different and conflicting necessities. One necessity is that each of the factors should think highly of itself and its duty, and act as if everything hung on itself and upon its own decision. That is a condition of efficiency; but it may also lead, if it is not checked, to self-sufficiency and arrogance. The other necessity is that each factor should keep in touch and harmony with the rest, acknowledging that they too have the right and duty to do their work and to be left free to do it effectively. This latter is the sovereign necessity; but the first necessity is only too apt to make itself particularly felt. The electorate, feeling its own importance, may claim to impose an "imperative mandate"; Parliament, with a collective pride, may seek to institute a system of parliamentary autocracy for the duration of its term, installing and evicting cabinets at will; a cabinet may attempt to vindicate sovereignty for itself, and may use its majority and its Whips to drill and discipline Parliament; or finally, and this is a danger which in the contemporary world is particularly apparent, a victorious party or combination of parties may claim the last word for a party caucus and for its manipulating managers. But a just and proper system of parliamentary democracy depends not only on a general spirit of give and take in the minds of the people at large: it also depends on a similar spirit, a spirit of balance and accommodation, among the four factors by and through which it works—party, electorate, Parliament, and cabinet; and the greater the ardor of each factor, the more difficult it is to secure such a spirit.

The exaggeration of party is a matter which is closely connected with the number of parties in a country. Here there are three possibilities. One is the system of a single party, which the Communist states of Eastern Europe regard as the basis of a true or popular democracy, based upon the people and acting for the people. Another is the system of multiple parties, common in a number of the states of Western Europe; a system which has, or may claim to have, the advantage of producing a true reflection of the varied currents of social thought, but which has also the disadvantage of making government uneasy and dependent on fluctuating combinations between a number of different parties. A third is the system of two parties, or at any rate two main parties, which is the system generally followed in Anglo-Saxon countries. It may be said that both of the two first possibilities are favorable to the exaggeration of party. A single party prevents that discussion, and that choice, between political alternatives which is a necessary condition of a free electorate: it establishes the open tyranny of one party, whether of the Right or Left. A system of multiple parties may seem to give a large possibility of choice to the electorate; but its ultimate effect may be the secret tyranny of a cabal which unites the leaders of several parties in an interested coalition and controls behind the scenes both the representative body and the nominal government. Nor is that all. If a system of multiple parties is accompanied, as it often is, by the device of proportional representation, it accentuates the ardor of each party, and stimulates all to press for their full pound of flesh and to urge their claims to the uttermost. The third possibility—that of a system of two parties, or at any rate two main parties—also has its defect. It reduces the choice of the electorate to no more than two alternatives: it eliminates shades and nuances, and substitutes in their place two gross averages of opinion: It may even be said to reduce the level of politics to that of football or baseball, with two contending sides each madly cheered and supported by its different partisans. Can a nation ever be one when it splits itself into two?

But whatever may be urged against the system of two parties, there is much to be said in its favor. Life, after all, is largely a matter of choice between two alternatives: there are generally two rival schools in philosophy, two rival views of painting, two rival opinions about music; and why should there not also be two rival views of politics? We have also to reflect that a system of two rival political parties is far from meaning that every voter is attached to one or the other: it leaves room for the floating or unattached voter, who may now give his vote to one and now to another of the two, and can thus bring about those changes and alterations of government which are as valuable and refreshing as changes of the weather. In this respect the system of two parties is more conducive to freedom and change than either of the other systems; for a single party seeks permanently to ensure a total vote for its policy from the whole of the population, and a system of multiple parties tends to enlist every citizen in a permanent and unwavering allegiance to his particular party. In a word, the system of two parties leaves room for a margin of imprecision, or an area of incalculability, which is a safety-valve in the working of a democratic State. . . .

There is a sovereign merit still to be mentioned which belongs to the system of two parties. Each party or side, within itself, is permeated by a force of attraction; but each, in its relation to the other, is equally marked by a force of repulsion. The term Her Majesty's Opposition is one of the most significant and important in British politics. It signifies that a single nation, one in a common allegiance to a common way of life symoblized by its Queen, is none the less also two—two as well as one, and two at the same time that it is one. Her Majesty has her actual advisers, who form the anticabinet. The existence of such an anticabinet, or organized opposition to the acting cabinet, is the salt of the British system of parliamentary democracy. It supplies the constant criticism which is as necessary as constructive creation. It fans the flame of discussion and keeps it bright and clear. It gives the possibility of an alternative government—an actual possibility, actually present and visible—to which the nation can look if it feels the need for a new hand at the helm. The general development of Her Majesty's Opposition, and the general recognition of its function (a recognition which has gone to the length of the parliamentary provision of a salary for its leader), are the clearest signs of the health of the British system of government. But this development, and this recognition, are connected with, and are the results of, the growing tendency towards a clear two-party system. An organized and coherent opposition is only possible under such a system; and an organized and coherent opposition is a necessary condition of healthy democratic discussion and of a proper balance of all the factors and organs of democracy.

Apart from the question of their number, another matter which affects the character of parties is the nature of their composition. Ideally, the cleavage between parties should be vertical, and not horizontal: in other words, party divisions should not follow the strata of class or religious differentiation, but should rather cut down deep through those strata and leave on either side of the cleavage a similar cross section of the nation. Each party will then seek, or at any rate tend, to represent a general view of the national interest, and neither will be committed to a single interest. It may seem, a priori, that a single party will include all interests; but in actual practice the single parties of the present century have been based on the interest of a class (the Fascist on the middle or lower middle class, and the Communist on the proletariat or "toiling masses"), and they have sought to adjust the whole community to the pattern of this particular interest. A system of multiple parties obviously tends to the representation of particular classes or sects; it splits the community not only into Left and Right, but also into different classes, different confessions, and different particular interests. Even a system of two parties may be a system of "two nations," and may split the community into a party of the poor, or the comparatively poor, and a party of the well-to-do. This is not actually the case in Britain, and it need never be the case. The Conservative Party is an all-class party, though more in the composition of its voting mass than in that of its parliamentary representatives, and the Labor Party, though based in the main on the industrial masses, is also a party including members of the professions and other sections of the nation: indeed it is to the interest of both parties, as well as to that of the nation, that they should spread a wide net, for the wider it is, the more their appeal and the greater the number of votes which they are likely to gain. At the same time it must be admitted that the electoral map of Britain, when it registers the result of a general election, has one alarming feature: it shows a clustering of Labor in densely packed areas of urban industry, and a dispersion of the other side over the great rural space of the country. We seem to be drifting into a state of division between the town and the country mouse; and there is peril in that division.

Another question suggested to the mind by any reflection on party systems is the question of the place of doctrine in the life and action of parties. Should a party elaborate a body of doctrine, expressed in a program, and should it seek to make its doctrine a fixed and permanent casing which encompasses and may cramp its life? Or should it rather be wedded to flexibility, and to ideas of progress and evolution; and should it accordingly abjure the expression of a creed, and be content to represent a general tendency and mental temper, with no precise definition in set terms and hard formulations? The question is one which vexes religious confessions as well as political parties; and in both cases there is more to be said for flexibility and evolution than for permanent expressions of doctrine and rigid sets of principle. A single party has a single doctrine or *Weltanschauung*, a single "general line" which all are expected to toe; a system of multiple parties, different as it may seem, may equally be a system of many hard-set doctrines, which harden themselves still more in their opposition and clash. It may be claimed as a merit for a two-party system that a party, seeking to increase the width of its appeal, progressively widens its scope and seeks to transcend old limitations and formulations. But it may also be said to be a demerit of such a system that a party seeks to deny or discredit the progress of the other, and attempts to limit and judge it by some form, or supposed form, of its past, so that the Conservative is condemned to be now what he was, or is supposed to have been, half a century ago, and the Labor candidate is equally condemned as still guilty of his past and outgrown extravagances, and as untaught and untrained by later experience. The chief enemy to the development of the temper and tendency of either party, under a system of two parties, is the refusal of the other party to acknowledge any development. On the other hand, when all is said that can be said in favor of development, the fact remains that there must be something of a hard inner core of steady principle in any party.

2. TOWARD A COMPARATIVE STUDY OF POLITICAL PARTIES

Sigmund Neumann

Functions of Political Parties Democratic and Dictatorial

It has often been stated that the primary task of political parties is to organize the chaotic public will. "They bring order out of the chaos of a multitude of voters" (Lord Bryce). They are brokers of ideas, constantly clarifying, systematizing, and expounding the party's doctrine. They are representatives of social interest groups, bridging the distance between the individual and the great community. They maximize the voter's education in the competitive scheme of at least a two-party system and sharpen his free choice. The coexistence of a competitor, therefore, is paramount to an effective democratic party system which presupposes that the final compromise will reflect the reasonable decision of a free electorate.

In fact, the basic assumption of democracy is the inevitability of differing views and the free operation of conflicting opinions. "The true democrat has a suspicion that he may not always be right," as W. Ivor Jennings remarked. Thus the opposition becomes the most important part of the parliament; its members are "critics by profession." It is not enough that Her Majesty's Opposition be highly respected by the ruling majority, but often its fruitful ideas are accepted—and, indeed, this is a wise course for the party in power to follow if it wants to remain there. Its political alternative represents not only the looming "Shadow Cabinet" but also an active participant in actual control.

The open forum of parliament becomes the clearinghouse for the policies that a state should follow. The political parties are the proper engine of such continuous plebiscite. They make the voters choose at least the lesser of two evils, thus forcing political differentiations into a few major channels. Yet important as such machinery of political concentration may be, the political services of the parties do not stop at that. What is even more essential, parties transform the private citizen himself. They make him a *zoon politikon*; they integrate him into the group.

From Sigmund Neumann, "Toward a Comparative Study of Political Parties," Reprinted from *Modern Political Parties*, ed., Sigmund Neumann, 396-416, excerpts. By permission of the University of Chicago Press. Copyrights 1956 by the University of Chicago. All rights reserved. Copyright under the International Copyright Union, 1956.

Every party has to present to the individual voter and to his powerful special-interest groups a picture of the community as an entity. It must constantly remind the citizen of this collective whole, adjust his wants to the needs of the community, and, if necessary, even ask sacrifices from him in the name of the community. Nor can even the so-called "class parties," which call upon only a specific part of the population, renounce this essential function. The outstanding example of such a class program, the *Communist Manifesto*, justifies its position with the claim that the united proletariat will represent the overwhelming majority and that its dictatorship will lead to a dissolution of all classes and therewith to the liberation of society as a whole. This second function differentiates the political party from a pressure group. Its specific interests must be fitted into the framework of the national collective. Wherever the policy-making parties do not succeed in this primary task, the modern state is in danger of deteriorating into a neofeudalism of powerful interest groups.

If the party in a democracy fulfils these two first functions of organizing the chaotic public will and educating the private citizen to political responsibility, then it can also lay claim to a third duty: to *represent the connecting link between government and public opinion*. Since democracies are pyramids built from below, the connection between leaders and followers becomes a necessity in the two-way traffic of democracy. It is the major function of the party to keep these lines of communication open and clear. Such a task makes the parties, if not the rulers, at least the controlling agencies of government in a representative democracy.

This crucial position is even more emphasized by the fourth function of a democratic party: *the selection of leaders*. Here as everywhere in a democracy, it is the competitive scheme, the choice between at least two oligarchies, which guarantees the quality of its leadership. Of course, such a selection presupposes an enlightened public, one qualified to make the right choice, and an intellectual climate appropriate to the functioning of democratic parties. Wherever these preconditions no longer prevail, the crisis of democracy is in the offing.

The crisis elements of democratic parties can be well perceived in the rise of dictatorial movements. In fact, dictatorial organizations often grow up within the democratic party system itself. They constitute a state within the state, alienated from its basic principles. And yet their rise is the expression of a basic lack within the society. . . . From now on, the argument between parties concerns fundamentals and a fight over ultimate issues. For these integrated political groups compromise becomes increasingly difficult, and so does any coalition with another party.

The main purpose of the fully developed totalitarian parties becomes the fight for a new political order, for a new society. Speaking a different language and living according to a different set of values, the partisans have to be segregated from the political and social body of the ruling class and society, so the party leaders decree. Otherwise the partisans may be enchanted and taken in by the old order, the destruction of which is the essential purpose of the "guarantors" of the new morrow.

With the rise of the dictatorial party, its competitors in politics necessarily become more inflexible too. Struggle assumes the quality of a religious war; the only possible outcome for any contestant seems to be overwhelming victory or ultimate annihilation. Such a situation explains the revolutionary functions of a dictatorial party before its seizure of power: it is, above all, the *revolutionary vanguard* of the future state.

The functions of the dictatorial parties in power, outwardly at least, do not appear to be different from the four features of their democratic counterparts. . . . Yet as their concepts of leaders and followers differ diametrically from democratic ideas, the meaning of these functions changes fundamentally. Organization of the chaotic will is fulfilled by a "monolithic control"; integration of the individual means "enforcement of conformity"; and, though these tasks are often directed by a "Ministry of Education and Enlightenment," the maintenance of communication between state and society is assured by a mere one-way propaganda stream from above. True, dictatorships also have to concern themselves with "public opinion." They must listen to the "voice of the people," especially since this is muted under the tyrant's rule. Thus the party serves through its secret agencies as a necessary listening post. Through such diverse services this leviathan apparatus, which claims at the outset to be the party to end all parties, becomes in fact the key instrument of modern totalitarianism.

All three functions, if successfully administered, secure the fourth and crucial purpose: the selection of leaders. Yet it is especially on this level of the creation, preservation, and extension of the ruling elite that the basic differences between the party systems become obvious.

Lenin's fight at the turn of the century for a small centralized revolutionary elite, as opposed to the Mensheviks' idea of a loose democratic mass

organization, laid the foundation for a disciplined castelike order. He thus anticipated what revolutionary parties experienced a generation later when they had to choose between thoroughly revolutionist cadres and a mass following.

Only in a "revolutionary situation" —i.e., when complete victory or the prospect of impending success brings a rush of adherents to the revolutionary cause—is it possible for such a radical party to win and to hold the masses. Revolutionary parties reckoning with a long struggle can count on only a small elite of unrelenting fighters who do not care for rewards today and who are ready to make the revolution their life's calling. Masses are in need of visible rewards. If they cannot reap the fruits now—or at least have reasonable expectation of doing so in the near future— they will leave the ranks. . . .

Toward a Classification of Parties

Since political parties are mainly concerned with the control of governmental power, the most obvious differentiation would be to distinguish the *in-group* from the *out-group*. Indeed, such a classification may point at some fundamental traits of political strategy and emphasize the advantage of a two-party system for clear-cut confrontation. It would divide the "haves" and the "have-nots" in politics. Thus the insider at the controls would be often identified with the status quo, the conservative tendencies, while the challenging outsider would usually be the party of change and reform.

One may even go further and recognize in these two opposing camps a classification which has been frequently applied by Continental writers as the possessor's *party of patronage* versus the defiant's *party of principles* and thereby indicate the danger points of the two parties: the corruption of the "ins" by power and the irresponsible dogmatism of the "outs."

In a wider comparative approach, the degree of proximity to power may also explain interesting variations in national party systems. Wherever parties are called upon for political decision-making, as in the Anglo-American democracies, they may well emphasize the day-by-day *expediency interests*. On the other hand, in nations where the parties have played only a subordinate role or where they are purposely kept from political key positions by the government, as was the case during the greater part of German history, parties may easily retreat to the fundamental principles of an all-inclusive "faith movement" (*Weltanschauungs-* or *Glaubens-Parteien*).

These different national positions may also suggest a division of parties of *platform* and of *program*. One may, however, observe that such a strict cleavage has become less significant in recent decades. The more the German parties have been drawn into responsible politics, especially in the contemporary attempt at a democratic government, the more they are forced to make daily decisions along lines of concrete interests. Contrariwise, the Western democracies have been increasingly confronted with fundamental issues of international reorientation, national planning, and individual soul-searching —all of which demand a basic ideological outlook. This interesting *rapprochement* of seemingly contradictory systems will have far-reaching consequences and deserves our most careful consideration. At this point we must mention that the traditional lines of demarcation between the parties of expedient interests and those of fundamental principles have been blurred.

In the light of these developments another classification is losing its sharp contours, the suggestive division of *parties of personages versus parties of programs*. Although this dichotomy has reappeared today, but in a different version, in the contrast between dictatorial and democratic rule, between personal and institutional government —parties of personages are of the past.

.   .   .

The reality of modern politics represents a much more complex picture than is suggested by the simple array of insiders and outsiders, of parties of patronage and parties of principles, of expediency interests and *Weltanschauung*, of personages and programs. Such precise but utterly imaginary partitions fail to reveal the inner dynamics and tensions of a functioning democracy. In fact, it is the inexhaustible mixture of all these elements that comprises the life of modern political parties—and perhaps escapes any rigid classification.

A more modest attempt at systematization simply follows the number of contestants in the political field and speaks of one-, two-, or multiparty systems. But some important facts of political organization and control can be derived from such a classification.

A careful analysis of the causes and consequences of the two-party system versus the multiparty regime must probe into the historical circumstances, social structures, and institutional arrangements which underlie the divergent national political settings. While it is generally agreed that a two-party rule promises greater efficiency for the democratic process, as the British and American cases prove, it is equally obvious that such a political setting cannot be easily transplanted into national communities which do not meet its preconditions and which therefore, by no mere oversight or accident, possess a different political organization.

Historical precedents may suggest the following favorable circumstances for a two-party development: social homogeneity, political continuity, an early sanction of responsible political parties striving for political control, and their orientation at one elective office (the United States presidency, the British premiership) as the desired prize.

Wherever fundamental cleavages in social structure evolve and continue to exist because of differences in nationalities, regions, religion, or class which are often fostered by outside influences like *irredenta* movements and revolutionary internationals; wherever political revolutions coincide with great social transformations, as in France, central and Eastern Europe, and the Near and Far East; wherever a controlling elite, through the divide-and -rule device, prevents parties from fulfilling their genuinely political functions of presenting clear-cut policy alternatives, as in Bismarck's strategies, for example; wherever the political machinery of a state diffuses the electorate's division by numerous choices —wherever any or all of these complicating factors enter the national political scene, a multiparty system finds its *raison d'être*. Obviously, it reflects in its more numerous groupings a fuller and more exacting picture of the peculiar features of a stratified society than a two-party system could ever present.

Once established, these different party systems have far-reaching consequences for the voting process and even more so for governmental decision-making. So far as elections go, in a two-party system both contenders will naturally compete for the shifting voter in the middle. Politics, therefore, will gravitate toward the center and the free-floating electoral bloc which is decisive for the winning or holding of a majority. The spectacle of a programmatic rapprochement, despite heated electoral campaigns, of the two main parties is not simply a trick of conniving politicians but a natural outcome of a party system that reflects a relatively stable order.

The double party has been called "a convenient system for contented peoples" who are agreed upon the general principles of the constitution and the policies of the government and feel not too intensely about measures over which they disagree. The fundamental cleavage over the slave issue broke for a time the efficacy of the American two-party system. The double party structure of modern England presupposed the reconciliation of the British Tories with the House of Hanover. Once the Glorious Revolution with its political institutions was recognized, they in turn could absorb the shock and major changes of the following social revolutions within their unchallenged political framework. Thus the miracle of British democracy in its combination of stability and progress was guaranteed. Once effectively established as a political institution, the two-party system reinforces and often perpetuates the trend toward conformity.

A multiparty system does not possess this unifying and centralizing order. On the contrary, yielding to its inability to produce a majority party in elections, its factions concentrate on the centrifugal forces of special-interest groups and may easily be directed at peripheral forces. Such diffusion of power, often emphasized by special electoral systems such as proportional representation (putting at high premium the true mirroring of all shades of public opinion), does not hold great promise for effective policy formation.

Policy-making in a two-party system is no doubt facilitated by its certain majorities and consequently its unmistakable party responsibilities. Yet even within the frame of the two major parties, a hidden multiparty system may often be detected with intra-party splits and factions or third parties, which may at times affect the crucial balance and enforce a break, new combinations, or compromises at the political front. In these critical moments the direct mandate of the people may be blurred by the parliamentary struggle for majorities until the voice of the electorate can be heard again.

What is exceptional in a two-party setting, however, becomes the rule under the procedures of a pluriparty system. By its very nature, it must transfer crucial decisions from a much-divided electorate to the parliament. This representative body in turn must content itself with a government by the formation of a coalition, attaining, after extended bickering, the compromise which in the two-party system is largely the voter's business to achieve within this own mind and political wisdom.

Even such a sketchy outline makes it obvious how much the character and policies of parties are defined by this formal division between two-party and multiparty systems. A classification along this line, therefore, proves to be quite suggestive and essential.

The differences are even more fundamental in the comparison of the one-party rule with the two-party and multiparty organizations. The character of the totalitarian rule indicates that a one-party system is a contradiction in terms. For clarity's sake it might be better to assign to this important contemporary phenomenon a different name, such as "political order." Modern usage, however, has coined the concept of the one-party state, and, if only for reasons of propagandistic appeal, the terminology has been accepted on the daily political fronts, both national and international. This being the case, one might recognize in the opposition of the one party versus the two and multiparties the fundamental cleavage of our time: *dictatorship versus democracy*. Along this dividing line all basic tenets of modern parties must be redefined: their structure and strategy, their leadership, their apparatus, their following, their techniques of mass communication, their national policies, and their international ties. Through the organization and practices of these contrasting party systems, in turn, the two great contenders over political control in our society stand fully revealed. The essence of democratic and dictatorial rule is embodied in the daily life of their parties. . . .

Modern parties have steadily enlarged their scope and power within the political community and have consequently changed their own functions and character. In place of a *party of individual representation*, our contemporary society increasingly shows a *party of social integration*.

This shift must be seen within the context of our changing society and its underlying philosophy. Three major stages can be observed in its development. Modern parties originated with the drive of a rising, self-conscious middle class that fought for liberation from the shackles of a feudal society and for representation to check monarchical absolutism. While the French Revolution officially proclaimed the end of this first phase of modern social development, the successful emancipation of rational man from the bonds of the *ancien régime* and its caste system proved to be only a transitional second stage. The individual, set free, was soon striving at reintegration into a new society. . . . We are still in the midst of this third phase. It constitutes the crisis of modern society.

It is against this background of crisis that a new concept of party is evolving. Its emergence and persistence, in fact, may well depend on the momentous character of social crisis. The well-balanced communities of the Scandinavian states and the Anglo-American world seem to be least affected by this new type, while it has found its most complete expression within nations in the grip of revolutions. The islands of social equilibrium, however, have shrunk, and the party of integration has no doubt beome a salient feature of our contemporary landscape.

The *party of individual representation* is characteristic of a society with a restricted political domain and only a limited degree of participation. Its membership activity is, for all practical purposes, limited to balloting, and the party organization (if existent at all) is dormant between election periods. Its main function is the selection of representatives, who, once chosen, are possessed of an absolutely "free mandate" and are in every respect responsible only to their own consciences. This conception of an ephemeral party as a mere electoral committee does not correspond to the political reality and practice of the modern mass democracy, a fact which in many countries has been recognized (though often most reluctantly) in the crucial controversy over party discipline and even in numerous court decisions codifying party regulations, responsibilities, and prerogatives. The fundamental concept of party, however, has hardly been challenged within democratic thinking.

Under the cover of such a persistent framework and rarely perceived even by circumspect political observers, a new type of party has emerged—the *party of integration*. The claim with which this party approaches its adherents is incomparably greater than that of the party of individual representation. It demands not only permanent dues-paying membership (which may be found to a smaller extent within the loose party of representation too) but, above all, an increasing influence over all spheres of the individual's daily life.

The first example of such a new party was presented by the Continental Socialists. Their organization has been jokingly characterized as extending from the cradle to the grave, from the workers' infant-care association to the atheists' cremation society; yet such a description articulates the intrinsic difference from the liberal party of representation, with its principle of "free recruitment" among a socially uncommitted, free-floating electorate (the bulk of which, in reality, may not be so independent). The following of the new movement is, indeed, much more clearly circumscribed by its permanent membership, the definite class alignment of its voting population, and its far-flung participation in over-all social affairs. The party can count on its adherents; it has taken over a good part of their social existence.

Despite such extensive organization and intensified ties of its partisans, the Socialist party (and in an even more limited way the Catholic movement and other democratic parties of integration) include only a small active core among its wider circle of mere dues-paying members and its even greater number of mere voters. In fact, this differentiation is at the base of the much-disputed "oligarchical" tendencies of modern mass parties which permit a relatively small group to decide the political fate of the disinterested and apathetic majority. Still, what is important is that the party in modern mass democracies has generally taken on an ever increasing area of commitments and responsibilities assuring the individual's share in society and incorporating him into the community. This is no mere usurpation of power by the politicians but the natural consequence of the extension of the public domain and the constantly increasing governmental functions in a reintegrated twentieth-century society.

In this sense the phenomenon of the *party of democratic integration* has become a matter of record. This fact makes it the more imperative to recognize its basic variance from the *party of total integration*, which has found its prototype in bolshevism, fascism, and National Socialism. This all-inclusive party demands the citizen's unconditional surrender. It denies not only the relative freedom of choice among the voters and followers but also any possibility of coalition and compromise among parties. It can perceive nothing but total seizure and exercise of power, undisputed acceptance of the party line, and monolithic rule. The rise of this absolutist police state decrees the end of democracy, of constitutionalism, of communal self-government, of Western man and his inalienable rights, of political parties.

. . .

Sociology of Political Parties

. . .

Although differing greatly in time and space, two main types of political leadership can be distinguished: *institutional* and *personal*. These are types roughly corresponding to the contrasting political systems, democracy and dictatorship. The pre-eminent elements of leadership in a democracy are institutional. This fact, of course, leads to a difference in democratic leadership according to varying institutional structures. The unlike character of the British prime minister, the French president of the council, and the United States president are a reflection of different institutional setups of these democratic governments and their respective party systems. This institutional character defines the personal qualities of democratic authority, its functions, its rise to eminence, its continuation, and its fluctuation and limitations in power. Deference, which is no doubt a basic desideratum of any leadership, derives largely from the leader's skills, the extent of his knowledge, judgment, and foresight, his strength of conviction, his policies, his ability to attain social cohesion and to give direction to social forces. Balance of mind, distaste for violence of expression, a faculty for spreading conciliation on all sides, become highly valued qualities of democratic leadership.

One should add, to enlarge upon Bagehot's famed remark, that the leader must be "an uncommon man of common opinions," which he articulates, intensifies, directs, and realizes through workable channels. This faculty of expressing the people's will points to a certain demagogical feature even in democratic leadership which is necessitated by the mass character of modern society. The pre-eminent elements of democratic authority, however, are institutional.

Dictatorial leadership is personal. Here again will be found variations due to national traditions, historical circumstances, and personality patterns; but all modern dictators have this in common: they are anti-institutional. In fact, their very rise indicates the weakening or nonexistence of political institutions, of a ruling class, of an accepted code of rules, of a belief in a rational order. The modern dictator is the substitute for institutions in the mass age of political confusion and social disintegration. He is, above all, the demagogue—the leader of the people, who, rising from the dark as an unknown soldier, breaks through society's institutional barriers. He does not stand for a positive program but only for himself. He is responsible to no man but to God and the nation (who are conveniently removed from any direct interference), and in his very irresponsibility he is revered by the emotional, rootless, and amorphous masses seeking mystery, devotion, and the miraculous. He is the wonder-performing *charismatic* leader whose charm of personality conceals conflicts of policy. The "state of the masses" is indeed the key to the acceptance of his myth.

Charismatic leadership and bureaucracy may well accompany each other. Even though it may seem inconsistent with the emotional dynamics of this personal ruler, his power rests on a strong party organization, an apparatus. In fact, the guardians of his machine, the "lieutenants," reveal the true character if the one-party system, its daily life, its divided rule, its inner tensions, its chance for survival and succession. Generally speaking, it is on this second level of political control that the multifarious functions of modern parties become apparent, the differences in degree and kind between the democratic and dictatorial parties are manifest, and the resilience, flexibility, and deep antagonisms of contemporary political organizations are tested.

Bureaucratization is a categorical fate of modern society, involving equally government, business, and political parties. This fact may be deplored for its social strains and its often serious consequences of hampering spontaneity and free play in human affairs; it is still an indisputable necessity inherent in an efficient, highly developed mass organization. It implies stratification and hierarchy of office, specialization and fragmentation of the citizen's role, centralization of government. It has become "the organizational weapon" of modern dictatorship. Yet its perils are not met by denying its existence or by warning of the inevitable destruction of the democratic fiber by the spider of administration. What must be stated carefully, however, are the manifold expressions it has found, the conditions under which this necessary phenomenon may choke the basic forces of a free society, and the safeguards which can and must be erected against such constriction today and tomorrow....

Variations in the character of those who are led are as important as those among those who lead, especially as the *concept of the masses* presents an even more elastic term. Leaving aside frequent moral connotations (such as "canaille," "the great unwashed," the "rebellious masses"), sharp distinctions should be made between the social variations of rural and urban groups, of scattered crowds and congregated mobs, of the latent and aroused masses, of the illiterate, numb, and untried and the educated, alert, skilled people. Different social classes invite a variety of stimuli and reactions. Political parties find an uneven appeal in various social strata, in accordance with their specific social experiences and historical conditions....

Next to the specific character of the rank and file, the people's role in politics will depend on the *size of organization.* The transition from aristocratic factions to modern mass parties no doubt necessitated the development of bureaucracies, as in any other large-scale organizations. All other factors being equal, this must diminish the individual member's potential in policy-making. Moreover, time, continuous effort, and skills are increasingly demanded for adequate legislative decision and subsequent administration. Naturally, these prerequisites lead to the predominance of the permanent and party professional over the political amateur. The problem of political organization, however, is not solved by abolishing the experts but by finding methods of checks and controls by an alert citizenry...

The *degree of participation* is a further key to the leader-followers relationship in political parties. Here again a preliminary exercise in definition is needed to clarify a politically charged and often purposely equivocal vocabulary. Ambiguity has become the secret weapon of modern autocrats. They will pride themselves on extending community enterprises as a genuine test of their "people's democracy." True, active involvement of a great number of party members can serve as a powerful counteracting force to oligarchical rule, yet democracy is not guaranteed by mere participation. If this means controlled and manipulated mass direction through the dictator's triple threat of all-embracing institutions, all-consuming fears, and an all-pervading propaganda, it can in fact become the most potent instrument of his lasting power. Indeed, so far as his rule aspires to a radical change in the societal structure, effective mass participation seems to be a prerequisite for the successful breaking of the traditional patterns, for channeling the people's discontent, and for preventing a counterrevolution. In this sense modern autocracies are still children of a democratic age; they are post-democratic dictatorships, and, because of that, they outdemonstrate any popular government in masterplanned, minutely organized, mass meetings.

Equally, if not more, important for democratic vitality is the party's ability to absorb and assimilate new social strata into the ruling class. Closely connected with this key problem is the much neglected phenomenon of the *succession in generations.* Many political revolutions have originated in this natural break between different political ages; the continuity of a political system, on the other hand, can well be measured in terms of its ability to guarantee a smooth and steady transition. This test of political wisdom and viability becomes manifest in the diverse selection and training of future leaders (and the mechanisms by which leaders can be retired). These procedures offer the most conclusive clue to the aims, character, and flexibility of the different party systems.

The *usual apprenticeship* of democratic aspirants through institutional channels of parliament, local government, and party organization is a selective process which tests particular qualifications: the capacity for effective statement, for framing legislation, for mastery in parliamentary debate, for teamwork, cooperation, and successful compromise. It offers a severe training and a slow rise to power—too slow for some young men in a hurry, who join extra-parliamentary movements that seem to promise a short cut to victory. The institutional path attracts certain personality types who may be groomed preferably by a definite educational system and who are more easily found in specific professions. The availability of trained political participants and, to use Max Weber's terminology, of "dispensable occupations" (lawyers, journalists, educators), which allow for career interruptions with even possible gains in skills and connections by such a political experience, will assure the filling of the necessary leadership reservoir. Equally important for the free flow of talent into political channels is a follow-up, a mechanism by which leaders can be retired and/or used for further advanced assignments without loss of craft and prestige. The rigidity of certain parties (and even more so, of many trade-unions) is often due to their petrified leadership which has no exit but oblivion....

Selection of leadership in modern autocracies meets with certain difficulties. . . . There is no natural competition in parliament or elsewhere to groom the dictator's lieutenants. Favoritism plays an important part in the selection, and especially in the higher brackets of the political hierarchy the leader's personal choice may even bring nonparty members into the inner council. The main channel, however is the party machine. Being a "charter member" of the party (the old guards of the first hour, the martyrs of the preceding "system's" prisons) is equivalent to a "safe" seat in a democratic parliament. These important qualities of the ardent fighters and trustworthy confidants may, however, at times become embarrassing after the seizure of power, and the "comrades of early and trying conspiracies" may be faced with purges and even the firing squad. . . .

The Party in a Pluralistic Society

This preliminary discussion of the sociology of political movements shows that a full definition of modern parties must include a clear understanding of the society of which they are a part and which they express. The nature and ethos of the ruling clique (military, managerial, intellectual, racial, religious, industrial, commercial, peasant, or proletarian, as the case may be), the status differentiation and degree of mobility (class or caste structure), the prevalent value system, the inner cohesion or crisis character of a nation—the complex interplay of these heterogeneous factors can alone indicate the extent of oligarchical trends or democratic participation within a political community. . . .

In fact, a high degree of diversity seems to create a favorable climate for a functioning democracy if it protects itself against the perils of castelike petrification and if it allows for a free interplay of its innumerable associations. And the varied parties serve as their forum.

Dictatorships, on the other hand, flourish among amorphous masses. If the natural groupings are not already pulverized, modern autocrats have to create a monolithic atmosphere, within which independent individuality and autonomous group life are submerged under the one-party rule and a "classless society" decrees "equality" before the tyrants. The fatal transformations in modern society—wars, inflation, depressions, and revolutions—prepared the ground and recruited the crucial strata of a dispossessed middle class, a propertyless peasantry, a rootless unemployed, and pugnacious partisans and perennial soldiers of fortune. Such constitute the social raw material of the rising autocracy, which systematically dismantles all free agencies and reduces them to the level of enforced conformity. And this means the end of a functioning democratic party system.

The democratic process has to respect and integrate the numerous special interests within a live society. This creates the intricate and fascinating interrelations between *parties* and *pressure groups*, which are not identical and do not exclude each other; they coexist in continuous interdependence. Parties are not merely the sum of all pressure groups; nor can the public simply dismiss the interests' proper functions by muckraking exposés of lobby activities. For a long time parties and pressure groups have had a bad press, largely because of a mistaken classical approach, which judged politics from the isolated individual's point of view. Once the social group is recognized as a proper starting point, the balance between the representation of homogeneous pressure groups (seeking influence) and the decision-making activities of heterogeneous parties (seeking office and reconciling the diverse forces within the state) becomes a major theme of national politics.

The techniques of interrelations differ in time and space. Pressure groups may try to establish or conquer parties, as has been the case with a number of European parties with strict class alignments or straight nationality backing. They may play the role of a free-floating vote bloc, seeking out the highest bidder, as practiced in Anglo-American patterns; they may extend their influence through divided representation in different parties (*Querverbindungen*); or they may concentrate on minor parties, pressing their special interests.

Whatever their methods, the strength of the "invisible government" as Wil-

liam Allen White called this consequential agglomeration of more than a hundred thousand associations of all types in this country, should not be underestimated. Their power rests largely on their singleness of purpose and their great degree of centralization. This directed appeal to specific concerns has evoked a most active response from the people, as the effective mass organizations of the trade-unions and employers' organizations in the Western world testify, while a deep-seated skepticism concerning the political parties prevails. Unaccountable to the public at large, the economic pressure groups have often overshadowed the political parties and have, in fact, hindered them in their primary task of integrating the special interests into the framework of the national whole. A merely descriptive analysis of what is happening on the political scene is misleading. It seems to confirm the make-believe of politics as the sum total of pressure-group activities. Constructive leadership, while recognizing their claims, must guard against their aggressions and, in the knowledge of their essential role, must lift the demands of the specific interests to the level of national needs. This is where effective parties come in.

$\cdot$ $\cdot$ $\cdot$

3.   A THEORY OF THE POLITICAL PARTY

Samuel J. Eldersveld

The political party is a social group, a system of meaningful and patterned

From Samuel J. Eldersveld, "A Theory of the Political Party," *Political Parties: A Behavioral Analysis*, (Chicago: Rand, McNally & Co., 1964), pp. 1-13, excerpts. By permission of the publisher.

activity within the larger society. It consists of a set of individuals populating specific roles and behaving as member-actors of a boundaried and identifiable social unit. Goals are perceived by these actors, tasks are assigned for and by them, and communication channels are maintained. The party is thus one social organism. But the party is also a polity, a miniature political system. It has an authority structure, although the manner in which authority is graded and legitimated may differ considerably from other social groups. The party has distinctive patterns of power distribution. It has a representative process, an electoral system, and subprocesses for recruiting leaders, defining goals, and resolving internal system conflicts. Above all, the party is a decision-making system, although, again, how "authoritative" the decision-making process is remains a subject of inquiry. The political party, thus, conforms to the common characteristics of social groups. Herbert Simon, for example, has defined a group as a system of "interdependent activity, encompassing at least several primary groups and usually characterized. . . by a high degree of rational direction of behavior towards ends that are objects of common acknowledgement and expectation." The party, as studied here, is such a group. It fulfills, at least minimally, these requirements, although we seek through empirical analysis to determine the degree to which "interdependent activity," "rationality," and "common acknowledgement" in fact exist.

In the study of the party as a social group, we are initially concerned with the empirical discovery of structural properties, those characteristic modes of activity which may distinguish the party as a social collectivity. To this end, it is necessary to develop and test empirical theory about the perspectives and behavior of individuals holding positions at all major levels of the hierarchy, their vertical and horizontal relationships with others in the group, and the meaning of this behavior for the subunits (or "primary groups") as well as for the total organization. Structure is people acting in relationship to others, not merely *some* actions and particular relationships, or *some* actors, for then only a segment of the structure will be revealed. The party is more than its executive elite, or campaign workers, or precinct activists, analyzed in isolation. It is a meaningful organizational system of interpersonal relationships. Concentration on those "in power," or the "inner circle," or the "activist cadre," while helpful and suggestive, cannot by itself lead to comprehension of the structure as a whole. Too much party research in America has had to settle for partial images of political reality.

In attempting to delineate the properties of the party, we assume that our knowledge of its tasks and roles in the larger political system will be enhanced. Parties came into existence to perform certain critical functions for the system, and derived their basic form in the process of implementing these functions. If one is interested in understanding the tasks presumably fulfilled by parties, it is necessary to analyze the party as a functioning structural subsystem. This is not to say that all party groups perform the same functions and possess identical structural properties. Social and political environmental conditions vary from one culture to the next. The same is true of "functional priorities." Parties are merely a particular structural response, therefore, to the needs of a social and political system in a particular milieu. . . .

Political party structures have certain common tendencies differentiating them from other groups such as families, churches, labor unions, business firms, lodges. This is a proposition not easily defended. In the long run it can be demonstrated only by the development of probable differentiae and the testing of these through empirical research. In taking the position that there are common structural tendencies, we do not mean to imply that party structures do not vary. They do, both in the same society and in different societies. But despite such variations which are primarily the product of particular adaptations to special environmental conditions, parties exhibit structural similarities in certain basic respects. We view the party as a specialized system of action in democratic societies, with a special meaning and purpose in the political and social order. It is distinguishable by its primary goal (to occupy at least some of the governmental leadership posts), by its competitive-electoral relationships with similar groups, and by its special pattern of public-support and adaptation strategies. . . .

The party must first be understood as a clientele-oriented structure. In contrast to the bureaucratic model, the party is almost by definition an open, informal, personalized system. Roberto Michels wrote long ago of the "omnibus tendency" of parties. He saw party as an "organization ever greedy for new members," adding, "the party no longer seeks to fight its opponents, but simply to outbid them." The result, claimed Michels, was that the party would "sacrifice its political virginity, by entering into promiscuous relationships with the most heterogeneous political elements. . . ." Although Michels was writing particularly about socialist parties a half-century ago, his observations are insightful and have been repeated by many scholars of party politics. The party is always "potential-clientele" conscious. It is open at its base to new recruits for party work as well as to nonactivist supporters. It is often open at the higher levels also, indeed, sometimes at the elite apex, if such a strategy will profit the party's power aspirations. Thus it is permeable and adaptive, even in societies with multiparty systems in which the probability of seducing the small number of "floating voters" is minimal. Singularly reliant on votes as the arithmetic of power, the party reflects structurally an inherent tendency toward joint advantage. The party is a mutually exploitative relationship—it is joined by those who would use it; it mobilizes for the sake of power those who would join it. This porous nature of the party—at its base, sides, and apex—has tremendous consequences for individual perspectives and organizational relationships. Where adaptation is maximal, internal managerial control is difficult, factional pluralism multiplied, operational efficiency likely to be impaired, and goal orientations and ideological consensus highly noncongruent; where adaptation is minimal, such consequences for internal control and perspectives will doubtless be less severe. This is the first theoretical dilemma the party must face.

The second empirical image follows from the first. The party is a structural system seeking to translate or convert (or be converted by) social and economic interests into political power directly. It consists of a set of socioeconomic interests groping for political recognition, articulation, and control. As such the party can be conceptualized as an alliance of substructures or subcoalitions. Many writers have implicitly recognized this character of the party organization. Charles Merriam made the point well 40 years ago:

Of great significance in the composition of any political party are the numerous types of social groupings. These are fundamental in any scientific study of the political party, and too great emphasis cannot be laid upon them. . . . The practical politician is never guilty of the omission of the study of social groupings, but the students of politics have sometimes proceeded as if parties were working in a social vacuum.

The subcoalitions within the party may be identified variously—in terms of geographical boundaries, on the basis of organizational status, as demographic or social categories, or on the basis of ideological division. In addition, there may be organizational entities almost completely self-reliant, such as the legislative wing of the party (or the congressman with his own "machine"), women and youth auxiliaries, a political club "movement," and affiliated business, labor, or farm suborganizations.

The party, in this image, exists as an intermediary group representing and exploiting multiple interests for the achievement of direct control over the power apparatus of the society. The party becomes inevitably, then, a conflict system. Conflict among the competing interests in the structure can be managed, channeled, avoided— in fact, the structure many times seems constituted to maximize conflict avoidance. But above all, and this is the unique structural characteristic of the party in this regard, conflict within the party must be tolerated. As a power-aspiring group, "greedy" for new followers, the party does not settle conflict; it defers the resolution of conflict. The party is thus no genuine mediator; it seeks to stabilize subcoalitional relationships and interactions so that these multiple interests will remain committed to the organization, after partial acquiescence to their demands, without permitting intergroup rivalries to collide with the party's grand design for power. Tension between the group goal and subcoalitional demands is, therefore, the second basic structural dilemma of the party. . . .

A third theoretical position concerning the pary's structural properties emerges with the question, What type of hierarchy or structure of power is a party? That the party is a hierarchy is generally not disputed, since certainly a coarchal pattern of perfectly equal power distribution does not exist. Whether the party structure is an "oligarchy," however, has been the subject of speculation since Michel's famous theory of the "iron law of oligarchy." Some insist that a minority inevitably assumes leadership and control of parties, with all the expected oligarchic phenomena which Michels predicted. Others note that even in the most carefully structured American party "machines," a reciprocal pattern of influence and responsibility obtains between the "boss' and his precinct captains. We do not wish to grapple with all the alleged features of oligarchy within the party. Rather, we take issue with the necessity of one crucial assumption in that "iron law," the assumption that control of the party structure is inexorably concentrated in the hands of a single leadership corps, the top, elite, managerial nucleus of the structure. In contrast to this theory we suggest the following alternative image of the pattern of control within the party.

The possibility clearly exists that a

special type of hierarchy obtains in parties—one which, to borrow Harold Lasswell and Abraham Kaplan's phrase, we will call *stratarchy*. The general characteristics of stratarchy are the proliferation of the ruling group and the diffusion of power prerogatives and power exercise. Rather than centralized "unity of command," or a general dilution of power throughout the structure, "strata commands" exist which operate with a varying, but considerable degree of, independence. Such allocation of command and control to specified "layer," or "echelon," authorities is a pragmatic necessity. The very heterogeneity of membership, and the subcoalitional system, make centralized control not only difficult but unwise. In the process of adaptation, then, the party develops its own hierarchical pattern of stratified devolution of responsibility for the settlement of conflicts, rather than jeopardize the viability of the total organization by carrying such conflicts to the top command levels of the party. Further, the party must cope with widely varying local milieus of opinion, tradition, and social structure, and this encourages the recognition and acceptance of local leadership, local strategy, local power. In addition, the desperate need in all parties for votes, which are scarcely mobilized at the apex of the hierarchy, results in at least some, if not pronounced, deference to the local structural strata where votes are won or lost. Thus, a kind of "balkanization" of power relations occurs, with variations in the extent of autonomy in middle and lower hierarchical strata from one habitat to the next. While admittedly party systems in different countries will vary in degree of stratarchy, exploratory research suggests the real

probability that there is a stratarchical element in all such systems, despite the custom of referring to them in such simple terms as "centralized," monolithic, or unitary.

The political party is thus to be visualized as a "reciprocal deference structure." Contrary to the bureaucratic and authoritarian models of social organization, the party is not a precisely ordered system of authority and influence from the top down, though as a "paper" structure it may give this appearance. The organization does not function through the issuance of directives from the top which are obeyed without question. Rather, there is tolerance of autonomy, local initiative, local inertia. The factors contributing to this property of the party are several: sparsity of activists, voluntary nature of recruitment for party work, limited rewards available to activists and irregularity of their loyalty. But, primarily, this "downward deference" stems from the absence of effective sanctions, the strong drive for votes, the instinctively adaptive tactics of success-minded party leaders, and the need for lower-echelon support. More than any other social organization, the critical action locus of the party structure is at its base. And since there is high potential for inefficiency, indifference, and displacement of group (leadership) goals with personal goals among activists at the base, leaders defer. In fact, the basis for the authority of the leadership of party organizations is one of the most puzzling to understand. It does not seem to be a function of expertise, or of role, or of normative expectations. Rather, the party structure appears to be characterized as a "rapport system." Rapport is basic to status. Rapport between the top elite, middle-level cadre, and local activists rests on mutual perspectives concerning the strategy of electoral success, or mutual tolerance of ineptness (and inaction) in the face of sure defeat. The relationship between the executive elite and the "hard-core" activists in the party structure is above all, therefore, one of accommodation—of "centralist" (leadership) drive and strategy for power to "localist" interests, demands, and support. In this structural context the party faces another crucial dilemma—the need for managerial efficiency while maintaining worker morale.

Closely related is a fourth major image which emphasizes the special type of elite careerism patterns found in the party. Here, again, we take issue with an important component in the theory of oligarchy, the picture of the party as possessing a single elite cadre, "one directive social group," well-organized, self-conscious, self-perpetuating, congruent, conspiring. In its place we suggest and empirically examine the possibility of another image of the party elite. We see the party elite as consisting of pluralized sets of separable "career classes" or "career categories," with considerable differentiation in congruence, communicative interchange, and self-consciousness. Furthermore, we hypothesize differently the character of "circulation" of the party elite, as well as the basis for the structural stability of the party in the face of such circulation. There is indeed a high turnover in party leadership at all levels of the hierarchy, just as individual mobility for the determined careerist can occur at unbelievable rates. But this is not a *pro forma* turnover, as the oligarchic theorists would contend, a circulation resulting from the "amalgamation" by the old elite of "new elite" elements which are considered

"safe." This is not primarily a process of absorption. It is often a process of genuine renovation, adaptation, and reconstitution of the subcoalitional balance of power within the party structure. Or it is often genuine evidence of the loss of power.

The party leader's basis of authority leans heavily on rapport, and yet is essentially quixotic, dependent as it is on an ever changing balance sheet of votes won and lost, as well as on the competitive struggle for power among the organizational subgroups with which he must contend. In addition, although party leadership cadres may indeed have some *esprit de corps*, this is quite different from that of a bureaucratic cadre. In the latter case, *esprit de corps* rests heavily on vocational security, professional associations, expectations of permanency, and a desire to protect the group from its environment. The party, however, is an open structure; tenure is unstable; personal relationships are uncertain. Thus power vanishes easily within a political party, but the saving grace is the existence of career groups of individuals who are not essentially aspiring to power. For many of these the party means "status," not "power," and the continuity of their commitment to party tasks contributes to stability in the face of constant flux and potential disequilibrium. The party structure, thus, has a peculiar career system which, despite insecurity of tenure and high circulation, does result in durability, due primarily to the continuous renewal of those separable career categories so indispensable to the fulfillment of party goals. But the dilemma of the party is clear, for it must accomplish the simultaneous fulfillment of "mobility" and "status" demands and satisfactions in an organization which is heterogeneous in membership, eclectic in ideology, and voluntaristic in motivational orientation.

These four images of the basic properties of the party structure are obviously not mutually exclusive. The argument here is that if the party as a social organization is distinctive from other organizational types, and we postulate that it is, then these tentative constructs may help identify its special character. It is not to be implied that all parties are equally characterized by these theoretical images. They are merely "dimensions," and party structures differ in the degree to which they approximate these properties. The coalitional character of certain party structures may be most relevant in certain locales; in others "reciprocal deference" and stratarchy may be more basic; and certainly parties vary in adaptiveness and clientele-consciousness. The suggestion is that an internal logic about the nature of party structure in a democratic system does exist, which theoretically differentiates it from other social structures. Two common elements in democratic societies contribute to the existence of party groups with these inherently unique structural styles: political power rests on votes; and groups compete for power. Where these components of the democratic system are strong, party groups will manifest their stylistic attributes maximally; where the components are weak, party attributes are also weak.

The specification of these structural properties should not lead to an analysis of the party in an intellectual vacuum, or to complete normative pessimism. In our opinion there are three major clusters of factors responsible for the party structure as it is. One such cluster consists of environmental pressures, both the socio-economic conditions with which the party must contend in a particular area, and the political history and climate of the area. The competitive conditions of political life interact with the social complexion of the area to impress on the party structure certain properties which are in a sense structural responses to environmental demands. Secondly, there is the "internal dynamic" cluster of variables, including the personal orientations and styles of political activism within the power process in a given area. This is the "political subculture" of the area—the normative and operational codes adhered to in the power process, communicated widely to participants in this process, and continually re-enforced by the system itself. The party and its leadership is but one segment of this subculture. Finally, the developmental or chronological component in the analysis of party structure, the factor of time, must be considered. Parties gradually evolve characteristic modes or properties which tend to become accepted and tolerated in a given area and culture. But change can and does occur, and it is possible that at critical points in time party structures do develop reorientations. Thus, although we are rather committed to accepting the basic theory outlined above, as having generalizable validity for modern-day parties in democratic societies, we accept the possibility that these, or their degree of manifestation at this point in time, are not fixed and unalterable. Human institutions do change. Social groups are dynamic. We are not locked into a structural system which is forever imprisoned by identical and constant social pressure.

4.   SOME FUNCTIONS OF THE POLITICAL MACHINE

Robert K. Merton

Some functions of the political machine.

Without presuming to enter into the variations of detail marking different political machines—a Tweed, Vare, Crump, Flynn, Hague are by no means identical types of bosses—we can briefly examine the functions more or less common to the political machine, as a generic type of social organization. We neither attempt to itemize all the diverse functions of the political machine nor imply that all these functions are similarly fulfilled by each and every machine.

The key structural function of the Boss is to organize, centralize and maintain in good working condition "the scattered fragments of power" which are at present dispersed through our political organization. By this centralized organization of political power, the boss and his apparatus can satisfy the needs of diverse subgroups in the larger community which are not adequately satisfied by legally devised and culturally approved social structures.

To understand the role of bossism and the machine, therefore, we must look at two types of sociological variables: 1) the *structural context* which

From Robert K. Merton, "Social Theory and Social Structure," *American Journal of Sociology,* (1945), 72-82, excerpts. Reprinted from *American Journal of Sociology* by permission of the University of Chicago Press. Copyright 1945 by the University of Chicago.

makes it difficult, if not impossible, for morally approved structures to fulfill essential social functions, thus leaving the door open for political machines (or their structural equivalents) to fulfill these functions and 2) the subgroups whose distinctive needs are left unsatisfied, except for the latent functions which the machine in fact fulfills.

Structural Context

The constitutional framework of American political organization specifically precludes the legal possibility of highly centralized power and, it has been noted, thus "discourages the growth of effective and responsible leadership. The framers of the Constitution, as Woodrow Wilson observed, set up the check and balance system 'to keep government at a sort of mechanical equipoise by means of a standing amicable contest among its several organic parts.' They distrusted power as dangerous to liberty: and therefore they spread it thin and erected barriers against its concentration." This dispersion of power is found not only at the national level but in local areas as well. "As a consequence." Sait goes on to observe, "when *the people or particular groups* among them demanded positive action, no one had adequate authority to act. The machine provided an antidote."

The constitutional dispersion of power not only makes for difficulty of effective decision and action but when action does occur it is defined and hemmed in by legalistic considerations. In consequence, there developed "a much *more human system* of partisan government, whose chief object soon became the circumvention of government by law. ... The lawlessness of the extra-official democracy was merely the counterpoise of the legalism of the official democracy. The lawyer having been permitted to subordinate democracy to the Law, the Boss had to be called in to extricate the victim, which he did after a fashion and for a consideration." ...

Put in more generalized terms, *the functional deficiencies of the official structure generate an alternative (unofficial) structure to fulfill existing needs somewhat more effectively.* Whatever its specific historical origins, the political machine persists as an apparatus for satisfying otherwise unfulfilled needs of diverse groups in the population. By turning to a few of these subgroups and their characteristic needs, we shall be led at once to a range of latent functions of the political machine.

Functions of the Political Machine for Diverse Subgroups

It is well known that one source of strength of the political machine derives from its roots in the local community and the neighborhood. The political machine does not regard the electorate as an amorphous, undifferentiated mass of voters. With a keen sociological intuition, the machine recognizes that the voter is a person living in a specific neighborhood, with specific personal problems and personal wants. Public issues are abstract and remote; private problems are extremely concrete and immediate. It is not through the generalized appeal to large public concerns that the machine operates, but through the direct, quasi-feudal relationships between local representatives of the machine and voters in their neighborhood. Elections are won in the precinct.

The machine welds its link with ordinary men and women by elaborate networks of personal relations. Politics is transformed into personalties. The precinct captain "must be a friend to every man assuming, if he does not feel, sympathy with the unfortunate, and utilizing in his good works the resources which the boss puts at his disposal." The precinct captain is forever a friend in need. In our prevailingly impersonal society, the machine, through its local agents, fulfills the important social *function of humanizing and personalizing all manner of assistance* to those in need. Foodbaskets and jobs, legal and extra-legal advice, setting to rights minor scrapes with the law, helping the bright poor boy to a political scholarship in a local college, looking after the bereaved —the whole range of crises when a feller needs a friend, and, above all, a friend who knows the score and who can do something about it,—all these find the ever-helpful precinct captain available in the pinch.

To assess this function of the political machine adequately, it is important to note not only that aid *is* provided but *the manner in which it is provided.* After all, other agencies do exist for dispensing such assistance. Welfare agencies, settlement houses, legal aid clinics, medical aid in free hospitals, public relief departments, immigration authorities—these and a multitude of other organizations are available to provide the most varied types of assistance. But in contrast to the professional techniques of the welfare worker which may typically represent in the mind of the recipient the cold, bureaucratic dispensation of limited aid following upon detailed investigation of *legal* claims to aid of the "client" are the unprofessional techniques of the precinct captain who asks no questions, exacts no compliance with legal rules of eligibility and does not "snoop" into private affairs.

For many, the loss of "self-respect" is too high a price for legalized assistance. In contrast to the gulf between the settlement house workers who so often come from a different social class, educational background and ethnic group, the precinct worker is "just one of us," who understands what it's all about. The condescending lady bountiful can hardly compete with the understanding friend in need. In *this struggle between alternative structures for fulfilling the nominally same function* of providing aid and support to those who need it, it is clearly the machine politician who is better integrated with the groups which he serves than the impersonal, professionalized, socially distant and legally constrained welfare worker. And since the politician can at times influence and manipulate the official organizations for the dispensation of assistance, whereas the welfare worker has practically no influence on the political machine, this only adds to his greater effectiveness. More colloquially and also, perhaps, more incisively, it was the Boston ward-leader, Martin Lomasny, who described this essential function to the curious Lincoln Steffens: "I think," said Lomasny, "that there's got to be in every ward somebody that any bloke can come to—no matter what he's done—and get help. *Help, you understand; none of your law and justice, but help.*"

The "deprived classes," then, constitute one subgroup for whom the political machine satisfies wants not adequately satisfied in the same fashion by the legitimate social structure.

For a second subgroup, that of business (primarily "big" business but also "small"), the political boss serves the function of providing those political privileges which entail immediate economic gains. Business corporations, among which the public utilities (railroads, local transportation and electric light companies, communications corporations) are simply the most conspicuous in this regard, seek special political dispensations which will enable them to stabilize their situation and to near their objective of maximizing profits. Interestingly enough, corporations often want to avoid a chaos of uncontrolled competition. They want the greater security of an economic czar who controls, regulates and organizes competition, providing that this czar is not a public official with his decisions subject to public scrutiny and public control. (The latter would be "government control," and hence taboo.) The political boss fulfills these requirements admirably.

Examined for a moment apart from any moral considerations, the political apparatus operated by the Boss is effectively designed to perform these functions with a minimum of inefficiency. Holding the strings of diverse governmental divisions, bureaus and agencies in his competent hands, the Boss rationalizes the relations between public and private business. He serves as the business community's ambassador in the otherwise alien (and sometimes unfriendly) realm of government. And, in strict business-like terms, he is well-paid for his economic services to his respectable business clients. In an article entitled, "An Apology to Graft," Lincoln Steffens suggested that "Our economic system, which held up riches, power and acclaim as prizes to men bold enough and able enough to buy corruptly timber, mines, oil fields and franchises and 'get away with it,' was at fault." And, in a conference with a hundred or so of Los Angeles business leaders, he described a fact well known to all of them: the Boss and his machine were an *integral part* of the organization of the economy. "You cannot build or operate a railroad, or a street railway, gas, water, or power company, develop and operate a mine, or get forests and cut timber on a large scale, or run any privileged business, without corrupting or joining in the corruption of the government. You tell me privately that you must, and here I am telling you semi-publicly that you must. And that is so all over the country. And that means that we have an organization of society in which, *for some reason*, you and your kind, the ablest, most intelligent, most imaginative, daring and resourceful leaders of society, are and must be against society and its laws and its all-around growth."

Since the demand for the services of special privileges are built into the structure of the society, the Boss fulfills diverse functions for this second subgroup of business-seeking-privilege. These "needs" of business, as presently constituted, are not adequately provided for by conventional and culturally approved social structures; consequently, the extra-legal but more-or-less efficient organization of the political machine comes to provide these services. To adopt an *exclusively* moral attitude toward the "corrupt political machine" is to lose sight of the very structural conditions which generate the "evil" that is so bitterly attacked. To adopt a functional outlook is to provide not an apologia for the political machines but a more solid basis for modifying or

eliminating the machine, *providing* specific structural arrangements are introduced either for eliminating these effective demands of the business community or, if that is the objective, of satisfying these demands through alternative means.

A third set of distinctive functions fulfilled by the political machine for a special subgroup is that of providing alternative channels of social mobility for those otherwise excluded from the more conventional avenues for personal "advancement." Both the sources of this special "need" (for social mobility) and the respect in which the political machine comes to help satisfy this need can be understood by examining the structure of the larger culture and society. As is well known, the American culture lays enormous emphasis on money and power as a "success" goal legitimate for all members of the society. By no means alone in our inventory of cultural goals, it still remains among the most heavily endowed with positive affect and value. However, certain subgroups and certain ecological areas are notable for the relative absence of opportunity for achieving these (monetary and power) types of success. They constitute, in short, sub-populations where the cultural emphasis upon pecuniary success has been absorbed, but where there is *little access to conventional and legitimate* means for attaining such success. The conventional occupational opportunities of persons in (such areas) are almost completely limited to manual labor. Given our cultural stigmatization of manual labor, and its correlate, the prestige of white-collar work, it is clear that the result is a tendency to achieve these culturally approved objectives *through whatever means are possible*. These people are on the one hand, "asked to orient their conduct toward the prospect of accumulating wealth [and power] and, on the other, they are largely denied effective opportunities to do so institutionally."

It is within this context of social structure that the political machine fulfills the basic function of providing avenues of social mobility for the otherwise disadvantaged. Within this context, even the corrupt political machine and the racket "represent the triumph of amoral intelligence over morally prescribed 'failure' when the channels of vertical mobility are closed or narrowed *in a society which places a high premium on economic affluence, [power] and social ascent for all its members.*" As one sociologist has noted on the basis of several years of close observation in a slum area:

The sociologist who dismisses racket and political organizations as deviations from desirable standards thereby neglects some of the major elements of slum life. . . . *He does not discover the functions they perform for the members* [of the groupings in the slum]. The Irish and later immigrant peoples have had the greatest difficulty in finding places for themselves in our urban social and economic structure. Does anyone believe that the immigrants and their children could have achieved their present degree of social mobility without gaining control of the political organization of some of our largest cities? The same is true of the racket organization. *Politics and the rackets have furnished an important means of social mobility for individuals, who, because of ethnic background and low class position,* are blocked from advancement in the "respectable" channels.

This, then, represents third type of function performed for a distinctive subgroup. This function, it may be noted in passing, is fulfilled by the *sheer* existence and operation of the political machine, for it is in the machine itself that these individuals and sub-groups find their culturally induced needs more or less satisfied. It refers to the services which the political apparatus provides for its own personnel. But seen in the wider social context we have set forth, it no longer appears as *merely* a means of self-aggrandizement for profit-hungry and power-hungry *individuals*, but as an organized provision for *subgroups* otherwise excluded from or handicapped in the race for "getting ahead."

Just as the political machine performs services for "legitimate" business, so it operates to perform not dissimilar services for "illegitimate" business: vice, crime and rackets. Once again, the basic sociological role of the machine in this respect can be more fully appreciated only if one temporarily abandons attitudes of moral indignation, to examine in all moral innocence the actual workings of the organization. In this light, it at once appears that the subgroup of the professional criminal, racketeer or gambler has basic similarities of organization, demands and operation to the subgroup of the industrialist, man of business or speculator. If there is a Lumber King or an Oil King, there is also a Vice King or a Racket King. If expansive legitimate business organizes administrative and financial syndicates to "rationalize" and to "integrate" diverse areas of production and business enterprise, so expansive rackets and crime organize syndicates to bring order to the otherwise chaotic areas of production of illicit goods and services. If legitimate business regards the proliferation of small business enterprises as wasteful and inefficient, substituting, for example, the giant chain stores for hundreds of corner groceries, so illegitimate business adopts the same businesslike attitude and syndicates crime and vice.

Finally, and in many respects,

most important, is the basic similarity, if not near-identity, of the economic role of "legitimate" business and of "illegitimate" business. *Both are in some degree concerned with the provision of goods and services for which there is an economic demand.* Morals aside, they are both business, industrial and professional enterprises, dispensing goods and services which some people want, for which there is a market in which goods and services are transformed into commodities. And, in a prevalently market society, we should expect appropriate enterprises to arise whenever there is a market demand for certain goods or services.

As is well known, vice, crime and the rackets *are* "big business." Consider only that there been have estimated to be about 500,000 professional prostitutes in the United States of 1950, and compare this with the approximately 200,000 physicians and 350,000 professional registered nurses. It is difficult to estimate which have the larger clientele: the professional men and women of medicine or the professional men and women of vice. It is, of course, difficult to estimate the economic assets, income, profits and dividends of illicit gambling in this country and to compare it with the economic assets, income, profits and dividends of, say, the shoe industry, but it is altogether possible that the two industries are about on a par. No precise figures exist on the annual expenditures on illicit narcotics, and it is probable that these are less than the expenditures on candy, but it is also probable that they are larger than the expenditure on books.

It takes but a moment's thought to recognize that, *in strictly economic terms,* there is no relevant difference between the provision of licit and of illicit goods and services. The liquor traffic illus-

trates this perfectly. It would be peculiar to argue that prior to 1920 (when the 18th amendment became effective), the provision of liquor constituted an economic service, that from 1920 to 1933, its production and sale no longer constituted an economic service dispensed in a market, and that from 1934 to the present, it once again took on a serviceable aspect. Or, it would be *economically* (not morally) absurd to suggest that the sale of boot-legged liquor in the dry state of Kansas is less a response to a market demand than the sale of publicly manufactured liquor in the neighboring wet state of Missouri. Examples of this sort can of course be multiplied many times over. Can it be held that in European countries, with registered and legalized prostitution, the prostitute contributes an economic service, whereas in this country, lacking legal sanction, the prostitute provides no such service? Or that the professional abortionist is in the economic market where he has approved legal status and that he is out of the economic market where he is legally taboo? Or that gambling satisfies a specific demand for entertainment in Nevada, where it constitutes the largest business enterprise of the larger cities in the state, but that it differs essentially in this respect from motion pictures in the neighboring state of California?

The failure to recognize that these businesses are only *morally* and not *economically* distinguishable from "legitimate" businesses has led to badly scrambled analysis. Once the economic identity of the two is recognized, we may anticipate that if the political machine performs functions for "legitimate big business' 'it will be all the more likely to perform not dissimilar functions for "illegitimate big business." And, of course, such is often the case.

The distinctive function of the political machine for their criminal, vice and racket clientele is to enable them to operate in satisfying the economic demands of a large market without due interference from the government. Just as big business may contribute funds to the political party war-chest to ensure a minimum of governmental interference, so with big rackets and big crime. In both instances, the political machine can, in varying degrees, provide "protection." In both instances, many features of the structural context are identical: 1) market demands for goods and services; 2) the operators' concern with maximizing gains from their enterprises; 3) the need for partial control of government which might otherwise interfere with these activities of businessmen; 4) the need for an efficient, powerful and centralized agency to provide an effective liaison of "business" with government.

Without assuming that the foregoing pages exhaust either the range of functions or the range of subgroups served by the political machine, we can at least see that *it presently fulfills some functions for these diverse subgroups which are not adequately fulfilled by culturally approved or more conventional structures.*

Several additional implications of the functional analysis of the political machine can be mentioned here only in passing, although they obviously require to be developed at length. First, the foregoing analysis has direct implications for *social engineering*. It helps explain why the periodic efforts at "political reform," turning the rascals out" and "cleaning political house" are typically (though not necessarily) short-lived and ineffectual. It exemplifies a basic theorem: *any attempt to eliminate an existing social structure without providing adequate alternative structures for fulfilling the functions previously fulfilled by*

the abolished organization is doomed to failure. (Needless to say, this theorem has much wider bearing than the one instance of the political machine.) When "political reform" confines itself to the manifest task of "turning the rascals out," it is engaging in little more than sociological magic. The reform may for a time bring new figures into the political limelight, it may serve the casual social function of re-assuring the electorate that the moral virtues remain intact and will ultimately triumph; it may actually effect a turnover in the personnel of the political machine; it may even, for a time, so curb the activities of the machine as to leave unsatisfied the many needs it has previously fulfilled. But, inevitably, unless the reform also involves a "re-forming" of the social and political structure such that the existing needs are satisfied by alternative structures or unless it involves a change which eliminates these needs altogether, the political machine will return to its integral place in the social scheme of things. *To seek social change, without due recognition of the manifest and latent functions performed by the social organization undergoing change, is to indulge in social ritual rather than social engineering.* The concepts of manifest and latent functions (or their equivalents) are indispensable elements in the theoretic repertoire of the social engineer. In this crucial sense, these concepts are not "merely" theoretical (in the abusive sense of the term), but are eminently practical. In the deliberate enactment of social change, they can be ignored only at the price of considerably heightening the risk of failure.

A second implication of this analysis of the political machine also has a bearing upon areas wider than the one we have considered. The paradox has often been noted that the supporters of the political machine include both the "respectable" business class elements who are, of course, opposed to the criminal or racketeer and the distinctly "unrespectable" elements of the underworld. And, at first appearance, this is cited as an instance of very strange bedfellows. The learned judge is not infrequently called upon to sentence the very racketeer beside whom he sat the night before at an informal dinner of the political bigwigs. The district attorney jostles the exonerated convict on his way to the back room where the Boss has called a meeting. The big business man may complain almost as bitterly as the big racketeer about the "extortionate" contributions to the party fund demanded by the Boss. Social opposites meet—in the smoke-filled room of the successful politician.

In the light of a functional analysis all this of course no longer seems paradoxical. Since the machine serves both the businessman and the criminal man, the two seemingly antipodal groups intersect. This points to a more general theorem: *the social functions of an organization help determine the structure (including the recruitment of personnel involved in the structure), just as the structure helps determine the effectiveness with which the functions are fulfilled.* In terms of social status, the business group and the criminal group are indeed poles apart. But status does not fully determine behavior and the inter-relations between groups. Functions modify these relations. Given their distinctive needs, the several subgroups in the large society are "integrated," whatever their personal desires or intentions, by the centralizing structure which serves these several needs. In a phrase with many implications which require further study, *structure affects function and function affects structure. . . .*

Party Systems

5. FEDERALISM AND THE PARTY SYSTEM

David Truman

   .   .   .

The basic political fact of federalism is that it creates separate, self-sustaining centers of power, privilege, and profit which may be sought and defended as desirable in themselves, as means of leverage upon elements in the political structure above and below, and as bases from which individuals may move

From David B. Truman, "Federalism and the Party System," *Federalism: Mature and Emergent,* ed. Arthur W. Macmahon, (New York: Doubleday & Company, Inc. 1955), pp. 122-34, excerpts. By permission of The Trustees of Columbia University, in the City of New York.

to places of greater influence and prestige in and out of government. This does not mean simply that a socio-economic interest group, dominant within a state or, more typically perhaps, a group of contiguous states, will utilize state powers to protect itself from assault both from within the area and from the national center. This is true enough; it merely restates the facts underlying the original choice of a federal rather than a unitary structure for the second American constitution, and it points to the familiar fact of sectional politics present through most of our history and recurrent with each wave of state creation.

The separate political existence of the state in the days of the nation's industrial and political maturity, on the other hand, provides effective access to the whole governmental structure for interest groups whose tactics may be local or sectional but whose scope is national. Separatism, whether within the federal system or in the form of a specious demand for making a governmental activity "independent of politics" at whatever level of the structure, has frequently been a refuge for interests bent on defensive or evasive action, and the "states' rights" argument has often had about it an air more of expediency than of principle. This is not new. But it is the fact of federalism which permits an interest group or other enterprise of national scope, in alliance with lesser interests which may be primarily local or sectional, to prevent or negate action on the national level and to insure inaction or indulgence in the states. It was not merely Yankee stubbornness and dedication to local self-government which in the thirties prevented federal action to foster integrated development of the Connecticut River Valley. Such sentiments may have been more than mere expedient romanticism, and they might alone have affected the outcome of the proposal and the fortunes of elected state officials and members of Congress, but they received significant support and direction from private utility interests whose reach was nationwide. Nor were the interests exclusively local or sectional, though such were allied at least peripherally, which induced the Congress to alter in favor of state action a Supreme Court decision asserting or permitting national control of insurance. These illustrations are not cited by way of indictment but merely of illustration. In the maturity of the federal systems the existence of the states as self-contained centers of power permits the use of them and associated party units by interests which are state or local only in a tactical sense. This is not equivalent to the separatism of a geographically defined interest, though it appears in the same garb and owes its significance as a technique to the continued existence of the states as power centers. Its effects on the party system are conducive to neither centralization nor cohesion at the national level.

In viewing the states as channels of access for interest groups, however, it is easy to forget that elective positions within the states, especially the governorships, are prizes in themselves and that the political "game" may be merely a means from the viewpoint of the interest group leader but is likely to be an end in itself for many of the more active partisans. It is perhaps a commentary on the instrumental, almost a-political attitudes of many academic observers of politics that they lay such stress upon the American parties as alliances of socio-economic interest groups. They are, of course, alliances of groups, but parties are not distinguishable exclusively or even primarily in terms of their socio-economic policy content. In varying but important measure they are purely political, focused upon securing and holding power for their leading elements as an end in itself. The grand patterns of sectional and perhaps class alliances which have successively dominated our presidential politics for periods lasting up to several decades can in the large view perhaps be explained most meaningfully in terms of socio-economic interest. But at shorter range the detailed patterns take on a more exclusively political appearance. There is here no intended implication of petty place-seeking but rather a suggestion that to aspire to be among those who govern and to associate for that objective as an end in itself is both normal and honorable. The evidence which indicates that enduring attachment to a party is for many voters a loyalty independent of, though not dissociated from, socioeconomic interest supports the assumption that similar attachments to party, clique, and faction exist among the more active elements in political organizations.

The significance of this point in the present context is that, given the multitude of elective positions in the system (only partially a consequence of federalism) and given the absence of a clearly defined and recognized path from one position to another in the loose hierarchy of political careers (a consequence more of a decentralized party system than directly of federalism itself), conflicting but interdependent clusters of loyalty and aspiration build up around various positions in the governmental structure. Thus, within a given "party," the career aspirations and prospects of a state governor, a United States Senator, and a member of the House of Representatives are likely to be ambiguous to one another or to others in the political structure with whom they must deal. Each may want one of the other offices; the governor and Senator may both have presidential ambitions which are mutually exclusive; the Senator or the Representative, though occupying a "national" office, may hope to move to the governorship and is likely to be far more closely dependent upon the state governor, from considerations either of preference or of expediency, than upon the leaders of the "parliamentary" party or upon a President bearing the same party designation. This is a simplified and hypothetical example, but it illustrates the role played by the offices established in the federal structure, and especially the state governor, in fractionating and decentralizing the party system, in encouraging the development of largely independent, hostile, and internally cohesive factional groupings. . . .

Three factors derived from the existence of the states as separate and largely self-sustaining power centers—channeling the claims of local socioeconomic interest groups, inviting their use as leverage against federal action by interests which are only tactically local, and providing for competing and frequently incompatible nuclei of decentralized intra-party conflict—are, of course, interrelated. In various combinations they go a long way toward indicating that there is something inherent in federalism which induces decentralization and lack of coherence in a party system.

But it is not sufficient merely to show that federalism has had some effect upon the nature of the party system. The important question of how much effect it has remains unanswered and to a precise degree unanswerable. It can easily be pointed out that decentralization and lack of cohesion frequently are apparent within the state parties, where factors other than federalism are influential. Could the like of these account in considerable measure for the peculiarities of the system as a whole? Would the American party system have developed essentially its present characteristics if the Founding Fathers had established a unitary constitution? The question is hypothetical but not irrelevant.

Before turning to an examination of some of the influences other than federalism that have molded the American parties, it may be instructive, or at least suggestive, to examine briefly two other federal systems, Canada and Australia, for evidence of similar effects of federal organization. The comparison cannot be conclusive, since, as in all such efforts, it is impossible to differentiate the effect of other influences and state in precise terms the consequences of basic constitutional structure. But contrasts may be revealing even when comparisons cannot be made with exactness.

In both Canada and Australia the major parties are obliged, especially in the former, to take account of the geographically defined differences which underlie the federal structure. Viable national political structures, as would be expected, must reckon with sectional issues, attitudes, and interests. Yet despite this obvious fact both have seen the development of national parties more centralized and considerably more cohesive than those in the United States.

In Canada there is considerable variation in the formal structures of the major parties, and within the parties the patterns differ from one province to another and between rural and urban constituencies, as in the United States. In Quebec, whose politics are not unlike those of the American South, parties are more loosely organized, and purely personal and factional influences have considerable significance. At the national level the only party organization of importance is the parliamentary party. Below that is the somewhat more complex provincial party organization and the constituency (riding) organization.

The fact of federalism introduces potential cleavages into the party system, yet normally the leader of the parliamentary party, especially if he is also Prime Minister, can count on the disciplined support of those elected with him, and a majority Government usually can survive throughout its permissible statutory life of five years. In Dominion elections, to be sure, it is not unusual for the outcome nationally to be affected by the existence of local or provincial hostilities clustered around other points in the federal structure and largely irrelevant to national questions.

Such centrifugal influences as exist within the Canadian parties seem to be associated, as in the United States, with decentralization of the nominating function and with the use of provincial governmental positions as points of resistance. Nominations for the Dominion parliament are made by the constituency organizations through various procedures generally lacking the complexity of their American equivalents, a point perhaps not without significance. These constituency organizations, perhaps especially in Quebec, are a good deal more independent in their decisions than are those in Britain, and the provincial and national parties have no formal or acknowledged power to withhold designations or to control the local decisions. A member of parliament who is not in the best of standing with the Government may be renominated if he nevertheless retains the confidence of the constituency committee, but this is less likely to occur if he is known to be in disfavor, and the national party leader may, especially if he is Prime Minister, be able to punish, by indirect means, the recalcitrant by seeing that he is deprived of his nomination. . . .

The Canadian party system thus shows the influences of the federal structure, but it is in rather sharp contrast to the United States in degree. This is not the place to attempt an exhaustive analysis of the reasons for the contrast, but one or two prominent factors should be cautiously mentioned. These seem to be associated with the parliament-cabinet system, operating under conditions at least analogous to those in Britain. In this connection it is tempting to seize upon the absence of a separation of powers as the crucial element, but as a simple constitutional fact it is not convincing. However, the consequence that it involves no separate popular election of the head of the government is significant, in that it implies narrowing and rather sharply defining the alternative lines of succession to the positions of principal influence. The subtle differences in the role of prime ministers, at the national level and in the provinces, flowing from retention of representatives of the Crown in the chief ceremonial positions, are not unimportant. But the chief fact seems to be that the positions of provincial prime ministers, to say nothing of a variety of other governmental and nongovernmental positions, are not points from which direct succession to the most important political post can take place. As a point of leverage the provincial prime ministership, or leadership of the minority party in a province, may be useful, but it is not readily convertible into peak national leadership. In fact, it appears that sectional hostilities are more likely to focus upon a provincial leader than upon a Dominion statesman. The advantages of political ambiguity, which adhere to the governor of an important state or to a presidential aspirant whose prominence rests on a nonpolitical career in the United States, lie with the experienced politician at the national level. This seems to produce a somewhat cooptative pattern of succession which, buttressed by a skillful and thoroughly un-British

use of patronage when the party is in power, increases dependence upon the party leader. In the hands of a gifted politician such as a Laurier or a Mackenzie King—historically not unimportant political facts in themselves—the system can produce long and durable national leadership and reduce the disruptive influences of federalism to a minimum. . . .

The main features of the Australian situation are succinctly expressed by Louise Overacker in the closing sentences of her informative study:

In spite of its federal structure and a strong sense of particularism among the member states, unified, disciplined parties with Commonwealth-wide organizations developed. Even the Senate, created to safeguard state interests, has become a body in which divisions are along strict party lines.

This state of affairs is traceable to the existence of the remarkable Australian Labor Party, not only in the sense that it applies most completely to that party but also because the A.L.P., far more than the Liberal Party in Canada, has developed a structural pattern to be imitated by other political groupings as well as a substantive position for them to react to.

Superficially the structure of the A.L.P. resembles the general pattern in Canada. However, the primary emphasis given to the movement has not only attached extraordinary importance at both the state and Commonwealth levels to the parliamentary caucus, which the elected member is pledged to support, but has also produced a federal structure of state and interstate conventions whose relations with the parliamentary parties in the matter of policy-making are not always clear or harmonious. . . .

But the chief significance of the Australian system for Americans is that matters of constitutional form are far less important than in Canada. The degree of discipline and of centralization which marks the A.L.P., and its rivals by partial adaptation, is fundamentally a reflection of underlying social conditions. Early land policies and patterns of settlement, imposed upon the peculiarities of Australian geography, and a course of economic development which restricted the emergence of a significant middle class and the dominance of middle-class values, resulted in the early appearance of a highly class-conscious labor movement unlike anything in the United States or Canada. Australian politics have been proportionally bitter and marked by lines of conflict drawn in class terms. Their significance is that these lines cut across geographic jurisdictions and minimize, even if they do not eliminate, the centrifugal effects of constitutional structure. These lines, moreover, are old, older than Australian federalism itself. As Overacker puts it, "Not only does the Australian Labor Party antedate federalism but in a sense it became a national party even before Australia was a nation."

The Canadian and Australian experiences thus seem to indicate that, although the structural fact of federalism produces tendencies toward decentralization and lack of cohesion in the party system, a variety of other political or social influences may minimize the effect of such tendencies sufficiently to permit the development of a centralized power to govern consistent with the degree of underlying popular consensus. In the American case, apparently, these additional political and social facts have accentuated or at least perpetuated the centrifugal tendencies.

It seems clear that the structural fact of federalism is not alone sufficient to account for the peculiar characteristics of the American party system, though it may be fundamental. Additional influences must be identified and accounted for. Yet any effort to identify the additional forces in the American experience and to assess their relative importance is, in a sense, likely to be artificial. It sets the analyst to the unenviable task of cutting apart what is a seamless web of multivariant and interdependent factors with the prospect that he will end up with a set of separate elements whose chief significance lies in their interaction.

The foregoing discussion of Canada and Australia suggests the relevance of the separation of powers, the constitutional arrangement which seems to attract the attention of critics most easily. If the present analysis is sound, however, it is not the partial constitutional isolation of executive from legislative functions or the accompanying system of checks and balances that is of chief interest. Attempts to encourage or to develop means for improving communication and collaboration between the White House and the Congress are, in this context, essentially palliatives, though commendably constructive ones of considerable potential significance. It is the separate election of chief executives at both levels, and perhaps all three, which seems relevant here. Governors have often succeeded in imposing their leadership upon state legislators and presidents have with varying degrees of success bridged the long mile from Capitol Hill to 1600 Pennsylvania Avenue. Nevertheless the separate election of chief executives has multiplied and thereby rendered ambiguous the lines of succession within the governmental structure, and ambiguity of this sort seems almost certain to encourage independence and parallelism in party structures rather than coherence and centralization. As long as Presidents may be recruited from Congress, from the governorships, or from the cabinet (as well as from outside of political life), and as long as men in any of these positions may reasonably aspire to any of the others, decentralization and lack of coherence are likely to appear in many subtle but significant ways. The hypothesis is rhetorical, but if gubernatorial aspirants could be recruited only from within the state legislature or only from among the principal executive positions and if presidents were drawn exclusively from the Senate, or, in Jeffersonian fashion, from the hierarchy of the cabinet, the reasons for independent and poorly articulated party structures would be reduced.

But if the separation of powers is relevant, it is not sufficient. Such elements of structure would not alone be controlling, particularly in face of the kinds of factors which originally produced a federal scheme and which give it vitality today. Looking broadly at such factors over the sweep of the years, one gets the impression that, with one great exception, our politics has been carried on at relatively low temperatures. Except for the conflicts leading up to the Civil War, the issues generally have been of moderate intensity or, when heated or persistent, have been considerably tempered by a timely improvement in prices or in the level of industrial and commercial activity. Operating in the context of a large domestic market and a rapidly expanding economy, unrestricted by the kinds of factors which stoked the fires of conflict in Australia, our politics has been occupied with parceling slices of a pie that has had a way of expanding when awkward choices were imminent,

not only over the relative sizes of the portions, but over who might partake and who must go without. Until very recently, moreover, our controversies have been for the most part domestic.

Our domestic, low-temperature quarrels have taken full cognizance of the geographically defined diversities which are still a reality within the country. In fact, the system has frequently exaggerated them; in a viable polity, and the survival value of the American scheme need not be argued, cleavages along local or sectional line are not likely to dominate the scene in the presence of intersecting issues of great significance, especially if the latter have their origin on the international plane. In the absence of such issues, and occasionally in default of a recognition of their import, Americans have been able to engage in locally or regionally based disputes which have not infrequently had the appearance of political luxury. The argument is not that all these geographically defined issues have been without substance, although some of them clearly have, but rather that their prominence is in part owing to the absence of more intense, intersecting issues and that collectively their impact on the party system has been decentralizing and disintegrative. These conditions, if this estimate is valid, may help account for tendencies toward a decentralized politics within many of the states as well as in the nation as a whole.

In no respect is the quality of American politics, in contrast with Australian, more clearly indicated than in the labor movement. No substantial proportion of American wage earners has ever developed strong class attitudes. Given our characteristically uninhibited methods of settling and exploiting a rich and virgin continent, the steadily expanding economy, and the resulting high social mobility, the dominant values of the society have been "middle-class" and individualistic. So thoroughly have these values been accepted by the wage-earning population that the labor movement throughout its history has been haunted by the problem of cohesion. For decades this problem was dealt with in the organized sector of labor more by a reliance on differences within the working-class population than on cleavages between class groupings. From the "plain people" movements of the eighteen-sixties to the industrial unionism of the nineteen-thirties and nineteen-forties, American workers have been more likely to divide along sectional, commodity, even ethnic and religious lines—all essentially decentralized—than to consolidate along the shadowy boundary of social class. For good or ill, the American political system has not been faced with the intersecting issues churned up by a class-conscious labor movement.

A further consequence of the low-temperature, domestic quality of American politics is the high visibility of the organized interest groups which have developed around the lines of cleavage and specialization in a complex, industrialized society. Many of these are local or sectional only in a tactical sense, as noted earlier, but all of them are on occasion highly significant, in the absence of other sorts of controversies, as elements in the calculations surrounding the nomination function, even though they may not be overtly active in this respect. Moreover, even when, in partial consequence of their own characteristically federal structures, they have been rent by divisive controversy, their local or state components are no less likely to be influential in the facilitation or disruption of political careers and in the determination of legislative action at state and national levels.

In this connection it is worth while to point out that a considerable element of localism has inevitably been injected into American politics, regardless of constitutional structure, by such factors as the patterns of immigration from Europe. Immigration itself has rarely provided a controversy of national scope, and nativist movements have been conspicuous on occasion but of no lasting significance. Ethnic issues as such, perhaps excluding the Negro question, have not had the impact on national politics that they have had, for example, in Canada. But with the tendency for individual nationality groupings to concentrate in particular areas, especially in the cities, and to find in their common rootlessness and frequently in the experience of discrimination and exploitation a basis in addition to national origin for cohesion and interdependence, they have constituted a means to power and influence for locally oriented political organizations outside and inside their own ranks.

It is these geographically defined factors, accentuated by a low-temperature, domestic politics, which give major force and relevance to the possibility of state control over the composition of the national governing bodies, through the electoral college and related means. Structural elements in the system—some, it is argued here, inherent in federalism—alone encourage an irreducible minimum of decentralization and disruption in the party system. But it is as these reflect the underlying pace of the political process and as they are harnessed to regionally differentiated issues and clusters of organization that they find their most impelling dynamic. . . .

6.   FOUR-PARTY POLITICS

James MacGregor Burns

We can conclude that the pattern of national politics is essentially a four-party pattern. The Democratic and Republican parties are each divided into congressional and presidential structures, with all the elements that comprise the Amercan type of party.

The division of Democrats and Republicans into two parties each is of course the immediate cause of the national four-party pattern. The four parties would not last long, however, if they lacked strong attitudinal bases in the electorate. They might not continue, for example, if people divided only over economic issues, for such a situation, combined with the tendency of politicians toward combinations, would normally produce two groupings, presumably of those who got smaller slices of the economic loaf against those who got bigger. At least two factors operate against such a simple two-way division in America.

One is the obvious fact that people divide over issues other than economic ones and—a crucial point—that the economic divisions are not congruent with the others. By "other issues" I mean those that have been variously called "moral" or "style" issues but that I will call "way-of-life" issues—that is, issues that pose choices about a nation's whole culture and way of

life and that cannot be calculated in terms of immediate and tangible economic return for specific groups of people. Taxes, wages, social security, farm prices, tariffs, public housing are examples of economic issues; while civil liberties, women's rights, disarmament, immigration, corruption in government, defense strategy, racial tolerance and integration, government, and religion are examples of way-of-life issues. The presumed motivational appeal of the former, Berelson, Lazarsfeld, and McPhee suggest, is self-interest of a relatively direct and tangible kind, while that of the latter is self-expression and self-gratification of a more subjective, symbolic, and projective kind. Issues do not fall neatly into the two categories. An expansion of civil rights, such as job opportunity, or of immigration of certain types of workers, or of certain types of defense activities, could mean economic benefits or deprivations for various groups as well as psychic benefits or deprivations for a wider public. But the difference between the two seems sharp enough to affect the shape of our party structure.

Data on the non-congruence of economic and way-of-life issues are limited but highly suggestive. Polls indicate that there has been in recent years little if any relationship between persons' relative positions on domestic and foreign issues. "An interventionist position in foreign affairs was as likely

From James MacGregor Burns, *The Deadlock of Democracy* (Englewood Cliffs, N.J.: Prentice-Hall, Inc., 1963) pp. 257-64 (Spectrum edition), excerpts. By permission of the publisher.

to be taken by a domestic conservative as by a domestic liberal" in 1956, report Campbell and associates, "and the relative isolationist was as likely to favor social welfare activities in Washington as he was to oppose them." By cross-tabulating distributions of responses in 1952 to an "international involvement" question and a "social welfare activity" question, Key finds four combinations of opinion: isolationist-liberal, internationalist-liberal, isolationist-conservative, internationalist-conservative (with the last the smallest of the four in numbers).

Evidence on the non-congruence of economic and domestic way-of-life issues is even more limited but still suggestive. Much of it stems from historians' observations. The political parties have usually had their "conscience" and "cotton" wings. Under Theodore Roosevelt the Republican party numbered hosts of high-income business and professional men who looked on their party mainly as a weapon to attack the moral and social evils of the day. The Democratic party in Bryan's and Wilson's days and also more recently has numbered not only hosts of economic reformers but also workers and farmers who took a hostile or stunted view of civil liberties, women's rights, civil rights, civic betterment, and other way-of-life problems.

A second root cause of the four-party pattern is the disarticulation of the national and state party systems, stemming from the workings of federalism in a sectional society combined with some of our special political arrangements. The impact of national politics on state and local politics in our sectional nation has been noted in these pages—the creation of one-party states and districts. Balance and competition at the national level, espe-

cially in presidential contests, helped produce local noncompetition and imbalance, most notably in the South and rural North. These one-party areas tended to be ignored by presidential candidates, who concentrated on the swing areas, and hence the one-party areas became less important to the presidential parties, but they received extra representation in Congress because of the seniority system, and hence became the buttress of the congressional parties.

This double cleavage, institutional and attitudinal, between the presidential parties and the congressional parties is largely responsible for the conflicting positions that a President, whether Democratic or Republican, and a Congress, whether Democratic or Republican controlled, take on the crucial affairs of state.

Willmore Kendall has pointed to the curious fact that the Executive "is able, with good show of reason, to put itself forward on any particular issue as the spokesman for... lofty and enlightened principle. ... The Executive tends, that is to say, to have the nation's ministers and publicists with it on 'peace,' the nation's professors and moralizers with it on desegregation, the nation's economists with it on fiscal policy and redistribution, the nation's political scientists with it on political reform and civil rights, etc." ... Congress, according to Professor Kendall, stresses other values; small group discussion in the community, deference to highly prestiged and presumably wiser citizens, and an anti-quixotic concern for the "realities, problems, the potential benefits and potential costs (and for whom?)" of presidential proposals. ...

The consequence of the four-party system is that American political leaders, in order to govern, must manage multiparty coalitions just as heads of coalition parliamentary regimes in Europe have traditionally done—as the French did, for example, before De Gaulle. But the task of governing in a sense is harder in the United States, for the leaders' job is not simply to pick up enough parliamentary votes to form a cabinet, or even just to pass a bill. They must bring together the right combination of presidential party and congressional party strength to accomplish a great variety of tasks day after day and year after year. And the leaders' job is further complicated by the fact that continuous, effective government policy-making is impossible without a strong working alliance between at least some combination of presidential and congressional parties. For the presidential side and the congressional side each wields power not only in its own "constitutional" orbit but in the opposite side's orbit as well.

The extent to which the congressional and presidential parties share the same powers and hence can block each other is extraordinary. The President has a broad range of legislative power besides his veto: he can issue executive orders that have the force of law; he can draw up with other nations executive agreements that are as controlling under international law as treaties ratified by the Senate; he can make war "by the push of a button" and let Congress ratify it later, if at all. But Congress inserts itself into the executive process too. The Senate can refuse to confirm appointments—even one lone Senator can induce the whole upper body to withhold approval through the device of "senatorial courtesy." The standing committees closely affect administrative arrangements through their control of policy, and the appropriations committees and subcommittees have a profound impact through their control of funds. The more "independent" an agency or commission may be of the President, the more dependent it may be on a committee or faction of Congress. The relation, of course, changes over time. After the Civil War Congress tried to control the Administration through such means as the Tenure of Office Act; the act is long since gone but not some of the motivation behind it. Today the Army Chief of Engineers has legislative authority to plan public works and report to Congress without clearing with the President.

In less obvious fields too, the two-party coalitions, the congressional and the presidential, maintain countervailing institutional apparatus. The President can publicize an issue and influence public opinion by appointing a "blue-ribbon" presidential commission controlled by the President's men, and he and his lieutenants can set into action other varieties of Administration inquiries, probes, and explorations. Congress at the same time has its standing committees, including the Un-American Activities Committee, which can investigate at the drop of a hat, and it can set up special committees to conduct grand investigations. . . .

This bewildering array of countervailing and overlapping powers compels American political leaders to piece together a new patch-work of party fragments, factional chieftains, congressional votes, constitutional usage, and bureaucratic officials in order to put through each major new program. Presidential party leaders do this through endless persuading, pressuring, manipulating, and bargaining. Congressional party leaders use the same methods to balk or modify

Administration proposals, and their task is all the easier because of the many points at which action can be slowed or stopped in the narrow, twisting, and crowded legislative channels. Since each set of parties, congressional or presidential, is a coalition itself, action depends on the alignment of coalition with coalition.

Not that the presidential and congressional party coalitions are of the same type. The former, to use Dahl's apt expression, is an "executive-centered coalition." The President has means of direction and discipline unmatched by the congressional parties or by the presidential party out of power. He has a public position, a command of the media, a control over personnel, and a direct electoral link with the people that enable him to maintain and exploit a somewhat hierarchical system in the presidential party. The congressional party is led by a coalition of parties, allied through their common attitudes and mutual dependence, and with an internal party system marked more by bargaining than by hierarchy. The essential operational process differs: the congressional reliance on committees, with their tendency to protect an existing consensus over the status quo, contrasts with the executive emphasis on single-leader activism. The out-of-power presidential party, to use Dahl's terminology, is a network of "independent sovereignties with spheres of influence." But even this network, inchoate though it is, has the attributes of party —ideology, program, leadership, machinery, and existing or potential electoral support.

Any one of the four parties can—and does—coalesce with any one of the others. We take for granted the coalition of the Democratic presidential and congressional parties, and of the two Republican parties—though often we should not. The durable alliance of the congressional parties has long been publicized by liberals as the "unholy alliance of Old Guard Republicans and Dixie Democrats" in Congress. Less obvious is another alliance, holy or unholy, between presidential Democrats and presidential Republicans. These parties occasionally combine in Congress, as Republicans from urban and suburban districts support the proposals of Democratic Presidents. But the main focus of the presidential party alliance is in the foreign policy and fiscal agencies. Roosevelt's enlistment of Stimson and Knox in his Cabinet in 1940, Truman's appointment of a host of Republicans to foreign-policy and foreign-aid agencies, Eisenhower's choice of Texas Democrat Robert Anderson as Secretary of the Treasury, and Kennedy's retention of Douglas Dillon and other Republicans from the Eisenhower Administration and his selection of an internationalist Republican, McGeorge Bundy, as an assistant, reflect a wide community of interest between the two parties. The alliance is consecrated in the name of "bipartisanship in foreign policy," or the hoary slogan "Party politics stops at the water's edge." What mainly stops at the water's edge is not party politics in general but congressional party politics in particular. The real "unholy alliance" to a good congressional Republican is the historic coalition between the internationalists in both parties. And the internationalist newspapers that approve so highly of foreign-policy bipartisanship today were never so enthusiastic about it in the 1920's and the early 1930's, when it represented a coalition of isolationists.

No political system is neutral—

certainly not the congressional and presidential. Power is inseparable from structure. It is not by chance that liberal and internationalist Presidents in this century have been "strong" Presidents, and that men like Taft and Harding are relegated to the ranks of the weak. The stronger the exertion of presidential power, the more liberal and internationalist it will be because of the make-up and dynamics of the presidential party. The stronger the exertion of congressional power, the more conservative and isolationist will be our national policy because of the structure of the congressional forces. The man who is all for liberalism and internationalism "as long as the President's power is not increased" (as for example in the trade agreements act) is a man who has not grasped the relation of ends and means of power and structure. The man who favors cutting down the powers of Congress because it is "slow and inefficient" is cutting down conservative influence, whether he wants to or not. The structure of coalition politics is inevitably the structure of "who gets what, when and how" in American national politics. As the Madisonian system in being, it is also the structure of slowdown and stalemate in American government.

7. LOCAL PARTY SYSTEMS: THEORETICAL CONSIDERATIONS AND A CASE ANALYSIS

J. Leiper Freeman

In searching for causal factors underlying local party systems, it is appropriate to resort to theories about party systems generally and to select factors which seem most likely to explain and to be universally applicable. Most of the literature on voting alignments, especially at other levels than the local community, emphasizes the following factors: (a) the social structure of the community, particularly in its cultural, religious, and economic aspects, and (b) the institutional prescriptions bearing upon political organization in the community. The present study adds to these (c) the factor of local attitudes toward national party structure, measured by what has been generally recognized as party identification. The local community cannot be presumed to possess the autonomy characteristic of the national political community in the family of national states. Hence national party identification must be underscored as a factor of high potential relevance in determining the nature of the local party system.

Following some of the implications of the preceding propositions, one can turn to the problem of why a given community manifests a particular type of party system. It would be especially

From J. Leiper Freeman, "Theoretical Considerations, and a Case Analysis," *American Journal of Sociology*, LXIV, 3 (Nov., 1958), 282–289.
Reprinted from American Journal of Sociology by permission of the University of Chicago Press. Copyright, 1958 by the University of Chicago.

useful to examine local communities having party systems which approximate the two-party model to determine what factors seem to underwrite that kind of system in the community rather than some variation of the multiparty model. As working propositions, one might expect that local multiparty systems exist more often where the following conditions prevail:

1. Where the national party identifications are weak and muddled and the cleavage between the two major parties is not attitudinally and organizationally dramatized in the community.
2. Where the social structure (ethnic, religious, economic) of the community is diffuse and in a state of change so as to lend little stability to social cleavages.
3. Where the local election laws prohibit the national parties from officially participating in local elections.

On the other hand, one might expect the local two-party model to be more frequently approximated under the following conditions:

1. Where the two national parties are both attitudinally and organizationally represented in the community with considerable strength.
2. Where the social structure of the community is characterized by one or more deep-seated cleavages related probably to urbanization, industrialization, and stratification of the cultural, religious, and economic structure.
3. Where the local election laws allow official participation of the national parties in local elections.

There is a further question which may be asked at this point: Which of the types of factors listed above is most relevant to the kind of party system that prevails? The hope of the municipal reform advocates—that they can shape the local party system primarily by alteration of the laws and thus sever the relationship between local electoral behavior and national party identification—seems predicated upon the assumption that institutional prescriptions are the controlling factors. On the other hand, some research into the determinants of national party systems emphasizes that the social structure is certainly more important than institutional formulas or laws in determining national party structure. Other research indicates that national party identification is important in determining presidential voting alignments, perhaps more so than any other single factor. Key has suggested that, while national and local partisanship are related, local partisans tend to exhibit some degree of autonomy relative to national nominees in their local voting alignments.

The hypotheses maintained here are that both national party identification and the social structure of the community will ordinarily be more determinative of the local party system than will be the laws governing local elections. As between the two more crucial factors—national party identification and social structure—it is difficult to state which will be the more important. This depends to some degree upon the relative congruence of the two, since one affects the other. To the extent that they are not congruent, however, one should expect that, when national party identification is less related to local party alignments, social cleavages in the community should be more strongly related to them. Hence the major consequence of local election laws attempting to keep national party identification from playing a part in local politics should be to enhance the effect of basic social cleavages upon the local party system.

"Bay City": A Variation of the Two-Party Model

The utility of the foregoing concepts and propositions can be demonstrated with respect to an example of a local two-party system in the case of "Bay City," pseudonym of a Massachusetts industrial city of nearly 50,000 population. Bay City is predominantly Democratic in national politics, but a strong Republican contingent remains from the earlier days of their dominance of affairs in the Bay State and in New England. Over the years the Republicans in Bay City slowly lost strength as the Democrats gained in the battle of political demography. Predominantly composed of ethnic groups of Protestant affiliation prior to 1928, the Republicans found themselves facing an even more united array of ethnic groups of Catholic affiliation among the Democrats after Al Smith's candidacy in that year. Buttressing this development was the higher birth rate among Catholics and the appeal of the Democratic party to industrial workers during the 1930–1950 period. In 1953 the Bay City Republican was typically Protestant, Yankee (of English, Scotch, or Welsh descent), white-collar, more educated, and older, while the Democrat was typically Catholic, non-Yankee (of French, Irish, or Italian descent), blue-collar, less educated, and younger.

Historically, Bay City's local politics was officially divorced from its national politics by several legal devices prior to the time the data on local party identification were obtained. In the early 1930's the city adopted a "non-partisan" election form in which local candidates could not compete under the labels of the national parties.

Furthermore, local elections were, by law, held in the odd-numbered years, a time when state and national races were not scheduled. In addition, a year prior to the time of the study the city adopted a "non-partisan" primary system for nominating candidates in local elections, prohibiting the formal use of local caucuses in the process.

Political parties persisted, nevertheless, in the vacuum left in local politics by the official absence of Democrats and Republicans. Two local mass caucuses operated under the titles "Progressives" and "Non-partisans." These two local parties composed the basic party system in Bay City's municipal politics for many years, although the Progressives were intermittently split by a "third-party" candidate. Knowledgeable informants among the Non-partisan hierarchy were frank to admit that splitting the Progressives was part of the strategy of "divide and rule." A united Progressive party could usually produce a comfortable majority. It is known that certain Non-partisans have not been above helping finance a discontented Progressive in his campaign as a third candidate. In sum, Bay City's local party structure basically conformed to the two-party model, with the minority party showing greater cohesion than the majority.

The data clearly show that this local party system was very strongly related to the national party system in the city. Not only was there a marked relationship between a citizen's identifying with the Democratic party in national politics and his preference for the Progressives in local politics but, the stronger his identification with the Democrats, the more likely his preference for the Progressives. Conversely, the same relation-

TABLE 1-1
BAY CITIZENS LOCAL PARTY PREFERENCES IN RELATION
TO THEIR NATIONAL PARTY IDENTIFICATIONS

	Bay Citizens National Party Identifications by Strength (Per Cent)				
	Strong Democrat	Weak Democrat	Neither	Weak Republican	Strong Republican
Bay Citizens local party preferences, by strength:					
Strong Progressive	70.6	26.6	7.9	7.4	4.4
Weak Progressive	16.7	21.3	10.1	14.8	4.4
Neither	7.9	42.5	53.9	31.5	8.3
Weak Non-partisan....	0.9	5.3	13.5	20.4	17.8
Strong Non-partisan ..	3.6	4.3	14.6	25.9	64.9
N	(329)	(94)	(89)	(54)	(180)

ship held between identifying as a Republican and preferring the local Non-partisans (see Table 1–1). Certainly, in a city where there are two organized and clearly competing national parties with which the local citizens identify in large numbers, a favorable base seems to be laid for a two-party system in local politics, even though the local parties may adopt deceptive appellations.

Leaving the effect of national partisanship momentarily, we ask what the social foundations of Bay City's two-party system were. They were what one might expect, given the close association shown between national and local party identification in the city. Distinct local partisan preferences were related to the following factors, considered one at a time: (*a*) the citizens' religious affiliations, Catholic versus Protestant; (*b*) their ethnic groups, Italian, French, Irish, Finnish, or Yankee (English, Scotch, Welsh) ancestry; (*c*) occupation, blue-collar versus white-collar; and (*d*) education, low (less than high school) versus high (high-school graduate or more). In each of the four categories of factors just mentioned, the one cited first is positively associated with preference for the local Progressive party (see

Table 1–2). In other words, the typical Bay City Progressive showed the same characteristics as did the typical Democrat described earlier in this article, and the typical Bay City Non-partisan similarly shared the characteristics of the typical Republican.

These social correlates of Bay City's local party system demonstrated that several factors possibly operated in addition to the national party identifications to support a local two-party alignment. The findings supported the proposition that a social structure in which certain cultural, religious, or economic dichotomies are strong furnishes a favorable base for a local two-party system. Yet, since the factors examined were known to be related to national party identification, it might have been that the local party system in Bay City had no discernible base other than the Democratic-Republican division. Therefore, it was necessary to examine the relation of these social factors to local party preference, holding national party identification constant.

In the main, Bay City data showed that, even with the type and strength of national party identification held constant, one major social factor— religious affiliation—produced a signif-

TABLE 1-2
LOCAL PARTY PREFERENCES OF BAY CITIZENS, IN RELATION TO (A) RELIGION, (B) ETHNICITY, (C) OCCUPATION, AND (D) EDUCATION (PER CENT)

| | a) Religion | | b) Ethnicity | | | | |
	Catholic	Protestant	Italian	French	Irish	Finnish	Yankee
Bay Citizens local party preferences by strength:							
Strong Progressive	51.8	14.2	58.5	45.2	42.8	35.9	19.8
Weak Progressive	17.3	7.1	17.0	14.0	18.7	17.2	10.3
Neither	18.8	18.3	11.3	22.9	22.0	18.7	15.7
Weak Non-partisan....	3.6	17.2	3.8	6.1	6.6	9.4	14.4
Strong Non-partian....	8.2	43.3	9.4	11.7	9.9	18.7	39.7
N	(439)	(268)	(53)	(179)	(91)	(64)	(146)

| | c) Occupation | | d) Education | |
	Blue-Collar	White-Collar	Less than High School	High School or More
Bay Citizens local party preferences by strength:				
Strong Progressive	44.1	22.4	44.1	27.0
Weak Progressive	12.9	14.6	13.2	13.8
Neither	19.4	20.9	21.3	17.0
Weak Non-partisan....	6.6	12.3	4.6	13.8
Strong Non-partisan ..	16.7	29.5	16.5	28.2
N	(441)	(267)	(430)	(311)

icant difference in citizens' preferences for a local party (see Table 1–3). Catholics gravitated toward the Progressives; Protestants, toward the Non-partisans. The local parties, then, were more than mere reflections of national party loyalties in the community arena. They also represented an adaptation of partisanship to a dominant local social and cultural cleavage.

No other factors produced local partisan differences within national party types as strongly and consistently as did religion. The next factor in order of strength was occupational status, with blue-collar workers tending more toward the Progressives than white-collar workers. Since occupational status was, however, strongly related to religious affiliation, the apparent effect of the former could be largely regarded as a by-product of the latter. Furthermore, education did not differentiate local partisans

within national party types as clearly as either religion or occupation. In fact, there was a slight indication that, the higher the education, the greater the tendency of national partisans to prefer their "same" parties locally, regardless of whether they were Democrats or Republicans. Presumably, the better educated person was a bit more capable of understanding the complexities of politics and therefore more capable of maintaining a consistent party position.

It should be stressed at this point that religious affiliation, as such, is a variable largely subsuming another important factor, ethnicity, which could not be treated adequately due to the limited number of cases in the sample. Religious affiliation should not be regarded here so much as a general index of doctrinal differences in the community as one of broad social groupings. The differences

TABLE 1-3
LOCAL PARTY PREFRENCES OF BAY CITIZENS IN RELATION TO (A) RELIGION, (B) OCCUPATION, AND (C) EDUCATION, WITH NATIONAL PARTY IDENTIFICATIONS HELD CONSTANT

	Bay Citizens National Party Identifications by Strength (Per Cent)									
	Strong Democratic		Weak Democratic		Neither		Weak Republican		Strong Republican	
	Cath.	Prot.	Cath.	Prot.	Cath.	Prot.	Cath.	Prot.	Cath.	Prot.
Bay Citizens local party preferences, by strength:										
Strong Progressive ..	72.4	59.5	28.1	25.9	9.6	6.5	11.5	3.8	16.7	2.1
Weak Progressive ..	16.7	16.7	24.6	18.5	15.4	0.0	26.9	3.8	3.3	4.2
Neither	7.3	11.9	40.3	44.4	57.7	41.9	23.1	34.6	13.3	7.0
Weak Non-partisan..	0.7	2.4	3.5	7.4	7.7	25.8	15.4	26.9	13.3	19.7
Strong Non-partisan.	2.5	9.5	3.5	3.7	9.6	25.8	23.1	30.8	53.3	66.9
N	(274)	(42)	(57)	(27)	(52)	(31)	(26)	(26)	(30)	(142)
	Blue Collar	White Collar	Blue Collar	White Collar	Blue Collar	White Collar	Blue Collar	White Collar	Blue Collar	White Collar
Local party:										
Strong Progressive ..	74.3	57.5	30.0	21.2	12.0	2.9	13.8	0.0	4.8	2.3
Weak Progressive ..	13.2	26.4	20.0	24.2	10.0	11.4	24.1	4.0	4.8	3.4
Neither	7.3	11.5	38.3	48.5	62.0	42.9	27.6	36.0	9.6	6.9
Weak Non-partisan..	0.5	2.3	5.0	6.1	8.0	22.9	20.7	20.0	18.1	18.4
Strong Non-partisan.	4.6	2.3	6.7	0.0	8.0	20.0	13.8	40.0	62.6	68.9
N	(219)	(87)	(60)	(33)	(50)	(35)	(29)	(25)	(83)	(87)
	Low*	High†	Low	High	Low	High	Low	High	Low	High
Local party:										
Strong Progressive ..	73.5	65.7	23.3	32.4	11.8	2.6	16.0	0.0	9.0	1.0
Weak Progressive ..	12.9	25.0	20.0	23.5	11.8	7.9	20.0	10.3	7.7	2.0
Neither	8.3	6.5	45.0	38.2	54.9	52.6	36.0	27.6	12.8	4.9
Weak Non-partisan..	0.5	1.9	5.0	5.9	11.8	15.8	12.0	27.6	9.0	24.5
Strong Non-partisan.	4.6	0.9	6.7	0.0	9.8	21.0	16.0	34.5	61.5	37.6
N	(216)	(108)	(60)	(34)	(51)	(38)	(25)	(29)	(78)	(102)

* Less than high-school graduate.
† High-school graduate or more.

evidenced among the ethnic groups (Table 1–2) in their attachment to local parties reflect a major cleavage between those ethnic types having Catholic affiliations and those having Protestant affiliations. Yet the evidence also warrants the speculation that ethnic attachments were related to local party preferences somewhat independently, too, within the two major religious categories of the city. This supports the contention often made in the city's political circles that the intermittent lack of cohesion in the Progressive party could be traced to competition among Italian, French, and Irish groups. Certainly, the possible defection of one or another ethnic segment of the Progressives was regarded by leaders of the Non-partisans as a major condition of their "divide and rule" strategy.

With the above qualifications in mind, certain general observations may be made about the local two-party system in Bay City. On the whole, it seemed primarily to be based upon national party identifications and religious affiliations within the community, with the former the stronger foundation, although the latter clearly functioned as an additional basis for local partisanship, especially where national party identification was nil. Specifically, among those citizens who identified with neither of the national parties, religion had its maximum effect in dividing people into the two local parties. It must also be emphasized that these two factors persevered in dividing "Bay Citizens" into a basically two-party system in local politics despite what might be considered nearly maximum legal provisions for so-called non-partisan local elections.

The Bay City variation of the two-party model therefore supports the following propositions:

1. Institutional devices are not likely to abolish a local two-party system in a city where attitudes toward the two major national parties are strongly structured and the relations between national and local party organizations are durable and persistent.

2. Insofar as legal devices may have some effect in disrupting the durable and persistent relationship between national and local party identifications, the foundations of the local party system will be altered in the direction of the dominant social divisions in the community. In Bay City's case this did not mean the destruction of the local two-party system but rather the conforming more closely to the divisions represented by Protestant and Catholic affiliations in the city. Divisions so represented were not necessarily of a doctrinal sort but rather were related to broad cleavages in the community deriving in part from ethnic and status differences which tended to coincide with different religious affiliations.

PART TWO

Political Parties:
Organization
and
Composition

Since the United States has a federal system, political power is decentralized; this is as true of the political parties as it is of the governmental structure. Rather than mere branch offices of a national organization the state parties are distinct entities of indeterminate autonomy whose relations with one another, and many of whose relations with the national party, strongly resemble those of sovereign states engaged in international relations. Furthermore, they themselves contain local organizations with which their relations may be *de jure* unitary, but are more often than not *de facto* federal. Powerful local organizations such as those in Chicago, Philadelphia, or Jersey City are quite as likely to dominate their respective state organizations as to be dominated by them. In a system of autonomous party organizations, those units nearest the source of power—the ballot box—tend to be strongest, although this should not be taken to mean that the controlling unit in party organizations is the precinct committee.

Both state and national parties serve as means of access to decision-making centers by those concerned. Arthur Schlesinger, Jr., maintains that to be successful an American party must have a multi-interest character, a require-ment dictated by the "brilliant and wonderful variety that is America." David B. Truman discusses the relationship between parties and interest groups, how they provide "access," and the differing balance of forces with-in a single political party.

From the standpoint of competition, the United States only faintly re-sembles the model of the two-party system. Quite apart from fluctuations in competitiveness at the national level, Austin Ranney points out that only half the states have genuine two-party competition; and more than half of those developed it only after World War II. He found further that insofar as party cohesiveness is an element of party competition, the state parties differ widely. At the local level, Elmer E. Cornwells, Jr., sees a decline in the power of the great city organizations stemming from the decline in immi-gration. The "bosses" who provided services to the unassimilated immi-grants were paid in votes. Immigration restrictions have largely deprived the bosses of their clientele, although interregional migration is still a factor. Cornwells' argument however does not account for the importance of sub-urban political machines that perform for constituents many services, albeit of a different nature from those undertaken by their earlier urban counter-parts. Louis C. Gawthrop notes the problem of the national "out-party" in establishing a national image despite its lack of internal cohesion and the change in its balance of power when the "presidential wing" leaves the White House.

Like other organizations, political parties require personnel to perform appropriate functions. Max Weber divides those who follow politics as a vocation into two categories based on their motivations and goals. Weber deals primarily with the professional politician, but James Q. Wilson sees another type, the amateur politician, developing. The commitment of the amateur, he believes, was more likely to be issue-oriented than that of the professional, with the possible consequence that in local politics questions of ideology and style become more important.

American Political Parties:
General

8. THE MULTI-INTEREST PARTY

Arthur Schlesinger, Jr.

A multi-interest party has several obvious advantages from the viewpoint of providing wise leadership. The first is that, since policy emerges from a wide consultation among various groups, it has a much better chance of corresponding to the needs of a diversified society and a sprawling nation. If government programs have to run the gauntlet of a variety of interests, the resulting process of criticism and modification increases the chance of producing policies which will genuinely serve the national interest. Of course, a single interest may be gifted with infallibility and thus not require the correction and chastening of other viewpoints; but this situation has not often arisen in the American democracy, where, as Jefferson has reminded us, we have not found angels to govern us.

The second advantage of the multi-interest party springs from the premium the coalition situation places on effective leadership. The driver with a team of fractious and competing horses must learn to impose his will if he is to stay on the road. Similarly a party leader who first must master

From Arthur Schlesinger, Jr., "The Multi-Interest Party," *The New Republic*, CXXX, 14 (April 5, 1954), 9–12, excerpts. By permission of the publisher. 1954, Harrison-Blaine of New Jersey, Inc.

his own coalition is more likely to develop the instincts and aptitudes which would enable him to lead the country. The potential viciousness of the multi-interest system lies in the possibility that a political leader might cater only to the interest groups and let the national welfare vanish in a scramble for special benefits. This is a real problem, and not to be underestimated. But the experience of controlling these tendencies only further develops capacities for national leadership. Nothing produces a more lively sense of the public interest than an awareness of the conflicts among special interests. The experience of directing a multi-interest party, in short, is unparalleled training for the experience of governing a multi-interest nation.

The third advantage of the multi-interest party springs from the premium the coalition situation places on ideas —that is, on thought and on *thinking*. This is only partly because the intellectuals, as a permanent minority group, will always be members of the multi-interest coalition. It is also because of the inherent need of the multi-interest party for policies, programs, formulas which will bind divergent groups together and reconcile their conflicting interests. The multi-interest party, in short, has both an urgent need for ideas and the people on hand who can work them out; and the result will be a much higher degree of intellectual activity and creativity.

The fourth advantage of the multi-interest party is that it has a better chance of winning consent for its policies. This is partly because its policies, developed from a concurrence of groups, are more likely to meet the needs of all; and partly because the multi-interest process of policy formation has a built-in tendency to

secure assent since no group in the country is likely to have the feeling of total exclusion. . . .

What are the consequences of single-interest government? The first consequence is surely a tendency to mistake a class interest for the national interest. No matter how much they may differ among themselves over minor issues, men of a single interest— whether business, labor, agriculture— have a set of common assumptions and beliefs. These assumptions and beliefs, though they may constitute an important part of American life, do not constitute its whole; and any policy based on the theory, for example, that business faith and experience do adequately represent the multifarious interests of American life is doomed to disaster. This is not the fault of businessmen. Probably no other single interest could do any better. It is the inevitable consequence when decisions are reached by men with a common background, common values and common objectives; no matter how high-minded and disinterested they may be personally, they can hardly escape identifying the welfare of their own group with the welfare of the nation— unless, that is, there are other people sitting around that table with equal authority and confidence who can speak up and say, "Hold on; wait a minute; let's consider what this will do to the farmers, or to the workers, or to the minority groups, or to civil liberties." The logic of single-interest government, in short, was stated with peculiar felicity and force by the Secretary of Defense when he said last winter [1953] that what was good for General Motors was good for the country.

The second consequence of single-interest government is to create tendencies toward weak executive leadership. If the job of the party leader is not to harmonize conflicting interests but to register a generally agreed-on view, then there is plainly less need for him to develop the resources of the Presidential power. That is probably one reason why, except for Lincoln and Theodore Roosevelt, all Republican Presidents have been what is technically known among political scientists as "weak" Presidents.

The third consequence of single-interest government is to create tendencies toward intellectual conformity and stagnation. This is partly because of the natural hostility between the major interest and the intellectuals (a hostility now deeply inbred in the case of the business community) and partly because the homogeneity of interests reduces the need for new formulations and new ideas.

The fourth consequence of single-interest government is to complicate the problem of winning assent. The farmers, workers, independent businessmen, eggheads, minority groups, etc., who feel that, in Mr. Burgess' phrase, *their* kind of people are not in power, are likely to regard with suspicion the proposals of a government that represents only Mr. Burgess' kind.

The Republican press has admitted fairly freely in recent months that most of these tendencies—weak executive leadership, intellectual apathy, popular dissatisfaction—are all too visible in this current experiment in single-interest government. And the incapacity of the new administration to develop national policies was strikingly illustrated when Attorney General Brownell, considered to be the political genius of the liberal wing of the party, dedicated himself to the enterprise accurately described by Adlai Stevenson as trying to take McCarthyism away from McCarthy. The Attorney General's suggestion that the former

President of the United States had knowingly appointed a Communist spy to high office was surely made, so to speak, in lieu of a more formal filing of a petition in intellectual bankruptcy.

Can the Republicans reverse their movement toward single-interest government? Is it too late for them to make their administration truly representative of the various interests in our pluralistic society? To do this, it must first be said, would require a major exertion of Presidential leadership, for the business community would have to be persuaded to relinquish part of its new power to lesser groups in society—especially to labor and the farmers. Such self-abnegation seems an unlikely eventuality. And it would appear, in consequence, that the general welfare and the national interest will continue to be served better in the future, as in the past, by a frankly multi-interest party.

But this argument contains warnings to the Democrats too. This is why I would insist that its basic thrust is neither anti-Republican nor antibusiness community. The Democrats must remember first that their party is not the property of a single section or a single interest; and, second, that being a receptacle is necessary, but it is not enough. The trick of political greatness is not to serve as a mechanism for whetting and gratifying group appetites. The problem is to develop an ardent sense of the national interest which includes and transcends the special interests within a framework of positive standards of decency and justice. This cannot be done by weak indulgence of class demand or sectional prejudice. It can only be done by hard work and by hard thought, by tolerance, by imagination, by a sense of responsibility and by a belief in the exercise of leadership.

The urgent necessity today—as always in our history—remains that of remembering the limitations and possibilities of man. If our government and our society are to work, they must rest, not on the presumed superior wisdom and infallibility of a single-interest, but on the diverse and reciprocally conditioned judgments of a plurality of interests; for this alone can faithfully represent the brilliant and wonderful variety that is America.

9. INTEREST GROUPS AND POLITICAL PARTIES

David B. Truman

The Basic Objective: Access

Power of any kind cannot be reached by a political interest group, or its leaders, without access to one or more key points of decision in the government. Access, therefore, becomes the facilitating intermediate objective of political interest groups. The development and improvement of such access is a common denominator of the tactics of all of them, frequently leading to efforts to exclude competing groups from equivalent access or to set up new decision points access to which can be monopolized by a particular group. Toward whatever institution of government we observe interest groups operating, the common feature of all their efforts is the attempt to achieve effective access to points of decision.

Key decision points may be explicitly established by the formal legal framework of the government, or they may lie in the gaps and interstices of the formal structure, protected by custom or by semi-obscurity. One key

From David B. Truman, "Interest Groups and Political Parties: Access and Involvements," *The Governmental Process* (New York Alfred A. Knopf, Inc., 1951) pp. 264-80, excerpts.

point may be at the president's elbow as he writes his message on the state of the Union; another may be in a smoke-filled room at a nominating convention; and a third almost literally may be in a legislative committee chairman's coat pocket, into which it is desired to slip a bill to prevent its being considered by the Congress. To describe the relative ease with which various groups gain access to such points of decision and to analyze the exploitation of such access through time is another way to describe the governmental institutions involved.

The importance of access to the machinery of government is formally recognized in the Constitution itself. Thus the First Amendment provides: "Congress shall make no law ... abridging ... the right of the people peaceably to assemble, and to petition the government for a redress of grievances." This provision, it should be noted, although an important safety valve, is a minimum guarantee and is essentially negative in character. Although Congress may not formally restrict access, the facts of the social structure, including established procedure, internal group politics, and the like, afford relatively greater ease of access to some groups as compared with others. Such will be a recurring theme of the next several chapters, but it may clarify the point to explore here some of its more general aspects.

Perhaps the most basic factor affecting access is the position of the group or its spokesman in the social structure. We encountered this element when discussing relative propaganda advantage in the preceding chapter. It is equally important here and for the same reasons. The deference accorded a high-status group not only facilitates the acceptance of its propaganda but also eases it approach to the government. Its petitions and claims may even in some instances appear less as demands or supplications and more as flattery of the official of whom a favor is asked. Such is likely to be the case when the legislative representative of a major corporation, of the American Bar Association, or of the Chamber of Commerce of the United States approaches a junior member of the legislature or an aspiring administrator. Even an official who shares the attitudes of a competing group may be flattered into aiding one of these high-status organizations. Even where flattery is not an influence, the high-status group is aided by the large proportion of key officials—legislative, executive, and judicial—whose class backgrounds are such that they have similar values, manners, and preconceptions. . . .

The Meanings of "Political Party"

The political party has come to be thought of as the instrumentality through which choices are made among aspirants for office. Access to this instrumentality, therefore, may be important to a political interest group, although, for reasons that will become apparent in succeeding pages, it cannot be the only, and may not be the most important, point of access to government. Group connections with the parties may be of the same type as those with other parts of the machinery of government; the latter may be either supplementary to, or alternative to, the contacts with party organizations. . . .

Some observers have interpreted the multiplication of organized political interest groups as evidence of the failure or decline of the political party in the United States. These, however, would not seem to be the most meaningful terms in which to state the situation. Clearly a change has taken place, a change in the character both of the interactions composing political parties and of those constituting the political interest groups. The initiative in promoting particular policies is apparently assumed more frequently by the latter, although precise evidence on the point is not available. But the functional relationship between the parties and interest groups remains the same. With limited local exceptions, some of which will be discussed shortly, no interest group or alliance of such groups has supplanted the party as a device for mobilizing majorities. The two types of group are still interdependent. The search for understanding, therefore, must concentrate upon the precise nature of the interactions, upon the character of this interdependence.

Serious difficulty is encountered in an effort to analyze the relations between parties and interest groups because the term "political party" has so many different meanings in this country. By "meanings," of course, we refer to the range and variety of behaviors that are called "political party" in different circumstances.

Even if one considers only the two major parties, the behavior patterns are fluid and inconsistent. The term does not have the same meaning at the national, state and local levels of government; it may not have the same meaning in two States or in two localities; finally, in the nation, in a single State, or in a single city the term may not have the same meaning at one point in time as at another, in one campaign year and in the next. It usually means in election campaigns something very different from what it means when applied to activities in a legislature. Less is known on the subject of these variations than would be desirable, but it is obvious that it is risky to speak of the relationships between political interest groups and "the political' party," since such relationships will vary in part according to differences in the bahavior that constitutes the party in different places and at different times.

The protean character of political parties will be apparent if the major political parties are examined as national aggregations. Herring has suggested that "the organization of the party on a national scale is most accurately envisaged in terms of a network of personal relations." He is not simply restating the obvious fact that all organizations are patterns of interpersonal relations. Rather, he means that the organization of the so-called national parties does not have much continuity of pattern, regardless of the persons who occupy various positions in the formalized structure. At a given period the organization is composed of the temporary, shifting relationships that a man or a handful of men have been able to establish with other individuals throughout all or part of the country. The formal, paper structure shows a hierarchy of committees running upward from the local voting precincts through the county, the State, and the senatorial and congressional campaign committees to the national committees. Actual lines of authority, however, do not correspond to this paper structure. The key men in the national party may not even be members of any of these committees. Even if some or all of them are, however, a committee at one level ordinarily has no control over one at the next lower level in the paper structure. The various committees actually are largely autonomous and are arranged in parallel, rather than in a hierarchy—units which become associated in temporary collaboration for the period of a campaign or a series of campaigns. . . .

One result of the kaleidoscopic pattern of national party organization is that the relationships that produce the vote for a president in a State or locality may be quite different from those that elect senators and congressmen, to say nothing of governors. In such circumstances it is accurate to say that the effective constituencies of the two sets of officials are different and even conflicting. The political interest groups supporting them are correspondingly different. The consequences for harmony between the President and Congress on matters of legislation, which will be explored in another chapter, are obvious. It is this sort of situation, in fact, that explains why interest groups, as Bentley and others have noted, encounter different degrees of resistance to their claims in the two houses of Congress and in the presidency and why they therefore work primarily through one or the other of these channels, whichever is more receptive.

The meaning of the term "political party" is even more obscure if the behaviors so designated are examined at the State level. Lack of correspondence between the constituencies of State and national officers is only one aspect of the matter. In certain States at certain times correspondence may be quite close, yet it may be virtually nonexistent in the same States at other times. In most States the pattern of activity that is given the label "party" involves securing the support of a majority of voters for at least some of the candidates running for office under the party banner, but in some this function is in no sense implied by the term. The major political parties in the States sometimes operate as units of a national organization, whereas at other times they go their own way; they are always autonomous. At some times and places they stage a co-ordinated assault upon every major elective office in the State; at others, each nominee makes a completely independent effort without help from a State party.

The factional struggles for control of a State party are not just clique rivalries, devoid of content. Depending on what faction is dominant and on the extent of its dominance, the party is likely to vary in the functions it performs and in the interests that it represents. For example, in recent years the so-called Grundy faction of the Pennsylvania Republican party has been made up primarily of elements in the rural counties and small towns rather than those in the major cities of Philadelphia and Pittsburgh. When it is dominant and its men are the nominees for all the State-wide offices, the organized support it receives in the major cities at the general election is likely to be *ad hoc* and improvised, or reflective of the habitual responses of voters to a party label. Nominees on the State-wide slate who are not of

this faction need to develop their own organization support in the election, as the dominant faction may not provide assistance and may even quietly aid the candidate of the opposition party. Moreover, when control of the State organization falls to the Grundy faction, the interests having access to the State party are likely to be quite different from those dominant in the urban centers. . . .

The heterogeneity of political parties in the United States is at its peak in the localities—cities, counties, legislative, and other election districts. At this level the party may be a unified organization capable of executing a co-ordinated campaign inclusive of all offices for which "party" nominees are running. Probably more often the candidate in each local constituency must organize a purely personal following that for all practical purposes becomes the party organization in that election district. When no such candidate presents himself, the party organization simply does not exist in the locality. This situation is particularly common in congressional districts, but it is not peculiar to them.

The local party organization at various times and places may be effectively tied in with the State and even the national organizations. As indicated earlier, however, the local organization is not therefore necessarily subordinate. It may be, in fact, the controlling element in the State party and synonymous with the national party in a particular State. Thus in Illinois the Cook County (Chicago) Democratic organization has long been the dominant force in the State party and usually has acted for it in the party councils at the national level. At times, however, its hegemony has been challenged by a governor or United States senator whose personal following may be more extensive and may even include some of the elements nominally part of the Cook County organization.

Party organizations in the localities are often almost completely autonomous, Gosnell's studies in Chicago, for example, disclosed the astonishing ease with which ward and precinct leaders were able to move with their supporters not only from one party faction to another but occasionally even from one party to another. Any well-disciplined faction from the precinct on up is likely to show independence. Such groupings may be the building blocks of more inclusive organizations, but they are exceedingly fractious and unruly ones. Moreover, the governmental officials whom they elect to State and national office are tied directly to these local constituency organizations, whether the public officials have made, or are made by, the district parties. Such officials are attached only tenuously to any more inclusive aggregaton. The activities of local party workers of the Eighth Congressional District of Virginia in the election of November, 1944, were a particularly open illustration of independence, but they were not remarkable in any other respect. These workers were urging those coming to the polls to "Vote for Howard Smith (Democrat) for Congress and Dewey for President." More cautious ones ones confined themselves to "Vote for Howard Smith for Congress and your choice for President." . . .

American Political Parties:
State and Local

10. PARTIES IN STATE POLITICS

Austin Ranney

Inter-Party Competition

Of all the variables studied in the analysis of state party politics, the one receiving the most attention from political scientists has been "inter-party competition": that is, the usual or "normal" distribution of popular votes and public offices between Republicans and Democrats. Most writers on the subject of state politics believe that a

From *Politics in the American States: A Comparative Analysis,* Herbert Jacob and Kenneth N. Vines, ed., Chapter 3, "Parties in State Politics" by Austin Ranney. Copyright © 1965, by Little, Brown and Company (Inc.), and reprinted by permission of the publisher.

state's competitiveness is significantly related to other characteristics of its parties and politics. Taking their lead from the pioneering works of V. O. Key, they generalize that the state parties facing the closest competition are likely to have the most centralized control of nominations, and the highest cohesion in state legislatures and in gubernatorial-legislative relations. Consequently, they are likely to be the most effective and responsible governing agencies. Thus we begin our analysis by categorizing the states according to degree of inter-party competition.

Dimensions and Measurement

In recent years a number of political scientists have developed various ways of measuring inter-party competition in the states. Each measure differs somewhat from the others in time period covered, offices for which elections are tabulated, and definitions of categories. All who try to measure inter-party competition, however, agree with Richard Dawson and James Robinson that it has three basic dimensions:

Proportion of Success: the per cent of the votes won by each party for state-wide offices and the per cent of seats in the legislature held by each.

Duration of Success: the length of time each party has controlled the statewide offices and/or the legislature.

Frequency of Divided Control: the proportion of time in which control of the governorship and legislature has been divided between the parties. . . .

For each state we first tabulated the percentages of the two-party popular vote for governor received by each party in each election, and the percentages of the seats in each house of the legislature held by each party in each legislative session.* From these tables we computed four basic figures: 1) the average per cent of the popular vote won by Democratic gubernatorial candidates; 2) the average per cent of the seats in the state senate held by the Democrats; 3) the average per cent of the seats in the state house of representatives held by the Democrats; and 4) the per cent of all terms for governor, senate, and house in which the Democrats had control.

*Since Minnesota and Nebraska have formally non-partisan legislatures, only their gubernatorial elections have been used to measure inter-party competition.

For each state we then averaged together all four percentages to produce an "index of competitiveness" carried to four decimal places. It has a possible range of .0000 (total Republican success) to 1.0000 (total Democratic success), with .5000 representing absolutely even two-party competition.

Finally, we listed the states in descending order of index numbers, and the resulting clusters suggested the following categories and definitions:

.9000 or higher: one-party Democratic
.7000 to .8999: modified one-party Democratic
.3000 to .6999: two-party
.1000 to .2999: modified one-party Republican
.0000 to .0999: one-party Republican

No state qualified as one-party Republican by these criteria. The states' distribution among the other four categories is given in Table 2–1, and their geographical distribution is shown in the map in Figure 2–1.

Some Warnings

The classifications in Table 2–1 and Figure 2–1 are likely to hold some surprises for most readers: for example, Arizona, the home of Barry Goldwater, is classified as modified one-party Democratic; Nebraska, on the other hand, is labeled two-party, while Wisconsin is called modified one-party Republican. Our classifications will raise fewer eyebrows if we bear in mind two warnings about what they mean.

First, they are based wholly on state offices. Hence while Arizona twice elected Goldwater Senator and voted for the Republican candidate for President in three of the four elections from 1948 to 1960, the Republicans never held more than 25 per cent of

Table 2-1
THE FIFTY STATES CLASSIFIED ACCORDING TO DEGREE
OF INTER-PARTY COMPETITION

One-Party Democratic	Modified One-Party Democratic	Two-Party		Modified One-Party Republican
South Carolina (1.0000)	Virginia (.8795)	Alaska (.6767)	Pennsylvania (.4050)	Wisconsin (.2997)
Georgia (.9915)	North Carolina (.8793)	Missouri (.6603)	California (.3930)	New Hampshire (.2680)
Louisiana (.9867)	Tennessee (.8715)	Rhode Island (.6327)	Nebraska (.3875)	Iowa (.2495)
Mississippi (.9805)	Oklahoma (.8193)	Washington (.5647)	Illinois (.3847)	Kansas (.2415)
Texas (.9590)	Kentucky (.7650)	Delaware (.5420)	Idaho (.3780)	Maine (.2405)
Alabama (.9565)	Arizona (.7490)	Nevada (.5263)	Michigan (.3770)	South Dakota (.2320)
Arkansas (.9427)	West Virginia (.7223)	Massachusetts (.5227)	New Jersey (.3605)	North Dakota (.1860)
Florida (.9220)	Maryland (.7137)	Hawaii (.4897)	Indiana (.3545)	Vermont (.1760)
	New Mexico (.7023)	Colorado (.4827)	Oregon (.3545)	
		Montana (.4695)	Ohio (.3523)	
		Minnesota (.4610)	Wyoming (.3470)	
		Utah (.4605)	New York (.3173)	
		Connecticut (.4420)		

the seats in the upper house or over 31 per cent of the seats in the lower house of the state legislature. Wisconsin, which at the present writing has a Democratic governor and two Democratic U.S. Senators, has seen Democratic control of either legislative house only once in eighteen opportunities in this period, and Democratic governors only three of nine terms. Florida voted for the Republican Presidential candidate in 1952, 1956, and 1960 and elected two Republican U.S. Representatives in 1962; but the Republicans never won the governorship or more than 7 per cent of the seats in either house of the legislature. These examples show that a state which has been highly

competitive for some national offices may have been much less so for state offices; and the latter are our primary concern here.

Second, any measurement such as ours is a snapshot of an object moving in time and hence does not always capture changes that may be occurring when the measurement is taken. Thus, Wisconsin and South Dakota are becoming more Democratic and Arizona and Florida more Republican; another measurement taken a decade hence may well change the classifications of all four states. All our present classification does is to indicate the relative competitiveness of the fifty states in the two decades after World War II.

FIGURE 2-1.

THE STATE PARTY SYSTEM

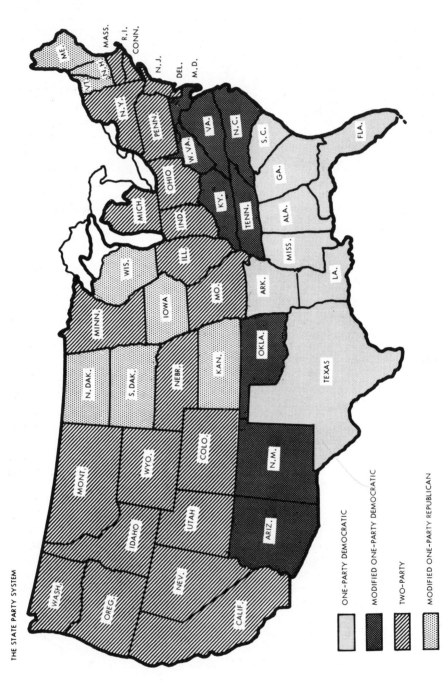

ONE-PARTY DEMOCRATIC

MODIFIED ONE-PARTY DEMOCRATIC

TWO-PARTY

MODIFIED ONE-PARTY REPUBLICAN

Alaska and Hawaii, not included in the map, are both two-party states.

Our next task, then, is to see whether the differences shown in Table 2–1 are significantly related to any other characteristics of the states in each category.

Correlates of Competitiveness

Most of the one-party and modified one-party states of both parties have had their present political colorations ever since the Civil War. . . . But the Civil War ended a century ago; how can it influence the party loyalties of so many voters in the 1960's? The answer seems to lie in the essential nature of party identification. The leading studies of voting behavior emphasize that the typical American acquires his party preference early in life, and it grows stronger the longer he holds it. Moreover, it is reinforced and activated by the similar preferences of his parents, his wife, and his friends and work associates, and living in a one-party atmosphere tends to corrode the loyalties of the few who identify with the minority party. Although a few individuals switch parties, perhaps because they move to new communities and/or change their socio-economic positions, *massive* switches take place only under such apocalyptic circumstances as the Civil War or the Great Depression of the early 1930's.

Given, then, the self-renewing and self-intensifying nature of party identification, it is not surprising that the deepest political cleavage in our history remains the basic source of party predominance in half our states. It is more surprising that the other half have two-party systems. After all, no fewer than seventeen fought for the Union in the war, one (Missouri) was a border state, and most of the others were settled by immigrants from the North. Why are they not also one-party or modified one-party Republican? Some of the answers are suggested by the data in Table 2–2.

The most striking contrast evident in Table 2–2 is the fact that the two-party states are substantially more urbanized than the states in the other three categories; and we may add that all the nation's cities with populations of over one million (New York, Chicago, Los Angeles, Philadelphia, and Detroit) are located in these states. The two-party states also have to a higher degree than the others the characteristics usually associated with urbanization: they have the highest median income, the highest percentage of labor force engaged in manufacturing and the lowest in agriculture, and the highest proportion of "foreign stock" (i.e., immigrants or children of immigrants).

When we compare the two-party states with the two groups of Democratic-dominated states we see that the former have a much smaller proportion of Negroes, and a larger proportion of foreign stock and Roman Catholics.

A more suggestive comparison, however, is that between the two-party states and the modified one-party Republican states; for if the Civil War were the sole source of present-day political loyalties, the two groups of states should be very similar. However, in certain respects they are at opposite extremes: the two-party states are the most urban and the Republican states the least; the two-party states are the least agricultural and the Republican states, the most.

All these comparisons are consistent with the general pattern of distribution of party strength *outside the South* noted by most commentators. Democratic support generally tends to be concentrated in big cities, for the minority eth-

Table 2-2
SOCIAL AND ECONOMIC CHARACTERISTICS OF STATES
BY DEGREE OF COMPETITIVENESS

Characteristic	One-Party Democratic	Modified One-Party Democratic	Two-Party	Modified One-Party Republican
Number of States	8	9	25	8
Per cent of population urban	55%	56%	69%	50%
Per cent of population living in cities over 100,000	18%	21%	21%	7%
Per cent of Negroes in population	27%	11%	5%	1%
Per cent of foreign stock in population	5%	6%	23%	21%
Per cent of Roman Catholics in population	18%	11%	23%	25%
Median income	$3982	$4814	$6034	$5060
Per cent of labor force in agriculture	9%	8%	7%	15%
Per cent of labor force in manufacturing	20%	19%	22%	20%

Source: *Congressional District Data Book* (Washington: Bureau of the Census, 1963).

nic groups and trade unionists who vote predominantly Democratic constitute the bulk of the big cities' populations. Republican voting strength tends to be concentrated in smaller towns and cities (i.e., those with populations from 2,500 to 100,000), for the "WASPs" (white, Anglo-Saxon Protestants) who vote predominantly Republican constitute the bulk of the small town populations. And the Northern rural farm areas are the most likely to switch back and forth between the two parties depending upon whether farms are prosperous (vote Republican) or depressed (vote Democratic). . . .

Party Government in the States

Structural Difficulties: Divided Party Control Between Governor and Legislature

Two essential prerequisites for responsible party government in the states are: 1) the majority party must control both the governorship and the legislature at any given time, or else it cannot be collectively responsible for how the government is run; and 2) there must be strong two-party competition so that the majority party may be turned out at any time when the voters decide it is time for a change.

However, the separate elections of the governor and the legislature endanger the first prerequisite, for they make it possible for the governor to be of one party and one or both houses of the legislature to be controlled by the other. This possibility, moreover, often becomes reality: from 1952 to 1962 in only sixteen states were the governor and both houses of the legislature controlled at all times by the same party. These were the Southern one-party and modified one-party states, and the Republican modified one-party states of Vermont and New Hampshire. The two-party states, on the other hand, had united party control only 50 per cent of the time. The result: the states most likely to satisfy the second prerequisite of party government are *least* likely to fulfill the first!

V. O. Key found the same pattern of divided control in the period from 1931 to 1952, and suggested several reasons for it. One is the apportionment of state legislatures, which, by overrepresenting rural areas and small towns and underrepresenting metropolitan areas, typically exaggerates Republican, strength and understates Democratic. Dramatic evidence of this is provided by the fact that since World War II the Democrats have never controlled the upper house of the legislature in such highly competitive states as Connecticut, Illinois, Indiana, Michigan, Nevada, New Jersey, and Wyoming. Therefore, if responsible party government were ever to operate in these states, the Republicans had to operate it, for the very structure of the state governments made it impossible for the Democrats to do so. The "apportionment revolution" growing from *Baker vs. Carr* may alter this situation somewhat in the Democrats' favor in the years ahead; but the concentration of Democratic votes in the metropolitan areas will probably sustain this anti-Democratic bias for a long time, and the resulting tendency to divided party control will persist.

A governor facing a legislature controlled by the opposition party does not invariably mean angry partisan wrangling and deadlock. If the governor carefully cultivates the opposition's legislative leaders, proposes a moderate program to which they have agreed, and in general plays down party politics and the independence of his office, the government may proceed about as smoothly as if all concerned were members of the same party. Such was the case with Democratic Governors Abraham Ribicoff of Connecticut and Robert Meyner of New Jersey in the 1950's. But men are not angels and politicians have to fight elections, so such cross-partisan harmony is rare. A more common story has been the bitter partisan conflict and resultant near-total deadlock between Democratic governors and Republican legislators that marked such administrations as those of G. Mennen Williams in Michigan in the 1950's, and Otto Kerner in Illinois and John Reynolds in Wisconsin in the early 1960's. All resulted in deadlocks over such basic matters as taxation, legislative apportionment, and executive appointments; and for a good part of the time the governments of all three states were brought to nearly complete standstills. In short, separation of powers, rural overrepresentation in legislatures, and close statewide two-party competition sometimes make for inter-party deadlock rather than responsible party government. . . .

Party Cohesion in State Legislatures

Another prerequisite of responsible party government is that the parties' legislators maintain high cohesion in their votes on legislative issues, for only in this way can the voters meaningfully hold the majority party—as opposed to individual legislators—responsible for what the legislature does or fails to do.

Party cohesion is generally very low in the one-party and modified one-party states, and tends to be higher in the two-party states. Its general relation to party competitiveness is illustrated in Table 2–3, which classifies the states in each of the categories of competitiveness according to their degree of party cohesion as reported by the Committee on Legislatures.

Table 2-3
LEGISLATIVE PARTY COHESION AND INTER-PARTY COMPETITION

Cohesion in the Two-Party States			Cohesion in the Modified One-Party States			Cohesion in the One-Party States		
Strong	Moderate	Weak	Strong	Moderate	Weak	Strong	Moderate	weak
Colo.	Ill.	Calif.	Iowa	N.H.	Ariz.			Ala.
Conn.	Mont.	Neb.†	Kans.	S.Dak.	Ky.			Ark.
Dela.	Nev.	Ore.	Md.	Vt.	Me.			Fla.
Ida.	Ohio		N.C.	Wis.	N.Dak.**			Ga.
Ind.	Utah		W.Va.		N.M.			La.
Mass.	Wash.				Okla.			Miss.
Mich.	Wyo.				Tenn.			S.C.
Minn.*					Va.			Tex.
Mo.								
N.J.								
N.Y.								
Pa.								
R.I.								

* Strong factional cohesion in non-partisan legislature.
† Weak factional cohesion in non-partisan legislature.
** Strong factional cohesion in dominant party.
Source: Adapted from Belle Zeller (ed.), *American State Legislatures*, Table 9, pp. 190–191 (Alaska and Hawaii not included).

Table 2–3 shows that more two-party states have strong cohesion than weak or moderate; more modified one-party states have weak cohesion than strong or moderate; and all eight one-party states have weak cohesion. So the degree of party competition is clearly one, but only one, factor affecting legislative cohesion.

Other factors have to do with the degree to which party divisions correspond with socio-economic divisions. Generally speaking, where the basic political conflict is that between metropolitan areas and small towns, and where most Democratic legislators are elected from the former and most Republicans from the latter, cohesion in both legislative parties tends to be high. Where party divisions do not coincide with metropolitan-small town conflict, however, party cohesion tends to be lower even where party competition is close. Thus in some state legislatures cohesion comes very close to the responsible-parties model, while in others it is considerably further away.

The Governor as Party Leader

Here we are concerned with [the governor's] position as leader of his party and the extent to which it helps him in his other roles. We should begin by distinguishing between his "outside" and "inside" roles.

In most states, whether one-party or two-party, the governor is usually (though not invariably) the principal leader and spokesman for his party in its relations with other state parties and with the national party. One evidence of this is the fact that the dominant figures in state delegations to national party conventions are usually governors rather than U.S. Senators, mayors, state chairmen, or other rivals. The reason is plain enough: most state parties see many advantages in presenting a united front in their operations in national party affairs, for this is the way to maximize their power. The governor is usually the logical person to act as their spokesman and chief strategist. This fact has sometimes misled outsiders to assume that the governor must be just as much in charge back home as he is at national conventions. But this is rarely the case.

We observed earlier that in some one-party and modified one-party states (e.g., Virginia, Louisiana, Vermont, and North Dakota) the dominant party is divided into two well organized, relatively cohesive and durable factions. Where this is the case, the governor can usually count upon regular support only from his fellow factionalists in the legislature; and, while he cannot be said to be the leader of the whole party for state purposes, he certainly has as much control over the machinery of government as any governor of a two-party state. In other one-party states (e.g., Florida, Oklahoma, and Mississippi) there are no durable factions, and the coalition that elects the governor usually has little carry-over in the legislature. As a result, the governor of such a state is the leader of his party in only the most nominal sense, and he must negotiate with factions in the legislature on an issue-by-issue basis to accomplish whatever he wishes to accomplish.

However, whether in a bifactional or multifactional state, the leadership of most governors in the one-party states is materially weakened by the fact that they are constitutionally prohibited from succeeding themselves: six of the eight one-party Democratic states have such prohibitions (only Arkansas and Texas do not), as well as six of the nine modified one-party Democratic states (only Arizona, Maryland, and New Mexico do not). By contrast, only three two-party states (Indiana, Missouri, and Pennsylvania) have comparable prohibitions and only four more (Alaska, Delaware, New Jersey, and Oregon) limit their governors to two terms.

Where the governor's term is limited, as it is in most of the Democratic states,

whatever leadership he may have had over his party when first elected is likely to dissipate as he nears the end of his term; for legislators and party chairmen alike know that he will soon be in a position where he can neither help nor hurt them very much.

A leading student of American governorship, Professor Coleman Ransone, sums up the party leadership of governors in the two-party states thus:

It is primarily because we do not really have party government at the state level that the governor must continue to play the role of the politician even after his election. . . . The idea of disciplined parties in the legislature who work with the governor to execute a party program is largely a none-too-effective myth at the state level. The governor is elected in an atmosphere of factional politics and he continues to operate in that atmosphere in his dealings with the legislature, with his department heads, and with the other members of the executive branch.

The principal reasons for this relative weakness of gubernatorial party leadership in the two-party states include: 1) the general decentralization of the state parties, which means that most county leaders and state legislators hold their positions by their own efforts and owe the governor nothing; 2) the frequency with which divided party control forces the governor to bargain with factions in the opposition party in the legislature and within the executive branch; 3) the fact that the use of his patronage and item-veto powers may well make at least as many enemies as friends. The upshot, Ransone concludes, is this:

There are situations in the two-party states in which the governorship and the legislature are controlled by the same party and where, given some party discipline, the governor may be able to make an appeal to the legislators on the basis of a party program. These situations, however, tend to be infrequent. . . . The American governor must concern himself with building legislative support from among clusters of legislative factions. In only a few states does the party actually play its traditional role. . . .

Changing Electoral Patterns in State Politics

The Growth of Inter-Party Competition

We noted earlier that the Civil War hammered most states' party alignments into forms that long seemed permanent. Since 1945, however, a number of hitherto one-party states have seen their second parties mount major challenges to the dominant parties. As a result, the nation's political landscape has come to look much different since V-J Day from the way it appeared before Pearl Harbor.

Perhaps the most dramatic instances have been the rise of Republican strength in a number of Southern and border states. We have already observed its effects on Presidential voting, but in some states it has operated in elections for other offices as well.

For example, in 1962 veteran Alabama Senator Lister Hill barely won re-election over Republican James D. Martin; Florida elected two Republican U.S. Representatives out of twelve; South Carolina gave over 40 per cent of its popular vote to a Republican candidate for the U.S. Senate for the first time since Reconstruction; Texas elected a second Republican U.S. Representative, and in 1961 Texas voters made John Tower the first Republican U.S. Senator from the state since Reconstruction; and Tennessee elected Republicans in three of its nine Congressional Districts. In all, 11 of 105 Southern U.S. Representatives were Republicans in the 88th Congress,

the highest number since the 1870's.

Only Oklahoma, to be sure, elected a Republican to any high *state* office—when it elected Henry Bellmon the first Republican governor in the state's history—so full two-party competition is still some distance off in most Southern and border states. Nevertheless, Southern Republicans are stronger today than they have been for a century, and they are likely to grow stronger.

Less dramatic but equally significant has been the rise of Democratic strength for state offices in a number of formerly solid Republican states. For example: Iowa elected Democratic governors in 1956, 1958, and 1962; Kansas did the same in 1956 and 1958; Maine elected Democratic governors in 1954, 1956, and 1958, and a Democratic U.S. Senator in 1958; New Hampshire elected both a Democratic governor and U. S. Senator in 1962; North Dakota returned a Democratic governor in 1960 and 1962, and a Democratic U.S. Senator in 1960; in South Dakota the Democrats not only won the governorship in 1958 and a U.S. Senatorship in 1962 but actually controlled one house of the legislature in 1958; Vermont elected a Democratic Congressman-at-Large in 1958 and a Democratic governor in 1962, the first Democrats elected to statewide office since 1854; and Wisconsin elected Democratic governors in 1958, 1960, and 1962, and Democratic U.S. Senators in 1958 and 1962. What the Democrats have lost in the South they have regained in the rural Midwest and Northeast.

We cannot now provide a complete and definitive explanation for these changes from traditional state political alignments. However, a major part of any such explanation will surely be interstate migration. Americans have always moved about within their country frequently and in large numbers, and the post-1954 era has witnessed one of the greatest migrations since the Civil War: the Bureau of the Census found that 12 per cent of the population over five years of age in 1960 had moved from one state to another since 1955!

Perhaps the most significant movement politically has been the parallel immigration of Northern whites into the South and emigration of Southern Negroes out of the South. One effect has been to reduce the proportion of Negroes in the Southern states' populations: in the decade from 1950 to 1960 the proportion of Negroes declined in all eight Democratic one-party states, the largest drops being from 27 to 18 per cent in Florida and from 43 to 35 per cent in South Carolina; the average drop for the eight states was 5.6 per cent. This Negro exodus has "lightened" many of the South's "black belts," which, according to Key, have always constituted the nucleus of Southern one-party politics. At the same time the influx of Northern whites, about half of whom were Republicans in the North and have remained so after moving to the South, has not only given Southern Republicans more votes; more significantly, it has greatly enlarged the pool of well-educated and active party supporters from which they can draw candidates for office and leaders of party organization. Both movements, accordingly, have encouraged a higher degree of inter-party competition in the South.

The other main post-war interstate migration has been the massive movement to the far West. The most spectacular instance, of course, is the growth of California from a population of 6,907,000 in 1940 to 15,717,000 in 1960, and a position as the most populous state in the Union by the mid-1960's. The Survey Research Center of the University of Michigan studied a sample of 588 western adults in 1956, and its findings tell us much about the post-war western immigrants and their impact on western politics. Slightly over twice as many came from the North as from the South. Those from the North were closely split between Democratic identifiers (39 per cent) and Republican (34 per cent), while those from the South were heavily Democratic (57 per cent to 20 per cent Republican). From one point of view, the net effect has been to make the West somewhat more Democratic than before; from another, it has sustained two-party competition, for Northern immigrants have supplied large numbers of Republicans, enough indeed to keep the region from the two-to-one lead the Democrats would probably have if the western electorate consisted entirely of persons born in the region and immigrants from the South.

Conclusions

We end where we began: in every state most elections are fought and most public offices are held by persons bearing the labels "Democratic" and "Republican"; but the meaning of the term "political parties" as applied to these aggregates varies considerably from one state to another. In the eight Southern one-party states "the Democratic party" is almost coterminous with the state itself; everyone is a Democrat; elections are not inter-party contests; and the Democratic party has as much "cohesion" and "responsibility" as the whole government, for they are one and the same.

In the seventeen modified one-party states, the "political parties" are somewhat more meaningful entities. Although most voters identify with the dominant party, a noticeable minority identifies with the other. Both parties nominate candidates in most elections, which thereby become genuine choices between parties; and occasionally a candidate of the second party wins. Much political conflict is fought out in the primaries and committees of the dominant party, but the presence of an organized party opposition ready to take over in case of schism or scandal makes the context of intra-party conflict substantially different from that in the one-party states.

In the two-party states each party musters a large segment of the population as its identifiers. Almost every election is contested by a Republican and a Democrat. In some two-party states there is high cohesion among both parties in the legislature and close cooperation between the governor and his fellow partisans. Such states, indeed, come closer than the national government to the responsible-party-government model. In other two-party states, however, the parties are a little, if any, more cohesive than in the modified one-party states. And we are as yet unable to say why two-party competition produces unified parties in some states but not in others.

Therefore, relatively even party competition seems to be a necessary—but not sufficient—condition for state parties to operate as unified governing agencies. Its post-war increase in many American states may help bring some of them nearer the responsible-parties ideal. But in other two-party states, two-party competition may, because of its combination with separation of powers and malapportionment of the legislatures, serve instead to intensify the partisan political deadlock and governmental paralysis which constitutes one of the principal barriers to making states into more effective units of government. Inter-party competition, in short, does make a difference; but the kind of difference it makes depends upon the context in which it operates. . . .

11. BOSSES, MACHINES, AND ETHNIC GROUPS

By Elmer E. Cornwell, Jr.

Relation of Machine to Immigration

The classic machine would probably not have been possible, and certainly would not have been so prominent a feature of the American political landscape, without the immigrant. Essential-

From Elmer E. Cornwell, Jr., "Bosses, Machines, and Ethnic Groups," *Annals of the American Academy of Political and Social Science,* CCCLIII (May, 1964) 27-39, excerpts. By permission of the publisher.

ly, any disciplined grass-roots political organization rests upon a docile mass base which has in some manner been rendered dependable, predictable, and manipulable. The rank and file of the Soviet Communist party is disciplined by a combination of ideological allegiance, fear, and hope of reward. The average party supporter in a liberal-democratic society cannot be so disciplined under ordinary circumstances, at least not for long. The newly arrived immigrant was a special case, however.

He was characteristically insecure, culturally and often linguistically alien, confused, and often in actual want. Thus, even if he had valued the franchise thrust upon him by his new political mentors, its careful exercise would have taken a low priority in his daily struggle for existence. In most cases, he did not value or even understand the political role into which he was being pushed.

Thus, it was the succeeding waves of immigrants that gave the urban political organizations the manipulable mass bases without which they could not have functioned as they did. And, until immigration dried up to a trickle in the 1920's, as one generation of newcomers began to espouse traditional American values of political independence, there was always a new group, often from a different country of origin, to which the machine could turn. As long as this continued to be possible, machines persisted, and once the immigrant base finally began to disappear, so did most of the bosses of the classic model. In a very real sense, then, the one phenomenon was dependent on the other. . . .

The point, then, is that, whereas in the cities the immigrants sold their political independence for the familiar currency of favors and aid, their rural native cousins were sometimes prompted to do the same, in part out of desire for cultural-religious as well as political, and perhaps at times economic, self-protection. Recollection of the Know-Nothing era of militant nativist activity a half-century earlier suggests that this kind of cultural-religious antagonism can be a very potent political force indeed. An analogous explanation could even be offered for the existence of machines in the South like that of Harry Byrd in Virginia, by simply substituting the perceived Negro threat for the danger of engulfment by foreigners in the

North. And, curiously enough, the two examples of reasonably thoroughgoing machine-like organizations that flourished in the otherwise inhospitable English soil—Joseph Chamberlain's Birmingham caucus and Archibald Salvidge's "machine" in Liverpool—also were at least indirectly related to the problem of Irish home rule, and, in Liverpool, to actual rivalry with Irish immigrants over religion and jobs.

In short, whatever else may be said about the conditions and forces that spawned the classic machine, this kind of disciplined political entity must rest at bottom on a clientele which has felt it necessary to exchange political independence—its votes, in a word—for something seen as more essential to its well-being and security. In general, such a group will be the product of some kind of socio-economic disequilibrium or cultural tension which finds its members in an insecure or seriously disadvantaged situation. Thus, the immigrant was willing to submit to the boss in exchange for aid—real or imagined—in gaining his foothold in the new environment, and the old-stock machine supporters, North or South, submitted in part for protection against swarming aliens or a potential Negro threat to white dominance.

The Classic Machine in Operation

It cannot be assumed that the process of machine exploitation of succeeding groups of newcomers was a smooth and simple operation. Any formal organization, political or otherwise, must maintain a continuing balance among a series of often contradictory forces. Its very existence rests on the success with which it achieves its objective—in the case of a political party, the winning of elections and, thus, power. In the long run, this success depends on the organization's continuing ability to tap fresh sources of support as time goes on and old reliances dwindle and may at times depend on keeping newly available resources away from its rival or rivals. For the machine, this has meant wooing each new ethnic contingent. Yet this process of growth and renewal will inevitably threaten the very position of many of the proprietors of the organization itself by recruiting rivals for their roles. Any organizational entity must not only achieve its corporate goals but, to survive, it must also satisfy the needs and desires of its members as individuals. If it fails in this, its supporters will vanish and its own objectives remain unattainable. Specifically, for the machine, this fact of organizational life often tempered missionary zeal and tempted its members to protect even an eroding *status quo*.

Usually the machine did yield in the long run to the political imperative that all groups of potential supporters must be wooed, if for no other reason than to keep them from the enemy. The short-term risk to the present leadership often must have appeared minimal. The plight of the newcomers was so pitiful, their needs so elemental, and their prospects of achieving security and independence so problematical in the foreseeable future that they must have appeared like a windfall to the machine proprietors. Thus, after initial hesitancy, the Irish were taken into Tammany and found their way into the ranks of the clientele of other big city party organizations.

The ways in which immigrant political support was purchased are familiar and need no elaborate review here. They had at least three kinds of needs which the ward heeler could fill on behalf of the party leadership. Above all, they needed the means of physical existence: jobs, loans, rent money, contributions of food or fuel to tide them over, and the like. Secondly, they needed a buffer against an unfamiliar state and its legal minions: help when they or their offspring got in trouble with the police, help in dealing with inspectors, in seeking pushcart licenses, or in other relations with the public bureaucracy. Finally, they needed the intangibles of friendship, sympathy, and social intercourse. These were available, variously, through contact with the precinct captain, the hospitality of the political clubhouse, the attendance of the neighborhood boss at wakes and weddings, and the annual ward outing.

As has often been noted, these kinds of services were not available, as they are today, at the hands of "United Fund" agencies, city welfare departments with their platoons of social workers, or through federal social security legislation. The sporadic and quite inadequate aid rendered by the boss and his lieutenants thus filled a vacuum. Their only rivals were the self-help associations which did spring up within each ethnic group as soon as available resources allowed a meager surplus to support burial societies and the like. The fact that the politicians acted from self-serving motives in distributing their largess, expecting and receiving a *quid pro quo*, is obvious but not wholly relevant. At least it was not relevant in judging the social importance of the services rendered. It was highly relevant, of course, in terms of the political power base thus acquired.

Some of the later arrivals following the pioneering Irish were in at least as great need of aid. The Irish did speak English and had had some experience with political action and representative institutions at home. This, plus the fact that they got here first, doubtless accounts for their rapid rise in the chosen party, the Democracy. The groups that followed, however, usually did not know English and bore the additional burden of a cultural heritage that had less in common with the American patterns they encountered than had been the case with the Irish. And, too, almost all groups, the Sons of Erin included, differed religiously from the basic Protestant consensus of their Anglo-Saxon predecessors.

As group followed group—not only into the country but into the rickety tenements and "river wards" reserved, as it were, for the latest arrivals—the processes of absorption became more complex. The Irish ward politicians doubtless had, if anything, more difficulty bridging the cultural and language gap to meet the newcomers than the "Yankees" had had in dealing with themselves some decades earlier. Also, while it may well be that the Yankees gave up their party committee posts fairly willingly to the Irish, because politics was not essential to their well-being either economically or psychologically, the Irish were in a rather different position when their turn came to move over and make room. They had not fully outgrown their dependence on politics for financial and psychic security. Thus, the conflicting demands of the machine for new sources of support versus the reluctance of the incumbents to encourage rivalry for their won positions, produced tension. In the long run, however, most of the new ethnic groups found their place in the party system. In some cases, as with the Italians, the Republicans, generally less skillful in these arts, won support by default when the Irish were especially inhospitable.

The Machine as Social Integrator

There is another side to the coin of machine dependence on the continuing flow of immigrants. The "invisible hand"—to use an analogy with Adam Smith's economics—which operated to produce social benefits out of the *quid pro quo* which the ward heelers exchanged for votes was at work in other ways, too. Henry Jones Ford noted in the 1890's, while discussing the role of party:

This nationalizing influence continues to produce results of the greatest social value, for in co-ordinating the various elements of the population for political purposes, party organization at the same time tends to fuse them into one mass of citizenship, pervaded by a common order of ideas and sentiments, and actuated by the same class of motives. This is probably the secret of the powerful solvent influence which American civilization exerts upon the enormous deposits of alien population thrown upon this country by the torrent of emigration.

Again, in other words, the selfish quest by the politician for electoral support and power was transmuted by the "invisible hand" into the major force integrating the immigrant into the community.

This process has had several facets. In the first place, the mere seeking out of the immigrants in quest of their support, the assistance rendered in getting them naturalized (when it was necessary to observe these legal niceties), and so forth were of considerable importance in laying the foundation for their more meaningful political participation later. In addition, the parties have progressively drawn into their own hierarchies and committee offices representatives of the various ethnic groups. The mechanics of this process were varied. In some cases, there doubtless emerged leaders of a particular group in one ward or neighborhood who, if given official party status, would automatically bring their followings along with them. On other occasions, new ethnic enclaves may have sought or even demanded representation in exchange for support. Perhaps prior to either of these, the machine sought to co-opt individuals who could speak the language and act as a cultural bridge between the party and the newcomers. Depending on the situation, it probably was essential to do this and impossible for precinct captains of a different background to develop adequate rapport. It is at this point that ethnic group rivalry in the organization becomes difficult. Gratitude to the boss for initial admission into the lower ranks of the hierarchy would be bound to change in time into demands, of growing insistence, for further recognition of the individual and his group.

These general patterns can to some extent be documented, at least illustratively. The tendency for the urban machines to reap the Irish vote and later much of the vote of more recent arrivals is well known. The process of infiltration by group representatives into party structure is harder to identify precisely. With this in mind, the author did a study of the members of party ward committees in Providence, Rhode Island, the findings of which may reflect trends elsewhere. Analysis of committee membership lists or their equivalent going back to the 1860's and 1870's showed initial overwhelming Anglo-Saxon majorities. For the Democrats, however, this majority gave way, between the 1880's and 1900, to a roughly 75 per cent Irish preponderance, while the Republican committees stayed "Yankee" until after the First World War. Then, in the 1920's, both parties simultaneously recruited Italian committeemen to replace some of the Irish and white Protestants, respectively. Today, both have varied, and roughly similar, proportions of all major groups in the city population. In other cities, the timing of shifts and the ethnic groups involved will have differed, but the general process and its relation to local patterns of immigration were doubtless similar. . . .

Politics for the machine politician never was an ideological enterprise or a matter of beliefs and principles. As someone once said, the boss had only seven principles, five loaves and two fishes. Rather, politics was an entrepreneurial vocation like any other business. Banfield and Wilson have written: "A political machine is a business organization in a particular field of business—getting votes and winning elections. As a Chicago machine boss once said . . . it is 'just like any sales organization trying to sell its product.'" The politician's aim was and is so to invest his supply of capital—jobs, favors, and the like—as to earn a profit, some of which he will take as "income" and the rest reinvest in quest of larger returns. In other words, the immigrant political leader took the one vocation open to him, politics, and made it into as close an approximation as he could of the more valued business callings in the society, from which he was effectively barred. He acted out the American success story in the only way open to him.

Obviously, the foregoing is not designed to portray the machine as a knight-errant rescuing American society from its willful folly. In the first place, the folly was not willful, and perhaps not folly. In the second, the boss's contribution toward making the melting pot melt should not be overrated. At the same time, many have testified— as does the record itself—to the almost unique ability of party as organization to bring people together across cultural and similar barriers. As Glazer and Moynihan have written of New York City:

> . . . political life itself emphasizes the ethnic character of the city, with its balanced tickets and its special appeals. . . . For those in the field itself, there is more contact across the ethnic lines, and the ethnic lines themselves mean less, than in other areas of the city's life.

Ticket-balancing, or United Nations politics, as it is sometimes called, is perhaps symbolic of the ultimate step in the process of granting group recognition and confirming the fact that something approaching intergroup equality has been achieved. Either, as with the Manhattan Borough presidency and the Negro group, certain prescriptive rights become established to a particular office or to one place on a city-wide ticket or ethnic allocation is made using the background of the head of the ticket as point of departure.

In short, the classic urban machine rested upon the immigrants, while at the same time it fostered their integration into American life. It also made, in the process, a major contribution to the over-all American political style. It is true that politics as a pragmatic entrepreneurial vocation owes much in America to the contributions of Burr, Van Buren, Weed, Marcy (to the victor belong the spoils), and, in a sense, to Andrew Jackson himself. Thus, Richard Hofstadter's attribution of one of the two central systems of political ethics in America to the immigrants is only partially valid. He is clearly correct, however, in suggesting that a

political style which stressed "personal obligations, and placed strong personal loyalties above allegiance to abstract codes of law or morals" was congenial to the machine politicians and their followers, and they made it their own, developing its full implications in the process. At the same time, the immigrant versus old stock cultural cleavage prompted the latter to espouse the more vigorously the typically middle-class, reformist style which stresses honesty, impartiality and efficiency. These two styles or ethics, since the late nineteenth century, have, by their interaction, shaped both the evolution of urban politics and the machinery of urban government.

The Decline of the Machine

The decline and fall of the boss as a political phenomenon has often been chronicled and explained. It is argued, *inter alia*, that reforms like the direct primary, non-partisan systems of election, voting machines and tightened registration requirements, and city-manager schemes often dealt crippling blows. In the aggregate, they doubtless did, though many exceptions can be found to prove the rule. One particular contribution of the reformers which has had unquestioned importance—though circumvention has not proven impossible—was the elimination of patronage with the installation of civil service based on the merit principle. And, generally, educational levels have risen, and occupational levels and incomes have risen as well. Even where patronage remains available, the latter development has rendered it less attractive, and to fewer people. Finally, and most often cited, there was the impact of the New Deal. Its installation of publicly sponsored welfare programs eliminated many of the rough-and-ready welfare functions of the precinct captain, though the more imaginative recouped part of their loss by helping to steer constituents through the bureaucratic maze, claiming credit for the benefits thus obtained.

Granting the importance of all of these developments, in the long run, the decline of immigration doubtless proved the most important blow to the traditional machine operation.

The Parties and the New Immigration

There are, of course, two major groups that do represent close parallels with the earlier influx and at the same time carry important differences. These are the Negroes who have been migrating in increasing numbers from the South to northern urban centers since the First World War and the Puerto Ricans who began coming to New York City, for the most part, after the Second World War. Both resemble their alien predecessors in the magnitude of their numbers, their basic and important cultural differences from the population into whose midst they are moving, an almost invariable need of assistance in adjusting to a new environment, and their potential impact on the political balance of forces.

The major points of difference are also worth noting. Both come bearing the credentials of American citizenship, which was not the case with the earlier groups. Though this factor should make for easier adjustment, other group characteristics operate to make acceptance more difficult. For the Negro, there is the fundamental problem of color, coupled with cultural characteristics which, though acquired ostensibly in the American environment, operate to make assimilation more difficult.

These include all the long deposit of servitude and enforced inferior status: loose marital ties and correspondingly weak family ties generally, a poverty of leadership potential, low literacy and skill levels, and the like. For the Puerto Ricans, there is language, plus differences of culture, and a partial color barrier which operates to cause at least some Spanish Americans to be classified—against their will—as Negroes. On balance, it is probably true that, so far as these two groups are concerned as groups, they face higher barriers to integration into American life than almost any earlier group save, possibly, the orientals.

But the society itself has changed enormously from the society to which the Irish, Italians, and Jews sought entrance. Urban areas are now equipped with facilities to which the newcomer can turn for aid that counterbalance to some degree the particular hostilities which members of these two groups arouse. There are now elaborate public welfare programs, there is Aid to Dependent Children for the many fatherless families, there are numerous private agencies and charities which stand ready to help, and, in the case of the Puerto Ricans, their land of origin has taken a unique interest in the welfare of its emigrants. There have even been legislative efforts to ban the discrimination in housing or employment which they encounter.

Though these facilities stand ready to ease aspects of the economic and social integration of these latest immigrants, there still remains the question of political absorption. Here, too, the situation today sharply differs from the past. The political parties now have neither the incentive nor the means with which to perform the functions they performed for the earlier immigrants. The machine in most affected areas is gone beyond recall, and there remain in its place party organizations that are hollow shells of their former strength and vigor. Party in general, given the proliferation of both public bureaucracies and the mass entertainment industry, has been pushed to the fringes of the average citizen's attention span and often to the fringes of the governing process itself. The debilitating impact of reform legislation contributed to the same end, needless to say. . . .

New York City, almost by traditional right, is *the* locale for the study of the behavior of American parties in relation to the immigrant. The 1960 census reported just over a million Negroes in New York City and somewhat more than 600,000 Puerto Ricans. In broad terms, it can be said that, since the days of Al Smith and Boss Murphy, New York politics have been long on confusion and fragmentation and short on centralized, disciplined organization. There was, therefore, little possibility that a relationship such as Representative Dawson worked out with his Negro clientele on the one hand and the leaders of the Cook County Democracy on the other could be developed in New York. Especially in Manhattan—which we shall take for analysis—one finds exemplified the more typical contemporary party situation: no dominating borough-wide authority save that in the hands of the mayor himself, hence a series of local feudal chiefs who are rarely willing to exchange their relative independence for the rather meager supplies of patronage available, and the whole system wracked periodically by factional feuding.

The Negro in New York, in apparent contrast to the Chicago situation, has been more fragmented in his political organization, has found little borough-wide structure with which to associate, but has made more spectacular symbolic gains in the party and city government. Representative Adam Clayton Powell, the rather erratic champion of the city's nonwhites, reaps vastly more national publicity for his espoused cause than the publicity-shy Congressman Dawson. How much this means in concrete benefits would be hard to determine. More significant is the fact that in 1953 a Negro, Hulan Jack, was elected for the first time to a major office in the city, that of Borough President of Manhattan. Powell had a major role in this, though he later broke with Jack. Since then, this position has become an accepted Negro prerogative. Other high positions have been filled by Negroes in the city administration in recent years.

Representation on Party Committees

A somewhat more useful basis for judging the reality of ethnic or racial group political absorption and power position than possession of some of these "commanding heights" (in Lenin's phrase) would be an analysis of the extent to which they had gained footholds in the lower and intermediate levels of the party organization. The ethnic proportions among Providence ward committee members cited above are a relatively accurate reflection of the nationality power relationships in city politics. For example, the fact that the Irish Democrats have held onto about half of the ward committee seats after yielding some places to Italians reflects the fact that they still have the dominant voice in the party. The rise of the Italians on the Republican side to the status of the largest single ethnic group also reflects their growing power.

Table 2–4 shows the approximate percentages of ethnic/racial representation in the total New York City population and, in the second column, the background of the Manhattan Democratic Assembly district leaders and coleaders insofar as these could be determined.

Table 2-4

COMPARISON OF ETHNIC PROPORTIONS IN POPULATION WITH DEMOCRATIC DISTRICT LEADERS IN MANHATTAN

	Approximate Percentage of New York City 1960 Population[a]	Percentage of Democratic Assembly District Leaders (N-66)
Negroes	14	21
Puerto Ricans	8	6
Jews	25±	38
Italians	17±	11
Irish	10±	9
Others	26±	15[b]
	100	100

[a]Population percentage estimates are from Nathan Glazer and D. P. Moynihan, *Beyond the Melting Pot* (Cambridge: Massachusetts Institute of Technology and Harvard Press, 1963). Only figures for Negroes and Puerto Ricans were given in the 1960 census. It was impossible to get ethnic group percentages for Manhattan alone.

[b]Includes Anglo-Saxon Protestants and others of unidentified background.

There are sixteen Assembly districts, but most are divided into two or three parts with a leader and coleader for each. There were some vacancies at the time the data were obtained. It can be seen that the Negro has done quite well by this measure of political integration in that the group has considerably more than the share of district leadership positions it would be entitled to on a strict population basis. The bulk of these Negroes preside over districts in or around Harlem, as might be expected—the 11th, 12th, 13th, 14th, and 16th Assembly districts. Of the eighteen occupied positions in these five Assembly districts, they hold twelve. There are two Negroes, one each in the 5th and 10th, to the west and east of Central Park, respectively, but none to the south of the Park at all.

In passing it might be noted that the other groups on the table each have something approximating their proportionate share of the leaderships. The Jewish contingent is disproportionately large, due in considerable measure to the fact that three-fifths of all the anti-Tammany "reform" leaders come from that part of the city population. True to what one knows about their situation in other cities, the Italians appear to be underrepresented. The Irish, however, even in view of the extreme difficulty in guessing their share of the city population, have far fewer positions than the prevailing myth of continuing Irish dominance of urban Democratic politics would suggest.

Turning now to the Puerto Ricans, they offer the best opportunity for assessing the ability of at least the Manhattan Democratic organization to absorb a genuinely new ethnic group. In Table 2–5, the backgrounds of the district leaders in the areas of heaviest Puerto Rican population are tabulated. Also included, in the last two columns, are figures on the personnel of the lowest level of "grass-roots" party organization, the election district captains. Out of the twelve district leader positions occupied at the time the data were obtained, four were held by Puerto Ricans, giving that group representation in three of the six most heavily Puerto Rican districts. Though only firsthand knowledge would indicate how effective these individuals are in representing their ethnic group and bargaining on its behalf, there is indication here of rather significant infiltration into the party structure. The figures for election district captains, where these could be obtained, point to the same conclusion. Except for the lower east side, where the proportion is

Table 2-5
AREAS OF HEAVY PUERTO RICAN[a] POPULATION

Area	Assembly District	District Leaders	Election District Captains	
			Total	Puerto Ricans
Lower East Side	4th, South	2 Jewish	29	7
East Harlem	10th, North	1 Puerto Rican and 1 Negro	16	9
	14th, South	2 Puerto Ricans	17	8
	14th, North	2 Negroes	—[b]	—[b]
	16th, South	1 Italian and 1 Puerto Rican	—[b]	—[b]
Upper West Side	13th, South	1 Italian and 1 Negro	52	23

[a]Puerto Rican population location was determined by plotting location of census tracts with at least 15 per cent Puerto Ricans and coloring these in according to density. There are scatterings in a few other parts of Manhattan as well.
[b]Data could not be obtained.

smaller, roughly half of these captains are also Puerto Rican, casting further doubt on common assumptions that the party in Manhattan is lagging seriously in making room for this latest group to arrive.

In general, both Table 2–4 and Table 2–5 suggest that the Puerto Ricans have secured, in the relatively short time since their arrival in large numbers, party offices roughly commensurate with their share of the population overall and in areas of high concentration. In addition, there are three state assemblymen from this group (two from East Harlem and one from the Bronx) and four or five with high positions in the city administration.

These achievements, obviously, as well as the district leaderships themselves and election district captaincies, can only be taken as rough indicators of the political progress of the group as a whole and are doubtless far less significant than they could have been viewed in the political setting of forty or fifty years ago when parties were central to the governing process and urban life generally. At the same time, they must be evaluated in light of the fact that New York State will not accept literacy in a language other than English (such as Spanish) as qualification to vote, and, thus, only some 150,000 to 175,000 of the total Puerto Rican group are on the rolls.

American Political Parties:
National

12. THE DILEMMA OF THE OUT-PARTY

Louis C. Gawthrop

I

The decentralized (and often disorganized) character of the American party system has consistently been a favorite topic of discussion in the literature of political science. "If you have to depend on a motley crew of feudal bands, welded together for the spoils of the quadrennial crusade," wrote Norton Long, "the inevitable disintegration and in-discipline [within the parties] must be expected."[1]

From Louis C. Gawthrop, original manuscript prepared for this volume.

[1] Norton Long, "Party Government and the United States," *Journal of Politics*, xiii (1951), 211.

While somewhat overstated, this description is suggestive; decentralization, disorganization, and, indeed, occasional disintegration have become almost standard characteristics of our brand of party politics, and all three symptoms are never better evidenced than when viewed in connection with the frustrating dilemmas which continually plague the party that does not control the Executive Branch of the Federal Government—the out-party.

In terms of basic party politics, the party which controls the Presidency— the in-party—enjoys, at the very least, an enormous symbolic advantage. To use Neustadt's terms, as long as the President can maintain his status, prestige, and reputation, his symbolic image as party leader will remain clear. In practical terms this generally means that even if the President has no taste for the intricacies of political party intrigue, the symbolic advantages of his position can be exploited and manipulated by his political deputies in order to maximize national party unity. However, unity is, itself, an imprecise and vague phrase. Franklin Roosevelt attempted to unify his party by personally involving himself in the now famous purge campaign of 1938; Dwight Eisenhower sought to unify his party by espousing his own brand of moderate Republicanism; and John Kennedy viewed unity in terms of a single executive-legislative perspective. The results in each instance were less than successful. However, despite the many personal, philosophical, and tactical differences which characterized these three Presidents, each was able to unify his own party nationally on the basis of his public policy decisions. The President's program *is* his party's program; in this sense the President automatically enjoys a virtual monopoly within his party over the choice and content of policy discussion. The monopoly is not absolute, of course; there is always an element of visible dissent within every in-party. However, the extent to which the President can command party cohesion in terms of policy decisions is probably the single most important factor which contributes to the integration of the party in power.

Conversely, this position of the President is probably the single most important factor which contributes to the disintegration of the out-party. Deprived control of the White House, who is to assume responsibility for the formulation and articulation of official policy pronouncements for the opposi-

tion party? One need only to examine the predicament of the Republican party following the last two Presidential elections to answer this question. In the aftermath of the 1960 election the usual patch-quilt pattern emerged. The image of "party" became dim as the appearance of cluster groups became more evident. The "voice" of the party came from many sources and in many directions. While Nixon, Rockefeller, Goldwater, and Eisenhower each offered his own views periodically as to what the party *should* do and what its position *should* be on a wide variety of issues, Senate Republican Leader Everett Dirksen and House Republican Leader Charles Halleck spoke frequently as to what the Party (i.e., Congressional Republicans) *was* in fact doing and what its position *was* on every Administration program. The inevitable confusion and intraparty competition was not atypical, of course. However, flagellation is a practice which few out-parties can afford to engage in extensively if any serious intention of regaining control of the Executive Branch is entertained. Thus, after extensive preparation, a concerted effort was made by a variety of cluster groups generally associated with the Eisenhower-wing to develop a consolidated party "voice" which would present a broader, more inclusive image than that presented by the "Ev and Charlie Show."

The initial public move in this direction came on June 30, 1962 with the formation of the Republican Citizens Committee following an all-day conference of GOP Governors, Congressional leaders, and former cabinet members at the Eisenhower farm in Gettysburg. The purpose of the Committee was twofold: first, to organize citizen groups in the urban areas of the nation in an effort to recapture the former Eisenhower supporters in these areas, and second, to engage in research which would lead to the development of positive party programs in the future. To implement the important second function, the Republican Citizens Committee established a Critical Issues Council on August 4, 1963, headed by Dr. Milton Eisenhower. The responsibility of this twenty-four-member group was to prepare and release policy statements which could be used to form the basis of a responsible opposition program. Until the Council suspended operations just before the 1964 nominating conventions began, it issued twelve position papers in such areas as national defense, foreign policy, domestic fiscal policy, public power, agriculture policy, civil rights, the population explosion, and the space program. On the basis of national newspaper coverage and editorial comments, extensive and generally favorable attention was given to the position papers released by the Council. Its primary purpose was to provide a focal point within the party around which the maximum number of cluster groups could coalesce in support of sensible, responsible, and rational policy pronouncements. In this respect it apparently succeeded. Unfortunately, with the nomination of Goldwater, the Critical Issues Council became the Dead Issues Council, and both it and the Republican Citizens Committee passed quietly from the scene.

After the 1964 Presidential election, the continued organizational plight of the Republicans steadily worsened. Not only did the election leave an intra-party rupture of major proportions, but President Johnson managed to maintain a high degree of support among Democratic and Republican voters nationally, as well as among Democratic and many Republican members of Congress. However, the most significant development of the 1964 aftermath was the rather rapid formation of several multi-clustered party groups within the first six months of 1965. The efforts by each group were designed to fill the leadership void which existed within the party and to formulate party policy. It was not surprising, therefore, that each of the groups reflected the major subgroupings evidenced within the party.

The Republican Governor's Association at its meeting on December 5, 1964 in Denver, Colorado decided to take a more active role in the policy-making of the national party. To this end it established a "Committee on Republican Party Policy" which was designed to develop policy positions for the national party and for the Association. A Washington office with full-time staff assistance was opened in September, 1965. The office is currently situated in the national headquarters building in order to maximize liaison between the Republican governors and the National Committee. Thus far, the Committee on Republican Party Policy has been relatively inactive, although it does mark the first attempt on the part of either party's Governors to involve themselves directly and formally in the national party's policy-making machinery.

A second effort of significant importance brought Congressional and non-Congressional party leaders together for the first time. The Republican Coordinating Committee was established on January 11, 1965 in an effort to provide unified leadership. This twenty-two-member group was presided over by the National Chairman, and included five governors (Smylie, Love, Rockefeller, Romney, and Scranton) and five former Presidential nominees (Eisenhower, Nixon, Goldwater, Dewey, and Landon). The remaining eleven positions on the Committee were filled by House and Senate Republican leaders. Five task forces were established to prepare policy papers covering major areas. The first of these reports was issued on June 1, 1965, and—along with all other subsequently released reports— was unanimously approved by the full Coordinating Committee. By April, 1966, seven additional members were invited to join the committee which raised its total membership to twenty-nine. In addition to the "charter" members noted above, the new appointees included one additional House Republican, a representative of the Republican State Legislator's Association, and five members of the Republican National Committee. The most significant effect of this enlargement was the proportional reduction of Congressional members on the Co-ordinating Committee.

The cause of moderate Republicanism in the wake of the 1964 election was revived by the Republicans for Progress established on February 3, 1965, with staff offices in Washington. This group was composed almost exclusively of former members of the Republican Citizens Committee, the Critical Issues Council, and the Committee to Elect Moderate Republicans. The declared aims of the Republicans for Progress were to assist in the election of moderate Republicans to Congress in 1966 and 1968, and to build a party image of progress and action to replace the conservative hue which was acquired as a result of the 1964 campaign. No Republican Congressmen or potential Presidential nominees were included in the forty-member group.

And, finally, the voice of conservative Republicans was recognized by the Free Society Association, Barry Goldwater, honorary chairman. Established on June 17, 1965 as a conservative educational group, its President, Denison Kitchel, announced and expected membership of 400,000-500,000 and an expected operating budget of $ 4-2.5 million annually. Although Goldwater flatly denied any covert attempt at starting a third party, the membership and budgetary statistics suggest that the Free Society has very little in common with the other groups discussed above.

In summary, the experience of the Republicans as the out-party since 1960, in attempting to solve the perplexing leadership and policy-making problems, has resulted in accomplishments which were significant and yet at the same time, inconclusive. They were significant in the sense that they revealed an awareness of the necessity for collective rather than individual leadership. The speed and relative ease which marked the formation of the Republican Coordinating Committee and the Republicans for Progress reflected this awareness as well as a willingness on the part of some factions (e.g., the Congressional leaders) to participate actively with other segments of the party which were usually ignored. On the other hand, the results are still inconclusive. Deep-seated traditions, prerogatives, and jealousies are hard to erase. Serious problems still persist which prevent the present out-party from developing a truly unified, national leadership and policy-making image. But the main point to be stressed is that the *collective* leadership pattern seems to have become a well-established principle of out-party organization management. Because of the importance of this development, special attention should be given to the first and longest sustained effort at collective out-party management, the Democratic Advisory Council.

II

Immediately after the 1956 Presidential election, Democratic National Chairman Paul Butler called a special meeting of the National Committee's Executive Council. Meeting in secret session on November 27, 1956, this group voted unanimously "to create a high-level advisory board to shape legislative proposals in line with the party's progressive, forward-looking platform. . ."[2] The task then confronting Butler was to set this newly-authorized advisory group into motion, and on December 5, 1956 he announced the names of twenty-one persons selected to serve as a group to be known formally as the Democratic Advisory Council (DAC). This list included Butler, as chairman of the DAC, five at-large members (ex-President Truman, Mrs. Franklin D. Roosevelt, John Battle, Adlai Stevenson, and Estes Kefauver), five members from the House of Representatives (Speaker Rayburn, Majority Leader McCormick, Carl Albert, Michael Kirwan, and Edith Green), five members from the Senate (Majority Leader Johnson, Mike Mansfield, George Smathers, Hubert Humphrey, and John F. Kennedy), and five other prominent Democratic officials (Governors Averell Harriman, G. Mennen Williams, Luther Hodges, Ernest McFarland, and Mayor Raymond Tucker of St. Louis).

Almost immediately the DAC—and Butler—was faced with its first major crisis. On December 8, 1956 Rayburn wired his reply to Butler. Speaking for the House Democratic leaders, Rayburn said:

We believe it would be a mistake and respectfully decline to serve on such a committee . . . It is the considered opinion of the four of us that it would be a mistake for the Democratic leadership of the House to join in any program that would place us to work with any committee outside of the House of Representatives.[3]

Following Rayburn's lead, Lyndon Johnson rejected Butler's offer, as did Mansfield, Smathers, and Kennedy.[4] Only Hubert Humphrey accepted the assignment. Governors John Battle (Va.) and Luther Hodges (N.C.) also declined to serve. Of the original group invited to serve on the Council, only nine accepted (ten including Butler): Truman, Mrs. Roosevelt, Stevenson, Kefauver, Humphrey, Harriman, Williams, McFarland, and Tucker. This prompted William S. White, then Washington Correspondent for the *New York Times*, to observe:

Democratic Congressional leaders have destroyed a movement by party liberals to put the national organization directly into legislative planning for the new Congress. The advisory body proposed for this purpose by the Executive committee will not function effectively and probably will never meet.[5]

Thus, with the Congressional leaders of the party refusing to participate, Butler was faced with the alternatives of abandoning the idea or proceeding with a group whose effectiveness would be decreased due to the absence of Congressional representation. Butler chose the latter course of action, and

---

[2] *The New York Times*, November 28, 1956.

[3] *Sunday Sun* (Baltimore) December 9, 1956. Edith Green subsequently withdrew from the DAC, although the telegram was signed only by the four other House members invited.
[4] Kennedy subsequently joined the Council along with Stuart Symington and Pat Brown.
[5] *The New York Times*, December 13, 1956.

added the fourteen member National Committee Executive Council and former U.S. Senator Herbert Lehman to replace those who had withdrawn. At the first meeting of the DAC on January 4, 1957, the membership agreed that the goals of the Council were: 1) to further the programs and principles of the Democratic party; 2) to provide a collective voice for the Democratic party; 3) to represent the millions of Democrats who were or were not represented in Congress; and 4) to formulate recommendations for policy and political strategy.[6]

Staff offices were obtained for the Council in Washington, and executive director was appointed, and a small operating budget was approved. During the period of its operation, the DAC usually held three of four formal meetings per year, and on these occasions, only the members themselves were permitted to attend. Council decisions were reached on the basis of a majority vote of the members *present*, and only in specifically authorized instances was the use of proxies permitted. No Council statement on a matter of public policy could be publicly released, however, without the approval of a majority of the *entire* membership. Decisions of the Council were *not* binding upon the individual members, and any member who dissented from any statement which was publicly released was entitled to have his dissent made public. Similarly, while the DAC could offer suggestions and advice to the National Committee and the National Chairman, these pronouncements were not binding. Also, any member who concurred with a policy statement issued by the Council was not bound by the contents of the statement in any

other capacity in which he served.

To aid the DAC in its formulation of public policy, an extensive network of advisory committees was established. The two major advisory committees were the Foreign Policy Committee and the Economic Policy Committee. The Foreign Policy group was composed of twenty-nine members, and was headed by the former Secretary of State, Dean Acheson. Paul Nitze was named Deputy Chairman. The Economic Policy Committee was directed by Professor John Kenneth Galbraith, as Chairman, and John I. Snyder, as Vice-Chairman. Twenty-three members were included in this group. In addition, five other groups were continuously engaged in research of interest to the Council. These included the Science and Technology Committee, Labor Committee, Urban and Suburban Committee, Health Policy Committee and Agriculture Committee. Thus, in the relatively short period of its operation (three-and-a-half years), the DAC gradually evolved into an organization which encompassed approximately 225 individuals.

From 1957 to 1960, the Council issued approximately fifty policy statements covering such subjects as foreign policy, national defense, national economy, unemployment, science and technology, natural resources, and agriculture. Reaction to these statements, and as a consequence, to the Council itself, depended on the subject matter of each particular statement. Thus, the Council's opinions on farm prices, right-to-work laws, and urban problems were limited in the scope of their appeal. On the other hand, Council statements encompassing broad national and international problems generally elicited wide response, and the DAC Executive Director, Charles Tyroler, III, was convinced that only

---

[6]The Democratic Advisory Council, *Plan of Operations*, mimeo., pp. 1-2.

international events and Presidential statements of the first magnitude commanded greater national press and editorial coverage than the major policy releases of the Council.

However, the DAC policy statements received virtually no public recognition from Congressional Democrats. During the 1958 congressional session the only indexed reference in the *Congressional Record* to the Council referred to two brief critical editorials. In the 1959 session criticism, primarily in the form of editorial comment inserted in the *Record* by Congressional Republicans, increased significantly. For the most part, Congressional Democrats remained silent and the extent of their acknowledgement of the DAC was limited to the occasional insertion in the *Record* of a Council statement. Actually, the Council exerted little effort, publicly, to heal the breach between it and the Congressional Democrats. For instance, in June, 1959, the DAC delivered a brief statement to the Congressional Democrats which noted that "time consuming efforts" had been made in Congress,

... to water down proposed legislation to the limits of what the President might accept, or to what might win the support of the two-thirds majority in each House necessary to override a Presidential veto.

"Republican obstructionism," the statement continued, made the Democratic task in Congress "doubly hard."

However, the people expect, and are entitled to have in this Congress more tangible results of the mandate they gave a Democratic majority last year than they have received to date.[7]

Democratic Congressional leaders

[7] *The New York Times*, June 15, 1959.

generally ignored the statement, although the Republican National Chairman, U.S. Senator Thurston Morton, suggested that the wisest decision the Council could make would be to disband.

Despite the extensive criticism directed at the DAC by Republicans in and out of Congress, on February 25, 1959, the Republican National Committee, then under the direction of Meade Alcorn, created an advisory committee of its own known as the Committee on Program and Progress. The purpose of this group was to provide a statement of the party's long-range objectives in all areas of political responsibility. The forty members (plus staff assistants) were divided into four "task forces," each covering a particular area of inquiry. At the end of six months of work, the chairman of the Committee on Program and Progress, Charles Percy, submitted a final, composite report to the National Chariman who succeeded Alcorn, Senator Thurston Morton. Following submission of its report, the Committee—which included several key Republican Congressional leaders in contrast to the DAC—dissolved. Nevertheless, one may legitimately conclude that the experience gained by the Republicans in this limited involvement with the advisory council technique proved valuable when, as already noted, they were once again faced with the realities of out-party status.

As for the DAC, while it did not follow Morton's advice to disband, it did gradually phase out of operation following the 1960 Democratic convention. Its final, and probably most significant action came in the preparation of the 1960 Democratic platform. Most of the platform was completed even before the delegates reached the convention site in Los Angeles. Chester

Bowles, the Platform Committee Chairman, as well as member of the DAC Foreign Policy Advisory Committee, informed the delegates,

The building of the platform ... began in 1957 with the formation of the Democratic Advisory Council and its various advisory committees. ... I believe that their reports constitute the most exhaustive political and economic and social studies ever made by any Democratic party anywhere.[8]

As is customary, National Chairman Paul Butler resigned from his position at the conclusion of the 1960 convention. In an attempt to heal the split between the Congressional and Presidential wings of the party, U.S. Senator Henry Jackson was named interim National Chairman. As an organized group, the last meeting of the DAC was held in May, 1960, although most of its members worked actively during the campaign for the Kennedy-Johnson ticket. On March 11, 1961, at the first formal meeting of the National Committee following the 1960 election, the new Democratic National Chairman, John Bailey, officially announced the end of the DAC. "It served a function," said Bailey who undoubtedly was aware of the fact that by the time he announced the demise of the Council, some fifteen-twenty former Council and advisory committee members had already been included in the new Administration. The DAC not only wrote a platform, but its position papers and policy statements, as well as many of its members, were, in a sense, commandeered by the Kennedy Administration and used as a springboard to develop in subsequent years a wide variety of public policy programs.

[8]Official Report of the Proceedings of the Democratic National Convention and Committee (Washington, 1964), pp. 62-63.

III

From this brief discussion of various out-party advisory groups, it seems apparent that the primary purpose of each was to accomplish one or more of the following goals: 1) to provide representation or recognition to voices within the party which were not sufficiently heard in Congress; 2) to provide an effective "amalgamated" policy-making center within the party; and/or 3) to provide a formidable and effective image of a responsible opposition party. Historically, *the fundamental* dilemma of the out-party has been its inability to achieve a satisfactory solution to the second goal mentioned above. In terms of the out-party efforts discussed in this essay, none—thus far, at any rate— has successfully blended the Congressional and Presidential orientations of the party into an effectively unified leadership pattern. The Congressional leaders of both parties have generally revealed extreme restraint in their endorsements of the various out-party organizational efforts.

In the case of the Republican Committee on Program and Progress, which did include the party's Congressional leaders, it should be noted that these individuals were asked to endorse a broad statement of long-range policy objectives to be achieved by the party by *1976*, not 1960. Thus, as Congressional leaders, they were neither committed, nor by virtue of their participation did they commit their Congressional colleagues to an immediate legislative program devised by a group of "outsiders." Even the promising start of the Republican Coordinating Committee was dimmed somewhat in view of the attitude reflected by House Leader Gerald Ford. Commenting on the fact that one of the Committee's task forces had completely ignored a controversy which existed at the time of its deliberations concerning the proposed repeal of section 14b of the Taft-Hartley Act, Ford stated that issues pending before Congress would not be discussed in task force reports because "Republicans in Congress would make Republican policy."[9]

One needs to understand the nature of the Congressional party as a mediate group[10] and the nature of Congressional leadership to realize that the intellectual gulf which separates the Congressional and Presidential wings of both parties involves something more than sheer "cussedness," or stubbornness on the part of a few "petty" politicians. The reluctance of Johnson, Rayburn, Dirksen, Halleck, and Ford to participate with enthusiasm in their party's advisory council ventures, when such ventures meant subordination of their own role in the policy-making decisions cannot be explained as the actions of "petty" men.

To a very real extent, the primary function of Congressional leaders is not to provide leadership in a dynamic, positive sense, as much as it is to maintain the stability of the Congressional system as it has evolved over the years. To insure the maintenance of the firmly entrenched set of Congressional values, attitudes, and norms certainly becomes one essential responsibility of Congressional leaders, and unfortunately these factors are not easily adapted to other, nonlegislative environments. In this sense, therefore, it seems reasonable to suggest that the dilemma of the out-party is basically one of accommodation. The extent to which a degree of accommodation can be achieved between the conflicting values, attitudes, and norms of the Congressional and Presidential groups will critically depend on the extent to which the traditional Congressional system can be altered to accommodate the vital political considerations that must be of primary importance and concern for any party that wishes to view itself as a truly national organization. The only alternative is out-party control by the Congressional leadership contingent, and although these individuals have been accorded an important role in our political system, this role does not extend—and, indeed, cannot be extended—to include a national leadership function. For this reason, Congressional out-party leaders must be prepared to share the task of directing the course of their party with other, non-Congressional party leaders.

The only hope for resolving the fundamental dilemma of the out-party is that the 1964 Republican Presidential nominee did not represent a significant segment of Congressional opinion—Democrat as well as Republican—when he wrote in his syndicated column, ". . .there is nothing more important for a national party than [control of] the national legislature. Even the Presidency is only co-equal in importance to the Congress."[11] If this statement does accurately reflect the dominant opinion of the majority of legislators in Congress, then the future of the out-party in American politics is bleak, indeed.

---

[9]*Congressional Quarterly Weekly Report*, XXIII, 24, 1122.

[10]As this term is used by David Truman in *The Congressional Party* (New York, Alfred A. Knopf, Inc., 1959).

[11]*Sunday Bulletin* (Philadelphia) August 15 1965.

Politicians

13. POLITICS AS A VOCATION

Max Weber

Now then, the boss is the figure who appears in the picture of this system of the plebiscitarian party machine. Who is the boss? He is a political capitalist entrepreneur who on his own account and at his own risk provides votes. He may have established his first relations as a lawyer or a saloon-keeper or as a proprietor of similar establishments, or perhaps as a creditor. From here he spins his threads out until he is able to "control" a certain number of votes. When he has come this far he establishes contact with the neighboring bosses, and through zeal, skill, and above all discretion, he attracts the attention of those who have already further advanced in the career, and then he climbs. The boss is indispensable to the organization of the party and the organization is centralized in his hands. He substantially provides the financial means. How does he get them? Well, partly by the contributions of the members, and especially by taxing the salaries of those officials who came into office through him and his party. Furthermore, there are bribes and tips. He who wishes to trespass with impunity

From Max Weber, *Essays in Sociology,* ed. and trans. Hans H. Gerth and C. Wright Mills. Copyright 1946 By Oxford University Press, Inc. pp. 107-27, excerpts. Reprinted by permission.

one of the many laws needs the boss's connivance and must pay for it; or else he will get into trouble. But this alone is not enough to accumulate the necessary capital for political enterprises. The boss is indispensable as the direct recipient of the money of great financial magnates, who would not entrust their money for election purposes to a paid party official, or to anyone else giving public account of his affairs. The boss, with his judicious discretion in financial matters, is the natural man for those capitalist circles who finance the election. The typical boss is an absolutely sober man. He does not seek social honor; the "professional" is despised in "respectable society." He seeks power alone, power as a source of money, but also power for power's sake. In contrast to the English leader, the American boss works in the dark. He is not heard speaking in public; he suggests to the speakers what they must say in expedient fashion. He himself, however, keeps silent. As a rule he accepts no office, except that of senator. For, since the senators, by virtue of the Constitution, participate in office patronage, the leading bosses often sit in person in this body. The distribution of offices is carried out, in the first place, according to services done for the party. But also, auctioning offices on financial bids often occurs and there are certain rates for individual offices; hence, a system of selling offices exists which, after all, has often been known also to the monarchies, the church-state included, of the seventeenth and eighteenth centuries.

The boss has no firm political "principles"; he is completely unprincipled in attitude and asks merely: What will capture votes? Frequently he is a rather poorly educated man. But as a rule he leads an inoffensive and correct private life. In his political morals, however, he naturally adjusts to the average ethical standards of political conduct, as a great many of us also may have done during the hoarding period in the field of economic ethics. That as a "professional" politician the boss is socially despised does not worry him. That he personally does not attain high federal offices, and does not wish to do so, has the frequent advantage that extra-party intellects, thus notables, may come into candidacy when the bosses believe they will have great appeal value at the polls. Hence the same old party notables do not run again and again, as is the case in Germany. Thus the structure of these unprincipled parties with their socially despised power-holders has aided able men to attain the Presidency—men who with us never would have come to the top. To be sure, the bosses resist an outsider who might jeopardize their sources of money and power. Yet in the competitive struggle to win the favor of the voters, the bosses frequently have had to condescend and accept candidates known to be opponents of corruption.

Thus there exists a strong capitalist party machine, strictly and thoroughly organized from top to bottom, and supported by clubs of extraordinary stability. These clubs, such as Tammany Hall, are like Knight orders. They seek profits solely through political control, especially of the municipal government, which is the most important object of booty. This structure of party life was made possible by the high degree of democracy in the United States—a "New Country." This connection, in turn, is the basis for the fact that the system is gradually dying out. America can no longer be governed only by dilettantes. Scarcely fifteen years ago, when American workers were asked why they allowed themselves to be governed by politicians whom they admitted they despised, the answer was: "We prefer having people in office whom we can spit upon, rather than a caste of officials who spit upon us, as is the case with you." This was the old point of view of American "democracy." Even then, the socialists had entirely different ideas and now the situation is no longer bearable. The dilettante administration does not suffice and the Civil Service Reform establishes an ever-increasing number of positions for life with pension rights. The reform works out in such a way that university-trained officials, just as incorruptible and quite as capable as our officials, get into office. Even now about 100,000 offices have ceased being objects of booty to be turned over after elections. Rather, the offices qualify their holders for pensions, and are based upon tested qualifications. The spoils system will thus gradually recede into the background and the nature of party leadership is then likely to be transformed also—but as yet, we do not know in what way. ...

Today, one cannot yet see in any way how the management of politics as a "vocation" will shape itself. Even less can one see along what avenue opportunities are opening to which political talents can be put for satisfactory political tasks. He who by his material circumstances is compelled to live "off" politics will almost always have to consider the alternative positions of the journalist or the party official as the typical direct avenues. Or, he must consider a position as representative of interest groups— such as a trade union, a chamber of commerce, a farm bureau, a craft association, a labor board, an employer's association, et cetera, or else a suitable municipal position. Nothing more than this can be said about this external aspect: in common with the journalist, the party official bears the odium of being *déclassé*. "Wage writer" or "wage speaker" will unfortunately always resound in his ears, even though the words remain unexpressed. He who is inwardly defenseless and unable to find the proper answer for himself had better stay away from this career. For in any case, besides grave temptations, it is an avenue that may constantly lead to disappointments. Now then, what inner enjoyments can this career offer and what personal conditions are presupposed for one who enters this avenue?

Well, first of all the career of politics grants a feeling of power. The knowledge of influencing men, of participating in power over them, and above all, the feeling of holding in one's hands a nerve fiber of historically important events can elevate the professional politician above everyday routine even when he is placed in formally modest positions. But now the question for him is: Through what qualities can I hope to do justice to this power (however narrowly circumscribed it may be in the individual case)? How can he hope to do justice to the responsibility that power imposes upon him? With this we enter the field of ethical questions, for that is where the problem belongs: What kind of a man must one be if he is to be allowed to put his hand on the wheel of history?

One can say that three pre-eminent qualities are decisive for the politician: passion, a feeling of responsibility, and a sense of proportion. ... To be sure, mere passion, however genuinely felt, is not enough. It does not make a politician, unless passion as devotion to a "cause" also makes responsibility to this cause the guiding star of action. And for this, a sense of proportion is needed. This is the decisive psychological quality of the politician: his ability to let realities work upon him with inner concentration and calmness. Hence his *distance* to things and men. "Lack of distance" *per se* is one of the deadly sins of every politician. It is one of those qualities the breeding of which will condemn the progeny of our intellectuals to political incapacity. For the problem is simply how can warm passion and a cool sense of proportion be forged together in one and the same soul? Politics is made with the head, not with other parts of the body or soul. And yet devotion to politics, if it is not to be frivolous intellectual play but rather genuinely human conduct, can be born and nourished from passion alone. However, that firm taming of the soul, which distinguishes the passionate politician and differentiates him from the "sterilely excited" and mere political dilettante, is possible only through habituation to detachment in every sense of the word. The "strength" of a political "personality" means, in the first place, the possession of these qualities of passion, responsibility, and proportion.

Therefore, daily and hourly, the politician inwardly has to overcome a quite trivial and all-too-human enemy: a quite vulgar vanity, the deadly enemy of all matter-of-fact devotion to a cause, and of all distance, in this case, of distance towards one's self.

Vanity is a very widespread quality and perhaps nobody is entirely free from it. In academic and scholarly circles, vanity is a sort of occupational disease, but precisely with the scholar, vanity—however disagreeably it may express itself—is relatively harmless; in the sense that as a rule it does not disturb scientific enterprise. With the politician the case is quite different. He works with the striving for power as an unavoidable means. Therefore, "power instinct," as is usually said, belongs indeed to his normal qualities. The sin against the lofty spirit of his vocation, however, begins where this striving for power ceases to be *objective* and becomes purely personal self-intoxication, instead of exclusively entering the service of "the cause." For ultimately there are only two kinds of deadly sins in the field of politics: lack of objectivity and—often but not always identical with it—irresponsibility. Vanity, the need personally to stand in the foreground as clearly as possible, strongly tempts the politician to commit one or both of these sins. This is more truly the case as the demagogue is compelled to count upon "effect." He therefore is constantly in danger of becoming an actor as well as taking lightly the responsibility for the outcome of his actions and of being concerned merely with the "impression" he makes. His lack of objectivity tempts him to strive for the glamorous semblance of power rather than for actual power. His irresponsibility, however, suggests that he enjoy power merely for power's sake without a substantive purpose. Although, or rather just because, power is the unavoidable means, and striving for power is one of the driving forces of all politics, there is no more harmful distortion of political force than the parvenu-like braggart with power, and the vain self-reflection in the feeling of power, and in general every worship of power *per se*. The mere "power politician" may get strong effects, but actually his work leads nowhere and is senseless. (Among us, too, an ardently promoted cult seeks to glorify him.) In this, the critics of "power politics" are absolutely right.

From the sudden inner collapse of typical representatives of this mentality, we can see what inner weakness and impotence hide behind this boastful but entirely empty gesture. It is a product of a shoddy and superficially blasé attitude towards the meaning of human conduct; and it has no relation whatsoever to the knowledge of tragedy with which all action, but especially political action, it truly interwoven.

The final result of political action often, no, even regularly, stands in completely inadequate and often even paradoxical relation to its original meaning. This is fundamental to all history, a point not to be proved in detail here. But because of this fact, the serving of a cause must not be absent if action is to have inner strength. Exactly what the cause, in the service of which the politician strives for power and uses power, looks like is a matter of faith. The politician may serve national, humanitarian, social, ethical, cultural, worldly, or religious ends. The politician may be sustained by a strong belief in "progress"—no matter in which sense—or he may coolly reject this kind of belief. He may claim to stand in the service of an "idea" or, rejecting this in principle, he may want to serve external ends of everyday life. However, some kind of faith must always exist. Otherwise, it is absolutely true that the curse of the creature's worthlessness overshadows even the externally strongest political successes. . . .

We must be clear about the fact that all ethically oriented conduct may be guided by one of two fundamentally differing and irreconcilably opposed maxims: conduct can be oriented to an "ethic of ultimate ends" or to an "ethic of responsibility." This is not to say that an ethic of ultimate ends is identical with irresponsibility, or that an ethic of responsibility is identical with unprincipled opportunism. Naturally nobody says that. However, there is an abysmal contrast between conduct that follows the maxim of an ethic of ultimate ends—that is, in religious terms, "The Christian does rightly and leaves the results with the Lord"—and conduct that follows the maxim of an ethic of responsibility, in which case one has to give an account of the foreseeable results of one's action.

You may demonstrate to a convinced syndicalist, believing in an ethic of ultimate ends, that his action will result in increasing the opportunities of reaction, in increasing the oppression of his class, and obstructing its ascent—and you will not make the slightest impression upon him. If an action of good intent leads to bad results, then, in the actor's eyes, not he but the world, or the stupidity of other men, or God's will who made them thus, is responsible for the evil. However a man who believes in an ethic of responsibility takes account of precisely the average deficiences of people; as Fichte has correctly said, he does not even have the right to presuppose their goodness and perfection. He does not feel in a position to burden others with the results of his own actions so far as he was able to foresee them; he will say: these results are ascribed to my action. The believer in an ethic of ultimate ends feels "responsible" only for seeing to it that the flame of pure intentions is not quenched: for example, the flame of protesting against the injustice of the social order. To rekindle the flame ever anew is the purpose of his quite irrational deeds, judged in view of their possible success. They are acts that can and shall have only exemplary value.

But even herewith the problem is not yet exhausted. No ethics in the world can dodge the fact that in numerous instances the attainment of "good" ends is bound to the fact that one must be willing to pay the price of using morally dubious means or at least dangerous ones—and facing the possibility or even the probability of evil ramifications. From no ethics in the world can it be concluded when and to what extent the ethically good purpose "justifies" the ethically dangerous means and ramifications. . . .

Surely, politics is made with the head, but it is certainly not made with the head alone. In this the proponents of an ethic of ultimate ends are right. One cannot prescribe to anyone whether he should follow an ethic of absolute ends or an ethic of responsibility, or when the one and when the other. One can say only this much: If in these times, which, in your opinion, are not times of "sterile" excitation—excitation is not, after all, genuine passion—if now suddenly the *Weltanschauungs*-politicians crop up *en masse* and pass the watchword, "The world is stupid and base, not I," "The responsibility for the consequences does not fall upon me but upon the others whom I serve and whose stupidity or baseness I shall eradicate,"

then I declare frankly that I would first inquire into the degree of inner poise backing this ethic of ultimate ends. I am under the impression that in nine out of ten cases I deal with windbags who do not fully realize what they take upon themselves but who intoxicate themselves with romantic sensations. From a human point of view this is not very interesting to me, nor does it move me profoundly. However, it is immensely moving when a *mature* man—no matter whether old or young in years—is aware of a responsibility for the consequences of his conduct and really feels such responsibility with heart and soul. He then acts by following an ethic of responsibility and somewhere he reaches the point where he says: "Here I stand; I can do no other." That is something genuinely human and moving. And every one of us who is not spiritually dead must realize the possibility of finding himself at some time in that position. In so far as this is true, an ethic of ultimate ends and an ethic of responsibility are not absolute contrasts but rather supplements, which only in unison constitute a genuine man—a man who *can* have the "calling for politics.". . .

14. THE AMATEUR DEMOCRAT
IN AMERICAN POLITICS

by James Q. Wilson

SINCE the Second World War a new kind of politician has appeared

From James Q. Wilson, "The Amateur Democrat in American Politics," in *Parliamentary Affairs*, XVI, 1, 73-86, excerpts. By permission of the Hansard Society for Parliamentary Government.

in large numbers in several of the biggest American cities. Although they are nowhere in control of their parties, these new politicians have played an important part in the defeat of the boss of Tammany Hall and have contributed to the election of several important officials: a governor in California, a mayor in New York City, and a state's attorney in Chicago. Their ambitions extended far beyond these offices, however, for they intend to alter fundamentally the character of the American party system, and accordingly of all governing institutions. They are found most prominently in the Democratic party but, in lesser numbers, they exercise influence among Republicans as well.

The new politicians are known by several names. In California, they are referred to, most generally, as the "club movement" and more specifically as the "CDC"—the California Democratic Council. In New York City they are called the "reformers" or sometimes the "Lehman group", after one of their chief sponsors, former Senator Herbert H. Lehman. In Illinois one group is known as the "IVI"—the Independent Voters of Illinois, a local affiliate of the Americans for Democratic Action—while another wing was called the "DFI"—the Democratic Federation of Illinois. Wherever they are found and whatever their name, however, they display certain common characteristics, and it is with these general traits that this study is concerned.

Although the traits these new politicians have in common are easy to list, it is difficult to find a single word which will describe them adequately and distinguish them from the more conventional politicians found in large cities. That they are so distinguished can scarcely be doubted. In every community where they are found in large numbers, a keen antipathy inevitably develops between the new and the conventional politicians. The former accuse the latter of being at best "hacks" and "organization

men" and at worst "bosses" and "machine leaders." The latter retort by describing the former as "dilettantes," "crackpots," "outsider," and "hypocritical do-gooders." Most of the new politicians in the Democratic party are also liberals, but it is not their liberalism that is their chief distinguishing characteristic. They can be found in the Republican party as well, and there they are likely to be extremely conservative. What is necessary is a definition that distinguishes the new from other politicians but which is applicable equally to liberals and conservatives.

The Nature of the Amateur

It is not his liberalism or his age, education, or class that sets the new politician apart and makes him worth studying. Rather, it is his outlook on politics, and the style of politics he practises. This is sensed by the politicians themselves; the conventional and new politicians, in almost every case, find it hard to "understand" one another or to "get along," even in those cases in which their interests or policies happen to coincide. Although in New York the new politicians are called "reformers," their counterparts in California are not reformers at all, for in these states they are not preoccupied with matters of reform. Nor, as we shall see, are they all "intellectuals" or "eggheads," although some of the new politicians are fond of describing themselves and their colleagues in these terms. Although no single word is completely satisfactory, the word which will be used in this study is "amateur."

By amateur is not meant a dabbler, a dilettante or an inept practitioner of some special skill; many amateur

Democrats have a highly sophisticated understanding of practical politics and have proved their skills in the only way that matters—by winning at the polls. Similarly, a good many undoubted professionals—by which word we mean all nonamateurs—are hopelessly incompetent and have proved themselves so in the only way that matters.

Nor does amateur here mean a person who is in politics for fun or as an avocation rather than for money or as a career. To be sure, most amateurs do get their incomes from sources other than politics and regard it as other than a career. But there are also many professionals, as the word will be used here, who do not make money out of politics and who think of it mainly as a game. In Chicago, of course, most professional politicians do as a rule have public jobs or get some income from politics, but this is not the case everywhere. In California few professionals other than those holding elective office are supported mainly by politics, and even in Manhattan there are as many or more workers in Tammany clubs who do not have political jobs as there are those who do.

An amateur is one who finds politics *intrinsically* interesting because it expresses a conception of the public interest. The amateur politician sees the political world more in terms of ideas and principles than in terms of persons. Politics is the determination of public policy, and public policy ought to be set deliberately rather than as the accidental by-product of a struggle for personal and party advantage. Issues ought to be settled on their merits; compromises by which one issue is settled other than on its merits are sometimes necessary, but they are never desirable. If the arena in

which the amateur acts is the city and the question at hand a limited one, his tendency is to endow, if he can, the issue with generality—either by making it a national issue or by finding in it wider implications. The amateur takes the outcome of politics—the determination of policies and the choice of officials—seriously, in the sense that he feels a direct concern for what he thinks are the ends these policies serve and the qualities these officials possess. He is not oblivious to considerations of partisan or personal advantage in assessing the outcome but (in the pure case) he dwells on the relation of outcome to his conception, be it vague or specific, of the public weal. Although politics may have attractions as a game of skill, it is never simply that.

The professional, on the other hand —even the "professional" who practises politics as a hobby rather than as a vocation—is preoccupied with the outcome of politics in terms of winning or losing. Politics, to him, consists of concrete questions and specific persons who must be dealt with in a manner that will "keep everybody happy" and thus minimize the possibility of defeat at the next election. The professional politician rarely broods about his function in society, the larger significance of the issues with which he deals, or the consistency of his procedures with some well-worked-out theory of democracy. Although he is not oblivious to the ends implied by political outcomes, he sees (or, since he is rarely given to theorizing, acts as if he sees) the good of society as the by-product of efforts that are aimed not at producing the good society, but at gaining power and place for one's self and one's party.

The amateur feels rewarded by having satisfied a felt obligation to "participate," and this satisfaction is greater the higher the value the amateur can attach to the ends which the outcomes of politics serve. The principal reward of the professional is to be found in the extrinsic satisfactions of participation—power, income, status, or the fun of the game. The ideal amateur has a "natural" response to politics; he sees each battle as a "crisis," and each victory as a triumph and each loss as a defeat for a cause. The professional tends, by contrast, to develop a certain detachment towards politics and a certain immunity to its excitement and its outcomes.

This distinction is, of course, somewhat overdrawn and its applicability tends to vary with the rank of the politician. Anyone with even a casual familiarity with amateur club politics in the Democratic party will object immediately that many so-called "amateurs," particularly those who seek elective office or who lead amateur clubs, are obviously and deeply ambitious, power-seeking, or eager for patronage in a way that is indistinguishable from the professional politician. This is true. Many, but not all, of the amateurs with long experience and personal stakes in politics acquire the habits and motives of the professional; indeed, it is entirely possible that an amateur club movement could not endure if there were not in it at least a few pseudo-amateurs who had made politics a career and who had a careerist's detachment about or even contempt for the "meaning" of politics. . . .

The source of. . .the behaviour of the amateur seems to be found in a "political ethic" which has been characteristic of the Anglo-Saxon, Yankee Protestant middle class in the United States and which is profoundly different from the political ethic of the immigrant, the Eastern and Southern European workers, and perhaps from that of the lower classes generally. Richard Hofstadter has given an excellent description of these competing political ethics in his book, *The Age of Reform*. One ethic, "founded upon the indigenous Yankee-Protestant political traditions, and upon middle-class life, assumed and demanded the constant, disinterested activity of the citizen in public affairs, argued that political life ought to be run, to a greater degree than it was, in accordance with general principles and abstract laws apart from and superior to personal needs, and expressed a common feeling that government should be in good part an effort to moralize the lives of individuals while economic life should be intimately related to the stimulation and development of individual character."

In contrast, "the other system, founded upon the European backgrounds of the immigrants, upon their unfamiliarity with independent political action, their familiarity with hierarchy and authority, and upon the urgent needs that so often grew out of their migration, took for granted that the political life of the individual would arise out of family needs, interpreted political and civic relations chiefly in terms of personal obligations, and placed strong personal loyalties above allegiance to abstract codes of laws and morals."

The political ethic of the immigrant became, of course, the basis of the big-city political machine, while the ethic of the Yankee Protestant became the basis for civic reform and assaults on that machine. Today, powerful, city-wide machines of the old style are hard to find; Chicago may be the only important example remaining. But the ethic of the machine persists, in modified form, in the habits of professional politicians for whom the value of organization and leadership are indisputable, personal loyalties and commitments remain indispensable, and the lower-class basis of the big-city electorate is unchanging. Similarly, contemporary amateur politicians are critical of the naivete of older reform efforts which sought to capture elective offices without first capturing the party organization. Nonetheless, the essence of the reform ethic persists: the desire to moralize public life, the effort to rationalize power with law, and the insistence that correct goals will be served only if goals are set and officials selected by correct procedures.

The political ethic of the followers of the professional politician places constraints on him entirely different from those placed on the amateur. These constraints are by and large unrelated to issues, the ends of government, the abstract desirability of citizen participation, or the need for the "better element" to control the party. Rather, the intangible rewards of the professional arise from the prestige, sociability, and personal loyalties which politics can provide: being a "big man" to one's neighbors, placing voters under an obligation to oneself, taking pride in the congratulations from the leader when one has "delivered" his district or precinct, or simply being able to meet regularly with one's neighbors and friends as one canvasses for votes of petition signatures and thus overcomes loneliness or boredom. An amateur may derive some of these satisfactions also, but not in a club where there is not at least a verbal concern for issues and "reform"; the professional, on the other hand, gets more out of politics precisely in those clubs where no one upsets pleas-

ant relations with issues and reforms. When an amateur club splits into factions, the issues at stake quickly become infused with ideology; when a professional club suffers from internal friction, it is in the nature of a family fight over ethnic claims, the division of patronage, or the conflict of personalities: in short, over the rupture of *personal* ties. For the amateur politician, personal ties are mediated through a nexus of general ideas; for the professional, they are direct. Thus, an essential aspect of an amateur's relation to politics is that he is what Robert K. Merton has called a "cosmopolitan;" the professional, on the other hand, is a "local."

A local, from whose ranks most professional politicians are drawn, is a person who is preoccupied with the local community to the exclusion of affairs outside his community. He is "parochial," and has lived in his community of many years, knows many people and is anxious to know more, and defines power in terms of interpersonal influence based on a network of friendships. He joins organizations which are local in order to avail himself of contacts and in order to associate himself with the broadest, most widely-accepted symbols of community integration. A cosmopolitan, on the other hand, is a person with minimal ties to the locality but a strong attachment to "the Great Society" of national and international problems, ideas, movements, fashions, and culture. He is often a recent arrival to the community and, if it is small, anxious to move on to large cities which are themselves "cosmopolitan." He is selective in his friendships, seeks out other cosmopolitans, joins organizations which have a professional and civic flavor, and endeavors to be influential through the display of his expertise and special skills. His attachment is to symbols which are not widely shared but esoteric and which are, thus, often divisive rather than integrating for the community as a whole. ...

The club movement has attracted many kinds of people to it, and no single description will suffice for all, but to a great extent the principal shared characteristics are precisely those which support the description of them as cosmopolitan, intellectually-orientated amateurs. For the most part, they are young, well-educated professional people, including a large number of women. In style of life, they are distinctly middle and upper-middle class: in mood and outlook, they are products of the generation which came of age after the Second World War and particularly after the Korean War; in political beliefs, they are almost entirely among the liberals of the left. They bring to politics a concern for ideas and ideals.

In Manhattan, between one-half and three-fourths of the members of three clubs studied were under forty years of age. Not only were they young, they were fairly recent arrivals to the city. Over three-fourths did not live in their present neighborhood before 1949, and between one-half and two-thirds did not live there before 1953. Many were raised in New York, but most had left home to attend a university and had only recently returned. Between two-thirds and three-fourths did not join their first political club until 1957 or later.

In two of the three clubs examined, over half of the members were of Jewish background; Catholics, on the other hand, were very few in number, never more than 10 per cent of the total. Only in one club did the proportion of married people exceed one-third; the rest were single, separated, or divorced. Those who were married often lacked children; although about 30 per cent of the members were married, only 10 per cent had a family. Most club members, at least the most active ones, appeared to be sufficiently young and lacking in extensive family or professional obligations so that a considerable amount of time and energy could be devoted to politics. Often husband and wife were both club members; presumably this reduced the problems which might result if one or the other were perennially absent on political tasks. The wives of volunteer politicians were not, unlike their Tammany counterparts, the kind of women who were likely to remain at home and raise children while husbands pre-empted all the diversions and excitement of political activity. Many of the married but childless women in reform politics were anxious not to let marriage and the demands of a husband's career compel them to give up their interests, "lose their personalities," or become absorbed by homely duties.

Professionally, lawyers represented between one-tenth and one-sixth of the membership but a much higher percentage (in one case, a half) of the officers and activists. Nearly a quarter of the members of two clubs were in what are described as the "communications" business—public relations, advertising, journalism, editing, publishing, radio, and television. There were often as many members from medicine (physicians, psychiatrists, nurses) as from law, a rather striking fact given the general beliefs about the reluctance of such persons to become associated with political or controversial causes. Business, service and clerical occupations accounted for one-fourth to one-third of the membership.

The backgrounds of the officers show even greater similarities. Officers were far more likely to be male, married, Jewish, and lawyers. In 1960 thirty-six men and women were nominated for office in the Lexington Democratic Club, the oldest of the reform organizations. Of the thirty-six, twenty-six were men and ten women. Thirty-four had graduated from college, and, of these, nineteen had attended the desirable schools of the Ivy League. The majority (twenty) had completed law school and were practising law in New York City (mostly with firms in and around Wall Street). Most of the rest were in public relations, advertising, the theatre, college teaching, radio, and television, and so on. Of the five who were in other businesses, most were associated with investment houses. In many cases, these young professionals were academically distinguished: there were sixteen instances of school honors, including five Phi Beta Kappa members, two teaching fellows, and at least two law review editors. Although no precise determination of ethnic background is available, a rough estimate based on family name suggests that there were about twenty or twenty-one Jewish and fifteen or sixteen non-Jewish candidates for office.

The ranks of the amateur politicians seem constantly to be replenished by new, young recruits as age, professional preoccupations, or family responsibilities cause older members to fall away. Many stay active in the movement only while they are still on the lower rungs of their career ladders. As a result, there is a high turnover of activists.

The Function of Parties

Political parties perform, to some degree, at least three functions in a democratic government. They recruit candidates, mobilize voters, and assemble power within the formal government. The first two functions are indispensable regardless of the precise nature of the political institutions; the third, on the other hand, varies with the extent to which elective officials have sufficient formal, legal power to operate the government. If legal power is badly fragmented among many independent elective officials and widely decentralized among many levels of government, the need for informal methods of assembling power becomes great. The political party is one, although by no means the only, mechanism for performing this task. If a single elective official has complete legal authority over all aspects of the government, then the need for informally assembling power is much less—ideally, zero. All three party functions will in some degree be performed differently by amateur as contrasted to professional politicians.

The professional, for whom politics primarily has extrinsic rewards, is preoccupied with maintaining his position in party and elective offices. Winning is essential, although sometimes electoral victory must be subordinated to maintaining the party organization. Candidates will be selected on the basis of their electoral appeal. A ticket will be constructed which maximizes this appeal by offering "representation" to candidates of important ethnic, religious, racial, and nationality groups and to important geographic regions and civil divisions. This is the "balanced" ticket. Since most voters support parties out of traditional allegiances, these traditional loyalties will be reinforced. Added to them will be appeals to "interests"—private advantage, sectional loyalties, and ethnic and nationality claims. Issues will be avoided except in the most general terms or where the party is confident that a majority supports its position. Should at the next election a contrary position on the same issue seem best suited for winning a majority, the party will try to change or at least mute its position. Votes will be mobilized not only by such appeals but also by personal contacts through precinct captains. These workers will appeal to the voter on the basis of party loyalty and personal friendship; sometimes material inducements (money, favors, jobs) will be offered. To the extent that the party can enable its candidates to win by providing them with these resources (loyalty to a party name, a balanced ticket, appeals to interests and the efforts of party workers), it places them under an obligation to it. Re-election without party support would be costly (in terms of money, time, effort, obtaining support from new groups in exchange for commitments to programs and so forth). Since the party enables the candidate, in effect, to economize, his behavior in office can be controlled to some extent by threatening not to reslate him for office if he acts independently. In this way, and through the distribution of patronage and money, the party is able to assemble power in the government.

The amateur politician, on the other hand, would in the ideal situation prefer to recruit candidates on the basis of their commitment to a set of policies. Voters would be mobilized by appeals to some set of principles or goals. The party would be held together and linked to the voter by a shared conception of the public interest. A politics of principle would necessarily attach little value to—and indeed would criticize—appeals to private, group or sectional interest. Private interests, which for the professional are the motive force of politics, the amateur would consider as irrelevant, irrational,

or immoral. The task of assembling power in the formal government would be met not by using sanctions to discipline elective officials, but by electing to those posts candidates who were committed to the policies of the party and who would therefore act in concert, not from coercion, but out of conviction. Amateur politicians thus seek to alter fundamentally the way in which the functions of parties are carried out. Instead of serving as neutral agents which mobilize majorities for whatever candidates and programs seem best suited to capturing public fancy, the parties would become the sources of program and the agents of social change. They would control the behavior of public officials by internalized convictions rather than external threats and for the purpose of realizing certain social policies rather than of enhancing the party's prospects for retaining power in the next election.

Few amateurs act completely in accord with the logic of their position and many professionals have modified their behavior to keep pace with a changing political situation. Because of the social mobility and economic affluence in America, resulting in a growing middle class which has assimilated older immigrant groups, more and more people have, in effect, abandoned the political ethic of the lower classes and adopted the ethic of the Yankees. Shrewd professional politicians, such as Mayor Richard J. Daley of Chicago, have adapted in part to this change by providing the image, if not the substance, of a politics of principle. They have sought out "blue ribbon" candidates and appealing civic causes with which to attract the votes of a growing middle class unresponsive to the inducements a patronage-fed precinct captain can offer. Banfield explains this in part by noting that, between 1948 and 1956, the proportion of the total Democratic vote in Cook County cast by the "inner wards" of Chicago declined from 37 to 31 per cent, while the proportion cast by that part of Cook County outside Chicago rose from 13 to 18 per cent. This ecological change compelled city bosses to devote more resources to attracting that vote which cannot be won by conventional precinct-captain appeals.

The fact that professional politicians are everywhere paying at least lip service to certain "reform" or good government programs as a result of profound changes in the character of the electorate goes far toward explaining what appears to be an anomaly in the record of the amateur politician in America. The amateur Democrat is, of course, a special case of the American municipal reformer—he is the reformer who has chosen to enter, capture and staff the political parties at the local level in order to realize goals that earlier reformers have tried to attain from outside the party. But, like the reformer, the amateur politican has lost most of his struggles for power. He is nowhere in control of his party and where he has contributed to the election of an important official—as in California and New York—he almost invariably discovers that the official does not feel bound by the amateur's demands. The anomaly is that, although the amateur—like the reformer generally—has lost the struggle for power, many of the measures he advocates have been adopted. Patronage is declining in importance, local government is vastly more honest and efficient today than thirty years ago, the parties are much more concerned with finding "good government" candidates and issues, the day of the "boss" is all but gone, and the "liberal" inclinations of most big-city

Democratic parties are practically assured.

The measures for which the amateurs have fought are being adopted, less because of the power of the amateurs than because of a change in the American electorate to which all politicians, professional and amateur, must respond—the steady diffusion of what Hofstadter has called the Yankee political ethic. With the continued affluence of America and her expanding investment in mass education, this ethic will undoubtedly come to characterize the political attitudes of an ever larger number of citizens. And, as is attested by the rise of local conservative clubs, the Young Americans for Freedom and the John Birch Society, the amateurs of the Republican party will enjoy an enhanced importance along with their colleagues among the Democrats.

Evaluating the Amateur Democrat

Since people who read books about politics are likely to be those who instinctively are sympathetic to the aims, if not the achievements, of amateur politicians, the contrast (necessarily over-simplified) between the amateur and the professional sketched here may make the choice appear an easy one. Politicians, one immediately feels, ought to be high-minded and committed to policies; they *ought* to "talk sense" to voters rather than rely on empty slogans, selfish appeals, and political pay-offs; elective officials *ought* to vote and act on the basis of conscience rather than at the dictate of party "bosses." But the choice is not a simple one. An amateur politics of principle may make the attainment of the certain highly-valued ends difficult or impossible, whereas politics of interest may, under certain circumstances, enable those ends to be realized much more easily. Institutions should be judged by the ends they serve, not by the motives of their members, and on this basis it is an open question whether the professional politican is not the person best equipped to operate a democratic government in a way that will produce desirable policies. A preoccupation with the propriety of methods, while a legitimate concern, can be carried too far. No one used the power of patronage more ruthlessly than Abraham Lincoln; no one appealed more cleverly or more successfully to "irrational" sentiments of nationalism and race pride than Fiorello H. La Guardia; no one relied more heavily on big-city machines than Franklin D. Roosevelt. Adlai Stevenson, the man who, more than anyone, has served as the patron saint of the amateur politicians, voiced similar concerns when he raised but did not answer these questions:

It does not belittle the movement to ask some questions, as a perceptive California friend of mine has done, about at least the West-Coast type of club development. What are the effects of an almost exclusively "ideological" political motivation? Is some degree of instability the likely price of a lack of the restraint of economic interest and of part-time interest in politics? What are the implications of all-out election campaigning by highly vocal groups who assume little responsibility for legislative follow-up of either their nominees or their programs? What is necessary to prevent hit-and-run politics—even by one's highest minded political friends? These seem to be worth-while questions.

PART THREE

Political Parties
and
The Electorate

By comparison with European democracies, unweighted percentages of the American electorate actually voting in elections have been low. Because of the concern of many people at this disclosure, President John F. Kennedy on March 30, 1963, appointed a commision to study the problems of registration and voter participation. The Commission in its *Report* suggested among other things that a number of legal barriers operated to prevent many people from voting, although the effect of an individual's lack of political involvement was recognized. When James A. Robinson and William H. Standing examined voter participation in Indiana, they found that voting tends to be higher: (a) in rural areas; (b) when the voters regard the offices to be filled as important; and (c) especially when a number of offices are to be filled at the same election. They did not find the competitiveness of the election critical. Philip K. Hastings, studying the non-voter in Pittsfield, Mass., found him generally uninformed and unwilling to think for himself—characteristics of the politically apathetic individual.

Are large-scale apathy and political alienation threats to a democratic system? Walter Dean Burnham believes they are. He calls for the integration of the politically alienated into the political universe. While he does not regard voting participation as a desideratum in itself, Seymour Lipset agrees that a low rate of participation may be a symptom of a more serious political malady. On the other hand, a strong case can be made against being concerned over the incidence of non-voting. Voter turn-out in competitive states in presidential elections is considerably higher than the national average. In addition to competitiveness, other factors influencing non-voting include illness, incarceration in penal or mental health institutions, illiteracy, and simple lack of intelligence. There are approximately as many American citizens with IQ's below 70 as above 130. Another factor is responsibility for registration: Whereas in the United States the individual is responsible, in Britain the state is responsible; a citizen must say, "No," twice to keep his name off the lists. As a result, in the 1964 British general election 99.5 per cent of the adult population was registered to vote. Comparative raw voting participation on figures are therefore untrustworthy indices to political interest and involvement in the United States. This is not to advocate a complacent attitude toward the political disenchantment which leads to apathy. It is rather to say it is simply not possible to conclude, using such data as a basis, that "half of the American electorate . . . is now more or less entirely outside the universe of active politics."

The relationship between the party and the electorate is a vital factor in the ability of a party to attract and mobilize voters. One aspect of that relationship is the nature of party membership. Maurice Duverger distinguishes between "mass parties," which include only active, card-carrying members, and "cadre parties," composed of a small group that relies on nonmembers or nominal members for their electoral support. United States parties are cadre parties. Voters appear to be predisposed to one of the parties for a variety of sociological reasons. Seymour Lipset finds religious, economic, and ethnic factors important. However despite an admitted class factor, he finds what he calls "upper-class liberalism" blurring the line between Republicans and Democrats. That voter predispositions within the American system are generally stable is shown by Philip E. Converse, et al., by their analysis of the 1960 election. The only major voting shifts observed were among Catholics switching to Kennedy and Protestants switching to Nixon, both presumably influenced by Mr. Kennedy's religion.

The question of why people vote as they do has provided one of the most fertile fields for political research. V. O. Key, Jr., and Frank Munger warn against too much emphasis on political sociology; they find an apparent traditional factor in voting behavior not readily explainable by the various sociological studies.

The Electorate

15. SOME CORRELATES OF VOTER PARTICIPATION: THE CASE OF INDIANA

Jams A. Robinson and William H. Standing

This article re-examines four familiar propositions about voter participation on the basis of general elections in Indiana for two periods, 1934 to 1944 and 1946 to 1956. (The independent variables in these propositions are *inter-party competition, urbanism, prestige of office, and totality of election appeal.* The relationship between two of these

variables and participation is the opposite of that observed in other studies, and the relationship between the other two and participation is less dramatic in Indiana than elsewhere.)

Inter-party Competition and Voter Participation

What is the relation of inter-party competition to voter participation? Do voters go to the polls in larger

From James A. Robinson and William H. Standing, "Some Correlates of Voter Participation: The Case of Indiana," *Journal of Politics,* XXII 1 (February, 1960), 96-111, excerpts. By permission of The Journal of Politics.

numbers for an election in which considerable doubt about the outcome exists than for one in which the result seems a foregone conclusion? To determine the relationship between competition and participation, safe and competitive electoral-situations were identified by tests designed for another study relating inter-party competition to the number of candidates in party primaries. The term, electoral-situation, means a general election held in a particular political subdivision for one office in a single year. Whereas most studies of this kind have determined safeness or competitiveness of elections by the size of majority, say 60 per cent, in previous elections or merely the immediately preceding election, our tests give primary emphasis to the *number* and *continuity* of elections won by a party. Second, we attempt to identify electoral-situations that are clearly safe and clearly competitive and put approximately one-half of the contested general elections in an unclassified category. . . .

When the electoral-situations in each of these categories had been identified, the next step was to compute the average percentage vote in all the situations within a category. These percentages were found by dividing *the total number of votes cast in all electoral-situations within a category* by *the total number of potential votes within that category*. The potential vote was defined as the population aged twenty-one or over. Data from the 1940 census were used for Period I and from the 1950 census for Period II.

These computations revealed that in Period I, 74.51 per cent voted in Competitive electoral-situations; 69.08 per cent voted in Safe Republican and 64.27 per cent voted in

Safe Democratic situations. The figure for Safe Democratic and Safe Republican combined was 66.18 per cent. Thus, for the years 1934–44 participation appears to have varied with the competitiveness of the contest. However, in Period II the relationship between competition and turnout was quite different. While participation in Competitive situations (60.59 per cent) was slightly higher than in Safe Democratic contests (60.19 per cent), it was slightly less than in Safe Republican (62.15 per cent). For all Safe situations in Period II the average turnout was 61.67 per cent, a full percent higher than Competitive situations.

By comparing experience in these two different periods, we are forced to qualify a generalization we might have given greater credence had we examined only one period. We are presently unable to say whether Period I or Period II is atypical, and we are also at a loss to explain the differences between the two periods. Our Competitive and Safe situations are "model" cases, that is clearly one or the other, so we are not inclined to regard the differences as an artifact of our classification scheme. The distribution of different kinds of situations among different election years is roughly proportional to the size of the different kinds of situations, so we cannot attribute the differences between periods to overweighting a particular election year or years. For the time being we are faced with an apparent exception to the proposition that participation depends on competition. V. O. Key also observed exceptions to the rule in Southern politics. He reports that the hypothesis the closer the vote the greater the turn-out must be modified "to take into account the fact that unless potential voters feel deeply about the issues, they will display a vast indifference no matter how close a race is predicted." Key was arguing that one-party systems do not formulate the issues in such a way as to activate the electorate as much as two-party systems. Nevertheless, a decline in concern about public problems might be a possible explanation for the difference between our findings in these two periods. (However, our data offer no support for this hypothesis other than the fact that the percentage of potential voters who actually voted was generally less in Period II.

Urbanism and Voter Participation

One of the traditional demographic variables in studies of political behavior is the urbanism of the population. However, the relation between urbanism and participation has differed between sample surveys and aggregate data studies. In national samples in three successive presidential years, metropolitan residents have shown a larger percentage participation than rural, while Key's analysis of election returns in Southern primaries reveals just the opposite, namely, that "metropolitan counties almost invariably have a substantially lower degree of voter interest, i.e., participation, than rural counties, other things being equal."

To relate urbanism to participation for Period I, the 92 Indiana counties were ranked according to density in 1940. The counties were then ranked according to average percentage vote in the presidential elections of 1936, 1940, and 1944. A correlation of these two rank-orders produced a coefficient of minus .53. A similar rank-order correlation was calculated between density and vote for prosecuting attorney in all counties in the non-presidential years, 1934, 1938, and 1942, and this produced a coefficient of minus .44. The same procedures were applied to Period II, with the substitution of the 1950 density figure and the exclusion, in one correlation, of ten counties which had no contests for prosecuting attorney in the nonpresidental years, 1946, 1950, and 1954. The correlation coefficients in this period were, for president and prosecuting attorney in nonpresidential years respectively, minus .51 and minus .65. Not only were all four correlations in the opposite direction from the national surveys, but they tended to be rather high. . . .

(Although it is not a one-to-one relationship, the general tendency in Indiana is that rural areas produce higher rates of voter participation than urban areas.) The present state of the data does not permit an analysis of the deviant cases such as Brown County, the most rural, which in Period I ranked seventh from the bottom in participation, or LaGrange, which had the second lowest rate of participation in the First Period and the lowest in the Second while ranking near (seventeenth) the bottom of the density scale. Nevertheless, these findings fail to conform to patterns of surveys which show greater participation among metropolitan than among rural voters. Instead, the relationship between urbanism and participation in Indiana over these twenty years corresponded more closely to what Key observed in Southern politics.

Prestige of Office and Voter Participation

Occasionally one reads in books on American politics that voters take greater interest in offices with high prestige than in those with low prestige. It is said that more people vote for President than for state and local offices, and frequently the implication is that the differences in participation for the two kinds of offices is considerable. ... A comparison of vote for President with that for governor and for prosecuting attorney will test the validity of the assertion that voters "taper off by voting for a few or none at all toward the bottom" of the ballot.

The effect of prestige of office on participation in Indiana for these two periods may be summarized as follows: vote for governor is nearly as high as that for president and in some counties exceeds that for President; participation for prosecuting attorney in presidential years falls off slightly from the high rate of voting for president and governor, but not very much. (Given the occasion to go to the polls, Indiana voters turn out in large numbers, and, if the experience with the offices of President, governor, and prosecuting attorney is representative, most of those who go vote for all places on the ballot. In short, the effect of prestige of office is apparent but slight.)

To elaborate, in Indiana the state-wide difference in the size of the vote for president and governor is quite small. The state-wide average vote for president in Period I was 77.4 per cent; for governor 77.2 per cent. In Period II the presidential races drew an average of 73.5 per cent and the gubernatorial contests 72.9 per cent.

The slight difference in turnout for these two offices is further revealed by examining county returns. For the three elections in Period I, the average vote for governor exceeded that for president in twenty-seven counties although never by more than 1.5 per cent. In the other sixty-five counties the average presidential vote was greater than the average vote for governor, but only in six was the presidential average more than 1 per cent above that for governor.

In Period II the turnout for governor remained close to the turn-out for president, but not so close as in Peroid I. In the elections of 1948, 1952, and 1956, the average vote for governor was higher than that for President in nine counties. Clark and Grant counties showed differences of 6.5 per cent and 11 per cent, but in the other seven, differences did not exceed 1.5 per cent. In the remaining eighty-three counties the average presidential turn-out was higher than the governor's. Thirty-one of these counties produced gubernatorial votes within 1 per cent of the vote for President; thirty-eight were within 2 per cent; fourteen showed more than 3 per cent difference, with White County's vote for governor nearly 12 per cent less than its turn-out for President. ...

Turning to the office of prosecuting attorney one finds that the difference between vote for that office in presidential years and vote for President is greater than the difference between vote for governor and vote for President. Almost uniformly voters participate in slightly smaller numbers in elections for prosecuting attorney than for either President or governor. In Period I, with the single exception of Carroll County, the average vote for President was higher than that for prosecuting attorney in all counties; there was no such exception in Period II. However, during Period I in fifty-six counties and during Period II in thirteen counties the average presecutting attorney vote was within 2 per cent of the presidential vote. In only six counties in Period I was the difference between average turnout for President and that for prosecuting attorney more than 5 per cent, and in Period II there were twenty-four counties whose average vote for President was more than 5 per cent above its average vote for governor.

Although the closeness of turn-out regardless of prestige of office is less striking in Period II than in Period I, this evidence from one state's electoral experience suggests that "voters' fatigue" may be neither chronic nor universal; that, in fact, in many electoral districts voters who come out to vote for offices with high prestige also vote for offices with low prestige. Unfortunately, we do not have data to explain why some counties show exceptionally greater interest in prosecuting attorney than in the presidency. Analysis of these deviant cases might suggest other conditions under which large numbers of people may become interested in local elections.

Totality of Election Appeal and Voter Participation

Another factor which is said to be related to participation is the com-

pleteness of the election appeal to the voter. One writer has suggested the following general rule of political behavior: "As between types of elections, a larger vote is generally cast for a given office in the presidential election than in other general elections." . . .

In Indiana presidential years make a larger appeal to participation, not only because the presidency is at stake, but also because the governorship and other state and county offices are filled simultaneously. In two of three presidential years a United States senator is also elected. With more offices to be filled, several of which possess high prestige, the totality of the election appeal would appear to be greater in presidential years than in other election years. But the election of the President is not the only contest enlarging the appeal.

Part of the relationship between appeal and participation can be demonstrated by comparing votes for the same office in presidential and nonpresidential years, as Key did with the election of governor in Ohio. Elections for prosecuting attorney in Indiana supply data for a similar comparison. During Period I there were six counties (Benton, Decatur, Jennings, Morgan, Ripley, and Rush) in which the average vote for prosecuting attorney was greater in non-presidential than in presidential years. In Period II, six counties (Harrison, Kosciusko, Morgan, Pike, Pulaski, and Starke) also had a higher average turnout for prosecuting attorney in non-presidential years than in presidential years. Only Morgan County was deviant in both periods, which leads one to believe that these aberrations are temporary rather than enduring characteristics of these counties. . . .

The fall-off between presidential and non-presidential year turn-out for the same office is further illustrated by these facts: in Period I in only thirty counties was the average vote in off-years within 6 per cent of that for presidential years; in off-year elections in Period II only fourteen counties were within 6 per cent of their turn-out in presidential years.

While participation in selecting prosecuting attorneys declines markedly between years of high and low election appeal, the difference is not as great as one might expect, given knowledge about other political systems. The decline is certainly less for the Indiana office of prosecuting attorney than for the Ohio governorship, a position of greater prestige. Only two counties in Period I and five in Period II showed a 20 per cent difference between presidential year and off-year vote for prosecuting attorney, but the state-wide difference in Ohio was nearly that much. As students of comparative politics will observe, the drop in voting participation between elections of great and less appeal in Indiana is slight in contrast to other political systems. For example, in Great Britain between 1946 and 1951, local elections produced turn-outs of approximately 40 per cent, while in the same areas, the turn-out at general elections tended to be twice as high. Thus, while we acknowledge differences in participation which appear to vary with differences in election appeal, we are more struck by the fact that the Indiana data reveal so little difference between the two kinds of election situations.

Summary

Four propositions about voter participation draw support from election data for three offices in Indiana during two successive ten-year periods. These propositions may be stated as follows:

1. *voter participation does not necessarily increase with the competitiveness of the electoral-situation;*
2. *voter participation increases with the rurality of the election jurisdiction;*
3. *voter participation increases with the prestige of office;*
4. *voter participation increases with the totality of election appeal.*

When these familiar hypotheses were replicated with Indiana data, the findings differed noticeably from those of studies of other political systems. Propositions #1 and #2 are precisely the opposite of conclusions in other studies, while #3 and #4 deserve to be stated a little less emphatically than if they applied to systems other than Indiana. This should demonstrate that it is not always futile to re-examine apparently shop-worn propositions nor unworthy to question the so-called "obvious." Further analysis and research presumably would aim at reconciling the discrepancies between ours and other findings by looking for basic difference from one political system to another and by specifying more particularly the conditions or parameters under which these conflicting phenomena occurred. One would expect to discover that when the basic conditions are the same, differences in turn-out among political systems are more apparent than real.

16. THE VOTER AND THE NON-VOTER

Philip K. Hastings

. . .

With certain demographic factors held constant, three groups of Pittsfield respondents differing from one another in frequency of voting were compared as to replies to the following:

1. Do voters and non-voters differ in the nature and extent of their political identification with a number of local leader (or authority) symbols?
2. With what income class do they identify themselves?
3. Is there a difference between them in degree of crystallization of their political attitudes?
4. Do voters and non-voters differ in their evaluation of political issues?
5. To what extent is general social isolation and immobility characteristic of the non-voter?
6. Is the non-voter significantly less informed than the voter on political matters?

As a preliminary, each of the Pittsfield respondents who had been an eligible

From Philip K. Hastings, "The Voter and the Non-Voter," AMERICAN JOURNAL OF SOCIOLO-GY, LXII 3, (November, 1956), 303-7. Reprinted from the American Journal of Sociology by permission of the University of Chicago Press. Copyright 1956 by the University of Chicago.

voter since 1948 was assigned to one of three groups divided on the basis of replies to two questions requiring them to recall how they voted and one on their voting intention. Group I, the voters, was composed of those who claimed that they had voted for President in 1948 and 1952 and who, as of September, 1954, expressed intention to vote in the 1954 Massachusetts senatorial, congressional, and gubernatorial elections. Group II, the non-voters, was made up of persons who said that they had not voted in either 1948 or 1952 for President and who in September, 1954, had made no decision regarding any of the 1954 elections about which they were questioned. Group III, the occasional voter, consisted of individuals who indicated actual or intended voting participation in at least two of the three elections. On a proportional basis, the three groups were equated as to age, sex, religion, education, and income.

That non-voting is but one indication of political apathy and a general withdrawal from community life was an assumption in the study. We expected that the non-voter's social isolation would be evident both in his overt behavior and in certain psychological attributes. We aimed to demonstrate empirically, with certain demographic factors held constant, that on both counts the non-voter differs significantly from the voter.

A composite measure dealing with different types of behavior was designed to test the non-voter's hypothesized isolation. As shown in Table 3–1, the sample was asked a series of questions designed to throw light on its involve-

Table 3-1
DECREE OF SOCIAL WITHDRAWAL AND IMMOBILITY*

Question: Have you ever—
a) Lived anywhere else but Pittsfield?
b) Had a job other than your present one?
c) Read a travel book?
d) Felt at election time that your vote didn't really count?
e) Openly disagreed with your boss on something?
f) Visited Canada?
g) Written to your congressman?
h) Thought of changing your present line of work?
i) Wished you were in politics?
j) Visited New York City?
k) Been a member of some Pittsfield group like the Red Cross, the P.T.A., the Elks, etc.?
l) Visited Chicago?
m) Listened to (or on TV) a news commentator like Elmer Davis, for example?
n) Read a newspaper editorial all the way through?

	Group I Voters (N-112)	Group II Non-Voters (N-44)	Group III Occasional Voters (N-57)
Mean score..	9.0	6.1†	7.9

* With the exception of item (d), each affirmative answer was assigned a score of 1. The score range was from 0 to 14, with the higher score indicating greater social involvement.
† The difference between the mean scores of Groups I and II is significant at the 5 per cent level of confidence.

ment in community life. The questions touched on: 1) physical or geographical mobility; 2) political behavior, aside from voting; 3) formal group activity; 4) exposure to politics in a medium of mass communication; and 5) vocational behavior. It was felt not only that the various questions should be simple and direct but that special care should be taken to avoid obliging the respondent to place himself in an unfavorable light. Further, since we sought a single index of general level of social involvement, by definition, it was necessary to devise a set of items with a wide range. Finally, it was clear that the value of the measure depended in part upon its power of discrimination within the total sample, specifically, between the voters and the non-voters.

The replies (Table 3–1) indicate, at least within the limits of our measure, a significant difference in the social involvement of the non-voter in comparison with the voter. This relationship is strengthened by data on Group III (the occasional voters), showing an average social involvement score which falls between those of the first two groups. With age, income, education, sex, and religion held constant, as voting decreased, so did social involvement in general.

The frequently demonstrated relationship between infrequent voting, uncertain attitudes, and meager information has often been accounted for by limited education. But we argued that failure to vote involves considerably more: that the non-voter literally does not perceive political stimuli whether factual data or controversial issues.

As Table 3–2 shows, the apathetic individual's ability to give correct answers to questions of fact on well-publicized political events was limited. Of eleven questions, Pittsfield's non-voters, on the average, could answer

Table 3-2
LEVEL OF INFORMATION*

QUESTION: I wonder if you happen to remember—

    a) About how many people live in Pittsfield?
    b) Whether Eisenhower or Stevenson won in Pittsfield in the 1952 elections?
    c) Who Roy Cohn is?
    d) Who ran against Governor Herter in 1952?
    e) Who L.K. Miller is?†
    f) Whether a pay raise for post-office workers was approved by Congress recently?
    g) Who Ralph Zwicker is?
    h) Whether Congress recently changed the Taft-Harley Law?
    i) Who is running against Heselton this year?
    j) Whether Congress voted, during the past year, to lower our taxes?
    k) Who Leonard Hall is?

	Group I Voters (N=112)	Group II Non-Voters (N=44)	Group III Occasional Voters (N=57)
Mean score..	13.0	5.7‡	10.0

* Each item was scored as follows: 0 = incorrect; 1 = partly correct; and 2 = totally correct. The score range was from 0 to 22.

† Editor of Pittsfield's only newspaper, The *Berkshire Eagle* (by and large, Republican-oriented).

‡ The difference between the mean scores of Groups I and II is significant at the 5 per cent level of confidence.

only three correctly, compared with seven correct replies by the voters. One might have expected that, with education held constant in the three groups, there would be insignificant differences in level of information. Yet this this was not the case.

A third variable hypothesized as correlated with non-voting was the crystallization of attitudes. As frequency of voting decreased, one would expect replies of "No opinion" to increase. And this is the case, as Table 3–3 shows.

What empirical data would give a more positive picture of the non-voter? To gain a better idea of the non-voter's personality, we went into each of the

Table 3-3
CRYSTALLIZATION OF ATTITUDES

(Per Cent)

	Group I Voters (N= 112)	Group II Non-Voters (N= 44)	Group III Occasional Voters (N= 57)
A. In your opinion does organized labor have a great deal of influence in the politics of this country, or doesn't it have very much influence?			
Great deal	65	43	58
Not much	22	25	25
No opinion	13	32*	17
B. Would you like to have McCarthy on your party ticket as the candidate for senator from Massachusetts?			
Yes	13	20	14
No	79	36	60
Depends	5	7	9
No opinion	3	37*	17
C. Would you favor making our Army and Navy smaller if this meant that you wouldn't have to pay so many taxes?			
Yes	6	14	11
No	89	55	81
Depends	2	9	7
No opinion	3	22*	1

* Items in which a percentage difference significant at the 5 per cent level of confidence or better exists between Groups I and II.

following questions: Are there differences between the voter and the non-voter in their selection and assessment of political issues of maximum concern? With which local economic stratum does the non-voter most frequently identify himself psychologically? What subjective relation exists between the non-voter and recognized community leaders?

We anticipated that the non-voter would tend to be a self- rather than environment-centered individual whose interest would focus primarily upon the political issues of most immediate and practical concern to him. Further, we expected that the non-voter experiences a sense of insecurity and inadequacy manifested in a comparatively great subjective dependence upon the local leaders. Definitive verification would require more than the techniques employed in the Pittsfield Project, and the following data are offered as the initial and tentative results.

It seemed likely that one indication of the non-voters' greater immediate and material self-interest would be the frequency with which they stress political issues of 1954 directly bearing on their economic well-being. The respondents were therefore presented a list of eight issues (Table 3–4), to be ranked in order of importance. The politically active respondents proved to be more concerned with foreign affairs; the non-voters, with taxation and the cost of living.

A corroborating finding was that six out of ten of the non-voters, when asked whether they considered themselves as wealthy, earning a little more than average, earning a little less than average, or poor, claimed to belong to one or the other of the latter two (Table 3–5). Essentially the opposite was found among the voters.

Those who are highly active politically tend to concern themselves with broad political issues that only indirectly and in the long run affected their daily lives and, although no different from non-voters in economic composition, identify themselves more frequently with the classes with higher incomes. For the comparatively inactive group, the findings on these two

Table 3-4
EVALUATION OF POLITICAL ISSUES

Political Issue	Percentage Difference between Groups I and II* Group I Non-Voters (N= 112)	Group II Voters (N= 44)
More aggression by Communist China (e.g., an invasion of Formosa)	+25	....
Threat of another world war..	+19	....
Corruption in government ..	+ 7	....
Government spending	+ 4	....
Amount of money I can earn (wages)	....	+ 1
McCarthy	....	+ 1
Level of taxation	....	+ 7
cost of living	....	+29

* The question on which Table 3–4 is based was: "[HAND CARD] Here is a list of problems that both the Democrats and the Republicans will be talking about during the election campaign this fall. As of now, which of these problems worries you *most?* Which worries you *second* most? *Third*, etc.? The card contained the issues as enumerated above. All the voters and non-voters replied, and the percentage differences here shown are differences in the frequency with which the issue was ranked No. 1 and No. 2 by the individuals in each group.

Table 3-5
ECONOMIC STRATA IDENTIFICATION (Per Cent)

	Group I Non-Voters (N= 112)	Group II Non-Voters (N= 44)	Group III Occasional Voters (N= 57)
Wealthy, or income a little above average..	65	40	52
Income a little below average, or poor	35	60*	48

* The percentage difference between Groups I and II is significant at the 5 per cent level of confidence.

counts indicated an opposite tendency.

To test our expectation that voters

and non-voters would differ in the extent to which they demonstrated a measure of political dependence upon individuals with comparatively high status (authority symbols), the following question was asked:

[HAND CARD] Here is a list of people whose opinions on politics you may or may not agree with. Could you tell us which people you *tend to agree with most* and, also, which you *tend to disagree with most?*

a) Other members of your family
b) Your priest or minister
c) Your boss (or your husband's)
d) The editor of the *Eagle*
e) Your close friends
f) Local labor union leaders
g) People who live in your neighborhood
h) Your (or your husband's) fellow workers

Of the eight individuals or groups included in the question, four were selected as having essentially equal status with the respondent and four as occupying relatively high status both in the community at large and in relation to most of the respondents. We anticipated that there would be insignificant differences in the comparative proportions of voters and non-voters indicating political agreement with those who were their equals in status but that among the non-voters significantly higher percentages would agree with their "superiors." With one exception ("your priest or minister"), the results (Table 3–6) bear out these expectations.

What can be inferred from these results? One might argue that they further reinforce the observation that the non-voter is generally a nonparticipant: these data suggest that he is perhaps not even willing to think for himself as far as political matters are

Table 3-6
POLITICAL IDENTIFICATION PATTERN (Per Cent)

Agree with Most	Group I Voters (N= 112)	Group II Non-Voters (N= 44)	Group III Occasional Voters (N= 57)
High status:			
The editor of the *Eagle*	41	79*	56
Your boss (or your husband's)	65	83*	85
Local labor union leaders	31	47*	39
Your priest or minister	86	78	92
Equal status:			
People who live in your neighborhood.	74	69	83
Members of your family	85	81	76
Your (or your husband's) fellow workers	74	74	88
Your close friends ...	80	77	81

* The percentage differences between Group I and II are significant at the 5 per cent level of confidence.

concerned. An alternative interpretation, however, is that the non-voter actually views those with high status in his community, whether they be the editor of the local paper, a labor leader, or his job superior, as politically knowledgeable people with whom to identify himself and to follow. One might speculate, although the Pittsfield data provide no empirical basis for this, that, to the extent that the non-voter depends politically upon the local authority or leader symbols, he betrays a personal sense of inadequacy and insecurity. Conceivably, this is a pervasive personality trait that in part defines the politically apathetic individual.

17. THE CHANGING SHAPE OF THE AMERICAN POLITICAL UNIVERSE

Walter Dean Burnham

. . .

The present shape and size of the American voting universe are, of course, largely the product of the 1928–1936 political realignment. Survey-research findings most closely approximate political reality as they relate to this next broad phase of American political evolution. But the characteristics of the present voting universe suggest rather forcefully that the New Deal realignment has been both incomplete and transitional. At present, about 44 per cent of the national electorate are core voters, another 16 or so are peripheral, and about 40 per cent are still outside the political system altogether. By nineteenth-century standards, indices of voter peripherality stand at very high levels. Party organizations remain at best only indifferently successful at mobilizing a stable, predictable mass base of support. . . .

The nineteenth-century American political system, for its day, was incomparably the most thoroughly democratized of any in the world. The development of vigorous party competition extended from individual localities to the nation itself. It involved the invention of the first organizational machinery—the caucus, the convention and the widely disseminated party press—which was designed to deal with large

From Walter Dean Burnham, "The Changing Shape of the American Political Universe," in *American Political Science Review*, LIX, 1, (March 1965), 7-28, excerpts. By permission of The American Political Science Association.

numbers of citizens rather than with semi-aristocratic parliamentary cliques. Sooner than the British, and at a time when Prussia protected its elites through its three-class electoral system, when each new change of regime in France brought with it a change in the size of the electorate and the nature of *le pays légal*, and when the basis of representation in Sweden was still the estate, Americans had elaborated not only the machinery and media of mass politics but a franchise which remarkably closely approached universal suffrage. Like the larger political culture of which it was an integral part, this system rested upon both broad consensual acceptance of middle-class social norms as ground rules and majoritarian settlement (in "critical" elections from time to time), once and for all, of deeply divisive substantive issues on which neither consensus nor further postponement of a showdown was possible. Within the limits so imposed it was apparently capable of coherent and decisive action. It especially permitted the explicit formulation of sectional issues and—though admittedly at the price of civil war—arrived at a clear-cut decision as to which of two incompatible sectional modes of social and economic organization was henceforth to prevail.

But after several decades of intensive industrialization a new dilemma of power, in many respects as grave as that which had eventuated in civil war, moved toward the stage of overt crisis. Prior to the closing years of the century the middle-class character of the political culture and the party system, coupled with the afterglow of the civil-war trauma, had permitted the penetration and control of the cadres of both major parties by the heavily concentrated power of our industrializing elites. But this control was inherently unstable, for if and when the social dislocations produced by the industrial revolution should in turn produce a grass-roots counterrevolution, the party whose clienteles were more vulnerable to the appeals of the counterrevolutionaries might be captured by them.

The take-off phase of industrialization has been a brutal and exploitative process everywhere, whether managed by capitalists or commissars. A vital functional political need during this phase is to provide adequate insulation of the industrializing elites from mass pressures, and to prevent their displacement by a coalition of those who are damaged by the processes of capital accumulation. This problem was effectively resolved in the Soviet Union under Lenin and Stalin by vesting a totalitarian monopoly of political power in the hands of Communist industrializing elites. In recent years developing nations have tended to rely upon less coercive devices such as nontotalitarian single-party systems or personalist dictatorship to meet that need, among others. The nineteenth-century European elites were provided a good deal of insulation by the persistence of feudal patterns of social deference and especially by the restriction of the right to vote to the middle and upper classes.

But in the United States the institutions of mass democratic politics and universal suffrage uniquely came into being *before* the onset of full-scale industrialization. The struggle for democracy in Europe was explicitly linked from the outset with the struggle for universal suffrage. The eventual success of this movement permitted the development in relatively sequential fashion of the forms of party organization which Duverger has described in detail. In the United States—ostensibly at least—the struggle for democracy had already been won, and remarkably painlessly, by the mid-nineteenth century. In consequence, the American industrializing elites were, and felt themselves to be, uniquely vulnerable to an anti-industrialist assault which could be carried out peacefully and in the absence of effective legal or customary sanctions by a citizenry possessing at least two generations' experience with political democracy.

This crisis of vulnerability reached its peak in the 1890's. Two major elements in the population bore the brunt of the exceptionally severe deprivations felt during this depression decade: the smaller cash-crop farmers of the Southern and Western "colonial" regions and the ethnically fragmented urban working class. . . .

The industrializers and their intellectual and legal spokesmen were acutely conscious that these two profoundly alienated groups might coalesce. Their alarm was apparently given quite tangible form when the agrarian insurgents captured control of the Democratic Party in 1896.

But the results of that great referendum revealed that the conservatives' fears and the anti-industrialists' hopes of putting together a winning coalition on a Jacksonian base were alike groundless. Not only did urban labor *not* flock to William Jennings Bryan, it repudiated the Democratic Party on an unprecedented scale throughout the industrialized Northeast. The intensity and permanence of this urban realignment was paralleled by the Democrats' failure to make significant inroads into Republican strength in the more diversified and depression-resistant farm areas east of the Missouri River, and by their nearly total collapse in rural New England. The Democratic-Populist effort to create a coalition of the dispossessed created instead the most enduringly sectional political alignment in American history—an alignment which eventually separated the Southern and Western agrarians and transformed the most industrially advanced region of the country into a bulwark of industrialist Republicanism.

This realignment brought victory beyond expectation to those who had sought to find some way of insulating American elites from mass pressures without formally disrupting the pre-existing democratic-pluralist political structure, without violence and without conspiracy. Of the factors involved in this victory three stand out as of particular importance. 1) The depression of 1893 began and deepened during a Democratic administration. Of course there is no way of ascertaining directly what part of the decisive minority which shifted its allegiance to the Republican Party reacted viscerally to the then incumbent party and failed to perceive that Cleveland and Bryan were diametrically opposed on the central policy issues of the day. But contemporary survey findings would tend to suggest that such a component in a realigning electorate might not be small. . . .

2) The Democratic platform and campaign were heavily weighted toward the interests and needs of an essentially rural and semi-colonial clientele. Considerably narrowed in its programmatic base from the farmer-labor Populist platform of 1892, the Democratic Party focused most of its campaign upon monetary inflation as a means of redressing the economic balance. . . .

Bryan's appeal at base was essentially Jacksonian—a call for a return to the simpler and more virtuous economic and political arrangements which he identified with that by-gone era. Such nostalgia could evoke a positive response among the native-stock rural elements whose political style and economic expectations had been shaped in the far-away past. But it could hardly seem a realistic political choice for the ethnically pluralist urban populations, large numbers of whom found such nostalgia meaningless since it related to nothing in their past or current experience. Programmatically, at least, these urbanites were presented with a two-way choice only one part of which seemed at all functionally related to the realities of an emergent industrial society. With the Democrats actually cast in the role of reactionaries despite the apparent radicalism of their platform and leader, and with no socialist alternative even thinkable in the context of the American political culture of the 1890s, the Republican Party alone retained some relevance to the urban setting. In this context, its massive triumph there was a foregone conclusion.

3) An extremely important aspect of any political realignment is the unusually intense mobilization of negative-reference-group sentiments during the course of the campaign. 1896 was typical in this respect. Profound antagonisms in culture and political style between the cosmopolitan, immigrant, wet, largely non-Protestant components of American urban populations and the parochial, dry, Anglo-Saxon Prot-

estant inhabitants of rural areas can be traced back at least to the 1840s. Bryan was virtually the archetype of the latter culture, and it would have been surprising had he not been the target of intense ethnocultural hostility from those who identified with the former. . . .

As Schattschneider has perceptively observed, the "system of 1896" was admirably suited to its primary function. One of its major working parts was a judiciary which proceeded first to manufacture the needed constitutional restraints on democratic political action—a development presaged by such decisions as the Minnesota railroad rate case of 1890 and the income tax cases of 1894–1895—and then to apply these restraints against certain sensitive categories of national and state economic legislation. Another of the new system's basic components was the control which the sectional alignment itself gave to the Republican Party, and through it the corporate business community, over the scope and direction of national public policy. Democracy was not only placed in judicial leading-strings, it was effectively placed out of commission—at least so far as two-party competition was concerned—in more than half of the states. Yet it was one of the greatest, if unacknowledged, contributions of the "system of 1896" that democratic forms, procedures and traditions continued to survive. Confronted with a narrowed scope of effective democratic options, an increasingly large proportion of the eligible adult population either left, failed to enter or—as was the case with Southern Negroes after the completion of the 1890–1904 disfranchisement movement in the Old Confederacy—was systematically excluded from the American voting universe. The results of this on

the exercise of the franchise have already been examined here in some detail. It was during this 1896–1932 era that the basic characteristics associated with today's mass electorate were formed.

These characteristics, as we have seen, have already far outlived the 1896 alignment itself. There seems to be no convincing evidence that they are being progressively liquidated at the present time. If the re-emergence of a competitive party politics and its at least partial orientation toward the broader needs of an urban, industrialized society were welcome fruits of the New Deal revolution, that revolution has apparently exhausted most of its potential for stimulating turn-out or party-oriented voting in America. The present state of affairs, to be sure, is not without its defenders. The civics-minded have tended to argue that the visible drift away from party-oriented voting among a growing minority of voters is a sign of increasing maturity in the electorate. Others have argued that mediocre rates of turnout in the United States, paralleled by the normally low salience of issues in our political campaigns, are indicative of a "politics of happiness." It is further contended that any sudden injection of large numbers of poorly socialized adults into the active voting universe could constitute a danger to the Republic.

But there is another side to this coin. The ultimate democratic purpose of issue-formulation in a campaign is to give the people at large the power to choose their and their agents' options. Moreover, so far as is known, the blunt alternative to party government is the concentration of political power, locally or nationally, in the hands of those who already possess concentrated economic power. If no adequate substitute for party as a means for mobilizing nonelite influence on the governing process has yet been discovered, the obvious growth of "image" and "personality" voting in recent decades should be a matter of some concern to those who would like to see a more complete restoration of the democratic process in the United States.

Moreover, recent studies—such as Murray Levin's examinations of the attitudes of the Boston and Massachusetts electorate—reveal that such phenomena as widespread ticket splitting may be associated quite readily with pervasive and remarkably intense feelings of political alienation. Convinced that both party organizations are hopelessly corrupt and out of reach of popular control, a minority which is large enough to hold the balance of power between Republicans and Democrats tends rather consistently to vote for the lesser, or lesser-known, of two evils. It takes a mordant variety of humor to find a kind of emergent voter maturity in this alienation. For Levin's data are difficult to square with the facile optimism underlying the civics approach to independent voting. So, for that matter, are the conclusions of survey research about the behavior of many so-called "independent" voters.

Findings such as these seem little more comforting to the proponents of the "politics of happiness" thesis. Granted the proposition that most people who have been immersed from birth in a given political system are apt to be unaware of alternatives whose explicit formulation that system inhibits, it is of course difficult to ascertain whether their issueless and apathetic political style is an outward sign of "real" happiness. We can surmise, however, that the kind of political alienation which Levin describes is incompatible with political happiness, whether real or fancied. A great many American voters, it would seem, are quite intelligent enough to perceive the deep contradiction which exists between the ideals of rhetorical democracy as preached in school and on the stump, and the actual day-to-day reality as that reality intrudes on his own *milieu*. Alienation arises from perception of that contradiction, and from the consequent feelings of individual political futility arising when the voter confronts an organization of politics which seems unable to produce minimally gratifying results. The concentration of socially deprived characteristics among the more than forty million adult Americans who today are altogether outside the voting universe suggests active alienation—or its passive equivalent, political apathy—on a scale quite unknown anywhere else in the Western world. Unless it is assumed as a kind of universal law that problems of existence which can be organized in political terms must fade out below a certain socio-economic level, this state of affairs is not inevitable. And if it is not inevitable, one may infer that the political system itself is responsible for its continued existence.

Yet such an assumption of fade-out is clearly untenable in view of what is known about patterns of voting participation in other democratic systems. Nor need it be assumed that substantial and rapid increases in American voting participation would necessarily, or even probably, involve the emergence of totalitarian mass movements. The possibility of such movements is a constant danger, to be sure, in any polity containing so high a proportion of apolitical elements in its potential electorate. But it would be unwise to respond to this possibility by merely expressing the comfortable hope that the apoliticals will remain apolitical, and by doing nothing to engage them in the system in a timely and orderly way. It is much more to the point to seek a way, if one can be found, to integrate the apolitical half of the American electorate into the political system before crisis arises. Such integration need not be out of the question. The United States, after all, enjoyed intense mass political involvement without totalitarian movements during the last part of the nineteenth century, as do other Western democracies today.

No integration of the apoliticals can be carried out without a price to be paid. Underlying the failure of political organizations more advanced than the nineteenth-century middle-class cadre party to develop in this country has been the deeper failure of any except middle-class social and political values to achieve full legitimacy in the American political culture. It may not now be possible for our polity to make so great a leap as to admit non-middle class values to political legitimacy and thus provide the preconditions for a more coherent and responsible mode of party organization. But such a leap may have to be made if full mobilization of the apolitical elements is to be achieved without the simultaneous emergence of manipulative radicalism of the left or the right. The heart of our contemporary political dilemma appears to lie in the conflict between this emergent need and the ideological individualism which continues so deeply to pervade our political culture. Yet the present situation perpetuates a standing danger that the half of the American electorate which is now more or less entirely outside the universe of active politics may someday be mobilized in substantial degree by totalitarian or quasi-totalitarian appeals. As the late President Kennedy seemed to intimate in his executive order establishing the Commission on Registration and Voting Participation, it also raises some questions about the legitimacy of the regime itself.

18. WHO VOTES AND WHO DOESN'T?

Seymour M. Lipset

Conclusions

A concern with the social roots of political participation should not lead us to ignore the consequences of different levels of participation for the stability of the democratic system. . . .

Both totalitarian states and Com-

From Seymour M. Lipset, *Political Man* (Garden City N.Y.; Doubleday & Co., Inc., 1960), pp 216-19.

munist trade-union leaders within democratic society are concerned with securing a high rate of participation among their citizens or members, because this means that the participants are reachable. One of the most important differences between a traditional conservative oligarchy or dictatorship and a totalitarian regime is that the former is relatively unconcerned about participation, while the latter demands it. David Riesman has perceptively noted that within a totalitarian society, political apathy may be a major barrier against the complete triumph of the system.

Democratic societies can exist with different levels of participation, although it is clear that varying consequences flow from them. Those who believe that democracy is best served by a high level of participation point to the fact that a democratic state, unlike a traditionalist oligarchy, must depend on the consent of its citizenry. And a state in which a large part of the population is apathetic, uninterested, and unaware is one in which consent cannot be taken for granted and in which consensus may actually be weak. Secondly, as the political scientist V. O. Key, Jr., has pointed out, when the vote is low, this almost always means that the socially and economically disadvantaged groups are underrepresented in government. The combination of a low vote and a relative lack of organization among the lower-status groups means that they will suffer from neglect by the politicians who will be receptive to the wishes of the more privileged, participating, and organized strata. Lack of participation and representation also reflects lack of effective citizenship and consequent lack of loyalty to the system as a whole.

But while the case for higher levels of participation may seem almost self-evident to believers in democracy, as we have come to know more about the characteristics of non-voters and the conditions under which nations secure high turn-outs, some people have questioned whether high participation actually is a good thing. One school of thought welcomes a low voting rate as evidence of the electorate's basic satisfaction with the way things are going. In 1936, the political scientist

Francis Wilson put it this way: "In a society in which only fifty per cent of the electorate participates it is clear that politics does satisfy in a way the desire of the mass of the individuals in the state. As the percentage of participation rises above, let us say, ninety per cent, it is apparent that the tensions of political struggle are stretching to the breaking point the will toward the constitutional." The same point was made a short time later by the foremost analyst of the determinants of political participation, the Swede Herbert Tingsten, in concluding his brilliant survey of voting statistics around the world. He pointed to the extremely high vote in various nations like Germany and Austria at the point when their democracies began to break down, and he suggested that a high turn-out was a symptom of the decline of consensus. David Riesman has argued also that apathy may reflect the fact that people have more interesting things to do with their time than indulge in politics, and suggests that governmental bodies and large-scale organizations function well in spite of great apathy.

Pessimistic conclusions about the effects of an increase in participation may also be reached from the research on the characteristics of non-voters. As early as 1928, the American political scientist W. B. Munro argued that increased participation might threaten the workings of democracy since non-voting was largely located among the most ignorant part of the electorate. And subsequent studies based on survey and questionnaire data . . . indicate that non-voters differ from voters in having authoritarian attitudes, cynical ideas about democracy and political parties, intolerant sentiments on deviant opinions and ethnic minorities, and in preferring strong leaders in government.

Many of the differences between voters and non-voters are, of course, a by-product of the fact that non-voting is concentrated among the least educated and poorest social groups. However, these variations in attitudes hold up even when the major social variables which have been found to affect voting turn-out—sex, age, religion, education, and income—are controlled. Thus in a study which controlled all of these factors, the psychologist Philip Hastings reported that, compared to the regular voter, the habitual non-voter withdraws from social activity, is more concerned with "immediate" issues than long-range ones, is "not even willing to think for himself as far as political matters are concerned" (manifested by his willingness to agree with his "superiors" on political matters) and in general exhibits "a personal sense of inadequacy and insecurity."

The evidence confirms Tingsten's thesis that a sudden increase in the size of the voting electorate probably reflects tension and serious governmental malfunctioning and also introduces as voters individuals whose social attitudes are unhealthy from the point of view of the requirements of the democratic system. On the other hand, a high vote is not necessarily bad. Many stable democratic nations—Australia, New Zealand, Great Britain, and the Scandinavian countries—have much higher rates of participation than does the United States. To the extent that the lower strata have been brought into electoral process *gradually* (through increased organization, an upgrading of the educational system, and a growth in their understanding of the relevance of government action to their interests), increased participation is undoubtedly a good thing for democracy. It is only when a major crisis or an effective authoritarian movement suddenly pulls the normally disaffected habitual non-voters into the political area that the system is threatened. Thus neither high nor low rates of participation and voting are in themselves good or bad for democracy; the extent and nature of that participation reflect other factors which determine far more decisively the system's chances to develop or survive. But the extent of apathy and the varying levels of participation of different segments of the population do clarify the underlying consensus and conflict within the political process. . . .

Electoral Parties

19. THE CONCEPT OF PARTY MEMBERSHIP

Maurice Duverger

. . .

The concept of member is linked with a particular notion of political party that was born at the beginning of the twentieth century along with Socialist parties and that has subsequently been imitated by others. It does not correspond to the old conception of party which flourished in the nineteenth century in parliamentary systems with a franchise based on a property qualification. The concept of membership is a result of the evolution which led from the cadre party to the mass party.

From Maurice Duverger, *Political Parties* (New York: John Wiley & Sons, Inc., 1954), pp. 63-70. By permission of the publisher

Cadre Parties and Mass Parties

The distinction between cadre and mass parties is not based upon their dimensions, upon the number of their members: the difference involved is not one of size but of structure. Consider, for example, the French Socialist party: in its eyes the recruiting of members is a fundamental activity, both from the political and the financial standpoints. In the first place, the party aims at the political education of the working class, at picking out from it an elite capable of taking over the government and the administration of the country: the members are therefore the very substance of the party, the stuff of its activity. Without members, the party would be like a teacher without pupils. Secondly, from the financial point of view, the party is essentially based upon the subscriptions paid by its members: the first duty of the branch is to ensure that they are regularly collected. In this way, the party gathers the funds required for its work of political education and for its day-to-day activity; in the same way it is enabled to finance electioneering: the financial and the political are here at one. This last point is fundamental: every electoral campaign represents considerable expense. The mass-party technique in effect replaces the capitalist financing of electioneering by democratic financing. Instead of appealing to a few big private donors, industrialists, bankers, or important merchants for funds to meet campaign expenses—which makes the candidate (and the person elected) dependent on them—the mass party spreads the burden over the largest possible number of members, each of whom contributes a modest sum. . . .

It is characteristic of the mass party that it appeals to the public: to the paying public who make it possible for the electoral campaign to be free from capitalist pressures; to the listening, active public which receives a political education and learns how to intervene in the life of the State.

The cadre party corresponds to a different conception: the grouping of notabilities for the preparation of elections, conducting campaigns, and maintaining contact with the candidates. Influential persons, in the first place, whose name, prestige, or connections can provide a backing for the candidate and secure him votes; experts, in the second place, who know how to handle the electors and how to organize a campaign; last of all financiers, who can

bring the sinews of war. Quality is the most important factor: extent of prestige, skill in technique, size of fortune. What the mass party secures by numbers, the cadre party achieves by selection. Adherence to it has therefore quite a different meaning: it is a completely personal act, based upon the aptitudes or the peculiar circumstances of a man; it is determined strictly by individual qualities. It is an act that is restricted to a few; it is dependent upon rigid and exclusive selection. If we define a member as one who signs an undertaking to the party and thereafter regularly pays his subscription, then cadre parties have no members. Some do make a show of recruiting after the contagious pattern of mass parties, but this is not to be taken seriously. The problem of the number of members belonging to the French Radical Socialist party is susceptible of no precise answer, simply because the problem itself is meaningless. The members of the Radical party cannot be counted, because the Radical party recruits no members, strictly speaking: it is a cadre party. American parties and the majority of European moderate and Conservative parties belong to the same category.

This distinction, though clear in theory, is not always easy to make in practice. As we have just noted, cadre parties sometimes admit ordinary members in imitation of mass parties. In fact, the practice is fairly widespread: there are few purely cadre parties. The others are not in practice far removed from them, but their outward form is likely to mislead the observer who must look beyond the official clauses laid down in the constitution or the declarations of the leaders. The absence of any syst m of registration of members or of any regular collection of subscriptions is a fairly reliable criterion; no true membership is conceivable in their absence, as we shall see. The vagueness of the figures put out can also be considered presumptive evidence: in 1950, the Turkish Democratic party claimed before the elections that it had "three or four million members." Obviously, it was referring to supporters; in actual fact, it was essentially a cadre party. In the same way, the distinction seems contradicted by the existence of indirect parties: mass parties which have no personal members. Consider the example of the Labour party: it was founded in 1900 to make it financially possible for working-class candidates to contest elections; from the financial point of view, the system is a mass-party system, election costs being met by Trade Unions, collectively. But this collective membership remains quite different from individual membership: it involves no true political enrollment and no personal pledge to the party. This profoundly alters the nature of the party and of membership, as we shall attempt to show in detail later. On the other hand, let us take the example of American parties in States which operate the system of "closed primaries" with registration of electors; they resemble mass parties from the political point of view. Participation in the primary, with the registration and pledges it involves, may be considered as an act of membership. Moreover, activity connected with the nomination of candidates presented at elections by a party constitutes one of the activities typical of party membership. But, in this particular instance, this is the sole activity: there is no activity which at all resembles the branch meetings of the mass parties. More particularly there is no regular system of subscription to provide for the financing of the party and of election campaigns: from the financial point of view these are clearly examples of the

cadre party. All things considered, the indirect party and the American party with closed primaries should be classified as semi-mass parties, though these examples must not be held to constitute a third category distinct from the two others because of their heterogeneous nature.

The distinction between cadre and mass parties corresponds to a difference in social and political substructure. In the beginning, it coincided on the whole with the replacement of a limited franchise by universal suffrage. In electoral systems based on a property qualification, which were the rule in the nineteenth century, parties obviously took on the form of cadre parties: there could be no question of enrolling the masses at a time when they had no political influence. Moreover, capitalist financing of elections appeared natural. Indeed, it has survived the property franchise. In point of fact, the coming of universal suffrage did not immediately lead to the arrival of true mass parties. The cadre parties simply attempted to make their organization more flexible by pretending to open their ranks to the masses. The Birmingham caucus system in the British Liberal party, the Primrose League in the Conservative party, the institution of primaries in America, correspond to this first stage. The problem was how to give the masses some scope for political activity and how to confer on the notabilities composing the caucus the air of having been popularly invested. In the first two cases some approach was made towards the mass party: there existed a system of formal membership as well as a periodic subscription. But the real life of the party was lived independently of the members: the Primrose League, an organization distinct from the party proper, aimed at social mixing; the primaries are limited to the nomination of candidates; the Birmingham caucus alone with its local branch foreshadowed a true mass party, but it proved to be no more than a passing experiment. The political and financial bases of the mass party were lacking. There was no question of rescuing candidates and elections from the clutches of capitalist finance, nor of educating the masses and making direct use in political life of their activity. The question was rather how to use the political and financial strength of the masses as an ancillary force. The first step had been taken, but only the first step.

The introduction of universal suffrage led almost every where(the United States excepted) to the development of Socialist parties which made the decisive transition, not always, however, at once. In France, for example, the first Socialist groups were not very different from the middle-class parties; registration of members, collection of subscriptions, autonomous financing of elections, developed only slowly. Development was even slower in Italy and in politically less-developed countries. Yet, at the outbreak of the 1914–1918 War, the European Socialist parties constituted great human communities profoundly different from the earlier cadre parties. A notable example is the German Social Democratic party which, with more than a million members and an annual budget of nearly two million marks, constituted a veritable state more powerful than some national states. It was the Marxist conception of the class party that led to such massive structures: if the party is the political expression of a class it must naturally seek to rally the whole of the class, to form it politically, to pick out the elites capable of leadership and administration. This effort of organization also made it possible to free the working class from the tutelage of middle-class parties: in order to put up independent working-class candidates at elections it was necessary to become independent of capitalist financing (except perhaps as a makeweight, the roles being reversed) and this was possible only with collective finances. To establish, in opposition to the middle-class political press, a working-class political press, it was necessary to collect funds and organize the distribution of the newspaper. Only a mass party could make these things possible.

This explains why the distinction between cadre and mass parties also corresponds approximately with the distinction between Right and Left, Middle-class and Workers' parties. The middle-class Right had no need, financial or political, to seek the organized support of the masses: it already had its elites, its personages, and its financial backers. It considered its own political education to be adequate. For these reasons, until the coming of Fascism, attempts to create mass Conservative parties have generally failed. The instinctive repugnance felt by the middle class for regimentation and collective action also played some part in the failures, just as the opposite tendency amongst the working class favored mass organization in Socialist parties. It would not be out of place to reiterate at this point some earlier observations. Nothing less than the development of Communism or of revolutionary tactics was required before the middle classes, realizing that cadre parties were inadequate, were to make serious attempts to create mass parties: in 1932, the National Socialist party had reached a membership of 800,000. This however really signified its breach with democracy. Under the electoral and parliamentary system cadre parties have generally been found sufficient by the

Right; in the struggle against the electoral and parliamentary system mass parties of the Fascist type have rarely shown the balance and stability of proletarian parties. They tend, moreover, as we shall see, to lose their pure mass-party characteristics.

Finally this distinction between cadre parties and mass parties coincides with differences arising out of the various kinds of party organization. Cadre parties correspond to the caucus parties, decentralized and weakly knit; mass parties to parties based on branches, more centralized and more firmly knit. Differences in recruiting technique follow from the differences in the kind of community to be fashioned. As for parties based upon cells or upon militia, they too are mass parties, but less definitely so. It is true that Communist and Fascist parties enrol the masses in as great numbers as do Socialist parties, even before their seizure of power and their transformation into the sole party: the German National Socialist party numbered 800,000 members in 1932, the French Communist party one million members in 1945, the Italian Communist party two million members in 1950. A development can however be traced. Periodically, Communist parties indulge in internal "purges," with the aim of banishing the lukewarm, the passive, the suspect; in this way quality again becomes more important than quantity. They tend moreover to exercise strict supervision of recruitment: some Socialist parties similarly provide for this kind of supervision, but the system is little applied by them whereas the Communists seem to be stricter. In Fascist parties the emphasis on quality is even more marked, more perhaps in their doctrine, which is clearly aristocratic, than in their practice: the enormous growth in numbers of the National Socialist party in the last years before the seizure of power can scarcely have permitted any serious "screening" of members.

In any case the general tendency is undeniable. It raises the problem of whether we are still dealing with true mass parties or whether there is a gradual evolution towards a new conception, a third category: devotee parties, more open than cadre parties, but more closed than mass parties. In the Leninist conception the party should not include the whole of the working class: it is only the advance guard, the fighting wing, the "most enlightened" section of the working class. This represents a change from the conception of the party as class; it is the party conceived as the elite. Fascist doctrines are even more definite on this point; anti-egalitarian and Nietzschean, fundamentally aristocratic, they view the party as an "Order," made up of the best, the most faithful, the most brave, the most suitable. The age of the masses is gone: we are in the age of elites. In consequence the meaning given to the term "member" tends to vary. Even within the party there are to be found concentric circles corresponding to different degrees of loyalty and activity. In the National Socialist party there was first of all the Party, then the S.A., then the S.S. In the Communist party the official doctrine is egalitarian and therefore opposed to such a hierarchy; however, it is possible to discern an "inner circle" that is reliable and permanent and around which is grouped the mass of ordinary members, often quite unreliable (the difference was very marked in the pre-war French Communist party). . . .

20. CLASSES AND PARTIES IN AMERICAN POLITICS

Seymour M. Lipset

It often comes as a shock, especially to Europeans, to be reminded that the first political parties in history with "labor" or "workingman" in their names developed in America in the 1820's and 1830's. The emphasis on "classlessness" in American political ideology has led many European and American political commentators to conclude that party divisions in America are less related to class cleavages than they are in other Western countries. Polling studies, however, belie this conclusion, showing that in every American election since 1936 (studies of the question were not made before then), the proportion voting Democratic increases sharply as one moves down the occupational or income ladder. In 1948 almost 80 per cent of the workers voted Democratic, a percentage which is higher than has ever been reported for left-wing parties in such countries as Britain, France, Italy, and Germany. Each year the lower-paid and less skilled workers are the most Democratic; even in 1952, two thirds of the unskilled workers were for Stevenson, though the proportion of all manual workers backing the Democrats dropped to 55 per cent in that year—a drop-off which was in large measure a result of Eisenhower's personal "above the parties"

From Seymour M. Lipset, *Political Man* (Garden City. N.Y.: Doubleday & Co., Inc., 1960.), pp. 301–322, excerpts.

appeal rather than a basic swing away from the Democratic party by the lower strata. . . .

In general, the bulk of the workers, even many who voted for Eisenhower in 1952 and 1956, still regard themselves as Democrats, and the results of the 1954 and 1958 congressional elections show that there has been no shift of the traditional Democratic voting base to the Republicans. Two thirds of the workers polled by Gallup in 1958 voted for a Democrat for Congress.

The same relationship between class, considered now as a very general differentiating factor, and party support exists within the middle and upper classes. The Democrats have been in a minority among the nonmanual strata, and, except among the intellectual professions, the Democratic proportion of the nonmanually occupied electorate declines inexorably with income and occupational status to the point where, according to one study, only 6 per cent of the heads of corporations with more than 10,000 employees are Democrats. Perhaps the best single example of the pervasiveness of status differences as a factor in American politics is the political allegiances of the chief executives of major American corporations. This study, done in 1955 by the Massachusetts Institute of Technology's Center for International Studies, and based on interviews with a systematic sample of one thousand such men, found that even within this upper economic group, the larger the company of which a man was an officer, the greater the likelihood that he was a Republican (see Table 3–7).

Table 3-7
RELATIONSHIP BETWEEN SIZE OF FIRM AND POLITICAL PARTY ALLEGIANCES OF CORPORATION EXECUTIVES—1955*

Size of Firm	Re-publican	Demo-cratic	Inde-pendent
More than 10,000 workers	84%	6%	10%
1,000–9,999	80	8	12
100–999	69	12	19

* Data supplied to author through the courtesy of the Center for International Studies of the Massachusetts Institute of Technology.

Consistent with these findings are the popular images of typical supporters of each party. The Gallup Poll, shortly before the 1958 congressional elections, asked a nation-wide sample what their picture of the typical Democrat was, and received these answers most frequently: "middle class . . . common people . . . a friend . . . an ordinary person . . . works for his wages . . . average person . . . someone who thinks of everybody." The typical Republican, in contrast, is "better class . . . well-to-do . . . big business-man . . . money voter . . . well-off financially . . . wealthy . . . higher class." . . .

Although most generalizations about the relationship of American parties to class differences are based on the variations in the backgrounds of their respective electorates, there is some as yet skimpy evidence that the same differences exist on the leadership level, particularly in the local community. A study of the backgrounds of candidates of nomination

for county office in local primaries in three counties in Indiana indicates a close correspondence between the characteristics of leaders and voters. While 76 per cent of those seeking Republican nominations were in professional or business-managerial occupations, 42 per cent of the Democratic aspirants were manual workers (see Table 3–8). In Milwaukee, Wisconsin, 54 per cent of the officers of the local Democratic party were manual workers or in sales and clerical positions. By contrast these groups represented only 10 per cent among the Republicans, whose leaders were largely professionals or ran business firms.

The relationship of socio-economic position to political behavior in America as elsewhere is reinforced by religious and ethnic factors. Surveys indicate that, among the Christian denominations, the higher the average income of the membership of a given church group, the more likely its members are to vote Republican. If Christian religious groups in the United States are ranked according to the average socio-economic status of their membership, they are, reading

Table 3-8
OCCUPATIONAL BACKGROUNDS OF CANDIDATES FOR NOMINATIONS FOR COUNTY OFFICE IN THREE INDIANA COUNTIES—1954*

Occupation	Republican Number	Republican Per cent	Democratic Number	Democratic Per cent
Professional	23	25.8	17	17.7
Managerial	45	50.6	25	26.0
Clerical-sales	8	9.0	10	10.4
Manual workers	11	12.4	40	41.7
Others	2	2.2	4	4.2
Totals	89	100.0	96	100.0

* Frank Munger, *Two-Party Politics in the State of Indiana* (unpublished M.S. thesis, Department of Government, Harvard University, 1955), p. 275; cited in V. O. Key, Jr., *Politics, Parties, and Pressure Groups* (New York: Crowell, 1958), p. 240.

from high to low, Congregational, Presbyterian, Episcopal, Methodist, Lutheran, Baptist, and Catholic—and this rank order is identical to the one produced when the denominations are ranked by propensity to vote Republican. This suggests that socio-economic status, rather than religious ideas, is the prime determinant of political values among different denominations. The fact that the Jews, who are one of the wealthiest religious groups in America, are shown by survey data to be most Democratic is probably due, as I have suggested earlier, to their sensitivity to ethnic discrimination and their lack of effective social intercourse with the upper-status groups in America. But religious beliefs or loyalties, and the political values associated with them, nevertheless seem to have some independent effect on voting behavior. Working-class Protestants belonging to the Congregational or Presbyterian churches are more likely to be Republicans than workers who are Baptist or Catholic. Conversely, wealthy Baptists or Catholics are more apt to be Democrats than equally rich Congregationalists or Episcopalians are.

Roughly speaking, the same differences appear between ethnic groups. Anglo-Saxons are more likely to be Republican than other Americans in the same class position who have a more recent immigrant background. Thus if an individual is middle class, Anglo-Saxon, and Protestant, he is very likely to be a Republican, whereas if he is working class, Catholic, and of recent immigrant stock, he will probably be a Democrat.

Even before the development of the two-party system in its present form, the political issues dividing the society tended to have a class character.

Free public schools, for example, did not emerge naturally and logically from the structure and values of American society. Rather, as one historian of American education, Ellwood P. Cubberley, has pointed out: "Excepting for the battle for the abolition of slavery, perhaps no question has ever been before the American people for settlement which caused so much feeling or aroused such bitter antagonism." In large part it was a struggle between liberals and conservatives in the modern sense of the term, although religious issues also played a strong role. "The friends of free schools were at first commonly regarded as fanatics, dangerous to the States, and the opponents of free schools were considered by them as old line conservatives or as selfish members of society." Among the arguments presented for free education was that "a common state school, equally open to all, would prevent that class differentiation so dangerous in a Republic;" while opponents of such schools argued that they "will make education too common, and will educate people out of their proper station in society . . . [and] would break down long-established and very desirable social barriers." On one side of the issue were the poorer classes; on the other, "the old aristocratic class . . . the conservatives of society . . . taxpayers." . . .

The evidence compiled by various social scientists indicates that the men of wealth and economic power in America have *never* given more than minority support to the Democrats. Dixon Ryan Fox, an analyst of New York politics in the first half of the nineteenth century, gathered considerable statistical data which show that the upper-class districts of the various cities of the state voted Federalist and Whig. He quotes a biographer of the wealthy merchants of New York who wrote in the 1860s:

It is a very common fact that for thirty-four years [since the revival of two-party politics in 1828] very few merchants of the first class have been Democrats. The mass of large and little merchants have, like a flock of sheep, gathered either in the Federalist, Whig, Clay, or Republican folds. The Democratic merchants could have easily been stored in a large Eighth Avenue railroad car.

A recent study by Mabel Newcomer of the political views of large business executives in 1900, 1925, and 1950 reports that in all three periods about three quarters of this group were Republicans. Even in 1925, a period not normally considered to be one of political class conflict in America, only 19 per cent of the executives were Democrats. These data certainly underestimate the Republican majority among business executives, since they are based on public party enrollment rather than voting preference and include many registered as southern Democrats who would be Republicans if they were not living in a one-party region. . . .

Party Policies Determined by Party Supporters

This division of Americans into supporters of one of two parties, one historically based on those who are poorer and the other on the more well to do, does not mean that the parties have always divided ideologically along traditional "left-right" political lines. Such issues did separate the parties in Jefferson's and Jackson's day, and also—for the most part— from 1896 to the present, although

there were some significant exceptions, like the elections of 1904 and the 1920s. However, even when the parties did not present opposing positions on conventional left-right lines, there have almost always been issues between them which reflected the differences in their social bases. For example, the Federalist-Whig-Republican party was less receptive to immigration in the nineteenth century than the Democratic party, and a Republican administration enacted the restrictive immigration legislation of the early 1920s. In general, the various nativist and anti-Catholic movements which have arisen at various periods in American history have been identified with the conservative parties on a local if not a national level.

Even the controversy over slavery reflected differences in class. The Northern urban lower-class groups before the Civil War tended to be anti-Negro and were uninterested in the struggle for abolition. In New York State the conservatives supported the right of free Negroes to vote in the state constitutional conventions of 1820 and 1846, while the major Democratic spokesmen either opposed, or were uninterested in, the extension of the suffrage to Negroes. The free Negroes, in turn, were supporters of the Federalist and Whig parties before 1850, and the freed slaves and their descendants remained loyal backers of the Republican party until the election of Roosevelt produced for the first time a Democratic administration which showed an interest in their problems. The Wilson Administration of 1913–1921, although liberal on other issues, reflected southern attitudes in its race-relations policies. The movements reflecting Protestant middle-class morality, such as those designed to prohibit liquor and gambling, or those concerned with the elimination of corruption in government, have also made headway largely through the conservative parties. In the controversies over prohibition in the twentieth century, the Democrats in the North were the "wet" party, while the Republicans were "dry." And in the prosperous 1920s the Democrats as the party of the lower strata and the Catholics ran the campaign of 1928 largely on the platform of repeal of prohibition.

The differences in the ethnic composition of their social bases have also been reflected in the foreign policy positions of the two parties. The one Democratic administration between 1861 and 1913—that of Grover Cleveland in the 1880s —opposed Great Britain on a number of issues and sympathized with the cause of Irish freedom. A recent study of the British immigrant in America shows that the British, though not viewed as a separate or alien ethnic group like arrivals from other countries, organized British clubs in the late nineteenth century as a means of fighting the political power of the Irish Democrats. These British associations gravitated toward the Republican party. Even during World War I, such differences affected American policy. Although Wilson was personally sympathetic to the cause of Britain and the Allies, the bulk of Americans of non-Anglo-Saxon background were hostile either to Britain or to Czarist Russia, and it was the Republican party, based on middle-class Anglo-Saxons, which advocated greater help to the Allies. Wilson, it should be remembered, fought the election of 1916 on an *anti*-war platform and won or held the support of the Irish, Jews, and Germans for the Democratic party.

The position of the two parties on foreign policy has not only reflected their ethnic bases, but on occasion has alienated part of them. Millions of Americans of Irish and German extraction clearly resented American entry into World War I. The Germans in particular suffered heavily as a result of social and economic discrimination during and after the war. Some analysts have suggested (although the statistical work to prove this has not been done) that the great Republican victory of 1920, in which Harding secured a larger percentage of the vote than any other Republican since the founding of the party, was in part at least a result of a shift away from the Democrats by members of ethnic groups who felt "betrayed" by Wilson's taking the country into war.

It is now largely forgotten that, in his early years of office, Franklin D. Roosevelt was an "isolationist," and that the Democratic party leadership in Congress acted as if it believed that America had been tricked into entering World War I by British propaganda and the manipulation of Wall Steet bankers. The neutrality act passed in Roosevelt's first term of office by an overwhelmingly Democratic Congress reflected isolationist and anti-British attitudes. In this respect the Democrats returned to their traditional role of representing the major ethnic groups.

The outbreak of World War II placed Roosevelt in the same dilemma that had faced Wilson earlier. He knew that he had to aid the Allies, but he also wanted to be re-elected. The fall of France left him with no alternative other than giving "all aid short of war;" but in the 1940 presidential campaign he still promised that the country would *not* go to war. This time, however, unlike 1916, the Republicans took the isolationist and pacifist position, largely as an election maneuver. Wendell Willkie was even more favorable to intervention than Roosevelt, yet he and his advisers apparently felt that their one hope of victory was to entice the Irish, German, and Italian voters, who were against intervention because of their national identification, away from the Democrats. Opinion-poll data for that year show that the Republicans were somewhat successful, since the Democratic vote did drop off greatly among these three groups. It was probably counterbalanced, at least in part, by a swing to Roosevelt among middle-class "Anglo-Saxons."

Ethnic reactions have also affected the handling of the Communist issue in the last decade. It should not be forgotten that Senator McCarthy was Irish had represented a state in which the influence of German-Americans is high. McCarthy, in his charges of Communist infiltration in the State Department, stressed that America was "betrayed" by men of upper-class Anglo-Saxon backgrounds, by the graduates of Harvard and other Ivy League schools. He was saying, in effect, to the isolationist ethnic groups which had been exposed to charges of "disloyalty" in the previous two wars, that the people who had really been disloyal were the upper-class Anglo-Saxons who had manipulated the United States into fighting the wrong enemy, and who had "lost the peace" to the Russians. In 1952 the Republicans made a strong foreign policy appeal to the ethnic groups, especially the Catholics and Germans. Eisenhower, like Willkie before him, allowed electoral expediency to modify his public state-

ments. And the election returns indicate that he made strong headway among middle-class Catholics, Germans, and Irish.

Upper-class Liberalism

Recent research by sociologists and historians has clarified some aspects of American politics which do not seem to fit a "class" interpretation of American history, like the fact, already noted, that the wealthier classes and their parties, the Whigs and Republicans, were more antislavery than the Democrats who were supported by the lower classes. Contemporary studies of political attitudes indicate that it is necessary to distinguish between so-called economic liberalism (issues concerned with the distribution of wealth and power) and noneconomic liberalism (issues concerned with civil liberties, race relations, and foreign affairs). The fundamental factor in noneconomic liberalism is not actually class, but education, general sophistication, and probably to a certain extent psychic security. But since these factors are strongly correlated with class, noneconomic liberalism is positively associated with social status (the wealthier are more tolerant), while economic liberalism is inversely correlated with social status (the poor are more leftist on such issues).

Actually within the conservative strata it has not been the wealthier classes in general which have led the political struggle for noneconomic liberalism, but rather those of established "old family" background as differentiated from the nouveaux riches. Before the Civil War most abolitionist leaders were, as David Donald has shown in *Lincoln Reconsidered*, "descended from old and socially dominant Northeastern families." Similarly, the leaders of the Progressive movement of the late nineteenth and early twentieth centuries, which arose within the Republican party and resisted the corrupt urban Democratic machines and the growth of big business trusts with their influence over Republican politicians, came from the same strata and family backgrounds as the abolitionists. In a real sense the abolitionists and Progressives have been the American Tory radicals—men of upper-class background and values, who as conservatives helped to democratize the society as part of their struggle against the vulgar *nouveau riche* businessman.

Tory radicalism has always been in difficulty in America since it has rarely dominated its natural outlet, the Republican party. After the broadening of adult suffrage in the 1820s and 1830s, American parties came under the control of professional politicians whose major concern was to win elections, secure and retain office, regardless of the means necessary to do so. Such an attitude fitted in well with those elements of the society like the *nouveaux riches* who were also concerned with *ends* (wealth and power) rather than with *means* (honor and status). In the nineteenth century many Americans of well-to-do background objected to both the politics based on the lower classes and immigrants (the Democrats), and the politics drawing its sustenance from the "new money-grubbing class" (the Republicans). As David Donald puts it: "They did not support radical economic reforms because [they] . . . had no serious quarrel with the capitalistic system of private ownership and control of property. What they did

question, and what they did rue, was the transfer of leadership to the wrong groups in society, and their appeal for reform was a strident call for their own class to re-exert its former social dominance."

The noneconomic liberalism of this group found its expression in issues like abolition, civil service reform, controlled immigration (so as to reduce urban corruption), and internationalism. In the twentieth century internationalism became the major issue. A large part of the leadership in internationalist local organizations advocating collective security seems to have come from members of old families, usually of Anglo-Saxon origin.

Though linked to the Whig and Republican parties, these upper-class liberals have been ready to help organize "third" parties whenever their issues have become salient. They played a major role in creating the demand for a new anti-slavery party before the Civil War; they played a dominant role in the effort to create a new Liberal Republican party in the 1870s designed to eliminate governmental corruption and enact civil service reform; they fostered the Progressive party of Theodore Roosevelt; and in the 1940s some of them, including their then leader, Wendell Willkie, seriously considered forming a new party. From the pre-Civil War abolitionist movement to the Committee to Defend America by Aiding the Allies (the William Allen White Committee) in 1940–1941, there is a thread of continuity: conservatives who have fought for the "noneconomic" values of honor and freedom, and who have occasionally deserted the traditional party allegiance of their class.

In recent decades the control of large corporations by college-educated men and the scions of established wealth rather than by the relatively uneducated *nouveaux riches* has created an alliance between economic power and traditional status. But this alliance has not meant that the Republican party has easily become the expression of sophisticated conservatism. Rather large sections of it have continued to express the reactionary sentiments of the small-town provincial middle classes. Since its centers of electoral strength, particularly during periods of Democratic dominance, are in the "provinces" rather than the large metropolitan cities, the Republican party can be more properly accused of being the agent of the small-town *bourgeoisie* than of big business.

The conflict between the values of the established upper class and sophisticated corporate wealth and those of small business and self-made wealth has led some observers to suggest that the true party of Tory radicalism in America is the Democratic party. It has achieved Disraeli's objective of a party based on the working class but led by the responsible "squires"— first Roosevelt of Groton and Harvard, and currently "Adlai Stevenson of Choate School and Princeton, G. Mennen Williams of Salisbury School and Princeton, John F. Kennedy of Choate and Harvard . . . and Averell Harriman of Groton and Yale." It is more likely, however, that Nelson Rockefeller, the liberal Republican Governor of New York, will ultimately prove to be the true representative of the revived pattern of direct participation in politics by members of the upper class—participation through their traditional party, the Republican. It is interesting to note in this connection that Mrs. Nelson Rockefeller, a cousin of Joseph Sill Clark, Philadelphia Social Registerite and former Democratic Mayor of Philadelphia, now U.S.Senator, was publicly registered as a member of a third party, New York's Liberal party, until recently.

The strong strain of Tory radicalism which has reappeared at crucial points in American history has served to reduce the tensions inherent in class and sectional cleavages. The Tory radicals, to use Richard Hofstadter's words describing the corporation lawyers who became leaders of the Progressive movement, have never wanted "a sharp change in the social structure, but rather the formation of a responsible elite which was to take charge of the popular impulse toward change, and direct it into moderate, and as they would have said, "constructive channels," a leadership occupying, as Brandeis aptly put it, a position of independence between the wealthy [self-interested businessmen] and the people, prepared to curb the excesses of either." From the standpoint of political stability, Tory radicalism has served to retain the loyalties of both the underprivileged out-groups who gain from needed reforms and the conservative strata who are outraged by the same measures. The participation of upper-class persons in liberal politics may also be seen as enlightened self-interest, since they are able to achieve needed reforms, exercise restraint, and, according to E. Digby Baltzell in *Philadelphia Gentleman*, "perpetuate upper-class influence on the functional class system as a whole by the very fact that they hold important positions within the new avenues to power." At the same time, their presence serves to blur the class lines separating the parties.

21. STABILITY AND CHANGE IN 1960: A REINSTATING ELECTION

Philip E. Converse, Angus Campbell, Warren E. Miller, Donald E. Stokes

The Basic Voting Strength of the Two Parties

We have found it of great explanatory value to think of election results as reflecting the interplay of two sets of forces: stable, long-term partisan dispositions and short-term forces specific to the immediate election situation. The long-term partisan dispositions are very adequately represented by our measures of party identification. The stability of these dispositions over time is a matter of empirical record. Their partisan division over any period, as it may favor one party or the other, provides the point from which one must start to understand any specific election. This underlying division of loyalties lends itself admirably to the goal of indicating what a "normal" vote would be, aside from specific forces associated with the immediate election.

In these terms, the basic Democratic majority in the nation is scarcely subject to dispute. Year in and year out since 1952, national samples of the American electorate have indicated

From Philip E. Converse, Angus Campbell, Warren E. Miller, and Donald E. Stokes, "Stability and Change in 1960: A Reinstating Election," *American Political Science Review*, LV 2 (June, 1961), 273-80. By permission of The American Political Science Association.

a preference for the Democratic party by a margin approaching 60–40. However, since no election in recent years has shown a Democratic margin of this magnitude, it would be as absurd to take a 60–40 Democratic majority for a baseline as it would be to work from the 1956 presidential vote. Actually there is little temptation to do so. Over the years large amounts of information have been accumulated on the behavior of people identifying with the two major parties, and it is clear that the realistic voting strength of the Democrats— and this is the sort of baseline which interests us—falls well short of a 60–40 majority. The fact that heavy Democratic majorities in the South are concealed by low voting turnout is but one factor which reduces realistic Democratic strength. Outside the South, as well, Democrats under the same conditions of short-term stimulation are less likely to vote than Republicans.

It is possible to manipulate the data in such a fashion as to take into account all of the significant discrepancies between nominal party identification and realistic voting strength. We thereby arrive at a picture of the vote division which could be expected in the normal presidential election, if short-term forces associated with the election favored neither party in particular, but stood at an equilibrium. In such circumstances, we would expect a Democratic proportion of the two-party popular vote to fall in the vicinity of 53–54 per cent. Outside of the South, such a vote would fall short of a 50–50 split with the Republicans; within the South there would be a strong Democratic majority exceeding a 2-to-1 division.

Short-term forces associated with a specific election may, according to their net partisan strength, send the actual vote in that election deviating to one side or the other of the equilibrium point. In 1952 and 1956 the popularity of Eisenhower constituted one such force, and this force was strongly pro-Republican. The distortions produced in the behaviors of party identifiers of different types have now become familiar. If the net partisan force is strong, as in 1956, identifiers of the favored party vote almost *en bloc*, without defection. The small group of "independents" who do not commit themselves to either party divide very disproportionately in favor of the advantaged party, instead of dividing their vote equally as in the equilibrium case. And members of the disfavored party defect in relatively large numbers, as Democrats did in 1956. A useful description of any specific election, then is an account of the short-term forces which have introduced these strains across the distribution of party identification.

In such a description, the existing division of deeper party loyalties is taken for granted. Its current character is not to be explained by the immediate political situation. The point is made most clearly by the 1960 election. The fact that the Democrats enjoyed a

standing majority was in no way a consequence of the personal duel between Kennedy and Nixon, for it was a majority created long before either candidate became salient as a national political figure, and long before most of the campaign "issues" of 1960 had taken shape. In this perspective, then, we can consider some of the forces which drew the 1960 vote away from its equilibrium state.

Short-Term Forces in the 1960 Election

Popular vote tallies show that Kennedy received 49.8 per cent of the two-party vote outside of the South, and 51.2 per cent of the popular vote cast in the South. The vote outside the South is almost 1 per cent more Democratic than our equilibrium estimates for this part of the nation. In the South, however, the Democratic deficit relative to the same baseline approaches 17 per cent. Naturally, some short-term forces may balance out so that no net advantage accrues to either party. But the comparisons between our baselines and the 1960 vote suggest that we should find some short-term forces which gave a very slight net advantage to Kennedy outside of the South, and yet which penalized him heavily within the South.

As in all elections that attract a wide degree of public attention, a number of short-term forces were certainly at work in 1960. A comprehensive assessment of these forces must await further analysis. However, there can be little doubt that the religious issue was the strongest single factor overlaid on basic partisan loyalities in the 1960 election, and we have focused most of our initial analyses in this area. Fortunately we know a great deal about the "normal" voting behavior within different religious categories, and can use this knowledge to provide baselines which aid in estimating the net effect of Kennedy's Catholicism upon his candidacy.

The Catholic Vote. As we have observed, the vote division among Catholics soared from a 50–50 split in the two Eisenhower contests to an 80–20 majority in the 1960 presidential vote. However, it is hard to attribute all of this increment simply to the Kennedy candidacy. In the 1958 election, when there were mild short-term economic forces favoring the Democratic party, the vote among Catholics went well over 70 per cent in that direction. Ever since our measurements of party identification began in 1952, only a small minority— less than 20 per cent—of Catholics in the nation have considered themselves as Republicans, although a fair portion have typically styled themselves as "Independents." Most of what attracted attention as a Republican trend among Catholics during the 1950's finds little support in our data, at least as a trend peculiar to Catholics. To be sure, many Democratic Catholics defected to vote for Eisenhower in 1952 and 1956. So did many Democratic Protestants. As a matter of fact, the defection rate among Democratic Catholics in 1952 was very slightly less than among Democratic Protestants, and in 1956 was very slightly more. In neither case do the differences exceed sampling error. There is some long-term evidence of a faint and slow erosion in the Catholic Democratic vote; but this has been proceeding at such a glacial pace that the 1956–1960 vote trends which we are treating here dwarf it completely. There is no reason to believe that the short-term personal "pull" exerted on Democrats generally by Eisenhower had a different strength for Catholics than for Protestants. The myths that have arisen to this effect seem to be primarily illusions stemming from the large proportion of Democrats who are Catholics. Their loss was painful in the two Eisenhower votes. But they were at the outset, and remained up to the first glimmer of the Kennedy candidacy, a strongly Democratic group.

We may specify this "normal" Democratic strength among Catholics by applying the same operations for Catholics alone that we have employed for the electorate as a whole. In the equilibrium case, it turns out that one would expect at least a 63 per cent Democratic margin among Catholics. The difference between 63 per cent and the 80 per cent which Kennedy achieved can provisionally be taken as an estimate of the increment in Democratic votes among Catholics above that which the normal, Protestant Democratic presidential candidate could have expected.

We can readily translate this 17 per cent vote gain into proportions of the total 1960 vote, taking into account levels of Catholic turn-out and the like. On such grounds, it appears that Kennedy won a vote bonus from Catholics amounting to about 4 per cent of the national two-party popular vote. This increment is, of course, very unequally divided between the South and the rest of the nation, owing simply to the sparse Catholic population in the South. Within the 1960 non-Southern electorate, Kennedy's net gain from the

Catholic increment amounts to better than 5 per cent of the two-party vote. The same· rate of gain represents less than 1 per cent of the Southern popular vote.

The Anti-Catholic Vote. Respondents talked to our interviewers with remarkable freedom about the Catholic factor during the fall of 1960. This is not to say that all respondents referred to it as a problem. There were even signs that some Protestant respondents were struggling to avoid mention of it although it was a matter of concern. Nonetheless, nearly 40 per cent of the sample voluntarily introduced the subject before any direct probing on our part in the early stages of the pre-election questionnaire. Since this figure certainly understates the proportion of the population for whom religion was a salient concern in 1960, it testifies rather eloquently to the importance of the factor in conscious political motivations during the fall campaign.

These discussions of the Catholic question, volunteered by our respondents, will, in time, provide more incisive descriptions of the short-term anti-Catholic forces important in the election. Our interest here, however, is to estimate the magnitude of anti-Catholic voting in terms of otherwise Democratic votes which Kennedy lost. In such an enterprise, our material on the political backgrounds of our respondents is most useful.

We focus, therefore, upon the simple rates of defection to Nixon among Protestants who were identified in 1960 with the Democratic party. As Figure 3–1 shows, this defection rate is strongly correlated with regularity of attendance at a Protestant church. Protestant Democrats who, by self-description, never attend church, and hence are not likely to have much identification with it, defected to Nixon only at a rate of 6 per cent. This rate, incidentally, is just about the "normal" defection rate which we would predict for both parties in the equilibrium case: it represents the scattered defections which occur for entirely idiosyncratic reasons in any election. Therefore, for Democrats who were nominal Protestants but outside the psychological orbit of their church, the short-term religious force set up by a Catholic candidacy had no visible impact. However, as soon as there is some evidence of identification with a Protestant church, the defection rate rises rapidly.

Although Protestant Independents are not included in Figure 3–1 they show the same gradient at a different level of the two-party vote division. The few Protestant Independents not attending church split close to the theoretically-expected 50–50 point. Then the Nixon vote rises to 61 per cent in the "seldom" category; to 72 per cent for the "often" category; and to 83 per cent for the Protestant Independents attending church regularly. This increment of Republican votes above the "normal" 50–50 division for Independents matches remarkably the increment of Republican votes above the "normal" figure of 6 per cent in the case of the Democrats.

We customarily find in our data certain substantial correlations between church attendance and political behavior. The correlation between church attendance and vote among Protestant Democrats and Independents is not, however, one of these. The strong associations seem linked in an obvious way to the 1960 election. We need not assume, of course, that each defection pictured here represents a sermon from the pulpit and an obedient member of the congregation. Social science theory assures us that whether through sermons, informal communication or a private sense of reserve toward Catholicism, the faithful Protestant would react more negatively to the presidential candidacy of a Catholic than would more indifferent Protestants. It remains notable, however, that Democrats who were at the same time regular Protestants defected to Nixon at rates far exceeding those which Eisenhower had attracted in 1952 or 1956.

We may use Figure 3–1 then, as a tool to estimate the magnitude of the anti-Catholic vote. It is easily argued that the area below the dotted line in Figure 3–1 represents "normal" defections within each category of church attendance, and that the votes represented by the triangle above the dotted line are votes which Kennedy lost on religious grounds. It is then a simple mechanical matter to convert this triangle into proportions of the popular vote for South and non-South.

On the surface, Figure 3–1 seems to say that the impact of the religious factor was very nearly the same, North and South, for the Southern gradient of defections is only slightly higher than the non-Southern gradient. If we think of the impact of short-term forces *on individuals* as a function of their party and religious loyalties, this conclusion is proper. Indeed, as we consider in later analyses the impact by different types of Protestantism, it may well be that the character of the impact will show no remaining regional difference whatever. However, to construe Figure 3–1 as suggesting

FIGURE 3-1.

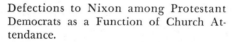

Defections to Nixon among Protestant Democrats as a Function of Church Attendance.

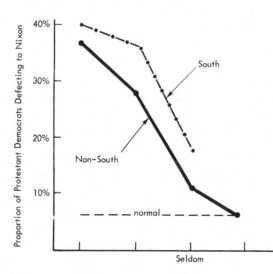

that the *magnitude* of the anti-Catholic effect was about the same in votes cast in North and South, is quite improper. The differences between the regions turn out to be substantial.

We must consider first that less than two-thirds of the active non-Southern electorate is Protestant, wheras within the South the electorate is almost completely (95 per cent) Protestant. Secondly, Protestants are more faithful church-goers in the South than outside it. Quite specifically, we find that over half of the Southern presidential vote is cast by Protestants who go to church regularly, whereas less than 20 per cent of the vote outside the South comes from regular, church-going Protestants. Finally, of the minority outside the South who are Protestant and attend church regularly, only a small proportion are Democratic identifiers; Republicans clearly predominate in this category. In the South, the situation is reversed, with regular Protestants being far more often than not Democratic identifiers.

This conjunction of regional differences means that the defecting votes represented in Figure 3–1 are of vastly different sizes, South and non-South. It turns out that outside the South regular, church-going Protestants who are Democrats cast only about 5 per cent of the total non-Southern vote. Within the South, however, regular church-going Protestants who are Democrats contributed over 35 per cent of the total Southern vote. Thus it is that the anti-Catholic impact in the South turns out to involve a much large share of the votes than elsewhere. The anti-Catholic vote in the South fulfills our search for a short-term force of strong net Republican strength in that region.

Summing up these apparent anti-Catholic votes as proportions of the total vote in the South, the non-South, and the nation as a whole, we can compare them with our estimations of the bonuses received by Kennedy from Catholics. Table 3–9 shows the balance sheet.

Table 3-9
OFFSETTING EFFECTS OF THE CATHOLIC ISSUE, 1960 DEMOCRATIC PRESIDENTIAL VOTE

Area	% of 2-party vote in area
Outside the South, Kennedy's "unexpected" . . .	
Gains from Catholics	5.2%
Losses from Protestant Democrats and Independents	−3.6
NET	+1.6%
Inside the South, Kennedy's "unexpected" . . .	
Gains from Catholics	0.7%
Losses from Protestant Democrats and Independents	−17.2
NET	−16.5%
For the *nation as a whole*, Kennedy's "unexpected" . . .	
Gains from Catholics	4.3%
Losses from Protestant Democrats and Independents	−6.5
NET	−2.2%

There is every reason to believe that these preliminary estimates underestimate the importance of religion in the 1960 vote and, in particular, underestimate the magnitude of the anti-Catholic vote. We have at no point taken account, for example, of the possiblity that certain Republican identifiers, exposed to short-term forces which would normally have produced defections to the Democrats, may have been inhibited from such defection by Kennedy's Catholicism. In the midwest there were signs of a "farm revolt" favoring the Democrats which failed to materialize in the presidential balloting. At lower levels on farm belt tickets one finds that major Democratic candidates consistently surpassed "normal" Democratic expectations. Yet Kennedy seems to have been peculiarly insulated from any of this profit-taking: in these areas he lagged behind other major Democrats by a rather consistent 5 per cent. It is difficult not to believe that at lower levels of office net short-term forces were favoring the Democrats, and Republican identifiers were defecting at unusual rates. Analyses may show that religion was a primary force inhibiting such defections at the presidential level.

Other early glimpses of our data also suggest the estimates of anti-Catholicism in Table 3–9 are conservative It is likely that a number of non-religious short-term forces generated by the campaign itself were favorable to Kennedy on balance. As a number of other surveys reported, Nixon held a substantial lead over Kennedy in the early stages. At the outset, Kennedy was little known to the public: he stood primarily as the Democratic candidate and a Catholic. As the campaign went on, other and non-religious aspects of the Kennedy image filled in, and the public impression was usually positive. In this crucial shift in sentiment during the campaign, the television debates probably played an important role. Although there were Democrats who reacted warmly to Nixon's performance, our materials show quite strikingly that the net response to the debates favored Kennedy, as has been commonly supposed. In case studies, a reading of interviews has already turned up numerous Protestants of varying partisanship who were much more impressed by Kennedy as a candidate than by Nixon, yet who

could not bring themselves to vote for a Catholic. In the measure that Kennedy's attractiveness as a candidate exceeded Nixon's and other short-term forces apart from religion were favoring the Democrats, the total popular vote should have been drawn to the Democratic side of the equilibrium point. The fact that it stayed instead on the Republican side may represent further damaging effects of religion for Kennedy.

Refined analyses at a later date will permit us to estimate more adequately the role which all the major motivational factors, including religion, played in the 1960 outcome. For the moment however, it is impressive the degree to which the surface characteristics of the 1960 election become intelligible even when viewed simply as the result of an "ancient" and enduring division of partisan loyalties overlaid by a short-term cross-current of religious motivation.

Normally we would expect a national vote falling as close to its equilibrium point as the 1960 case to be a relatively low-turnout election. That is, a vote near the equilibrium point suggests either weak short-term forces or else a balance of stronger forces creating conflict in individuals and thereby lowering their motivation to vote. It is rare that forces strong enough to compel indifferent citizens to come out and vote do not also favor one party over the other quite categorically.

In 1960, however, the motivational picture underlying the vote was somewhat different, and can best be understood by separating the Protestant South from the rest of the nation. In the South, of course, a strong and unidirectional short-term force was reflected in a sharp departure from equilibrium and a surge in turn-out, as fits normal expectations. What is abnormal is that this strong Republican short-term force raised motivation in a Democratic preserve, rather than diluting it through conflict. It is likely that conflict *was* created, especially where Democratic partisanship was strong. "Strong" Democrats in our sample made virtually no contribution to the 1960 rise in Southern turn-out. The increase came from weaker Democrats, whose participation increased so radically over 1952 and 1956 that their turnout even surpassed that of strong Democrats in very exceptional fashion. For these voters, it seems likely that such forces as anti-Catholic feelings rapidly overcame relatively weak party loyalties and left strong motivation to turn out.

While turnout elsewhere did not show the same remarkable surge which appeared in the South, it remained at the fairly high level characteristic of the 1952 and 1956 elections, despite a partisan division of the vote near the regional equilibrium point. Strong balancing forces appear to have been in operation which did not create much conflict within individuals. The reason is clear: to the degree that religious motivations were engaged, forces were conflicting between groups rather than within individuals. Non-Southern Catholics, predominantly Democratic, were exposed to strong unidirectional short-term forces motivating them to get out and vote for Kennedy. Non-Southern Protestants, predominantly Republican, were exposed to contrary forces, at least where Protestant religious fidelity was strong. Thus the vote fell near the equilibrium point, but there was rather high turn-out as well.

The other surface characteristics of the election are equally intelligible in these terms. Despite his position as majority candidate, Kennedy very nearly lost and tended to run behind his ticket. In the Northeast, where concentrations of Catholics are greatest, his relation to the rest of the ticket was not generally unfavorable. The penalty he suffered becomes visible and consistent in the Midwest, where Catholics are fewer and Protestant church attendance is more regular. In the South, and for the same reasons, the differences between the Kennedy vote and that of other Democrats become large indeed. Everywhere, if one compares 1956 vote statistics with 1960 statistics, the course of political change is closely associated with the religious composition of voting units.

There was some relief even outside the more committed Democratic circles when the Kennedy victory, slight though it was, demonstrated that a Catholic was not in practice barred from the White House. Yet it would be naive to suppose that a Catholic candidate no longer suffers any initial disadvantage before the American electorate as a result of his creed. Not only did Kennedy possess a type of personal appeal which the television debates permitted him to exploit in unusual measure, but he was also the candidate of a party enjoying a fundamental majority in the land. Even the combination of these circumstances was barely sufficient to give him a popular vote victory. Lacking such a strong underlying majority, which Al Smith most certainly lacked in 1928, it is doubtful that the most attractive of Catholic presidential candidates in 1960 would have had much chance of success. It remains to be seen how far the experience of a Catholic president may diminish the disadvantage another time.

The 1960 election in historical perspective

In a publication which appeared a few months prior to the 1960 elections we posed the question of "how long a party can hope to hold the White House if it does not have a majority of the party-identified electorate." We had identified the two Eisenhower victories as "deviating elections," in which short-term forces had brought about the defeat of the majority party. We had not found any evidence in our 1952 or 1956 studies that these short-term forces were producing any significant realignment in the basic partisan commitments of the electorate. We felt that unless such a realignment did occur, "the minority party [could] not hope to continue its tenure in office over a very extended period."

We now know that the eight-year Eisenhower period ended with no basic change in the proportions of the public who identify themselves as Republican, Democrat, or Independent. If there had been an opportunity in 1952 for the Republican party to rewin the majority status it had held prior to 1932, it failed to capitalize on it. The Democratic party remained the majority party and the 1960 election returned it to the presidency. It was, to extend the nomenclature of our earlier publication, a "reinstating" election, one in which the party enjoying a majority of party identifiers returns to power. The 1960 election was remarkable not in the fact that the majority party was reinstated but that its return to power was accomplished by such a narrow margin.

We had recognized the possibility that "the unfolding of national and international events and the appearance of new political figures" might swing the vote away from its natural equilibrium. We now see that such a deflection did occur and that it very nearly cost the majority party the election.

It may be argued that the deficit the Democratic presidential candidate suffered from his normal expectation did not derive from damaging circumstances which were specific to the 1960 election but from a progressive weakening in the willingness of some Democratic partisans to support their ticket at the presidential level. It has been suggested that some voters who consider themselves to be Democrats and customarily favor Democratic candidates at the lower levels of office may have come during the Eisenhower period to have a perverse interest in favoring Republican candidates for president, either because of notions of party balance in government, because of local considerations in their states, or simply out of admiration for Eisenhower.

Important differences no doubt exist between voting at the presidential level and voting for a congressman. Our studies have shown, for example, that the popular vote for lesser offices is a more party-determined vote than the vote for president and varies around the normal equilibrium vote figure within a much narrower range than does the presidential vote. However, the supposition that Kennedy failed to win a normal Democratic majority because of a cadre of Democrats who are covertly Republican in their presidential voting is not supported by our data.

. . . [T]he over-all shift in partisanship of the vote between 1956 and 1960 cannot be explained as a simple unilateral movement of erstwhile Eisenhower Democrats. The election did not depend, as was often supposed, upon the number of Eisenhower Democrats whom Nixon could retain as "covert Republicans." Our panel materials show that if Nixon had been forced to depend only upon the Eisenhower Democrats whom he retained, he would have suffered a convincing 54–46 defeat, assuming that other Democrats had continued to vote for Kennedy. He did not suffer such a defeat because he drew a new stream of Democratic defections nearly sufficient to put him in the White House.

The patterns of short-term forces in the 1960 election were independent of those shaping the 1956 election, then, in the sense that they affected a new set of people, on new grounds. There were Democrats susceptible to Eisenhower in 1956; there were Democrats sensitive to religion in 1960: the two sets of people do not intersect much more than one would expect by chance. In short, there is little evidence that the two Eisenhower elections had created a set of Democrats peculiarly disposed to vote for a Republican presidential candidate.

Analysis of our 1960 data is not sufficiently complete to enable us to describe the entire pattern of forces to which the electorate was reacting on Election Day. We do not know, for example, what the partisan impact of international affairs, which had favored the Republican candidate so strongly in the preceding two elections, was in the 1960 election. We do not know the effect of the Negro discrimination issues. We do not know in detail as yet how the personal attributes of the major candidates, other than their religious affiliations, were evaluated by the public. We feel confident, however, that we will not find any short-term force which moved as large a fraction of the 1960 electorate as did the issue of a Catholic president. This was the major cause of the net departure of the vote totals from the division which the comparative underlying strength of the two parties in 1960 would have led us to expect. After two consecutive "deviating" elections won at a presidential level by the minority party, the 1960 election reinstated the Democratic party. But short-term forces generated by the immediate 1960 situation once again favored the Republicans on balance, and the difference in votes which separated this "reinstating election" from a third "deviating election" was slight indeed.

Voting Behavior

22. SOCIAL DETERMINISM AND ELECTORAL DECISION: THE CASE OF INDIANA

V. O. Key, Jr. and Frank Munger

The style set in the Erie County study of voting, *The People's Choice*, threatens to take the politics out of the study of electoral behavior. The theoretical heart of *The People's Choice* rests in the contention that "social characteristics determine political preference." Professor Lazarsfeld and his associates, prudent as they are, do not let so bald a statement

From V. O. Key, Jr., and Frank Munger, " Social Determinism and Electoral Decision: The Case of Indiana," in *American Voting Behavior,* eds. Eugene Burdick and Arthur J. Brodbeck (New York: Free Press of Glencoe, Inc., 1959), pp. 281-99, excerpts. Reprinted with permission of The Free Press. Copyright (c) 1959 by The Free Press, a Corporation.

stand without qualification or exception. Yet almost inevitably from this basic view, which is usually not put so explicitly, there develops a school of analysis that tends to divert attention from critical elements of electoral decision. The focus of analysis under the doctrine of social determinism comes to rest broadly on the capacity of the "nonpolitical group" to induce conformity to its political standards by the individual voter.

At bottom the tendency of the theory of group or social determinism is to equate the people's choice with individual choice. Perhaps the collective electoral decision, the people's choice, is merely the sum of individual choices. If enough were understood about individual decisions, by addition the collective political decision of the electorate would be comprehended. Yet when attention centers on the individual elector as he is led to decision by the compulsion of his nonpolitical group, the tendency is to lose sight of significant elements that both affect and relate individual decisions to the political aggregate. The study of electoral behavior then becomes only a special case of the more general problem of group inducement of individual behavior in accord with group norms. As such it does not invariably throw much light on the broad nature of electoral decision in the sense of decisions by the electorate as a whole.

The purpose here is not to dissent from *The People's Choice*. It is rather to raise the question whether its fundamental propositions do not provide a base on which, if enough effort were devoted to the matter, a supplementary theoretical structure might be erected that would bring politics into the study of electoral behavior. A few of the possible directions of development are here indicated through questions suggested by an examination of the voting record of Indiana. The simplest of techniques permits the analysis of a variety of types of electoral situations and suggests interpretations not so likely to emerge from the close observation of a single campaign. Parenthetically, it ought to be made explicit that such crude manipulation of aggregate electoral data is not urged as a substitute for the refined techniques of observation and analysis employed in *The People's Choice*. . . .

Traditional Partisan Attachments: A Bench Mark For Analysis

. . . Explicit attention to the time dimension of electoral decision would probably bring to light a variety of characteristics not readily perceptible by the observation of a single case. Illustrative is the difficulty of obtaining a satisfactory estimate of the nature and significance of traditional or habitual partisan attachments by interviewing a sample at a particular point in time. Often electoral decision is not an action whose outcome is in doubt but a reaffirmation of past decisions, at least for the community as a whole. For generations the Democrats may carry this county and the Republicans may predominate in an adjacent county.

The potency of these traditional attachments may be inferred from the maps in Figure 3–2 which show the distribution of Indiana presidential vote by counties in 1868 and 1900. Although the pattern of 1868 did not move unchanged from election to election to 1900, an astonishing parallelism appears in the county-by-county division of party strength at the two widely separated points in time. Thirty-six of the state's ninety-two counties were over 50 per cent Democratic at both elections; forty-five were under 50 per cent Democratic at both elections.

Apparently the persistent pattern of party division represented a crystallization of attitudes at the time of the Civil War mainly along lines separating areas with different sources of settlement. The southern half of the state, peopled chiefly from the southern states, contained in 1868 and 1900

FIGURE 3-2.

The Traditional Vote: Democratic Percentage of the Two-Party Presidential Vote
in Indiana, 1868.

Democratic Percentage of Two-Party Presidential Vote

FIGURE 3-3.

The Traditional Vote: Democratic Percentage of the Two-Party Presidential Vote in Indiana, 1900.

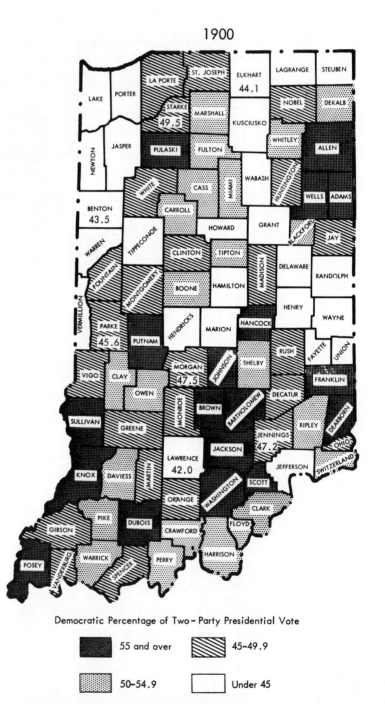

1900

Democratic Percentage of Two-Party Presidential Vote

55 and over   45-49.9

50-54.9   Under 45

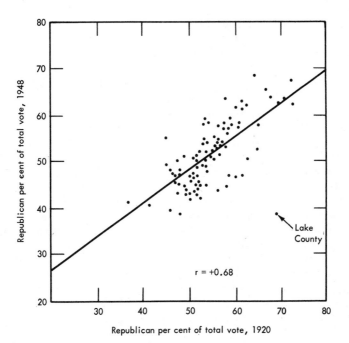

FIGURE 3-4.

The Traditional Vote: Relation Between Republican Percentage of Total Presidential Vote in 1920 and 1948 by Counties in Indiana.

most of the Democratic strongholds. Other Democratic areas find a partial explanation in the greater attractiveness of that party to newcomers from abroad. Dearborn, Franklin, Adams, Allen, and Pulaski counties all had large German populations as did Dubois in the south. The Republicanism of certain blocks of counties was related also to the sectional origins of settlers. The block of 1868–1900 Republican counties in east central Indiana was settled by Quakers, whose cultural center was Richmond in Wayne County. Their antislavery sentiments and perhaps other reasons as well made them early converts to Republicanism. Other strongly Republican areas in the northern part of the state had drawn heavily from Federalist and Whig areas of the Northeast. Many of the oddities in detail of the territorial distribution of party strength find explanation in like terms.

From 1868 to 1900 the potency of traditional party attachments may have been much greater than now, yet such community traits persist as is demonstrated by the scatter-diagram in Figure 3–3. The diagram relates the Republican percentage of the total presidential vote by county in 1920 to the corresponding percentage in 1948. Although most counties were more Democratic in 1948 than in 1920, a substantial correlation, +0.689, existed between the Republican percentages for the two elections. Generally where the Republicans were strong in 1920, they were relatively strong in 1948; where the Democrats were weak in 1920, they were relatively weak in 1948.

The analytical model that centers attention on the campaign as a period of decision obviously obscures a significant dimension of the electoral process. In fact, there tends to be a standing decision by the community, although as a descriptive term "section" has connotations of deliberate choice that are apt to be misleading. The "decision" may simply represent the balance between two opposing party groups each with striking powers of self-perpetuation. Their original formation may have in some instances represented a simple transplantation of partisan attachments. In others the dominant classes of the community allied themselves with the party whose policies of the moment were most akin to their inclinations. Doubtless great contests and stirring events intensified and renewed partisan loyalties. The clustering of interests, career lines, and community sentiments about the dominant party gives it a powerful capacity for survival.

The relevance of all this to the theoretical problem is that it raises the question whether one needs to supplement the doctrine that "social characteristics determine political preference." May there not also be a political group with to some extent an independence of exterior determinants of membership and attachment? Obviously a simple reconciliation of the persistence of party groupings and the notion of social determinism would be to assert that the stability of "interests" and people associated with geography produces a parallel continuity of partisan attachment. Yet the long persistence of county patterns of party affiliation despite changes in "interest" and the disappearance of issues that created the pattern, and the existence of contrasting partisan patterns in essentially similar counties, point toward a "political" grouping at least to some extent independent of other social groupings. . . .

In any case the traditional pattern of voting provides a bench mark for the identification and analysis of particular electoral shifts. Electoral decision may be fundamentally a question of whether to depart from pre-existing decision. Under what circumstances does the electorate, or parts of it, choose to deviate from old habits of action? Does the nature of these "decisions" differ from election to election, situation to situation?

Durable Alterations in Partisan Division

Even the most cursory analysis of shifts in party strength from the more or less viscous pattern of traditional behavior suggests that an understanding of the process of electoral decision (and of popular government) must rest on a differentiation of types of electoral decision in the sense of elections as collective decision. It also suggests lines for the supplementation of the theory that "social characteristics determine political preference" to make it a more useful tool for political analysis.

Evidently one type of electoral decision consists in a more or less durable shift in the traditional partisan division within a community. The manner in which such realignments occur should be instructive to advocates of party reconstruction as well as suggestive for speculation about the nature of the party system. This type of alteration is not the work of a moment but may take place in a series of steps spread over a considerable period of time. Or at least such would be the conclusion if the Indiana data mean anything beyond the particular situation.

To identify areas undergoing a secular change in party division one must separate the electoral movements

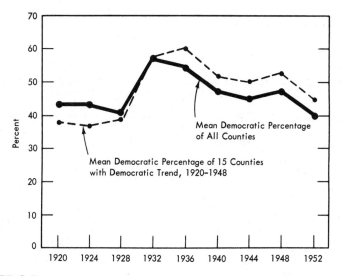

FIGURE 3-5.

Secular Shift in Partisan Attachment: Mean Democratic Percentage of Two-Party Presidential Vote for all Indiana Counties and for Fifteen Counties with the Most Marked Democratic Growth, 1920-52.

that occur from election to election from those that seem to represent a long-term trend. The long-term tendency of the areas undergoing durable re-alignment presumably will be retarded or accelerated by those factors peculiar to each election which affect them as well as those areas not touched by the secular trend. A crude separation of short-term movements and long-term trends is accomplished by the arrangement of the data in Figure 3–4. From 1920 to 1948 in fifteen Indiana counties the Democratic proportion of the two-party presidential vote increased by 10 percentage points or more. In the chart the average Democratic percentage of these counties is plotted alongside the average Democratic percentage of all counties of the state. Although the fifteen counties evidently felt the election-to-election influences common to all counties, their long-term divergence as a group from the mean of all counties moved them in a sequence of steps over sixteen years

from a Republican position to a new and relatively stable pattern of division above the Democratic average for all counties. The shifting counties were more affected by the LaFollette candidacy in 1924 than were the rest of the state's counties. As a group, they withstood the general trend toward Hoover in 1928. In 1932 they moved Democratic as did all other counties but at a slightly higher rate. In 1936 their divergent trend continued and apparently that election fixed a new equilibrium in partisan division. In effect, the analysis segregates out areas undergoing a secular trend that creates a "new traditional" pattern. If the cyclical component of the fifteen-county series in Figure 3–4 were to be removed, the residual secular trend would show a gradual upward movement from 1924 to 1936 after which the series would flatten out.

The phenomenon recorded in the chart has interest purely for its isolation of a secular movement from one party

FIGURE 3-6.

Impact of the 1928 Campaign: Shift from 1924 to 1928 in the Republican Percentage of Total Presidential Vote in Four Types of Indiana Counties.

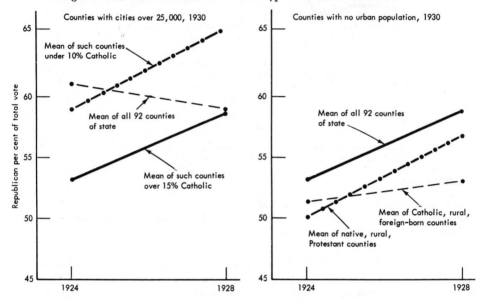

toward the other. Only a panel study over a long period could determine the detailed nature of the secular change, yet from the aggregate statistics some surmises are possible. To the extent that the shift reflected a net change in partisan attachment rather than differentials in accretions to the two parties, it probably occurred by the cumulation of individual shifts. Some persons became disenchanted with the major parties in 1924 and voted for LaFollette. Others were recruited by the Democrats on liquor and religious issues in 1928. The depression made permanent as well as temporary Democratic converts in 1932. The impact of the New Deal program completed the process in 1936. Party realignment may be accomplished under some circumstances by a series of steps.

If this aggregate analysis identifies a type of electoral shift, can it be brought under the doctrine that "social characteristics determine political preference" or do we need a supplementary theory? If social characteristics determine political preference, it would be supposed that a set of secular social changes occurred in our fifteen counties and guided their political reorientation. Most of the fifteen counties either included within their limits considerable cities or were within the zone of influence of such cities. Yet not all counties containing such cities underwent enough partisan change to be included in the group. Most of the counties enjoyed a continuing growth of urban population and of industry, and in some instances notable addition to the electorate occurred with the coming of age of sons and daughters of immigrants.

It seems most improbable that changes in social characteristics occurred as rapidly as did political change during the period 1924–1936. To fill in one theoretical gap one could posit the existence of a lag in the adjustment of political preference to social characteristics, i.e., that it took some time for political attitude to catch up with urbanization and industrialization. Under some circumstances the process of social determinism may encounter formidable friction in remolding political orientation. . . .

Short-Term Disturbances of Partisan Patterns: the Relativity of Social Determinism

Another elaboration of the doctrine of social determinism is suggested by observation of the short-term shifts in partisan strength. Evidently at some moments in time these shifts are associated with a particular social characteristic; at other times that characteristic will be unimportant as a determinant. At one time one social characteristic may seem to fix election results; at another time another will predominate.

Again rough analyses of the Indiana data may illustrate the argument. The charts in Figure 3–5 indicate the movement of the mean of the Republican percentage of the total presidential vote from 1924 to 1928 in four types of counties. In the urban counties with relatively small proportions of their population Roman Catholic, the Republicans gained sharply while their proportion of the vote declined in urban counties with the highest proportions of Roman Catholic population. In the rural counties with the highest proportions of native-born Protestant population, a much sharper Republican gain occurred than in rural counties with relatively high proportions of Catholic and foreign-born.

Obviously these aggregate figures do not establish that Protestants moved from Democratic to Republican ranks from 1924 to 1928. Nevertheless, it is

FIGURE 3-7.

National Origin and the Vote: Democratic Percentage of the Two-Party Vote for President and Governor in Dubois and Clark Counties, Indiana, 1936-48.

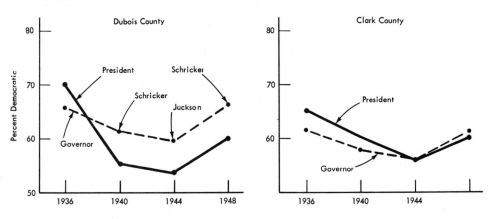

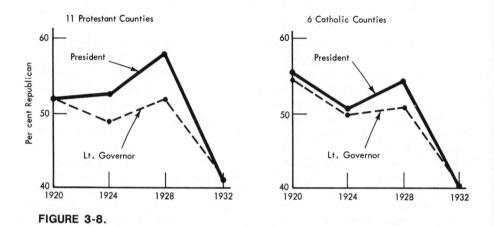

FIGURE 3-8.

Mean Republican Percentage of the Total Vote for President and Lieutenant-Governor in Selected Protestant and Catholic Counties in Indiana, 1920-32.

most probable that a shift associated with religion and related factors occurred. To the extent that the data indicate electoral decisions associated with such social attributes, they point toward an additional elaboration of the theory of social determinism. The social characteristics of our contrasting counties changed very little over the period 1924 to 1928. If these characteristics determined political preference, they acquired a political significance, at least for some people, in 1928 that they lacked in 1924.

The same sorts of propositions find further illustration in the voting behavior of German and non-German counties. Although most Indiana counties from 1936 to 1940 shifted to some degree away from the Democrats, the supposition is that voters of German origin were especially antagonized by Roosevelt's policy toward the Reich. In 1940 Henry Schricker ran as the Democratic candidate for governor. Of German origin, he was reputed to have a potent appeal to voters of that nationality. If the social characteristic of national origin moved in higher degree into the zone of political relevance in 1940, it would be supposed that German voters

would support Schricker in higher degree than Roosevelt while the non-German groups would probably give about the same proportion of their vote to both gubernatorial and presidential candidates.

Insofar as election returns give a clue to group voting behavior the graphs in Figure 3–6 support the proposition. The chart compares Dubois County, in high degree Germanic in origin, with Clark County, an area with relatively fewer citizens of German origin. Dissatisfaction with foreign policy presumably accounted for the especially sharp drop in Dubois in the vote for the Democratic presidential candidate in 1940. The higher vote in that county for Democratic candidates for governor probably reflected primarily a loyalty to the state Democratic ticket unaffected by national policy and perhaps to some extent the special appeal of Henry Schricker, who ran in both 1940 and 1948. On the other hand, in Clark County the Democratic presidential and gubernatorial candidates polled more nearly the same percentages of the vote.

The relativity of social determinism is further illustrated by a type of fluctuation in party strength in which voters are apparently drawn away from their usual party preference by the issue or events of a particular campaign only to return to the fold when the repelling peculiarities of the election disappear. It might be supposed, for example, that in 1928 some persons who usually voted Democratic supported Hoover in preference to Smith yet returned to their party when the commotion subsided. A rough test of the proposition is provided by the data in Figure 3–7, which shows the mean Republican percentage of the total vote for President and for Lieutenant-Governor of another pair of contrasting groups of counties from 1920 to 1932. Note in particular that the predominantly Protestant rural counties reported about twice as wide a net splitting of tickets to the advantage of Hoover as did otherwise comparable counties with relatively large Catholic populations. In both types of counties the gaps between the state and national votes disappeared in 1932. Such aggregate figures, of course, do not tell us who crossed party lines, whether gross ticket splitting was greater in one set of counties than in the other, or whether ticket splitting was higher at one election than another. Yet the differentials strongly suggest that Protestant Democrats and perhaps Catholic Republicans responded to the situation in 1928 by splitting their tickets. After the religious issue subsided, national and local party appeals were more nearly congruent and ticket splitting declined.

The data have an incidental utility in sharper definition of the "independent" voter. Insofar as ticket splitting is regarded as a manifestation of "independence," one type of independence apparently is not a generalized objectivity of judgment but a response of particular classes of voters to the particular issues of the day. The quantity and incidence of this type of voting would be expected to differ from time to time with the issues and personalities of the moment.

All these illustrative analyses in a sense support the doctrine of social determinism of political preference yet they also point to the need for correlative theory. Social characteristics gain a political significance when political alternatives tend to parallel differentials in social attribute. One attribute may be of political significance at one time and another at another. That significance may well be the product of events and actions entirely outside the group concerned. Politicians may, in effect, invest group attributes with political significance. Appeals to group interest, prejudice, and pride are part of the stock-in-trade of the politician who often labors mightily to make the voter conscious of his social characteristics in order that they may determine his political preference. . . .

Unexplained Elements of Decision: the General Drift of Sentiment

While the interaction of the structure of political alternatives and cleavages in social characteristics undoubtedly bears significantly on electoral decision, the preceding analyses implicitly suggest that social determinism may account for only part of the movement of the electorate from party to party over each four-year period. Social groups that move into the zone of political relevance in a particular campaign may transfer their loyalties in a relatively high degree, but it seems not unlikely that in many elections most groups move in the same direction. If this could be demonstrated, it would suggest the existence of some political

Table 3-10
NUMBER OF INDIANA COUNTIES WITH INCREASING OR DECLINING
DEMOCRATIC PERCENTAGE OF TWO-PARTY PRESIDENTIAL VOTE, 1928-52

Period	Increasing Democratic Percentage	Declining Democratic Percentage	No Percentage Change	Total
1928–32	92	0	0	92
1932–36	23	68	1	92
1936–40	0	92	0	92
1940–44	3	89	0	92
1944–48	87	5	0	92
1948–52	0	92	0	92

X factor or factors which may, in most elections, play the determinative role in political decision.

The evidence on the proposition is extremely thin. Obviously the facts differ from election to election, yet it seems fairly plain that in many four-year periods a general drift of sentiment occurs that is shared to some degree by people of all sorts of social characteristics. Some of the charts point in that direction. Some broader possibilities are suggested by the data in Table 3–10, which shows the direction of movement from presidential election to presidential election from 1928 to 1952 of all the counties of Indiana. It will be observed that the more common pattern was for most of the counties to move in the same direction. A sharp deviation from this uniformity occurred in 1936 which was a crucial election in reshaping the traditional composition of the Democratic following, as was indicated by Figure 3–2.

The figures of Table 3–10 only show, of course, that the people of geographical units as a whole moved in the same direction in most elections. Only insofar as social differentiation is associated with geography do the figures give ground for supposing that various sorts of social groups moved in the same direction. A series of sample surveys covering the same period as the table would be necessary to deter-

mine the answer to that question. Yet scattered evidence suggests that it is not uncommon for people of the most diverse social groups to shift their political sentiments in the same direction. Decisions, i.e., to change, may well be conditioned, at least in some elections, by factors more or less independent of social characteristics. It could be that persons of different characteristics shift in the same direction for different reasons, yet that seems inadequate to account for the drastic shifts affecting all types of persons in some elections. Whatever the explanations may be, it seems clear that the search has to extend beyond the tendency of nonpolitical groups to enforce their norms on their members.

Comment

A major burden of the argument has been that the isolation of the electorate from the total governing process and its subjection to microscopic analysis tends to make electoral study a nonpolitical endeavor. That isolation tends, perhaps not of necessity but because of the blinders on perception associated with the method, to divorce the subjects of microscopic examination from their place in the larger political situation. Hence, all the studies of so-called "political behavior" do not add impressively to our comprehension of the awesome process by which the community or nation makes decisions at the ballot box.

It has been suggested that a fruitful avenue of development might be to seek to bridge the gap between microanalysis and macroanalysis, to the improvement of both. Much further refinement of our knowledge of the place of social characteristics in electoral decision, for example, would probably quickly follow once the setting of political alternatives and the matrix of objective conditions within which these determinants operate were brought more specifically into the field of observation. It seems apparent that social characteristics move into and out of the zone of political relevance, that they "explain" the actions of some people and not those of others, and that insofar as social characteristics determine political preference they encounter considerable friction.

Some of the difficulties of theory and analysis will be solved in due course, doubtless in a serendipitous manner, as the number of studies multiplies. New types of election situations will be analyzed; provisional generalizations will be modified to account for new situations; and the process will be repeated. By the observation of a greater variety of types of situations it may be possible to tie the study of electoral behavior more directly to the workings of the state. Such a linkage might enable us to talk with a bit more information about the conditions under which an electorate can most effectively perform its decision-making role in the governing process. What are the consequences, for example, of the subjection of differing proportions of the vote to determination by specified social characteristics? Of the existence of a greater or lesser proportion of the elec-

torate loyal to party? Of the intensification of particular types of group loyalties? Of the decay of others? Of the introduction of particular types of issues into the electoral arena? Of integration or atomization of the structure of leadership? Of variations in the range of electoral indifference and in the intensity of electoral involvement?

Another point that recurs is a note of doubt about the doctrine that social characteristics determine political preference. There can be no doubt that there is at times a high degree of association between readily identifiable social characteristics and political preference. At the extreme position it might be argued that political preference is a hitchhiker on social characteristics. Yet there seems to be always a very considerable part of the electorate for which no readily isolable social characteristic "explains" political preference. The query may be raised whether a rather serious void does not exist in the theory. Is there some sort of political order or system of loyalties more or less independent of the identifications of citizens and electors with these nonpolitical groups to which we have an index in their social characteristics? The identification and analysis of the political role of the voter may present considerable difficulty in research design, yet if there is no political community, if citizens, or many of them, have no political role more or less autonomous from their other roles, a good many centuries of political speculation, both hortatory and otherwise, has been beside the point. Some of the considerable variance unaccounted for by social determination might be removed by attempts to analyze the nature of the individual's identification with the community and the nation, the character of his identification with political party, his perception of the political world, his general orientation toward complexes of policy questions, his conception of his role as a voter and as a citizen. There may well be, for a part of the electorate at least, roles, identifications, and preferences of a purely political nature with quite as much reality as his "social characteristics." Perhaps some common denominator ties together the archetype Republican and the Republican unskilled laborer who always turns up in the survey.

In research the answers one gets depend in part on the kinds of questions he asks. If one inquires about social characteristics and political preference, he finds out about social characteristics and political preference. If one puts other sorts of questions into the research mill, he might well bring out other and more complex characteristics of the process of electoral decision. It might well turn out that the emerging picture would be one of an electorate, or at least of a great many electors, now struggling with great questions, now whipped into a frenzy or into fear by the demagogue, now voting against its own imputed short-term interest, now acting without check or restraint, now weighing as best it may the welfare of the community, all more or less in accord with classical democratic theory.

PART FOUR

POLITICAL PARTIES AS ELECTORAL ORGANIZATIONS

In its quest for votes a political party necessarily must choose an electoral strategy. Its choice of a candidate is a key aspect of its strategy; the identity and appeal of the candidate in turn affect the kind of strategy the party can use in the general election. Only a few states provide that parties will select their candidates in conventions; in those that do not, parties sometimes go to great lengths to avoid contests in the primary. Party leaders have assumed that a strenuous primary campaign weakens the party's chances in the general election. Andrew Hacker finds little evidence to support that assumption —candidates appear to do about as well whether they had won a "divisive" or an easy primary. Similarly, scholars and politicians have made a number of assumptions regarding political strategy in presidential elections. Philip E. Converse, *et al.*, examine a number of them in light of the 1964 election. They find: (a) there was no conservative "stay-at-home" vote when "liberal" Republicans ran; (b) the apparent distribution of opinion within the Republican Party was part of the general American political continuum; (c) there were significant differences between party activists and nonactivists. All these illustrate the centripetal nature of the United States party system.

Does knowledge of the results of presidential election voting in eastern states affect the outcome in states whose polls close hours later—will the returns from New York influence voting in California or Hawaii? Harold Mendelsohn finds no differences in voting changes among those voters who had an opportunity to know the voting results in the eastern states when compared with those who had not.

To the individual voter the electoral process does not look quite the same as it does to the state organization. To Talcott Parsons, the electoral process is a social system in which his input—his vote—is correlated with an output—action he wants government to take. The two-party system simply simplifies his choice.

Political parties and political campaigns require a great deal of money. Herbert E. Alexander discusses some problems of party financing, applying them to the 1964 election. Considering the same topic from a slightly different angle, Alexander Heard suggests congressional legislation to prevent abuses in raising and spending money and to broaden the base of private political contributions.

Nominations

23. DOES A "DIVISIVE" PRIMARY HARM A CANDIDATE'S ELECTION CHANCES?

Andrew Hacker

It is a rare election year when the nation's attention is not focussed on at least one party primary where the struggle for the nomination is highly competitive and the result a matter of doubt until the last precincts are reported. In many such cases the other party has settled on its own standard-bearer and thus sits back contentedly while the opposition wages its internecine battle before a rapt public. In recent years as varied personages as Estes Kefauver,

From Andrew Hacker, "Does a Divisive Primary Harm a Candidate's Election Chances?" *American Political Science Review*, Vol. 59, No. 1 (March, 1965), 105-10, excerpts. By permission of the American Political Science Association.

Richard Nixon, and Charles Percy found themselves engaged in a hard-fought primary campaign to secure their nomination or renomination for state office.

Nixon's subsequent defeat in the 1962 race for the California governorship, and in a lesser degree Percy's 1964 experience in Illinois, served to illustrate the conventional view that the party whose candidate is obliged to fight a hard primary campaign has an important strike against it upon entering the general election. Common sense, if nothing else, suggests that the very existence of such a primary produces or symbolizes fissures among a party's supporters. The supposition also arises that those who backed the primary loser in the Spring may be less than enthusiastic about aiding his vanquisher in the Fall. And there is reason to believe that voters who are committed to neither party may wonder whether the party that needed to go to the polls to resolve its own leadership problems is fit to hold public office.

The validity of these common sense assumptions can be tested by juxtaposing the experience of candidates in their primary and general elections. The period to be considered here runs from 1956 through to 1964, and the offices contested are those of governor and senator. . . .

"Divisive" Primaries

A "divisive" primary is here defined as one where the winning candidate received less than 65 per cent of the total votes cast.

Between 1956 and 1964 there were 220 elections for senator and governor in the thirty-one states. In ninety-four of these both candidates had token primaries; in twenty-seven both had divisive primary contests; and in ninety-nine one candidate had only token opposition while the other had a divisive fight in the primaries. Lumping together the first two categories, it may be assumed that in 121 of the 220 elections, at least so far as their primary experience was concerned, the candidates entered the general election on an equal footing. These elections can be used as a "control" group, and it will be referred to again in the concluding section. But in order to analyze the influence of a divisive primary, our attention should first be directed to the ninety-nine elections where one of the two candidates had had only a token primary.

In these ninety-nine cases, the opponent who underwent a divisive primary was the loser in the general election in sixty-eight instances and the winner in only thirty-one. Thus in almost 70 per cent of these elections it was the candidate who had to fight for his nomination who went down to a November defeat. From these figures it is easy enough to jump to the conclusion that the candidate emerging from a divisive primary stood a better than two-to-one chance of being defeated at the general election. On the other hand it appears that almost one-third of the divisive primary candidates managed to pick up the pieces and emerge victorious over an opponent who had had little or no trouble at the primary stage himself. Hence some inquiry must be made into the conditions under which some candidates with a divisive primary behind them went on to subsequent victory while others suffered defeat. . . .

The Office

Senatorial and gubernatorial elections differ in just about as many respects as they are similar. It is well understood, for example, that an incumbent senator stands a far better chance of re-election than does an incumbent governor. The senator can make his public reputation on national and international issues; most of his enemies on these have no vote in his state. The American governorship is a highly visible and vulnerable office locally, and the man who occupies it is often the scapegoat for all manner of parochial political grievances when he is so temerarious as to request a renewed vote of confidence. . . .

Looking at their previous primary experience it develops that a gubernatorial candidate who fought a divi-

Table 4-1

OFFICE AND ELECTION OUTCOME

Fate of "divisive" candidate	Senator (N=49)	Gover- nor (N=50)	Total (N=99)
	per cent	per cent	per cent
Lost	73	64	69
Won	27	36	31
	—	—	—
	100	100	100

sive primary stood a better chance of winning the general election than a senatorial candidate with a similar fight behind him. In absolute numbers this means that eighteen candidates won the governorship even after a hard-fought primary whereas only thirteen senatorial candidates survived to victory. What is noteworthy, and this will be amplified later on, is that no less than eight of the winning governors were challengers facing incumbents, while this was the case with only three of the senatorial aspirants. In other words the experience of a divisive primary behind a gubernatorial candidate can be compensated for, at least in part, by the fact that his opponent is an incumbent governor who, despite his own token primary, stands a good chance of being defeated just because he is governor.

The State

A variety of schemes and systems have been used to classify states by party, each with its own criteria and merits. To classify the thirty-one states here being studied as either "Democratic" or "Republican" it was simply asked how many of the statewide elec-

tions between 1956 and 1964 were won by each party's candidate in each state. If a majority of these elections were won, say, by Republicans then the state was listed as "Republican." This was the case with eleven states, and the "Democratic" label was assigned to sixteen others. Four states were, for present purposes, put to one side since both parties there won an equal number of statewide contests.

Using this classification the candidates may be categorized as running in "friendly" or "hostile" territory. Any Democrat campaigning in Utah, for example, obviously has an uphill road to travel, no matter what kind of primary experience he had; and the same is true for any Republican aspirant in Washington or Nevada. Of the ninety-nine elections being examined, ten took place in the four states where the parties struck an even balance, leaving eighty-nine to be analyzed here.

What is most striking in Table 4–2 is that only eleven percentage points separate the electoral outcomes of candidates running in friendly as opposed to hostile states. It is not surprising that three-quarters of the candidates who had survived divisive primaries then went down to defeat in a general election in unfriendly territory—the surprise here is rather that as many as 25 per cent of such candidates won at all. However, sixty-one of the eighty-nine candidates were running in states already sympathetic to their party and this presumed advantage did not prevent almost two-thirds of them from being defeated anyway. Apparently, then, the advantage of running in a friendly state is not sufficient to compensate for having undergone a divisive primary. It should be noted, further, that of these candidates who lost in friendly territory about equal propor-

tions were aspirants for the governorship and a seat in the Senate.

The key difference between those
who won and those who lost in friendly

Table 4-2
STATUS OF STATE AND
ELECTION OUTCOME

Fate of "divisive" candidate	"Friendly" (N=61)	"Hos- tile" (N=28)	Total (N=89)
	per cent	per cent	per cent
Lost	64	75	67
Won	36	25	33
	—	—	—
	100	100	100

states lies in whether or not the candidate was an incumbent. . . . Thus the
losers, whether they ran in friendly
or in hostile states, were chiefly challengers who were running against
incumbents. This condition of incumbency, or its lack, will be examined
next. It only remains to remark that
primary contests are twice as apt to
occur in a party situated in friendly
territory. Only on twenty-eight occasions out of the eighty-nine did the
underdog party, already at a disadvantage in terms of popular appeal,
have a divisive primary.

Incumbency

It is a rule of thumb that in elections
where a challenger faces an incumbent
the latter begins the race with an
advantage. Thus if the survivor of a
divisive primary is subsequently defeated the reason may have less to do
with his primary experience than with
the status of the opponent he faced at
the general election. An incumbent
was involved in seventy-five contests.
. . . Most of these candidates were
challengers and most of them went

down to defeat. Indeed only eleven of
these aspirants, faced with the double
disadvantage of a divisive primary and
of running against an incumbent,
managed to win at all. In contrast,
most of the fifteen incumbents who had
had divisive primaries won. It has
already been noted that being or not
being an incumbent has more to do
with a candidate's electoral chances
than the friendliness or hostility of the
state in which he is running. By the
same token there may be some value in
inquiring whether the office involved
makes any difference in the security
apparently offered by incumbency. . . .

[O]f the six incumbents who lost
five were sitting governors and only
one was a senator. At the same time, of
the eleven double-disadvantaged challengers who won, only three were
senators and eight were aspirants for a
governorship. This of course goes far
toward underlining the volatile character of the office of governor: if it is
relatively easy for a challenger to come
by, it is also quite easy to depart from
once he is there. . . .

The Primary

Some primaries are more competitive than others; some are a veritable
free-for-all while others are well structured contests between two prominent
contenders. There were, for example,
no less than nine aspirants for the
Kansas Republican gubernatorial nomination in 1964, and the front-runner
received less than 30 per cent of the
primary vote. In contrast the Illinois
Republican gubernatorial primary ballot that year had only two names
and the winner, Charles Percy, secured
more than 60 per cent of the votes.

Hence it might be thought that
candidates who gain their nomination

by securing a majority of the primary vote would fare better at the general election than their counterparts who won the candidacy with only a plurality. (None of the thirty-one states except Idaho had a run-off primary.) This, however, was not the case. Of the candidates who won their nominations with a majority vote in the primary, 71 per cent went on to lose in the general election; whereas of those who secured only a plurality in the primary, 68 per cent lost their general election. The difference, only three percentage points, is insignificant and it suggests that there are equal disadvantages in either leading a large field by a small margin (which shows that no one has a commanding popularity) or in running ahead of one or more competitors by a relatively larger margin (which, if the margin is less than 65 per cent, shows a polarized opposition).

Rather more interesting is the influence of the extent of voter turn-out in the primary on subsequent election results. The absolute number of people turning out to vote is not a very meaningful measure due to the differential standards of Presidential and mid-term years. Moreover local or national personalities and issues can be the cause of high primary participation; once in the booth, voters will usually go ahead and cast a ballot in any senatorial or gubernatorial contests that are in progress at the same time, even though these alone might not have brought them out. What can be evaluated, however, is the relation between the number of voters participating in a party's primary and the number who vote for that party's candidate in the general election. Thus the November vote may be used as a norm against which to measure the size of the primary turn-out in the preceding spring.

Voting in the general election, to be sure, varies markedly as between Presidential and other years. However, of the ninety-nine elections being examined here, half were in each category: forty-five took place in 1956, 1960, and 1964, while forty-four were in the intervening years.

Turn-out at a primary was classed as "high" if the total number of primary voters—regardless of which contender they voted for in the primary—was over 50 per cent of the primary winner's subsequent election showing. . . . The figures in Table 4–3 reveal that candidates who survived divisive primaries where the turn-out was high

Table 4-3
PRIMARY TURN-OUT AND ELECTION OUTCOME

Fate of " divisive " candidate	"Low" Turn- Out (N=35)	"High" Turn- Out (N=64)	Total (N=99)
	per cent	per cent	per cent
Lost	74	66	69
Won	26	34	31
	—	—	—
	100	100	100

actually went on to do better in the general election than those who won in primaries having low participation. Over a third of those in the high turn-out primaries fared well, compared with just about a quarter of those who emerged from primaries with low turn-outs. This may seem curious, as a higher turn-out might suggest a greater degree of interest and therefore the potentiality of greater intra-party tensions.

As a matter of arithmetic, a high primary turn-out of, say, 70 per cent may simply denote that the party's candidate did very poorly at the general election. If the 70 per cent stands for

70,000 primary voters in relation to 100,000 general election voters—while the opposition party was getting, say, 200,000 votes at that election—then a highly participative primary is not very impressive. But the point is that 34 per cent of the high primary candidates did in fact win, so the high turn-outs in their primaries are to be measured against what were majorities at the general election. At all events it appears that a high primary turn-out, despite the divisive character of that balloting, is a better augury for a candidate than one that is sparsely attended. For despite the struggle taking place in the primary a high turn-out seems to indicate wide interest in the party's fortunes and thus some likelihood that this interest will be translated into support of the primary winner.

Finally it should be noted that turn-outs are higher in gubernatorial than in senatorial primaries. The average participation in contests for Senate nominations was 55.1 per cent whereas when the candidacy for a governorship was at stake the primary turn-outs averaged 64.0 per cent. Even when we allow for the years in which these races took place—for a slightly higher proportion of the Senate elections were in Presidential years—the contest for the governorship still aroused more public interest in the primaries. Indeed the difference of nine percentage points just noted remained steady in both Presidential and off-years. This is more evidence of the governor's higher visibility, and it shows that he is a figure of interest at the primary stage no less than at the general election.

A Controlled Conclusion

Does a divisive primary place a candidate at a disadvantage as against an opponent who had smooth sailing in

Table 4-4
TYPES OF ELECTIONS AND OUTCOMES

	Elections With One Candidate Having a "Divisive Primary"	Elections With Both Candidates on Equal Terms
	per cent	per cent
A. *Office Contested*	(N=99)	(N=121)
Governor	51	48
Senator	49	52
	100	100
B. *Status of State*	(N=89)	(N=104)
Winner in "Friendly" State	69	68
Winner in "Hostile" State	31	32
	100	100
C. *Status of Candidate*	(N=75)	(N=78)
Winner the incumbent	77	72
Winner the challenger	23	28
	100	100

securing his nomination? The record as thus far reported would seem to suggest that a prior experience of a hard-fought primary is a handicap. For in the ninety-nine elections examined, sixty-eight were lost by the candidate with a divisive primary behind him. The tabulations, to be sure, showed that gubernatorial candidates, candidates running in friendly states, candidates who won their nominations in primaries with high turn-outs, and—most particularly —candidates who were incumbents, were all more apt to win. The winners, however, constituted only 31 per cent of the group being studied whereas, *ceteris paribus*, they would have constituted about 50 per cent.

It is therefore in order to compare these ninety-nine elections with a parallel set of such contests where "other things" were, as near as may be, equal.

These are the 121 elections where both candidates were at an equal advantage, at least so far as their experience in the primary was concerned. In this group, either both candidates had undergone a divisive primary or both had had token primaries. Table 4–4 compares the status of the winners in the two groups of elections. . . .

Accordingly, it appears that a divisive primary, in and of itself, bears little relation to a candidate's prospects at the general election. The sorts of candidates who win and lose are much the same in contests where one or neither or both of the contenders have first undergone a divisive primary. Every election inexorably produces one winner and one loser. The conditions associated with victory and defeat are chiefly the traditional ones of incumbency and the party-orientation of the state in which the election is held. This study has sought to throw some light on which candidates who have had divisive primaries are more likely to win or to lose. But its chief conclusion is that their prospects would have been much the same even if they had had no difficulties at all in securing their nominations.

[*Editor's note: The 1964 Blatt-Musmanno contest for the Democratic nomination for United State Senator from Pennsylvania provides a sidelight on Prof. Hacker's article. While Judge Musmanno was the organization candidate, Miss Blatt had been Secretary of the State Committee for years and was supported by parts of the state organization. The bitterness engendered by the primary fight was not permitted to fade; the Philadelphia Democratic organization challenged the outcome in the courts in proceedings which lasted throughout the summer and into the fall. The incumbent Republican Senator, Hugh Scott, was able to use the Democratic charges and evidence against his opponent during his campaign. Furthermore, elements of the Democratic organization, especially in Philadelphia, "cut" Miss Blatt on election day. While President Johnson carried Pennsylvania by 1,457,000 votes, Miss Blatt lost by 71,000.*]

Campaigns

24. ELECTORAL MYTH AND REALITY : THE 1964 ELECTION

Philip E. Converse, Aage R. Clausen, and Warren E. Miller

Certainly no one questioned the importance of ideological differences in the factional dispute that split the Republican Party along liberal-conservative lines with an enduring bitterness unmatched in decades. Indeed, these three prime elements of the 1964 election—faction, ideology, and the contest for votes—became intertwined after the manner of a classic script. That is, the "outer" ideological wing of a party captures its nomination, leaving a

From Philip E. Converse, Aage R. Clausen, and Warren E. Miller, "Electoral Myth and Reality: The 1964 Election," *American Political Science Review*, LIX, 2 (June, 1965), 321-35, excerpts. By permission of the American Political Science Association.

vacuum toward the center of gravity of national opinion. This vacuum is gleefully filled by the opposing party without any loss of votes from its own side of the spectrum. The outcome, logically and inexorably, is a landslide at the polls.

With a script so clearly written in advance, the outsider would naturally ask why any party controlled by rational strategists should choose a course likely to lead to such massive repudiation in its name. The answers to this question in the 1964 case are not particularly obscure, although they can be made at numerous levels. One answer, of course, is that Republican Party strategists were themselves in deep disagreement as to just what script was relevant: many recognized the classic script and predicted the eventual outcome, with all of its attendant losses for other Republican candidates, in deadly accuracy.

For the factional dispute within Republican ranks involved not only an ideological clash, but also major differences in the perception of that political reality which becomes important in winning votes and elections. The Goldwater faction was told by its Republican adversaries, as the conservative wing had been told for years, that a Goldwater could not conceivably defeat a Democratic President, and would instead greatly damage the party ticket at all levels. The Goldwater group countered that a victory for their man was entirely plausible despite the danger signals of the spring polls and the normal difficulties of challenging an incumbent. It is not clear how sincere or wide-spread this confidence was: some statements sounded as though the Goldwater candidacy had little chance of winning but would at least provide a forum for the conservative philosophy, along with control of the Republican Party. But even in their more pessimistic moments, the Goldwater people would argue that while victory might be difficult, they certainly saw no reason to believe that Goldwater would do worse than any other Republican challenger, or encounter the electoral disaster the liberals were predicting.

Similarly, at the San Francisco nominating convention, his opponents vehemently charged that Goldwater was a "minority candidate," even among Republicans in this country. In another direct clash of perceptions, Senator Goldwater is said to have remarked to a group of Midwestern delegates, "What the minority [the convention liberals] can't get through their heads is that this is a true representation of the Republican Party." ...

The Myth of the Stay-At-Home Republicans

... At an ideological level, the conservative wing coined the epithet "me-tooism" to ridicule the liberals for their refusal to reject Democratic innovations of the New and Fair Deal eras root and branch. The liberals, it was charged, were slowly selling out the fundamental principles on which earlier days of G.O.P. ascendancy had been based.

This accusation of ideological "flabbiness" was not, however, compelling of itself without some further comment on the problem of winning votes. As a consequence, a theory became widely current among conservative Republicans that G.O.P. difficulties in maintaining much contact with the White House were in fact directly tied to the "me-tooist" flavor of its presidential candidates. Republicans running for that office tended to lose not because there was any lack of potential Republican votes (as the superficial observer might have thought), but because many of the "real" Republicans were sufficiently offended by "me-tooism" that they simply didn't bother to vote at all. Nominate a true Republican rather than a Tweedledee, the theory went, and enough of these stay-at-homes would return to the polls to put him into the White House.

As such theories go, this contention was remarkably verifiable. That is, the critic need not argue that few Republicans were disappointed by the nominees of their party, for disappointment in itself is irrelevant for argument. The question is simply whether or not Republicans, however disappointed, did continue to turn out and vote even for "me-tooist" candidates through this period—a matter much easier to ascertain. Nor is there any point in arguing that there were *never* any stray Republicans who in the last analysis vented their frustrations by refusing to go to the polls. Undoubtedly there were. But the theory hinges less on the question as to whether such people existed, than on the contention that they existed in significant numbers: not merely several hundred or several thousand or even a few hundred thousand, but in the millions needed to overcome the persistent Democratic majorities.

Such a pool of potential voters would be large enough to be discriminated reliably in most sample surveys. And we know of no reputable sample surveys at any time in this period that gave any shred of reason to believe that this significant pool of stay-at-home Republicans existed. Indeed, such findings as were relevant pointed massively in the opposite direction. From 1944 on, for example, one can contrast turn-out rates between Democrats and Republicans of comparable strengths of identification. And over election after election featuring "me-tooist" Republican nominees, one finds that turn-out rates are consistently higher —and often much higher—on the Republican side. Indeed, each time we isolate that polar minority who not only have an intense commitment to the Republican Party, but whose commitment is of a highly sensitive ideological sort, turn-out typically reaches proportions staggering for the American system: 96 per cent, 98 per cent—levels almost implausible in view of registration difficulties, travel, sickness, and other accidents which can keep the most devoted American from the polls upon occasion. More impressive still, we find that in 1952 those Republicans who

reported during the campaign that they would have preferred the "conservative" Taft over the "liberal" Eisenhower—exactly those Republicans to whom the theory refers—actually turned out at much *higher* rates to vote for Eisenhower in the November election (94 per cent) than did the set of Republicans who indicated satisfaction with Eisenhower's nomination (84 per cent).

These brief observations do not begin to exhaust the evidence, none of which lends any support whatever to the theory of a silent pool of frustrated conservative Republicans. . . .

The Minority Candidate of A Minority Party

The charge of the liberal wing of the G.O.P. that Goldwater not only was unattractive to Democrats and Independents but was not even the majority preference of Republicans was a particularly severe allegation in view of the constraints under which the Republican Party has been obliged to operate in recent years. It has been the consensus of observers for quite some time that the Republican Party is a minority party in the affections of the American public. Our relevant data collections at frequent intervals since 1952 have left little question in our minds both as to the minority status of the Republicans, and as to the stability of that status during this epoch. For most of this time, our estimates would suggest that in terms of underlying loyalties, the Democrats could expect to receive, all other things equal, something in the neighborhood of 54 per cent of the national popular vote; and if any change has been occurring in this figure in the past 15 years, it is that this Democratic majority is slowly increasing. In practical terms, this means that a Democratic candidate need not have much attraction for grass-roots Republicans: he can win easily if he can but carry the votes of a reasonable share of independents, and has general appeal for Democrats. A Republican candidate, on the other hand, can only win at the national level by drawing nearly monolithic support from Republicans, attracting the votes of a lion's share of independents, and inducing unusual defection among the less committed Democratic identifiers as well. The latter was the Eisenhower formula, and one which Nixon had nearly succeeded in following in 1960. More generally, the liberal wing of the Republican Party had sought candidates with this kind of broad appeal throughout this period. In this light, the question of Goldwater's popularity was serious: for if a minority party nominates a figure enjoying only minority support within his own party, it is an obvious invitation to disaster. . . .

Table 4–5 speaks for itself as to Goldwater's attractiveness as a candidate. Clearly Goldwater's problem was not that he was still too little known: he received mentions from a wider proportion of the electorate than any of his competitors. But for much of the electorate he was an object of antagonism even in January, 1964. And among grass-roots Republicans, where his strength was concentrated, he remained fourth in a field of six. . . .

No evidence from polls of the period, moreover, suggests that Goldwater's popularity showed any sudden increase, even among Republicans, in the short interval between the final primary and the San Francisco convention. In interviewing our sample of the national electorate in September and October, we asked respondents to recall their reactions to the decisions of the Repub-

Table 4-5
PREFERENCES FOR THE REPUBLICAN PRESIDENTIAL NOMINATION AMONG SELECTED SEGMENTS OF THE ELECTORATE, JANUARY, 1964

	Per cent mentions[a]	Score across total electorate[b]	Score within "Minimal Majority": all Independents and Republicans[b]	Score among all Republicans[b]
	per cent			
Nixon	42	+25	+32	+37
Lodge	10	+11	+13	+13
Romney	11	+ 9	+11	+10
Rockefeller	49	+19	+10	+ 1
Scranton	11	+ 7	+ 6	+ 5
Goldwater	54	− 8	− 5	+ 9

a The percentage entered represents the proportion of individuals in the total sample mentioning the Republican leader indicated, either as one of two best or one of two very bad candidates.

b Each mention of a leader as the "best" candidate received a score of + 2. Each mention as second best received a score of + 1. The first-mentioned "bad" candidate received a score of − 2. Any negative second mentions were scored − 1. The entries in the table represent the net balance of positive or negative scores for the leader, expressed as a proportion of the maximum possible positive score an individual would have received had he been awarded all of the "best" choices given by the indicated segment of the electorate.

lican convention, including the identity of the candidates they had preferred at the time the convention began, as well as their gratification, indifference or disappointment at the outcome. While these responses suffer the inevitable frailties of any retrospective accounts that go back over an evolving situation, the social and political lines of support and antagonism for the various major contestants in July as reported during the campaign bear so close a resemblance to the lines of support visible in the January, 1964 data, as to make it unlikely that they are badly distorted by selective recollection, *post hoc* rationalization, and the like. . . .

In sum, then, it is hard to turn up any bit of evidence to challenge the conclusion that Goldwater was, in rather startling degree, a minority candidate within a minority party. If his camp actually believed that the San Francisco delegates represented a true cross-section of grass-roots Republican sentiment, then they had grossly misunderstood the situation. There was, however, at least one extenuating circumstance: the support among Republican citizens for other candidates than Goldwater was split badly among the four or five other leading candidates. Thus while any of several pairs of other candidates had grass-roots party support at convention time which would have outnumbered the Goldwater faction quite readily, the fact remains that the 20 per cent Goldwater support represented a plurality for any single candidate.

However this may be, disappointment at the convention outcome in 1964 had radically different consequences in November than the comparable disappointments among Republicans in 1952. As we have seen above, the former Taft supporters in that year turned out at the polls in near-perfect proportions and cast a very faithful Republican vote for Eisenhower. In 1964, however, the widespread defections among Republicans necessary to account for the Johnson landslide tended to follow rather closely the lines of lingering discontent with the nomination.

These recollections of San Francisco varied according to the different camps in which rank-and-file Republicans

had located themselves at the time. So, for example, about three Lodge supporters in four reported they were unhappy with the Goldwater nomination; for Rockefeller supporters, the figure was closer to two in three. Slightly over half of the Nixon supporters, however, indicated that they thought Goldwater was "nearly as good" as their man, Nixon. With minor departures, similar patterns marked the ultimate defections to Johnson among these varying Republicans. Since Nixon supporters were, like Goldwater's, more frequently "strong" Republicans than the adherents of some of the camps, lower defection rates here were only to be expected. However, defections to Johnson among Republicans who had preferred Nixon at convention time remained about double what could be expected from past norms for Republicans of this particular mixture of strengths of identification. Over three times as many Republicans for Lodge and Scranton defected to Johnson as parallel "normal" expectations would suggest, and—perhaps surprisingly—defections among Republicans who expressed no pre-convention favorite at all were in this range as well. Most extreme were the Rockefeller and Romney supporters, with defection rates at the polls exceeding expectation by a factor of greater than four.

These differences across the several non-Goldwater camps are intriguing, in part because they appear related to reactions of the various G.O.P. leaders to the Goldwater candidacy. That is, of the set of major Republicans under discussion, Nixon took greatest pains to maintain relations with the Goldwater group before the convention, and undertook to help unify the party behind him after the nomination. Therefore it seems fitting that dismay at the nomination was least in his camp, and defections relatively limited. Neither Rockefeller nor Romney made any major show of reconciliation after the nomination, and subsequently went to some lengths to dissociate themselves from the Goldwater aspects of the Republican campaign.

Yet if it were true that nothing more than a "follow-the-leader" response is needed to account for these variations in defection rates among Republicans, the data would cast a somewhat differ-ent light on the question of conflicting perceptions between liberal and conservative wings of Goldwater's voting strength. For in such a case the Senator's problem would have been less one of gross overestimates of his strength, than of self-fulfilling prophecy on the part of the disgruntled liberal leaders. In other words, they first refused to support Goldwater on grounds that he could not win enough votes, and then proceeded to withhold in large quantities the votes of their "followers" to assure exactly this outcome. . . .

Nixon supporters, while unmistakably different, looked more nearly like the Goldwater people than the adherents of any of the other camps. Next in order moving away from the Goldwater position were the Scranton and Lodge followers, and the Rockefeller and Romney adherents show slightly more liberal positions still. Ideological differences, therefore, plainly existed between grass-roots supporters of the various factions, and these differences were indeed correlated with defections from a Goldwater vote. This does not exclude the possibility that the defections might have been lessened by a genuine "unity" move on the part of more liberal Republican leaders. It indicates nevertheless that the desertions were rooted not only in leader-follower behavior, but in a more per-sonal sense of ideological distance between many rank-and-file Republicans and the Goldwater faction—a distance that would have produced increased defections quite apart from examples set by the leadership.

However this may be, it was a significant feature of the election that the customary post-convention reconciliation between party factions was in the 1964 Republican case lack-lustre at best, and at many levels simply nonexistent. Many of the liberals wished to avoid the Goldwater platform. At the same time, Goldwater seemed to do less than most candidates in making it easy for the dissident brethren to return to the fold. Among several possible reasons, one may have been that in the blueprint laid out by Goldwater strategists for a November victory, the support of most of these leaders did not appear to be critical.

Campaign Strategy:
The South as Republican Target

The strategy of the Goldwater camp for a November victory was both simple and relatively selective. Goldwater felt, to begin with, that he could hold on to essentially the same states that Nixon had won in 1960. This meant a clean sweep of the populous states of the Pacific Coast, most of the Mountain and Plains states, and a scattering east of the Mississippi. To reap the additional electoral votes for victory, Goldwater believed that the way lay open, under proper circumstances, for the Republican Party to make further major inroads in the once solidly Democratic South. The plan implied that Goldwater could largely afford to write off the populous industrial states of the Northeast and some, if not all, of the Midwest —a matter which greatly reduced the importance of the dissident liberal Republican bloc. And it represented a dramatic departure from any past Republican strategy in making of the South a fulcrum for victory.

Such a strategy was not only unusual but, against the long sweep of American electoral history, it might even be thought of as implausible. Yet it was no hastily devised scheme. For years Goldwater had participated in the Congressional coalition between conservative Republicans and Southern Democrats. The same drive for ideological neatness that led him to call for the reorganization of American politics into "Conservative" and "Liberal" parties impressed upon him the grotesque incongruity of a Democratic South. The South had no reason to be a Democratic bastion; by all of its affinities and traditions, it should long since have become Republican. Part of the problem lay with the national Republican Party, which, in the control of the Northeastern bloc, had failed to present national-level candidates making clear that Republicanism was the natural home of the Southern voter. This had been a frustrating fact since Goldwater's entry into national politics—a period during which political observers had frequently predicted an imminent partisan realignment of the South; but gains in the region, while very obvious, had remained rather modest. In discussions of Republican difficulty in recapturing majority status in the land, Goldwater had opined that the Party had to learn to "go hunting in the pond where the ducks are"—the South. As bitterness began to mount in that region toward the civil rights pressures of the Kennedy Administration, the time seemed more ripe

than ever for the presentation of a purely conservative Republican candidate who could appeal to the Southern ethos in a most direct way, thereby breaking the Democratic hold on the region in one dramatic and decisive stroke. . . .

After the votes were counted, what was the success of this strategy? The verdict must come in two halves. From one point of view, the strategy was a brilliant success, and it left its imprint on the geographical voting returns with greater strength than any other of what we have called "short-term forces" in the 1964 election. One crude way of separating these immediate or new effects from those better attributable to long-term standing loyalties is to create a different of kind electoral map, entering state by state or region by region the departure of a particular presidential vote in a more Republican or more Democratic direction than the normal voting of the area involved. A map so constructed for 1964, with pro-Goldwater deviations regarded as "high ground" and pro-Johnson deviations as "low," would show one primary "tilt" or gradient across the nation. The very lowest ground would appear in the northern reaches of New England, and the gradient would move upward with fair regularity all the way west to the Pacific Coast. The same gradient would appear, but much more sharply tilted still, as one moved southward to the Gulf of Mexico. In other words, Goldwater's regional emphases were indeed profoundly reflected in the vote.

As soon as one leaves the relative question of the regional and the geographic, however, the strategy was a dismal failure. For while the whole continent tilted in the expected direction, the strong Democratic tide nationally left virtually all of the country submerged under what from a Goldwater point of view was "sea level"—the 50–50 mark in popular votes. In terms of electoral votes, Goldwater was stranded on a few islands which remained above the tide on the outer Southern and South-western fringe of the continent. These islands represented stunning "firsts" or dramatic historic reversals in states like Georgia, Alabama, Mississippi, and South Carolina. But their historic interest did not bring Goldwater any closer to the presidency.

Indeed, while Goldwater scored sharp Republican gains through the "Black Belt" of the deepest South, his assault on the South as a whole produced rather pathetic results. All observers agree, for example, that the South has been drifting away from its old status as a one-party Democratic bastion for at least two decades, if not for five or more. Hence Goldwater could have hoped to profit from four years more of this drift than Nixon, and a decade more than Eisenhower. Secondly, all observers are equally agreed that not only in the Black Belt but well north into the Border States of the South, civil rights was the prime political issue, and there is no doubt where the mass white population stood on the matter. Our data from the late 1950s and the early 1960s have consistently made clear that the potential of this issue for dramatic partisan realignment in the South had been muffled because of lack of clarity in the eyes of the mass population, prior to 1964, that either of the two major national parties offered much hope to the Southern white. It was exactly this ambiguity that Goldwater set out to remove by providing a clear party differentiation on civil rights at the national level. Putting these two ingredients together, the actual 1964 election results from the South as a whole might seem astonishing. For Goldwater actually did less well in the region than either Nixon in 1960 or Eisenhower in 1952 and 1956. One has to return at least to 1948 to find a comparably poor showing for a Republican presidential canditate; and there are reasonable treatments of the 1948 Thurmond vote which would send one back to 1944 for a parallel. Given the fact that Gold-water wooed the South so straightfor-wardly, and injected the new and potent ingredient of clear party differentiation on civil rights into the 1964 picture, this retrogression of Republican popular voting strength for a presidential candidate back to levels of the 1940's may seem quite incomprehensible.

A possible explanation, although one that we can summarily reject, would be that the clear party differ-entiation on civil (or "states'") rights which Goldwater tried to communi-cate failed to come across to the mass voters. Perhaps to the dismay of the liberal wing of the Republicans, however, the communication was near-perfect. ...

The Southern vote for Goldwater becomes intelligible if we add three elements to the consideration. First, while civil rights lent an important new pro-Goldwater force to the situa-tion, various strong short-term forces which had pushed the Southern electorate in a pro-Republican direc-tion in 1952, 1956, and 1960 were no longer present. We have argued else-where that the popular vote for Eisen-hower and Nixon in the South was a very misleading index of the degree of solid Republican advance there. While our data do show the Republican Party inching forward in the affections of mass Southern voters, the pace has been slow; the South remains a preponderantly Democratic region. In 1952 and 1956, the Southern presidential vote swung far to the Republican side of normal for the region, just as it did in all other parts of the United States. In 1960, with the Eisenhower appeal gone, other regions moved back toward the Democrats as we expected. This return toward normal was almost invisible in the South, since a new and offsetting short-term force—Kennedy's Catholicism—had arisen which was peculiarly repugnant to the Southern population with its concentration (Louisiana excepted) of devout and fundamentalist Protestants. Thus if any other of the Republican aspirants had run in 1964, we might have expected a delayed return toward a much more normally Democratic vote in the South. From this point of view, the injection of a new civil rights differentiation by Goldwater did not occur in a void, but was something of a replacement for other forces which had kept the Southern vote extended in a remarkably pro-Republican direction for three consecutive presidential elections.

Once we take this into account, the Republican retrogression is less perplexing, although intuitively we would expect civil rights to have an impact on the Southern voter more potent than either Eisenhower's appeal or fear of a Catholic president. It is here that the second and third considerations enter. While Goldwater's civil rights position drew Southern whites toward the Republicans, Negroes both South and North moved monolithically toward the Democrats. Although Southern Negro voting was still limited by registration difficulties, it increased over 1960 and was almost unanimously

Democratic for the first time. If this sudden new increment of Negro votes could be removed from the Southern totals, the Goldwater vote proportion would undoubtedly appear to be a slight progression, rather than a retrogression, over the Eisenhower and Nixon votes.

Finally, it must be recognized that civil rights, while the primary issue in the South, was not the only one. Beyond civil rights, Southerners reacted negatively to the Goldwater positions much as their fellow citizens elsewhere. Many Southern white respondents said in effect: "Goldwater is right on the black man, and that is very important. But he is so wrong on everything else I can't bring myself to vote for him." From this point of view, the civil rights issue did indeed have a powerful impact in the South: without it, the 1964 Goldwater vote probably would not only have slipped to normal Republican levels, but would have veered as elsewhere to the pro-Democratic side. The more general ideological appeal to what Goldwater saw as Southern "conservatism" aside from the Negro question, did not have major impact. . . .

The Election "Post-Mortem"

Up to this point we have referred only vaguely to the many negative reactions Goldwater occasioned in all sectors of the country, which tended to dim out isolated attractions he did present. The Goldwater "image" was indeed phenomenally unfavorable. We have measured such images in the past, among other ways, by tallying the simple number of favorable and unfavorable references made by respondents to broad questions inviting them to say what they like and dislike about each of the candidates. Typically, American voters have tended on balance to speak favorably, even about candidates they were about to send down to defeat. The least favorable image we have seen—in Adlai Stevenson's second try in 1956 —involved only about 52 per cent of all responses that were favorable. Less than 35 per cent of the Goldwater references were favorable. . . .

We have sifted Johnson and Goldwater references into categories more or less purely reflecting "policy" as opposed to "personality" significance. Among the most pure policy references, Johnson's were favorable by an 80–20 margin, visibly ahead of the 69–31 balance of his total image. Mentions of Goldwater policies ran less than 30–70 favorable, thereby trailing the rest of his image slightly. In general, the farther one moves from pure policy to pure personality, Johnson's advantage declines. His "wheeler-dealer" style and the aura of conflicts-of-interest which dogged him during the campaign came through to dilute his attractiveness. Against this backdrop, Goldwater's personal "integrity" and "sincerity" drew praise. Throughout, the data suggest that Johnson was carried along to an image nearly as positive as Eisenhower's best, less by his personal characteristics than by the policies with which he was associated (many of them identified by respondents as continuations from the Kennedy Administration). For Goldwater, if anything, the reverse was true.

Aside from civil rights and a faint flutter of approval brought by Goldwater's latter-day stand against immorality, none of his major positions was attractive to voters outside the most hard-core Republican ranks. In general, the mass of public opinion has been quite unsympathetic to traditional Republican thinking in areas of social welfare and other domestic problems for several decades. A major Goldwater theme involved attacks against the increasingly heavy hand of "big government," yet this struck little in the way of a responsive chord. Most Americans in the more numerous occupational strata do not appear to feel the governmental presence (save for local civil rights situations) in any oppressive or day-to-day manner, and as a consequence simply have no reactions to the area which have any motivational significance. Among those more aware of the practices and potentials of federal government, a slight majority feels that if anything, governmental services and protections are inadequate rather than overdone. Thus for better or for worse, such contentions on Goldwater's part had little popular resonance.

Goldwater's failure to make much capital of domestic policy was not uncharacteristic of a Republican presidential candidate. What was new for a Republican, however, was his performance in the area of foreign policy. In a degree often overlooked, the 1950's were a period during which, from the point of view of many Americans inattentive to the finer lines of politics and reacting to the parties in terms of gross associations and moods, something of an uneasy equilibrium prevailed between the two major parties. Much more often than not, for these Americans the Democratic Party was the party of prosperity and good times, but also the party more likely to blunder into war. The Republican Party, conversely, was more skilled in maintaining peace, but brought with it depression and hard times.

The foreign policies proposed by Goldwater and refracted through the press and other commentators, shifted this image more dramatically than one might have thought possible (Table 4–6). Setting aside the large mass of voters who throughout the period did not see any particular

Table 4-6
PERCEPTIONS AS TO THE PARTY MOST LIKELY TO KEEP THE UNITED STATES OUT OF WAR IN THE ENSUING FOUR YEARS

	1956	1960	1964
	per cent	per cent	per cent
Democrats would handle better	7	15	38
No party difference	45	46	46
Republicans would handle better	40	29	12
Don't know, not ascertained	8	10	4
	100	100	100

differences between the parties in foreign policy capability, the balance of expectations in the area favored the Republicans by better than a 5–1 margin in 1956. This margin deteriorated somewhat in the late stage of the Eisenhower Administration, but remained at an imposing 2–1 edge. During the Goldwater campaign it reversed itself to a 3–1 margin favoring the Democrats.

Thus to the many ways of describing the public's repudiation of the Goldwater candidacy, another may be added: between a party of prosperity and peace, as against a party of depression and war, there is little room for hesitation.

Levels of Public Opinion and The Bases for Misperception

From at least one point of view, it is less interesting that Goldwater lost the 1964 election than that he thought

he had a chance to win. What most of our descriptions of the election year have had in common is a sort of chronic miscalculation of electoral reality: miscalculations of standing strength, of new strength that might be won, and of what appeals were necessary to win that new strength. Since "electoral reality" is at many points a nest of uncertainties, and since we are told that in the face of uncertainty personal needs are likely to color perceptions the more strongly, there is little surprising in the fact that Goldwater overestimated his strength and drawing power. But as these misperceptions of Goldwater and his aides went grossly beyond what many observers felt were the margins of uncertainty, they deserve closer comment.

Rather than write off these perceptions as figments of imagination, let us suppose that to persist in the way many electoral misperceptions of the right wing have persisted, there must be some sustaining reality bases; and let us ask instead what such bases might be. For "public opinion" is a protean thing, and we shall discover that there are perfectly sound ways of measuring public opinion during the 1964 campaign which, instead of illustrating Johnson's towering lead in the opinion polls, would actually have shown Goldwater enjoying a slight margin. . . .

If we accept letter-writing for the moment then as a relevant indicator of public opinion, we see a rather marvelous change in the state of political affairs. In Figure 4–1 (a), instead of trailing Johnson sadly in the anonymous crowd in mid-campaign, Goldwater holds a visible lead. Moving back to the time of the San Francisco convention (b), Goldwater is no longer the candidate of a small minority among Republicans and Independents, but rather is the toast of an absolute majority, even counting "no preferences" against him. In (c), we discover that not only is a vast majority of the public interested in the problem of the growing strength of the federal government, but those upset by this growing strength outnumber their opponents by a ratio approaching 3 to 1! In Figure 4–1 (d), the displacement of "letter opinion" from public opinion is much less, in part because the item wording brought a relatively consensual response. However, it is clear that Goldwater's "hard" inclinations in foreign policy are somewhat overrepresented as well in the letter-writing public.

In some ways, Figure 4–1 (e) contains more grist than any of the others, however. First, the very form of the distributions of ideological preference differs rather dramatically. Where "public opinion" is concerned, nearly half the population falls in the "zero" category, making no effective distinction whatever between conservatives and liberals. In addition, the clustering around this zero-point is very tight: over three-quarters of the population is located within one category of the zero-point. The distribution of "letter opinion," however, is quite different. The central mode of indifference or ignorance shrinks dramatically, and voices from more extreme positions on the continuum gain in strength. Other analyses show that virtually all letter-writers rank very high on measures we have used of ideological sensitivity. Hence those who remain toward the middle of the continuum in the right half of Figure 4–1 (e) are not there through indifference or ignorance: they understand the ideological al-

ternatives and place themselves toward the middle of the road with forethought. And, as the bimodal shape of the distribution suggests, political discourse becomes most notably a dialogue between very mild liberals and ultra-conservatives.

It is to the world of letter opinion or one like it that the Goldwater campaign, in its original design, was addressed. At least until its late stages, it assumed an electorate with near-total ideological comprehension and sensitivity. The appeal to the Southern conservative tradition in any abstract vein was indeed joyfully received in the South, and created great ferment among a part of the Southern population. Except as this theme became concretized in day-to-day problems with Negroes, however, the part of the population affected was tiny, even though in the letter-writing and related senses it was so visible as to appear to be "most of the South," politically speaking.

Similarly, the distribution of the population in this world of letter opinion helped maintain persistent overestimations of strength. Empirically speaking, the center of Goldwater support lay roughly in the third bar of the figure on the conservative side. It weakened rapidly with any further steps toward the center, and was relatively solid in the outer two bars of the graph. If one looks at "letter opinion" with this zone in mind, it would appear that the base of standing Goldwater support was very substantial. Goldwater hoped to firm up the support on his side of the center sufficiently to create a majority, and in this figure it would have taken only a modest extension of influence to achieve this. In the world of public opinion relevant for mass elections, however, the dis-

FIGURE 4-1.

Public Opinion as Measured by People or Political Letters.

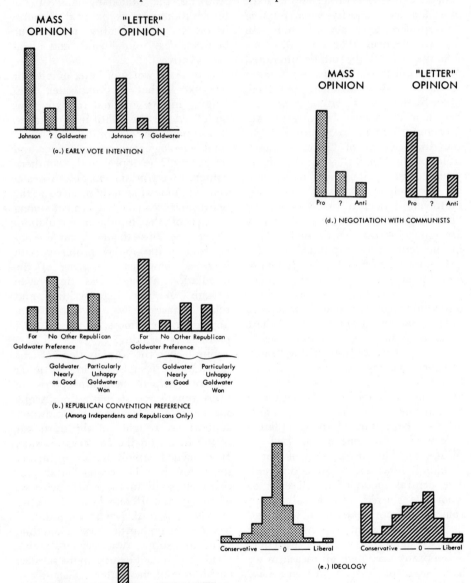

(a.) EARLY VOTE INTENTION

(d.) NEGOTIATION WITH COMMUNISTS

(b.) REPUBLICAN CONVENTION PREFERENCE
(Among Independents and Republicans Only)

(e.) IDEOLOGY

(c.) FEDERAL GOVERNMENT GETTING TOO STRONG?

tribution of actual and potential support was radically different. Rather than starting from a solid base of support on the conservative wing, the initial springboard was scarcely populated at all. To win a majority, a much deeper penetration into the center would have been required. . . .

25. BALLOTS AND BROADCASTS: EXPOSURE TO ELECTION BROADCASTS AND TERMINAL VOTING DECISIONS

Harold Mendelsohn

Introduction

The Problem, Research Objectives, and Methods

This report presents highlights from the findings of a study of influences to which a sample of California voters was exposed or could have been exposed before they cast their ballots on Election Day, November 3, 1964. Because these were last-day influences, we have adopted, for convenience, the expresssion "terminal influences." We will be concerned in this paper primarily with the effects of election returns broadcast over radio or television. . . . Allegations have been made by various writers, social observers, critics, and politicians that the broadcasting of election news from the eastern seaboard on Election Day will cause western voters variously:

1. To change their vote intentions in order to vote for the indicated winner;
2. To change their vote intentions in order to vote for the indicated loser;

3. To slacken their efforts to persuade others to vote;

4. To increase their efforts to persuade others to vote;
5. To vote though they had intended not to vote;
6. To abstain from voting though they had intended to vote.

Whether it is argued that election broadcasts create a bandwagon effect for the indicated winner, foster an underdog effect on behalf of the indicated loser, increase or inhibit persuasive efforts to "get out the vote," or alter a person's intention to vote or not to vote, one major assumption underlies the notion that voters may be influenced by election broadcasts prior to voting: exposure to election broadcasts before voting is sufficient to lead the potential voter to behave on Election Day in a manner other than the way he had intended to behave prior to the broadcasts. Essential to the investigation of the possible effects of election broadcasts on the terminal voting decision process is an examination of 1) whether, and if so 2) in what manner, exposure to such broadcasts does indeed serve to neutralize prior commitments so that the actual

Presented at the 1965 Annual Conference American Association for Public Opinion Research, May 14, 1965.

votes do not reflect previous voting plans and intentions, to crystallize undecided votes in one or the other direction, and to mobilize or depress efforts to vote oneself or to "get out the vote." . . .

Time of Voting and Salience of Broadcasts

Before introducting the variable of exposure to network election coverage, let us consider the times of day at which our sample voted. Together with other data, this will provide us with some indication of the salience which our voters attribute to such broadcasts in the terminal decision-making process.

We divided our sample of 1.689 voters into three groups, as follows:

1. *Early Voters* who voted prior to 2:30 p.m. PST, *before* it was possible to attend election broadcasts. There were 1,044 persons (62 per cent of the sample) in this group.

2. *Mid-Afternoon Voters* who voted between 2:30 p.m. and 4:30 p.m. PST, when it was possible for them to have heard only local, or cursory, inconclusive returns before actually voting. There were 170 such voters (10 per cent of our sample).*

3. *Late Voters* who voted after 4:30 p.m. PST, and thus could have seen or heard sizable tallies and predictions. There were 475 voters (28 per cent of our sample) in this group.

---

*According to the *The New York Times*, the National Broadcasting Company presented the first conditional forecast at 3:48 p.m. PST, stating that President Johnson would probably receive between 60 per cent and 70 per cent of the popular vote. At 6:04 p.m. PST the Columbia Broadcasting System announced the first substantive "Vote Profile Analysis" forecast of a conclusive Johnson victory.

The important point to note here, of course, is that 62 per cent of our sample of voters literally could not have been influenced by exposure to broadcast returns because they voted well before the broadcasts began. An additional 10 per cent, who voted between 2:30 p.m. and 4:30 p.m., could have been exposed before voting only to relatively cursory election reports.

The 475 Late Voters could, of course, have been exposed to broadcasts including predictions and large tallies. But only 196, or 41 per cent of them, actually were so exposed *prior to voting*. More than half of this group who could have seen or heard broadcasts simply didn't. The ones who did represent only 12 per cent of our *total* sample. Put another way, only 12 per cent of our sample made themselves available to broadcasts which could have induced vote switching resulting in direct bandwagon or underdog effects. Of course, these data do not indicate whether any significant number of intended late voters heard or saw broadcasts and as a result decided not to vote at all, thus creating indirect bandwagon or underdog effects. This question will be discussed a little later in this paper. . . .

The Late Voter

It will be recalled that 475 persons in the sample voted after 4:30 p.m. PST on Election Day at a time when the opportunity to hear or see pre-voting election broadcasts was maximal. For this reason the Late Voters constitute one of the key groups in an investigation of possible broadcast-attributed bandwagon or underdog effects.

Analysis reveals that the Late Voter voted almost precisely as did the rest of our sample for whom adequate

Table 4-7
VOTING INTENTION AND ACTUAL VOTES BY TIME OF DAY

	Early Voters Number	Per cent	Mid-Afternoon Voters Number	Per cent	Late Voters Number	Per cent
Voted as Intended	743	97	110	95	321	96
Switched from Nov. 2 Intention	5	1	4	3	5	2
Intended to vote for either Goldwater or Johnson, refused to disclose actual vote	15	2	2	2	7	2
	763	100	116	100	333	100

information is available. In the case of both President Johnson and Senator Goldwater, 96 per cent of the late voters who were *not* exposed to election broadcasts before voting cast their ballots according to their previous intention, and 97 per cent of those who *were* exposed did likewise.

Only five Late Voters defected from their announced intention to the opposite camp, and only three of these were exposed to election broadcasts before voting. Of these three, Johnson gained one and Goldwater two, which in percentage terms amounted to a two per cent loss on each side. It should be noted that Johnson also lost two per cent (two) of his previously announced adherents who were *not* exposed. This miniscule number of switchers defies interpretation. There is no reliable evidence that switching is more common among those who witnessed election broadcasts (three, or two per cent) than among those who did not (two, or one per cent). If the switching among the exposed was due to the broadcasts, its two-directional movement cancelled out any net effects. In any case, to talk of bandwagon or underdog effects on the basis of such figures is obviously ridiculous, except to note that clearly neither effect occurred in any magnitude.

The absence of any clear effect even holds for Late Voters who recalled hearing radio or television tallies or predictions, clearly forecasting a Johnson victory. The data are so similar to those which have just been presented that it seems purposeless to report them here. In brief, each candidate lost one voter who had heard actual vote tallies, and each lost one who had heard forecasts or predictions.

It is interesting to consider why Late Voter adherents of both Goldwater and Johnson continued to vote for their candidates even after they had heard that Johnson's victory was assured. It would seem that exposure to the election broadcasts wherein information regarding a Johnson victory was presented either had no effect upon such voters or served simply to reinforce pre-election commitments in both camps. In particular, the fact that such information does not seem to have upset prior commitments to Senator Goldwater suggests the operation of a curious psychological dynamic. Since well over nine out of every ten late Goldwater Intenders carried out their commitments to the obvious loser, it is evident that knowledge of his impending loss was not assimilated psychologically as a meaningful reason for abandoning him. Our qualitative data, obtained from twenty depth interviews, indicate that witnessing broadcast predictions or actual announcements of an election winner may strengthen the determination among certain of the indicated loser's partisans to support him nevertheless—come what may.

Here, then, is a psychological consideration arguing against the operation of broadcast-generated conversions. This consideration supplements our quantitative data, which show that in California in 1964, explicit prior commitment was capable of immunizing nearly all late voting partisans—regardless of whether they were on the winner's or loser's side—to broadcast information about the developing resolution of the national election.

By way of review, we have now examined not only the large sample, but also three key groups: the Switchers, the Last-Day Deciders, and the Late Voters. In none of these did we find any evidence of either a bandwagon or underdog effect of any magnitude.

We have seen occasional miniscule differences, involving one or two voters, which may or may not represent the manifestation of a tiny underdog or bandwagon effect. This exploratory study was not designed to possess the statistical power to interpret such miniscule variations. Reliance on variations of this magnitude would require a panel study employing a gigantic sample.

Persuasion and Abstention

Let us now consider two other aspects of exposure to election broadcasts—namely the possibilities that they: 1) may have slackened or increased the efforts of partisans to get others to vote; and 2) that they may have inhibited voting itself.

Persuasion

It is impossible to discuss these data fully in the time available. Suffice it to say that the information gathered from the California voters offered no evidence of importance to sustain the hypothesis that pre-voting exposure to broadcasts served to inhibit Election Day political activity. Let me touch on two examples.

A full fifth (341) of the voters in the sample reported that as a consequence of attending Election Day broadcasts, they personally urged others to vote (simply to vote, not necessarily for one or another candidate). Conversely, only three of the 1,689 voters studied admitted that they tried to convince others *not* to vote as a result of hearing Election Day broadcasts.

Fourteen per cent of the sample (235) reported that as a result of hearing the broadcasts, they had urged others to vote for the candidate of the other's choice, and six per cent (102) reported that they had urged others to change their vote intentions.

In *all* of these persuasion activities, Goldwater voters were proportionately more numerous than Johnson voters. Within the design of this study, however, there is no way of knowing to what degree, if any, this greater activity on the part of Goldwater adherents was stimulated by the broadcast returns, and to what degree it simply reflected a more vigorous campaign than the Johnson adherents were waging.

What we can say is that as a result of the election broadcasts a considerable number of people spoke to others about voting. These would-be persuaders urged others to vote far more often than they urged them not to vote. They also urged people to stay with their chosen candidates far more often than they urged switching.

Abstention

The data obtained offer no reason to believe that exposure to election broadcasts kept eligible voters who had intended to vote for a president from actually doing so.

Of the 1,704 people who stated in Wave I that they intended to vote, fifteen, or approximately one per cent, subsequently failed to vote. Of these fifteen persons:

—Five had stated that they would vote for Senator Goldwater;
—Three had planned to vote for President Johnson;
—Four were "undecided" about whom to support;
—Three refused to disclose their preferred candidate.

It must also be remembered that of twenty persons who said they would not vote or did not know if they would vote, nine subsequently did.

To determine whether exposure to election broadcasts had led to abstention by the fifteen persons who intended to vote but did not vote, these fifteen persons were asked in Wave II, "What, if anything, happened in the past twenty-four hours or so that made you *not* vote?"

In reply not one of the fifteen mentioned exposure to election broadcasts. Only six had, in fact, been exposed, and they stated that the election returns they had heard had had no influence at all on their decisions not to vote.

The reasons for abstention given by these fifteen non-voters who had planned to vote . . . fall into five general categories:

1. Physical or psychological incapacity;
2. Preoccupation with other matters; delay in getting to the polls;
3. Ineligibility to vote;
4. Indifference regarding the outcome of the election;
5. Disenchantment with the candidates.

It should also be noted that at least five of the fifteen abstainers had little interest in national politics; three had not voted in 1960, though eligible to do so, and two others said they had voted in 1960 but could not remember for whom.

Conclusion

It is clear that among the Californians studied, exposure to election broadcasts on November 3, 1964, did not create discrepancies between prior commitments and ultimate choices. Nor did we find any evidence that election broadcasts deterred persons who planned to vote for a President from actually doing so.

By and large, well over nine out of ten voters in the study who had committed themselves to either Presidential candidate before Election Day voted accordingly, regardless of whether they heard election broadcasts prior to voting or not. Negligible switching, which occurred in both directions, could not be traced to prevoting exposure to election broadcasts.

Nor was the relatively higher proportion of votes accorded Johnson by the handful of election broadcast-exposed Last-Day Deciders really indicative of a bandwagon effect in any serious sense of the term.

The conclusion that stands out is that there is no evidence from the research to support the contention that eastern network coverage of the unfolding national voting pattern on November 3, 1964 was responsible either for a bandwagon or underdog effect among the voters studied.

Presidential Elections

26. VOTING

Talcott Parsons

... I think it is legitimate to consider the voting process by which Presidents are elected as authentically a *social system*. It is a set of processes of action and interaction which may be treated in terms of specific modes of interdependence which can be analytically separated from other influences. Furthermore, in our system, the Presidency is the focus of integration of the political system as a whole. Of course the concrete data that will be reviewed are affected by factors

From: Talcott Parsons, "Voting," *American Voting Behavior*, eds., Eugene Burdick and Arthur J. Brodbeck (New York: Free Press of Glencoe, Inc., 1959), pp., 87-93, excerpts. Reprinted with permission of the Free Press.

emanating from outside this particular system—including the other voting processes in other subsystems of the political structure. But in principle this is true of any social system that is a subsystem of a larger one, i.e., less than the total society.

To return to the substantive discussion, the main function of political organizations is the facilitation of effective action on collective levels. The two-party system may be regarded as a mechanism that makes possible a certain balance between effectiveness through relative centralization of power, and mobilization of support from different sources in such a way that there is genuine contingency—the supporter is offered a real alternative. Dictatorships naturally are different; their concern is to avoid losing support lest the opposition become dangerous, and there is a strong tendency to use coercive measures in coping with actual or feared opposition. But the two-party system as has often been pointed out, makes it possible for the holders of power to be changed without upsetting the system. Naturally this depends on definite institutional conditions, notably the acceptance of electoral results by the losing side without impairment of basic loyalties, and the restraint of winners from using their power to suppress opposition. It depends overwhelmingly on the firm institutionalization of such "rules of the game."

All this I take for granted. The point of present interest is that the two-party system, as distinguished from a many party system or one of an indefinite number of shifting factions, has certain implications for the structure of support in its relation to leadership. This way of structuring the situation forces a high level of *generalization* of support on the one side, of responsibility on the other. This is particularly true in a society with a social structure as diverse as the American, in economic, class, occupational, regional, ethnic, religious, and other terms. Support, focusing on the Presidency, must be given to one of two party candidates: the alternative is a "protest" vote for a minority-party candidate, or nonparticipation altogether. Many votes are motivated by more particularized considerations having to do with specific interest groups, etc. But *whatever* their motiva-

tion on lower levels of generality, all the votes have to be *counted* as support for the party candidate and his administration, and on some level for the power of the party in Congress. This point brings out in one context very sharply the difference in significance between the problem of the *motivation* of the individual voter, and of the *consequences* of his vote for the political system.

A word may now be said about the line of differentiation between the two major parties. This line is less one of ideological "principle," and more pragmatic, than is the case in European politics. A broad line can, however, be discerned. I would like to characterize this distinction as that between "right" and "left" in a sense appropriate to American conditions. The focus of the American right in this sense is the organization of the free-enterprise economy. This is by no means "conservative" in a general social sense; it is in fact the main center of dynamic development in the society. But it is *politically* conservative because the economy is institutionalized on a private-enterprise basis in such a way that positive political action can readily be defined as threatening to interfere with the conditions of operation of this type of economy. Connected with the "business" interest in this sense are various other elements with a tendency to fear innovative change, notably in our recent history the rural-small town elements of a large part of the country.

The "left" on the other hand, has been the focus of those elements predisposed to favor positive action on the political level, who have been favorable to "reform" of various sorts, to control of the economy, to promotion of "welfare," and not least to "interventionism" in foreign affairs. On a broad basis this distinction adequately characterizes the *main* line of distinction between Republican and Democratic tendencies. Of course the Solid South has been a special case, and at the present time major processes of realignment seem to be going on. It is my judgment, however, that the realignments will result, not in substituting a new major axis, but in reshuffling the elements involved in the support groups about the present axis. Business will continue to be the major focus of the more conservative party.

In our system the party leader, as candidate and as President, must appeal to a variety of diverse groups and interests for the support necessary to elect. He must come up with some balance involving compromises and creative syntheses. The general meaning of the aggregate of the support he receives cannot be more than the endorsement of a broad *direction* of action for the polity. More specific interests can be endorsed only as they fit the general direction; they always stand in competition with others. There can never be any "absolute" commitment to particular interest—economic, ideological, religious, or other—because this would lead to burning of bridges connecting with other elements necessary for an effective support-coalition, elements that would not "go along" with such a commitment. For example, in pre-Nazi Germany the Center party was definitely committed to represent the interests of the Catholic Church. It had considerable range for maneuver, but was prevented by this commitment from becoming a genuine national party in a religiously divided society. Similarly, an American Catholic party under our system could not conceivably become one of the two general parties.

Let us return to the parallel with the input-output boundary of the economy. What I have called the generalization of support is parallel to the "mobility of labor," the readiness to cooperate in the production of goods and services that do not themselves satisfy one's own personal needs or those of one's family. The individual worker must in an important sense relinquish control of the product of his labor. Similarly the political supporter, in our case the voter, must not claim direct control of the consequences of his vote; if he did, political support would be reduced to a "barter" basis and the political integration of a complex social system would become inpossible. What then does the voter receive which is analogous to the money income of the worker? He receives the expectation that many *kinds* of measures that he approves will be implemented if his candidate wins, but without exact specification of particular policies. The directional orientation of a party candidate is a kind of political "currency" which, if he wins, will improve the probabilities that a *kind* of direct political action, over which the voter does not have direct control but which *in general* he favors, will be taken. In taking money wages for his work and relinquishing control of the product, the worker evidences "faith" that by spending the money he will be able to get something he values as much or more than the product of his work. Similarly the voter evidences faith that, if his candidate wins, the "way things will go" will be relatively in accord with his wishes, but he cannot directly control the specific decisions that will be taken.

This generalized support is, I have noted, a fundamental ingredient of power. It, along with the other ingredients, is used to help produce concrete decisions, binding on the collectivity, which are analogous to specific goods. The support is necessary because without it the decisions could not be responsible, i.e., could not be made to "stick." But if the support is to be of any "use," its consequences must eventuate in concrete decisions that deal effectively with the real problems of the collectivity. The quality and quantity of these decisions and of their consequences in turn justify the acts of faith involved in giving political support. But it is the *aggregate value* of such decisions, not their particularities, which is the basis of the community's political "income" from its commitments of support.

Perhaps it is worth while to carry the parallel between the economic and the political one step further. The keynote of economic organization has rightly been said to be the division of labor. Through it the individual "producer" makes a sacrifice and receives a gain. The sacrifice is essentially one of self-contained independence; he can no longer meet his own needs from his own efforts and resources. The gain is one of "efficiency." He gets more by pooling competence and resources with others than if each operated alone on a self-sufficient basis. In the political case the axis is the differentiation of responsibility. The giver of support makes a sacrifice—loss of immediate control

of collective decisions that affect his own interest; he "delegates" this control to the holders of power. But he also receives a gain, which is his share in the benefits of the *effectiveness* with which collective action can be taken. If the responsibility of every voter, including the President, for collective action were exactly equal, in effect *no* collective action would be taken at all. But in exchange for this gain the voter has to take his chances that the *particular* decisions in which he is most directly interested will be forthcoming. . . .

It follows, I think, from the above analysis that there are certain further conditions necessary to the successful operation of a democratic two-party system. These conditions may be stated in the following four propositions:

1. There must be mechanisms by which the average voter can come to a "responsible decision that is meaningful to him. He must not, in too many cases, withdraw to non-voting, nor be too susceptible to appeals that would be grossly disruptive of the stability of the system. Since the intellectual problems involved in a rational solution are not practicably soluble, my thesis is that the mechanisms are typically nonrational. They involve stabilization of political attitudes *in terms of association with other members of the principal solidary groups in which the voter is involved.* In terms of party affiliation this may be called "traditionalism." The traditionalistic operation of nonrational mechanisms is a condition of the stability of the system. That they root in the solidary groupings of the society follows from the fact that support is mobilized from the integration subsystem of the society.

2. Pure traditionalism, however,

would result in a rigidity of the system which would be incompatible both with the shift of conditions under which problems of public goal-specification and attainment must be posed and with the necessity, for a two-party system, that there be realistic opportunities for each party to win in its bid for leadership through the election of a President. A certain proportion of voters must shift from time to time in party allegiance, if a flexible balance is to be maintained. The data show that this takes place mainly through what has been called above the "indifference" reaction—the voting change of people under cross-pressures who show relatively low levels of interest in the campaign and have difficulty in making their decisions. This finding will be interpreted as in line with the importance of solidary groupings as foci of political loyalties. It is a mechanism which on the whole minimizes the dangers of instability, inherent in political shifting. But it is primarily a condition of effective attainment of *new* goals as they become salient.

3. Under two-party conditions a limited polarization of the electorate is essential—a choice between only two realistic alternatives is offered. This means that the inherently divisive potentialities of political power-struggle are increased. There must clearly be mechanisms which prevent this polarization from producing a progressively deepening rift in the electorate. In the subsequent discussion, it will be shown that there are two main foci of such mechanisms. First, there is the supra-party consensus referred to above, which institutionalizes the duality of party organization, prescribing rules of political fair play. Second, there is the involvement of voting with the solidary groups in the society in such a way that, though there is a correlation, there is no *exact* correspondence between political polarization and other bases of differentiation. Hence, pushing the implications of political difference too far activates the solidarities between adherents of the two parties which exist on other, nonpolitical, bases so that members of the political majority come to defend those who share other of their interests but differ from them politically. These mechanisms serve the effective integration of the system.

4. American society is not static, but dynamically evolving. The political system must be adapted to this fact and must include mechanisms of adjustment to social change. Under American conditions the main autonomous processes of social change do not operate through government, but largely through the development of the economy. The business element, which is the core of this process of change, tends to be politically conservative because positive use of the powers of government has been felt, since the early thirties, to imply interference with the process. The left, on the other hand, is relatively residual, tending to gather together those elements in the society on whom the problems and difficulties arising from the dynamic process impinge, and who see in governmental action an opportunity to remedy their situations. There must be mechanisms in the political system which mediate the balance between right and left without running the risk that either set of elements will be oppressively overwhelmed by the other. They are mechanisms that are essential to adapt the system to *changes in the structure of the society*. . . .

Political Finance

27. FINANCING THE 1964 ELECTION

Herbert E. Alexander

Introduction

The financing of the presidential campaigns of 1964 contrasted sharply with the voting patterns: the victory of Lyndon Baines Johnson was built on a narrow financial base but a broad electoral base; the Barry Goldwater candidacy had a broad

From Herbert E. Alexander, *Financing The 1964 Election*, (Princeton, N. J.: Citizens' Research Foundation, 1966), pp. 7-17, 121-25, excerpts.

financial but a narrow electoral base. The contrast was put in more vivid terms by John M. Bailey, Chairman of the Democratic National Committee (DNC) when he said the Republicans ". . . wound up with a vote deficit and a financial surplus," while the Democrats had a vote surplus and a financial deficit.

Political costs continued to escalate in 1964 at both the national and other levels. To take one outstanding example: There were dramatic increases in television *and* radio costs from 1960 to 1964. Broadcast costs are easily measurable, thanks to the surveys of political broadcasting conducted by the Federal Communications Commission. Other political costs by category of expenditure are not so easily ascertained. Since 1956, there has been no Congressional investigation of campaign funds, as there had been in earlier presidential election years, to gather data and summarize findings. Accordingly, the only systematic attempt to obtain data from official fund reports was made privately, and only for national-level committees which filed reports as legally required with the Clerk of the House of Representatives. These reports furnish basic data on costs of the presidential campaigns. But they fail to reflect expenses incurred at the state and local levels on behalf of the national party tickets—and they lack much more, as will be seen. Hence a statement of national costs from these sources alone gives an incomplete and possibly distorted view. With this caveat in mind, 1964 financial patterns can be described and conclusions drawn.

The 107 committees operating at the national level reported spending $34.8 million in 1964, as shown in Table 4–8. This is more than twice the $17.2 million spent in 1956—only eight years before—and represents a 39 per cent increase from the $25 million spent in 1960.

Major party national campaign costs in 1964, disrgarding spending by labor and miscellaneous committees, were $29.2 million or 41 cents per voter for the two parties combined for the 70,642,496 votes cast in the presidential election. This compares with roughly 32 cents per vote cast in the 1960 presidential election. A study comparing costs in presidential years 1912–1928 showed that though direct expenditures of the two national committees rose from $2.9 million in 1912 to $7.2 million in 1928, the cost per presidential vote cast remained between 19 and 20 cents—at the same time that the price level rose 40 per cent. Costs in 1952 were 18 cents per presidential vote cast, and in 1956, 19 cents.

Table 4-8
SUMMARY OF POLITICAL SPENDING AT THE NATIONAL LEVEL, 1964
(in thousands of dollars)

Committees[a]	Gross Reported Disbursements[b]	Known Debt	Total Campaign Costs	Transfers to Candidates & Committees	Direct Expenditures[c]
18 Republican	$17,187	$ —	$17,187	$1,163	$16,026
32 Democratic	10,973	1,000	11,973	3,216	8,757
31 Labor	3,665	—	3,665	2,940	725
26 Miscellaneous	1,963	—	1,963	889	1,074
107 Total	$33,788	$1,000	$34,788	$8,208	$26,582

[a]The number of national-level committees increased from 70 in 1960, but the same criteria were used in identifying them.

[b]Data derived from reports filed with the Clerk of the United States House of Representatives.

[c]Details on all categories of expenditures were not obtained from the campaign fund reports. Hence direct expenditures were determined by subtracting from total campaign costs all transfers of funds out. Though the totals in this column may be subject to error, enough evidence is available to indicate that the totals represent fair approximations.

The fairest index reflecting fully the dollar value of presidential campaign activities at the national level in other years has been direct expenditures plus deficits. Table 4–8 has been constructed to combine direct spending and deficits in the "Direct Expenditures" column; accordingly, in dollar terms, the comparison is between Republican spending of $16 million and Democratic spending of $8.8 million plus labor spending of $726,000. Using this index for 1964, as shown in Table 4–9, Republican expenditures at the national level exceeded those

of Democratic transfers—an unusually large amount. Labor also transferred more than twice as much money as in 1960, while decreasing direct spending somewhat. Since the Republicans transferred only $1.2 million—about the same level as in 1960—their direct national spending for campaign activities in 1964 is proportionally greater.

Despite the seeming Republican advantage in spending, the Democrats have never in recent times conducted such a well-financed national campaign as in 1964. Spurred by the President's

Table 4-9
RATIOS OF NATIONAL-LEVEL DIRECT SPENDING PLUS DEFICITS, 1956, 1960 AND 1964 (in percentages)

	1956	1960	1964
Republican Committees:	59	49	63
Democratic Committees:	37	47	34
Labor Committees:	4	4	3
Total on behalf of Democrats:	41	51	37
	100	100	100

of the Democrats and labor combined, reinstating an advantage the Republicans held in 1952 and 1956, but not in 1960 when Democratic-labor spending totaled more than Republican spending. For 1964 the ratio of Republican advantage over the combination is 63:37, which is a higher ratio than in 1956. Given their greater gross receipts and expenditures in 1964, naturally the ratio favors the Republicans, while *significant Democratic spending by groups and Congressional candidates utilizing national-level Democratic money is not included in this computation.* In effect, the index eliminates duplication for both parties by subtracting from total costs their expenditures which go to other committees or candidates for spending. This requires subtracting $3.2 million

Club, which throughout the country had about 4,000 members (including some disenchanted Republicans) contributing at least $1,000 each, they raised more money than ever before, reporting receipts totaling over $11 million, or $4 million more than in 1960. At the same time, Democratic spokesmen stated there was a deficit of $1 million or more at the national level, a figure that compares favorably with the larger $3.8 million deficit incurred in 1960. But this stated deficit must be seen in the context of Democratic spending patterns.

Democratic spending reported under federal law was only about 10 per cent more than reported Democratic expenditures on behalf of John F. Kennedy in 1960. But in 1964 there was considerable additional money available at the state level for use at the direction of the national campaign. Using an old practice of secreting funds in certain states, where they need not be reported in Washington under common interpretations of federal law, Democratic leaders will not divulge how much more was raised or spent—though they admit to some. And state reporting requirements are so varied and loose that the complete picture cannot be known.

The Democratic reports filed in Washington failed to reflect fully certain Democratic funds raised through $1000-a-year-memberships in the President's Clubs of New York and California, and the national share of a series of $100-a-plate dinners addressed by President Johnson in several states. The President's Clubs of New York and California did not file reports in Washington though sizeable portions of their funds were transferred to committees which did report as required by federal law. But national shares of funds in California, Michigan, Minnesota and perhaps other states were left in the states to be expended in those states for the presidential campaign at the command of the DNC. Thus they were never reported in Washington and are not included in our totals.

Democrats raised enough at the national level be able to contribute $2.3 million to state groups for registration drives and other pupposes, to give twice as much to candidates for Congress as in 1960, and to divert certain state funds to congressional campaigns and to registration drives that would benefit the party at all levels. Clearly, the Democrats were not concerned about incurring some debts that probably could be paid off

quickly later, if they could thereby extend the predicted presidential landslide to other offices.

The financial base of Democratic support was comprised mostly of a wide geographic and occupational diversity of large contributors. About 69 per cent of the dollar value of total individual contributions came in sums of $500 and over. Compared with the Republican financial base, which included unparalleled numbers of small contributors, the Democratic base was narrow indeed and can be considered broad only in relation to times past when there were only a handful of very large contributors who financed campaigns; and only in relation to the Republican's smaller number of large contributors.

The Republicans at the national level were able to maintain financial support from many of their usual sources, but they broadened their appeal dramatically through massive direct mail drives and effective television appeals for funds. Neither method had heretofore been very successful in national fund raising, but in 1964 the Republicans received an unprecedented 32 per cent of total income from direct mail and almost 14 per cent from TV appeals. The Republicans raised $18.5 million, over $7 million more than was raised in 1960. Most of these additional funds came from an unusual outpouring of about 650,000 contributions of less than $100, raised by direct mail and TV appeals. Only 28 per cent of the dollar value of Republican individual contributions came in sums of $500 and over.

Compared with 1952, the Goldwater financial support was notable. In that earlier year, the Eisenhower candidacy drew wide electoral support in the general election, yet the RNC claimed only 17,500 contributors and the national Citizens for Eisenhower-Nixon claimed about 20,000 contributors.

It was remarkable indeed that so much was raised from so many in view of the widespread belief that Senator Goldwater would not win the election—a condition that usually hinders fund-raising appeals. In addition, some normally Republican sources of funds were closed to Goldwater, and some actually aided the Johnson campaign. The Republicans were the "out" party, usually considered a disadvantage, especially in seeking contributions from special interests. And the campaigns for the presidential nomination were expensive, draining off more than $10 million. The roughly $15 million spent for the Republican presidential election campaign (excluding the national-level congressional costs) and the $10 million spent in seeking the Republican nomination total over $25 million in out-of-pocket expenses alone for an office that few thought Republicans could win.

To some extent, the large number of contributors to national-level Republican committees must have reflected the political polarization within the Republican Party in 1964. Goldwater supporters tended to give directly to Washington to avoid normal Republican state finance channels whereby funds would be shared with moderate candidates for other offices. Nor were moderate Republicans anxious to have portions of their funds shared with the national campaign, so individual moderate candidates and not state party committees benefited from their contributions.

The Democrats in 1964 probably spent about half as much as the Republican presidential pre- and post-

nomination costs. But given their control of the Presidency, the advantages of controlling government forums that attract media attention, their favorable public opinion poll results, and the fact that the only pre-nomination costs were spent in three states in contesting the presidential candidacy of Governor Wallace of Alabama, they did not need to spend more. Given these advantages, they could have operated a non-deficit campaign, but they chose instead to increase spending for registration and Congressional campaigns and thus ended with some debts. Yet with their national dominance in the Executive and Legislative branches, and other favorable factors, they attracted funds far in excess of the Truman, Stevenson, and Kennedy candidacies.

Along with dollar increases went increases in the number of national-level committees—from 70 in 1960 to 107 in 1964—reporting as required by federal law with the Clerk of the House of Representatives. In 1960 the Democrats had operated with only 13 national-level committees, though some of these subsumed various professional, ethnic, and other divisions; in 1964, each division was organized as a separate committee, and 32 different committees operated. The number of Republican committees increased by only one from 1960 to 1964. The number of reporting labor committees increased by 10, perhaps because of widespread labor opposition to Senator Goldwater. The number of miscellaneous committees increased from 19 to 26, probably a reflection of the growth of independent committees organized to give assistance in dollars and services to candidates for Congress.

Total national level campaign costs for 1960, over $34,800,000 when combined for all groups, nevertheless exclude amounts spent by or on behalf of Senatorial and Congressional candidates at state and local levels. The totals do not include expenditures made in connection with nomination campaigns either in primary or convention nor those made for state, county, municipal or other offices. Expenditures made by state and local party or non-party committees on behalf of the presidential tickets are not reflected, nor are cost equivalents of the free broadcast time provided to the presidential and vice-presidential candidates.

Responsible estimates of some of these exclusions have been obtained—often graciously given on a voluntary basis—and will be reported as we proceed. If all exclusions were known, it would be possible to determine total political costs at all levels for 1964. In the absence of sufficient supporting data at other than the national level, it is impossible to make a firm estimate. Indications of increased costs—some demonstrated in this paper unless offset by decreased spending elsewhere—presumably sent 1964 totals to about $200 million at all levels, as shown in the following estimates:

$200 million in 1964
$175 million in 1960
$155 million in 1956
$140 million in 1952

Spending for all election contests undoubtedly made 1964 the most expensive election year in history But the national estimate seems realistic bearing in mind such factors as the following:

the increase in the national-level totals;

increases in political broadcasting, literature and mailing costs to be noted later;

the Republican presidential pre-nomination costs which far exceeded the Democratic ones in 1960;

the notable Goldwater grass-roots activity in certain regions;

special efforts in many states to gain control of state legislatures in order to control reapportionment;

the general price rise of about 5 per cent since 1960.

Off-setting reductions in expenditures are hard to find.

Comparison and Conclusions

During the period of Democratic ascendancy from 1932 to 1952, the Republicans consistently spent more money in presidential campaigns than did the Democrats. During the Eisenhower campaigns, the pattern of greater Republican spending continued. In 1960, the Democrats went deeply into debt to spend as much as the Republicans spent, though the G.O.P. also incurred a small deficit. In 1964, the Republicans surged ahead again while reporting a surplus; the Democrats went into debt though they raised more than ever before.

Most striking is the long-term growth in Democratic financial support from low points in the presidential elections in 1948 and 1956. From 1960 to 1964 the dollar value of contributions received in sums of $500 increased more than two-and-one-half times, while total receipts from all sources more than doubled from 1956 to 1964. Significant are the changing bases of Democratic financial support, accentuated in 1964 by the easy willingness of certain businessmen and nominal Republicans to join the President's Club or otherwise contribute to Democratic committees. Of equal importance is the decrease in emphasis on small contributors, on the Democratic National Committee Sustaining Fund and on the national Dollars for Democrats program. One wonders whether the unusual degree of secrecy regarding aspects of Democratic financing is related to the improved ability of the party in power to attract increased funds. With 1964 funds available and not needed for a winning presidential campaign, the trends to increasing national-level payments for both local registration drives and campaigns for Congress surely are meaningful in terms of the nationalization of American politics; now some state and local Democraic organizations and candidates are obligated to the national party for money and assistance, and the potential effects on party responsibility will be most interesting to observe.

Republican experience in 1964 was marked by the breakdown of the unified fund-raising structure developed in recent decades. On one hand there was little change from 1960 to 1964 in the number of large contributors, though in geographic terms there were indications in 1964 of increased financial support in the South and Southwest, and decreases in parts of the North and East. On the other hand, an unparalleled number of small contributors responded to massive mail drives and TV appeals. The response was partly due to the special appeal of Senator Goldwater to enthusiasts, but also the large investment of time, energy and money which the Republicans since 1962 have consciously devoted to building a national Sustaining Fund. Its development beyond 1964 will surely test Republican ingenuity and signal its financial health. In 1964, the Republicans raised so much money they ended with a surplus, giving the Goldwater command its one clear and unqualified achievement—financial soundness in the 1964 campaign. In a sense, the Republicans were caught up by their own petard—they felt they could not indulge in deficit party financing while complaining of deficit governmental financing.

The comparative financial picture of the two major parties since 1960 is instructive. In that year the Democrats and Republicans at the national level each spent roughly $10 million. Neither was able to raise that much through either regular party or citizens committee channels, so both had deficits; the Democratic deficit was $3,820,000, and the Republican debt was $700,000. In 1961, the Republicans raised slightly over $2 million, and in 1962, about $3.2 million; in both years, they spent about as much as they raised.

Democratic figures are not comparable for 1961 or 1962 because of the special effort to retire the large 1960 debt. Amounts raised and spent to reduce the deficit and for annual operating expenses are so intermingled as to be indistinguishable. As old debts are paid, certain unpaid current operating expenses become new debt. By mid-1962, the 1960 Democratic debt of $3.8 million had been rolled over and retired. At the end of 1962, a new debt of $400,000 had been incurred, but in early 1963 that was erased.

In the period of over three years, from January 1, 1960 to March 1, 1963, the Democrats and the Republicans at the national level each raised roughly $15 million. From Inauguration Day, 1961, to March 1, 1963, the Democrats raised almost twice as much as the Republicans, permitting retirement of a larger debt while carrying on roughly equivalent operations. Similarly, while incumbents in 1960, the Republicans raised over $3 million more at the national level for the presidential election than the Democrats did. The sudden Democratic affluence following the 1960 election contrasts greatly with the decade of the 1950's, when the Democrats were constantly in debt, and the Republicans, controlling the Administration, consistently outraised and outspent them.

In 1963, the Republicans moved ahead, according to reports filed in Washington; the Republicans raised $3.3 million and spent $3.7 million, while the Democrats reported raising $2.2 million and spending $2.5 million. The Republican advantage resulted in significant part from the immediate and subsequent success of the RNC Sustaining Fund, without which Republican totals would not have been so substantial. However not included in Democratic national-level totals are funds raised in 1962–63 by the President's Club of New York, which did not file in Washington but did in Albany. For these two years, the N.Y. group raised about $1.1 million and transferred about $500,000 to the DNC in Washington, which included the transfers in its reports. The remainder of the New York President's Club funds were diverted to help pay off N.Y. mayorality (1961) and gubernatorial (1962) deficits, and the DNC returned small amounts to the N.Y. Democratic State Committee. However, had the N.Y. President's Club totals been added to the national Democratic totals, the national Republican lead in income would have been erased.

Experience in recent years, particularly in 1964, has served to put in perspective some widely held notions about aspects of political finance:

That large amounts in small sums could not be raised by direct mail. This was proved untenable by the immediate and

developing success of the RNC Sustaining Fund from 1962 on.

That large amounts in small sums could not be raised by televised appeals for funds. The Goldwater campaign experienced extraordinary success with TV appeals.

That money is difficult to raise for a candidate with unfavorable poll results. The Goldwater campaign experienced unsuccessful polls and successful fund raising.

That the "out" party is disadvantaged in fund raising. Yet Republicans at the national level reported raising more than the Democrats reported.

That the drain of funds into expensive pre-nomination contests cuts into fund-raising ability in the general election campaign. The Republicans in 1964 spent much more than did the Democrats in 1960 in the prenomination period, yet raised more than could be effectively spent in the general election in 1964 and ended with a surplus.

That Democrats attract fewer large contributors and fewer big businessmen than Republicans. There was a dramatic switch in traditional party appeals in 1964.

While some of these propositions may have resulted mainly from a unique Goldwater phenomenon, or in the context of the Johnson-Goldwater confrontation, the fact that they happened at all confirms that given certain conditions, such results are possible; as more is learned about the conditions under which such exceptions occur, presumably even exceptions to a rule could prove susceptible to imitation.

This chapter began with a contrast and can end with one as well. Whereas the Republicans during the presidential election complained of unhappy press relations and unfairness in the media, they were frank with the media about their finances. On the other hand, the Democrats, enjoying generally good press relations, were less than candid about their financial operations —and the press did not generally press hard for answers to questions about national party and campaign finances.

The Issues of Public Policy

In 1961, President Kennedy established a nine-member bipartisan Commission on Campaign Costs, which reported to him in April 1962. With some exceptions, the Commission advocated the course of expanding the financial base of support for the parties. President Kennedy twice proposed the legislative recommendations of the Commission to the Congress, but President Johnson failed to follow through in any known respect for two years, until he stated in his 1966 State of the Union address the following:

As the process of election becomes more complex and costly, we must make it possible for those without personal wealth to enter public life without being obligated to a few large contributors. Therefore, I will submit legislation to revise the present unrealistic restrictions on contributions; to prohibit the endless proliferation of committees, bringing local and State committees under the act; to attach strong teeth and severe penalties to the requirement of full disclosure of contributions, and to broaden the participation of the people, through added tax incentives, to stimulate small contributions to the party and to the candidate of their choice.

The specific recommendations have not been made public at this writing. President Johnson also proposed a four-year term for U. S. Representatives, a recommendation with significant implications for political finance.

The President's Commission proposed a system of limited tax credits and deductions for political contributions, designed to give an incentive to the potential donor. A tax deduction in another form passed the Senate, but not the House. Some businessmen have favored the proposals; however, organized labor has opposed aspects of the plan.

During 1964, in lieu of debates between the presidential candidates, the Democrats appeared willing to pay for whatever broadcast time they desired, so long as this forced the Republicans to do likewise. Accordingly, Section 315 of the Federal Communications Act was not suspended for the presidential and vice-presidential campaigns; political broadcast costs for these offices were substantially higher than in 1960; and no steps were taken to alleviate financial pressures on the parties resulting from the high costs.

The President's Commission recommended a limited subsidy to provide federal funds for the President-elect and Vice-President-elect to cover certain expenses from Election Day until Inauguration Day. This proposal limits financial pressures upon the parties at a time following a campaign when there may already be deficits to pay off, by permitting the Federal government to assume limited costs for the new President in selecting and assembling his administration and in preparing to assume responsibility for government. Legislation to effect this change passed both Houses of Congress and was signed into law by President Johnson. Funds were thus available for paying salaries of the Vice-President-elect's staff during the transition period, permitting Senator Humphrey to resign his Senate seat to allow the early appointment of his successor.

The Commission failed to endorse the concept popular in other democracies that registration and voting drives are proper or exclusive functions of government. Yet if financial pressures on parties and candidates are to be relieved in America by other than tax incentives, the next step will likely be in the direction of government assistance in bipartisan registration and voting drives. Labor unions and corporations have undertaken registration programs which, though selective, help to reduce direct party costs.

President Kennedy had agreed to call a nonpartisan White House Conference on Campaign Finance to focus attention on the problems of financing presidential campaigns, and to signalize certain new approaches that would be made during 1964. Following President Kennedy's assassination, higher governmental policies and priorities occupied President Johnson, valuable time was lost, and no programs were carried on.

Before President Johnson spoke out on the subject, the Republican Coordinating Committee, in a task force paper entitled, "Toward Fair Elections in America," urged reasonable deduction from Federal income tax for contributions to parties and their nominees, the removal of limitations on committee, Senatorial and Congressional candidate expenditures, and changes in the regulation of political broadcasting. The Republican leadership's answer to the 1966 State of the Union address again endorsed legislative attention to political finance. Thus, a year after 1964 experience, expressions of concern at the highest levels of leadership in both parties were made.

As the Great Society embarks upon a new program to regulate political finance, its direction, duration, effects and effectiveness remain to be seen, as does the response of the Congress.

28. A NEW APPROACH TO CAMPAIGN FINANCES

Alexander Heard

President Kennedy has again asked Congress for legislation to encourage private donations to Presidential election campaigns. He wants to give political contributors a break with their income taxes by making gifts of up to $500 a year to a Presidential campaign deductible from taxable income. (This concession is like that a

From Alexander Heard, "A New Approach to Campaign Finances, "New York Times Magazine (Oct. 6, 1963), pp. 50, 94, 96, 98, excerpts. Copyright 1963 by The New York Times Company. Reprinted by permission.

taxpayer now gets when he gives to educational and religious causes.) As an alternative, contributors, like those who do not itemize their deductions, would be permitted to take a tax credit—to be subtracted from the amount of tax owed—of one-half the total of their political gifts up to a maximum credit of $10 per year.

Although attitudes on Capitol Hill are discouraging, the favorable editorial comment these proposals evoked and Mr. Kennedy's persistence with them are proof that the problem they were designed to meet is still very much alive.

Raising campaign funds has been a pressing difficulty for generations, but it assumed new dimensions in 1960 when expenditures reported by Democratic and Republican national campaign groups rose 55 per cent over the total recorded four years before. Most telling of all, nearly one-fourth of the $20,000,000 spent in 1960 had to be put on the cuff. At the end of the campaign, the Republicans owed $700,000 and the Democrats an unprecedented $3,820,000.

The burden of raising such sums weighs heavily on the political parties and the methods they use are often open to serious objections. They must rely, for example, on individuals and organizations with special political interests for large amounts of cash.

In setting up a bipartisan Presidential Commission on Campaign Costs in 1961 to recommend appropriate legislation, President Kennedy again expressed his conviction that "it is not healthy for the democratic process— or for the ethical standards in our government—to keep our national candidates in [the present] condition of dependence." Other recent Presidential candidates agree with him. Messrs. Dewey, Eisenhower, Nixon, Stevenson and Truman all endorsed the commission's unanimous 12-point report, which recommended, among other measures, tax incentives of the kind Mr. Kennedy has been trying to get Congress to introduce. (Both national party chairmen gave the report their blessing, too.) . . .

Congressional inaction stems from three different roots. In the first place, most politicians and special-interest groups operating successfully under existing conditions naturally

do not want to see them changed. Under the President's plan, campaign contributions, to be eligible for income-tax deduction or credit, would have to be made to the national committee of a party whose Presidential candidate appeared on the ballot in at least ten states or to a state committee designated by the national committee, one in each state. Many state and local politicians see this as a threat to the present distribution of political power.

They usually oppose moves that might substantially increase the fund-raising ability of national committees at their own expense, and they usually oppose steps that might centralize control over party funds—and the tax-incentive proposals threaten to do both.

The lack of positive support from labor leaders for the President's tax incentives may be because contributions to labor political committees would not be eligible for such benefits. And if the money-raising capacity of the parties is improved, the relative importance of labor's help to Democratic candidates could diminish, thus weakening its tactical position. Some leaders of "volunteer" political committees which campaign alongside the regular party committees are also wary of any move that might strengthen the official organization—as are those unhappy about the leadership given their party.

Opponents of the tax-*deduction* proposal, moreover, point out that well-to-do contributors would gain an unfair advantage. Given the graduated income tax, the net cost of a political gift would go down as the taxpayer's income went up. In contrast, people with smaller incomes taking a standard tax deduction would gain no benefit at all. On the other hand, opponents of a tax *credit* fear it would give a powerful weapon to leaders of mass organizations who could use it to dragoon their followers into making campaign contributions. In both cases, the threat of shift in political power is sensed.

The second cause of Congressional inaction lies in the fact that even when the necessity for reform is conceded—or cannot be ignored—the *means* of reform prove to be controversial.

For example, some persons who share the President's desire to reform campaign finance are opposed to cluttering up the tax structure further with yet another deduction and credit. Moreover, there are still those who believe that taxation should be used solely to raise revenue and not as a tool of social or political reform. Others object because they view the diversion of taxes as contributing to a greater federal deficit, or because they are opposed in principle to an indirect federal subsidy of campaign expenditures.

The third main source of legislative inertia is the lack of political sex appeal in the whole issue of campaign finance. There is little popular concern and few political activists in or out of Congress feel that their interests are sufficiently affected to make them push for public support of reform. It is, therefore, both commendable and courageous of President Kennedy to take a determined initiative in this lonely sphere. He is the only President in recent history to concern himself seriously with the matter.

For those seeking change, the solution obviously has to be sought at two levels: First, wider public understanding and interest must be awakened, and second, the search must continue for legislative proposals that will

accomplish the desired objectives with the least opposition. . . .

Nonpartisan and bipartisan fund-raising plans take various forms. Some industrial concerns encourage their employees to give to the party of their choice by arranging automatic deduction from wages. The Internal Revenue Service, following a recommendation from the Commission on Campaign Costs, ruled last year that certain expenditures for impartial political activities of equal benefit to both parties (TV debates, for example) can be deducted as a business expense. A non-partisan foundation has been proposed that would receive tax-deductible contributions and use the money to inform the electorate about campaign issues and personalities.

Most discussed of all the proposals in recent years have been those for indirect or direct government subsidy, partly, perhaps, because ample precedent for both can be found in the states and in foreign democratic nations. The direct subsidies suggested have ranged from outright payments of cash to the parties (Presidents Theodore Roosevelt and Harry Truman) to the provision of federally financed campaign services—broadcast time, postal mailings, transportation and so on.

The objections include many of those already prompted by the idea of tax incentives—an indirect subsidy—but there are others as well. Some argue that to ease financial burdens in this fashion would lead to less popular participation in party affairs. The need to get out and scramble for funds and the general atmosphere of financial strain surrounding campaign operations contribute, it is said, to a more meaningful involvement of ordinary citizens in the parties. If adequate funds were assured from outside, party bureaucracies might develop that would be impervious to the wishes of the rank and file—rich and poor alike. In addition, opponents claim that public money would not get where it was supposed to go, and that the party in power would surely be favored.

When he sent up his tax proposals this year, the President hinted that he might be looking for an additional approach. He called attention to a "matching-incentive" plan that had been mentioned but not recommended in the report of the commission. Senators Maurine Neuberger (Democrat) and Clifford Case (Republican) subsequently embodied such a plan in a bill they introduced in Congress.

Under a matching-incentive plan, small contributions raised from the public by approved political committees would be deposited with the United States Treasury. There they would be matched by an equal amount from federal revenues and the combined total made available to the committee making the original deposit. The money would be used only to meet approved expenses, payments being made by Government checks direct to the providers of the goods or services.

Limited to small gifts of perhaps $10 per person per year, the plan would spur party fund-raising by insuring that the amount of money the parties received would still be determined by the number of voluntary contributions they succeeded in attracting. Payment by federal check would also make sure the money got where it was supposed to go. The safeguards built into Government fiscal operations —and the unusual scrutiny to which these funds would be subjected—would prevent any partisan administration of the system.

Further advantages are that Congress could limit the amount of money to be matched and control the uses to which it was put. The scheme would not restrict the parties' freedom to raise and spend other moneys, however, nor would it prevent individuals from contributing as much as they do now. And the plan could also be used to aid candidates for other offices besides President—an advantage that might increase its acceptability in Congress. . . .

PART FIVE

Party
and
Governmental Power

American students of Congressional voting behavior have unduly mini-
mized the role of party in formulating and determining public policy in the
United States. For decades they have noted a lack of party discipline, a
tendency of members of one party to vote with the majority of members of
the opposite party on almost every issue.

Recent studies, however—even before the 89th Congress—suggest that
party membership is gaining importance in Congressional decisions, both of
the House and Senate collectively and of the individual member. In his
study of committee assignments in the House, Nicholas A. Masters points
to one major factor in this development: the party leaders now dominate
the system of assignment to committees. By way of illustration, Richard F.
Fenno, Jr., notes that after the Democratic landslide in the 1958 Congressional elections six Democratic vacancies existed on the House Committee
on Education and Labor. All six were filled by naming freshmen Democrats
who had been supported for election by organized labor; they were given
preference over Southern Democrats who applied for membership on the
Committee.

This trend is borne out by the study of Donald R. Matthews on party leadership in the U.S. Senate and underlined by that of Robert E. Dowse and Trevor Smith on discipline in the House of Commons. Matthews concludes that while discipline strictly considered may be weak, party identification is strong, and that the individual Senator's party affiliation is a major influence in his voting pattern. Even though party leaders lack the power to *order* Senators to vote in a certain way, they can make life in the Senate more comfortable and rewarding for those who do. Voting in the British House of Commons always takes place under the shadow of rigid discipline, but in practice a variety of leader-follower relationships develop there as well. Dowse and Smith point out, for example, that only a minority of Members of Parliament are interested in any particular piece of legislation; the vast majority accept the leadership's position simply because such support is an integral part of the British system. Having had two opportunities to influence the form of legislation before its formal introduction, the interested minority in most cases considers them sufficient. Thus voluntarism akin to that in the United States rather than heavy-handed discipline in the form of "three-line whips" characterizes voting in the House of Commons.

From the time Lord Bryce likened American political parties to two empty bottles, the "conventional wisdom" held that differences between the two major parties were few and minor, if not actually nonexistent. In a careful study Herbert McClosky and his colleagues discover that the old impression required considerable reinterpretation. Although they find that policy differences between Republican and Democratic *followers* are comparatively small, though discernible, they find marked differences between leaders so great that Republican followers are actually nearer ideologically to the Democratic leaders than to their own! Robert McKenzie emphasizes this when he states that in 1964 there was a higher ideological content in the American presidential than in the British general election. He stresses that the British electorate was presented with a proper question—Shall Labour or the Conservatives run the Government, rather than—Shall British Government be capitalist or socialist? Comparing various aspects of British and American political practice, Malcolm Shaw suggest that while ideological differences may have declined, there are still important differences between the Labour and Conservative Parties in the power of party leaders, class attitudes, and political style.

Section

1

Party in the Legislative Process

29. COMMITTEE ASSIGNMENTS

Nicholas A. Masters

The Committees-on-Committees

In one of the more notable features of the reorganization of Congress in 1911, each party created a committee-on-committees to distribute committee assignments, on the theory, still asserted, that a party committee offers at least an opportunity for all party members to receive suitable assignments. Such a committee would go a long way toward eliminating the arbitrary judgments of the Speaker who, in the past, had used

From Nicholas A. Masters, "Committee Assignments," Robert L. Peabody and Nelson W. Polsby, eds., *New Perspectives on the House of Representatives* (Skokie, Ill.: Rand McNally & Co., 1963), pp. 35-44, excerpts. By permission of the publishers.

committee assignments as rewards and punishments, to help insure his control of pending legislation.

Though both parties use a committee for this purpose, their methods of selecting its members differ. Each committee therefore needs separate treatment, with comparisons from time to time.

Democrats

By custom the Democratic members of the House Ways and Means Committee, together with the Speaker and Majority Floor Leader (or the Minority Floor Leader when Democrats are in

215

the minority), have constituted the committee-on-committees since 1911. This arrangement is evidently an outgrowth of the former practice of selecting the chairman of Ways and Means as the Majority Floor Leader. Because the Democratic members serve in this dual capacity, and although they are formally designated by the Democratic caucus, they are in fact self-perpetuating. The Speaker and Majority Floor Leader participate extensively in the Committee's deliberations and, of course, have considerable influence on the decisions.

The method of organizing the work of the Committee-on-committees in the 86th Congress was typical. Each member of the Committee was assigned a geographical zone within which his own district lies. (See Table 5-1) All zones except two were geographically contiguous. Requests for committee assignments coming from members were handled by their respective zone committeeman. For example, Representative Aime Forand from Rhode Island was responsible for the assignment and reassignment requests of all Democratic representatives from districts within his zone, which includes, in addition to his own state, Connecticut, Maine, Massachusetts, and Vermont. As can be seen from Table 5-1, each zone representative served an average of approximately eighteen members.

Although committee deliberations are closed, the procedure followed is well known among most House members. Each zone representative, speaking in order of seniority, nominates candidates from his zone for the various committee vacancies, usually with supporting arguments. Thereupon the Committee votes on each of the vacancies, and the nominee receiving the highest number of votes is designated to fill it.

The volume of work before the Committee varies, depending chiefly on the changes resulting from the preceding election. Almost always, however, there are more applications than vacancies; in the 86th Congress one hundred twenty-four applications were made for seventy-five places to be filled. The major committees were naturally most in demand; applications exceeded vacancies for all committees except District of Columbia, House Administration, Merchant Marine and Fisheries, Post Office and Civil Service, and Science and Astronautics—all regarded as lesser committees. Applicants usually list their order of preference, taking into account not only their personal desires but also advice from other members and their own assessments of where they stand the best chance to land at least an acceptable assignment. Without encouragement from above, an applicant, however much he might prefer to be on the Appropriations Committee, say, would hardly bother (or venture) to ask for what he realizes he has virtually no chance of getting.

Much more than committee structure and manner of procedure is involved in making assignments. Animating and guiding these formal mechanisms are the norms and customs observed when assignments are sought. The pervasive seniority rule, for example, works in a manner not commonly appreciated. Members seeking assignments, and particularly freshmen, channel their requests through the "dean" or senior member of their state party delegation. In negotiations between the Committee-on-committees and the applicants he plays a crucially important role in securing assignments.

Table 5-1
**HOUSE DEMOCRATIC COMMITTEE-ON-COMMITTEES AND ZONE
ASSIGNMENTS, 86th CONGRESS**

Committee Member	Zone	Dems. in State Del.	Fresh-men	Committee Member	Zone	Dems. in State Del.	Fresh-men
Mills (Ark.)	Ark.	6	(1)	Herlong (Fla.)	Fla.	7	(0)
	Del.	1	(1)		Ga.		
	Kans.	3	(2)			10	(0)
	Okla.	5	(0)			17	(0)
		15	(4)	Ikard (Texas)	Texas	21	(1)
Forand (R.I.)	R.I.	2	(0)		N.Mex.	2	(1)
	Conn.	6	(6)			23	(2)
	Me.	2	(1)				
	Mass.	8	(1)	Frazier (Tenn.)	Tenn.	7	(0)
	Vt.	1	(1)		N.C.	11	(1)
		19	(9)			18	(1)
King (Calif.)	Calif.	16	(4)	Machrowicz	Mich.	7	(1)
	Alas.	1	(1)	(Mich.)	Ind.	8	(6)
	Ariz.	1	(0)		Ohio	9	(3)
	Nev.	1	(0)			24	(10)
	Utah	1	(1)				
		20	(6)	Metcalf (Mont.)	Mont.	2	(0)
					Colo.	3	(1)
O'Brien (Ill.)	Ill.	14	(4)		Idaho	1	(0)
	Wis.	5	(2)		Nebr.	2	(2)
		19	(6)		N.Dak.	1	(1)
					Ore.	3	(0)
					S.Dak.	1	(0)
Boggs (La.)	La.	8	(1)		Wash.	1	(0)
	Ala.	9	(0)			14	(4)
	Miss.	6	(0)				
		23	(1)	Green (Pa.)	Pa.	16	(4)
Keogh (N.Y.)	N.Y.	19	(2)		N.J.	5	(2)
		19	(2)			21	(6)
Harrison (Va.)	Va.	8	(1)	Watts (Ky.)	Ky.	7	(2)
	S.C.	6	(0)		Md.	7	(3)
		14	(1)		W.Va.	5	(2)
Karsten (Mo.)	Mo.	10	(0)			19	(7)
	Iowa	4	(3)	Total		283	(63)
	Minn.	4	(1)				
		18	(4)				

It is his special responsibility to see that his members receive adequate representation on the various committees. In performing this task, he tries to protect or maintain the delegation's place on a major committee when a vacancy occurs and the seat has previously been held by a member of the delegation; he consults with, and advises, the members of his delegation seeking assignments as to what their chances are, and which committee assignments he will support for them. The dean's decisions must be made in consideration of the needs of his state, the qualifications of his own members, and the necessity for adjusting the requests among his members to prevent duplication on committees. It falls to his lot also to discourage and dissuade members who have unrealistic designs on the major committees—Appropriations, Rules, and Ways and Means.

The importance of the deans of the state delegations may be illustrated negatively. Connecticut, for the first time since 1936, elected six freshman Democrats in 1958. Since the entire delegation was composed of freshmen, no senior member could serve as the dean and apparently there was no time or forethought to form an agreement to become part of an area delegation. So when the committee assignments were made, only one of the six, Chester Bowles, felt that he had been given as good representation as he was entitled to. Bowles got the assignment of his choice, Foreign Affairs. Frank Kowalski was assigned to Armed Services because of his extensive military experience although it was not an assignment he wanted. The remaining four were given committee places they did not prefer, namely Science and Astronautics, Education and Labor, Government Operations, and a dual appointment to the District of Columbia and Post Office and Civil Service Committees. Several dissatisfied Connecticut congressmen complained, two of them quite bitterly, that their committee positions would not help them to be re-elected—that they had received the "left over" assignments. These assignments had not been made from any desire to penalize them, but apparently because they were orphans with no dean or senior member to fight for their preferences or look after their interests.

If the Democratic Committee-on-committees is judged as a system of collective responsibility among men of equal status, then it is clear that the use of members of a permanent standing committee for this purpose has had almost the opposite effect. Each member does not carry equal weight on the committee. The status and rank of each Democratic member of Ways and Means are carried over to the Committee-on-committees. The ranking Democrat serves as chairman and the status of the other ranking members is unquestionably enhanced by the fact that they also serve as Ways and Means subcommittee chairmen when the Democrats are in the majority. These are the senior members in an institution that respects seniority.

Ways and Means members have had considerable congressional experience prior to their assignment. For the period 1913 to 1958, only five of eighty-six assignments to this Committee were given to congressmen without any seniority; and each of these five had had previous, but interrupted, congressional service. On the average, members have served at least three consecutive terms prior to being placed on the Committee, and the average is closer to five terms if computations are based simply on prior, rather than continuous, service before selection. The stability of the Committee's membership is also increased by the fact that, although a congressman may sometimes shrink from its responsibilities, only one member has ever left the Committee by his own request. What turnover there is results from death, resignation, or loss of party control, rather than from transfers or election defeat.

For a key functioning unit of the

Democratic party's legislative apparatus, so much continuity in the Committee-on-committees makes it ill-designed for flexibility and responsiveness to electoral changes and public opinion trends. Rather, it is more analogous to a firmly entrenched bureaucracy, not completely immune but well insulated, and capable of considerable resistance to any pressures placed upon it.

Republicans

The Republican Committee-on-committees is specially set up for its function and is responsible for no other. It is composed of one member from each state having Republican representation in the House; thereby, a lone Republican from any state is automatically included. Each state delegation determines its member on the Committee. This method might be thought to provide an opportunity to select a new member for each new Congress, but the normal pattern, on the contrary, is for the senior member of the delegation, usually the dean, to assume membership on the Committee and hold it as long as he desires or remains in Congress. Table 5-2 shows the membership of the Republican Committee-on-committees for the 86th Congress.

The point is sometimes argued that

Table 5-2
HOUSE REPUBLICAN COMMITTEE-ON-COMMITTEES, 86TH CONGRESS

State	Member	Votes	State	Member	Votes
Arizona	John J. Rhodes	1	New Jersey	Frank C. Osmers	9
California	James Utt	14	New York	Mrs. K. St. George	24
Colorado	J. Edgar Chenoweth	1	North Carolina	Chas. R. Jonas	1
Florida	William C. Cramer	1	North Dakota	Don L. Short	1
Idaho	Hamer Budge	1	Ohio	Clarence J. Brown	14
Illinois	Leo E. Allen	11	Oklahoma	Page Belcher	1
Indiana	E. Ross Adair	3	Oregon	Walter Norblad	1
Iowa	Charles B. Hoeven	4	Pennsylvania	Richard Simpson	14
Kansas	Edward H. Rees	3	South Dakota	E. Y. Berry	1
Kentucky	Eugene Siler	1	Tennessee	Howard H. Baker	2
Maine	Clifford G. McIntire	1	Texas	Bruce Alger	1
Massachusetts	William H. Bates	6	Utah	Henry A. Dixon	1
Michigan	Clare E. Hoffman	11	Virginia	Joel T. Broyhill	2
Minnesota	H. Carl Anderson	5	Washington	Jack Westland	6
Missouri	Thomas B. Curtis	1	West Virginia	Arch A. Moore	1
Nebraska	Phil Weaver	2	Wisconsin	John W. Byrnes	5
New Hampshire	Perkins Bass	2	Wyoming	E. Keith Thomson	1
			Total—153		

SUBCOMMITTEE APPOINTED BY MINORITY LEADER

State	Member	Votes	Seniority
California	James Utt	14	4 consecutive terms
Idaho	Hamer H. Budge	1	5 consecutive terms
Illinois	Leo E. Allen	11	14 consecutive terms
Michigan	Clare E. Hoffman	11	13 consecutive terms
New Jersey	Frank C. Osmers	9	7 non-consecutive terms
New York	Katharine St. George	24	7 consecutive terms
North Carolina	Charles Raper Jonas	1	4 consecutive terms
Ohio	Clarence J. Brown	14	11 consecutive terms
Pennsylvania	Richard M. Simpson	14	7 consecutive terms
	Total—99		

the Republicans make it possible for each state delegation to assume a greater share of the organizational responsibility than the Democratic committee assignment process allows, and consequently that the decentralized Republican method is much more responsible to electoral changes. Actual Republican practice tends to contradict this argument. For the Republicans allow each representative on the Committee-on-committees to cast as many votes as there are Republicans in his delegation. This concentrates the power over committee assignments in the hands of the senior members from the large state delegations. In the 86th Congress, members from seven states—California, Illinois, Michigan, New Jersey, New York, Ohio, and Pennsylvania—controlled 97 of the 153 committee votes.

Not to mask the realities of power, the Republican committee assignments are handled by a Subcommittee which, in the 86th Congress for example, was composed of the senior members from these seven states and two others, with one vote each, evidently added to give a voice to large geographical areas (intermountain and southern) that would otherwise have gone entirely unrepresented. Together the Subcommittee members controlled about two-thirds of the full committee's votes. None of them had served less than four terms in Congress. By custom the Subcommittee is appointed by the Minority Leader (or Speaker, as the case may be) on the authority granted by a resolution of the full Committee. The resolution leaves the membership of the Subcommittee apparently at the discretion of the party leader, but the example just given shows how far he is hemmed in by the practice of appointing the same members from the larger delegations each time a new

Congress convenes. The change in the minority leadership in the 86th Congress had no discernible effect on this part of the organizational process.

The Subcommittee receives and considers *all* applications for assignment and transfer, and the full Committee invariably accepts all of its recommendations. Subcommittee sessions are informal and each member is free to speak for or against any assignment. Information on newly elected members is obtained from the Republican Congressional Campaign Committee and the party leaders pride themselves on having extensive konwledge not only of the professional and personal backgrounds of their colleagues, but also of the constituencies they represent. Members of the full Committee who are not on the Subcommittee are entitled to participate in the determinations if they desire, but they seldom do.

Republicans from small states sometimes object that as a result of the system of proportional voting and large-state domination of the Subcommittee they have no real voice in committee assignments and are often overlooked for assignments to the better committees. Along the same line they complain that the Republican procedure allows no mechanism whereby the small state delegations can combine their voting power in the Committee-on-committees. The critics point to the Democratic practice of letting smaller state delegations select a joint dean in order to be able to negotiate for committee assignments from a position of strength.

Actually, the principal difference between Republican and Democratic practice in formal organization is that the Republicans have built into their system a voting formula that rewards heavy Republican areas; the Democrats offer no comparable leverage to the large delegations. Nor is it likely the Democrats would even consider such a plan as long as the seniority system prevails. For it would only lessen the power of the Southern Democrats by putting more control over committee assignments into the hands of the larger northern, midwestern, and western delegations, with their very different traditions and interests. . . .

Despite these differences the arrangements in both parties for handling committee assignments have one basic feature in common. Both committees-on-committees are so constituted as to be virtually immune to immediate pressures brought about by electoral changes. This is no accident. Its justification rests on a number of considerations congenial to the norms and customs of the entire body. If junior or freshman members had the responsibility for making committee assignments they would immediately be thrust into difficult and delicate positions, particularly in deciding on transfer requests from senior members. Such decisions might well be controversial enough to damage permanently a junior member's career within the legislature and possibly outside of it. In private as well as public life, organizations seldom allow the newcomer—unfamiliar with the subtleties and the institutional trappings of the process—to make important personnel decisions; and committee assignments are party personnel decisions of the most crucial importance. Senior members simply would not willingly tolerate decisions made in this way. If forced to do so, the pressures, roadblocks and penalties they could evoke might be so severe and difficult to overcome that order in the whole legislative process might be endangered. The system has evolved as it has for these reasons, as well as for more positive benefits, such as the desire

to rely on the more knowledgeable judgments of those with greater experience in the legislature.

Finally, the system is intended to give the process a tone of moderation and detachment. Members with seniority are less threatened by an election two years hence, being less subject to the vicissitudes of a competitive district. After years of experience in a collective body, senior members are readier to recognize the need for compromise and adjustment if work is to be done. Although competitive ambitions among members may be intense, prolonged debate over committee assignments would delay the conduct of legislative business which is already too long delayed by the employment of existing institutional and parliamentary devices.

The Role of Party Leaders

The role of the party leaders in making committee assignments is difficult to define; no simple definition fits all the realities. Generally speaking, the leadership of each party in the House is formidable and independent to a great degree, though the leaders' power varies with their personal relations with the other members. David Truman explains the dependence of the rank-and-file upon the party leaders as follows:

The machinery of the House and of its parties is normally available to the ordinary member only, so to speak, on its own terms, because the source of its strength is also the source of its disabilities, namely, numbers. In a House of 435 or in a body roughly half that size, as one of the parties, there is a tendency . . . for the real and formal leadership closely to coincide. A formal, standardized system of communication and control is indispensable to the conduct of affairs in a body of that size . . . This standardization of the communication structure implies that initiative tends to be centralized or at least that there are central controls on the flow of business. These the rank-and-file member cannot command or, as sometimes happens in the Senate, supplant. Hence, excepting some aspects of his own voting decisions, the independence of the ordinary member is restricted.

The Democratic and Republican leaders not only play the principal role in the selection of the members of their respective committees-on-committees, but their personal judgments also tend to become the norm for major committee assignments. In practice, the leadership of both parties is directly involved in assignments to all the major committees, though the leaders do not usually concern themselves with applicants to lesser ones.

The party leaders use their power over committee assignments variously, to reward members who have been loyal and cooperative, and to reinforce the strength of their own positions by rewarding members whose loyalty may be suspected but whose strength may no longer be safely disregarded. Party leaders working with the committee-on-committees have in a number of instances offered important committee positions to members with demonstrated followings who were regarded as prospective threats. Such offers are made for the obvious purpose of securing cooperation, and so are frequently labelled as "sell-outs" or "the buying-off process" by some discontented members. Value judgments on particular cases will vary with individual viewpoints, but it must be recognized that Congress is not the only place where adjustments in the power structure are designed to accommodate or to absorb potentially strong rivals. . . .

30. THE HOUSE OF REPRESENTATIVES AND FEDERAL AID TO EDUCATION

Richard F. Fenno, Jr.

. . .

Membership

Conflict within the Committee on Education and Labor is, ultimately, not a conflict among issues but among individual members. The selection of committee members is, therefore, criti-

From Richard F. Fenno, Jr., "The House of Representatives and Federal Aid to Education," *New Perspectives on the House of Representatives,* Robert L. Peabody and Nelson W. Polsby eds., (Skokie. III.: Rand McNally & Co., 1963), pp.201-5. By permission of the publisher.

cal in determining the degree, if not the main lines, of internal conflict. The net result has been that the members of the House committee come from among those in their respective parties who already are in the widest disagreement on the issues of federal aid. The people who control assignments to the committee exercise considerable care. On the Republican side, new House members are ordinarily discouraged from applying for this committee unless their convictions are firm, their talents for combat considerable, and their districts reasonably safe. Those who cannot be dissuaded and those who must be solicited tend to lean toward the more conservative wing of their party. A rather senior Republican said that he advises anyone who desires a political career to stay off the Committee—unless he is deeply committed. Of himself, he said:

My people didn't vote for me. They voted for what I stood for, my principles. I was elected as a conservative, and that's a wonderful thing. . . . It's an awfully unpopular committee. I take a terrible pounding. But my future is behind me, and I don't give a good God damn.

"I'm the kind of person," echoed an equally conservative freshman member, "who jumps right into these hot spots. So I figured if this was the most controversial committee in the House, I'd like to get on it." When the leadership has to fill a slot with a member who has not applied, it may try to ascertain his views beforehand. One member explained:

Halleck called a friend of mine in ——— and said, "What kind of a guy is this——? We're thinking of putting him on Education and Labor, but we need someone who'll stand up, someone we can count on who won't waver in his views." My friend replied, "You don't have to worry about ———."

On the Democratic side, too, members are strongly issue-oriented, personally contentious, and vigorously committed. They tend to represent the more liberal elements of their party. Party leaders produce this result both by encouraging the appointment of labor-oriented congressmen and by discouraging the appointment of southerners. To an individual representing a manufacturing or mining constit-uency, a place on the committee dealing with labor matters will have positive electoral advantages. Many Democratic members (fifteen of nineteen in 1961) received financial assistance from the trade unions, and all of these are dependent upon labor support at the polls. Union lobbyists sometimes actively intercede with the Democratic committee selectors on behalf of congressmen known to be sympathetic to them. On the other hand, no more than four (and usually fewer) southern Democrats have ever been placed on the committee at one time—despite the pleas of the southern committee members. No pretense is made at representativeness on this score; in 1961, 38 per cent of all Democratic congressmen (99 of 263) came from the eleven southern states, but only 11 per cent (two of nineteen) of the committee members did.

Despite the most careful attention to their appointment, the Democratic members of the committee constitute an extraordinarily heterogeneous group. They are personally much more predisposed to intra-party conflicts than are the Republicans. Moreover, if there is a unifying bond among most of them, it is a bond on the issues of labor, not education. The Republicans on the committee in 1961, however, were all male, non-southern, non-border-state, and Protestant—whatever their differences. They were all white, and not one of them represented a constituency with a nonwhite population of 10 per cent or over. Though 17 per cent of the Roman Catholic House members were Republicans, of these, none was on the committee. The 1961 Democratic members, by contrast, included two women, two southerners, two border-state members, seven Roman Catholics, and two Jews. The chairman was a Negro, and four Democrats represented constituencies with nonwhite populations of over 10 per cent. These demographic differences are overlaid with vast differences in personality and political style. Together they make consensus-building on the Democratic side especially hazardous, particularly on the issues of school integration and private school assistance.

The combined result of Republican and Democratic appointment practices, which is most significant for this study, is not only that they guarantee sharp ideological and partisan division on the committee, but that they intensify internal committee division. The *Congressional Quarterly* selected ten roll-call votes in 1961 to distinguish those House members who supported a larger federal role in the nation's economic and social life (*i.e.*, liberals) and those House members who opposed a larger federal role (*i.e.*, conservatives). A majority of committee Democrats (twelve of nineteen) voted on every occasion to expand government activity, and a majority of committee Republicans (seven of twelve) voted on every occasion in opposition to this expansion.

Moreover, if the voting percentages are scaled, every Democratic committee member voted more often for an expanded federal role than did any of the Republicans.

These ideological and partisan differences inside the committee are significantly greater than differences on the same issues in the House as a whole. Whereas average percentages among House Democrats were 78 per cent in favor of a larger federal role and 21 per cent against, committee Democrats averaged 91 per cent in favor and 8 per cent against. House Republicans averaged 12 per cent in favor and 87 per cent opposed, whereas committee Republicans averaged 7 per cent in favor and 93 per cent opposed. See Table 5-3.

Given the considerable degree of inflexibility within party groups, the ratio of Democrats to Republicans has assumed considerable importance. During the years of Republican control, it was certain that no bill would emerge from the committee. During the years of Democratic majorities, a coalition of Republicans plus southern Democrats could prevent committee

Table 5-3

IDEOLOGICAL REPRESENTATIVENESS OF COMMITTEE ON EDUCATION AND LABOR, 1961

	Votes For Expanded Federal Role (10 Roll Calls)	Votes Against Expanded Federal Role (10 Roll Calls)	Index of Ideological Representativeness*
	(Mean Percentage)		
All House Democrats	78	21	+57
House Education and Labor Committee Democrats	91	8	+83
All House Republicans	12	87	−75
House Education and Labor Committee Republicans	7	93	−86

Source: *Congressional Quarterly*, XIX (October 20, 1961), 1751–63.
* The Index of Ideological Representativeness constitutes the difference between the mean percentage of votes in favor of an expanded federal role and the mean percentage of those opposed.

action. Until the Eighty-sixth Congress in January, 1959, the Republicans plus the southern Democrats constituted a majority—hence a controlling influence whenever they could agree. In 1959, following the sweeping Democratic congressional victory of the previous November, the liberal Democrats and their interest-group allies succeeded in breaking the long-standing coalition majority. They persuaded Speaker Rayburn to recommend a new party ratio of twenty Democrats to ten Republicans instead of the previous seventeen Democrats to thirteen Republicans. Under the previous arrangements, thirteen Republicans plus Chairman Barden and Phil Landrum (Ga.) could create a tie vote. A third, a more liberal southerner, Carl Elliott of Alabama, one of the committee's few education specialists, was placed in a strategic position at the ideological center of the committee and in the eye of most internal storms. Six new Democrats, all supported by organized labor, were given committee membership in 1959; those southerners who applied were turned down. This membership change constitutes one of the landmarks of the federal aid controversy in Congress. . . .

31. PARTY LEADERSHIP

Donald R. Matthews

The Role of Parties in the Senate

According to popular mythology, the Democratic and Republican parties formulate "principles" and select candidates who "stand" on them at election time. Then "the people" choose the party which most nearly represents their opinions at the polls. The victorious party, backed by a popular "mandate," enacts the program into legislation. If the majority party fails to live up to its commitments or if the people, on second thought, do not care for its policies they may be defeated at the next election.

The realities of American party

From Donald R. Matthews, *U. S. Senators and Their World.* (Chapel Hill, N. C.: U. of North Carolina Press, 1960), pp. 119-29. By permission of the publisher.

politics are different. The parties are loose coalitions of state and local organizations with divergent policy aims, leadership groups, and electoral followings. Senators who belong to the same national party are elected at different times, by different electorates, on different platforms. Both Senate parties contain "liberals" and "conservatives," "radicals" and "reactionaries," no matter how these much abused terms are defined. Nevertheless, the ideological center of gravity of the two parties *is* different; the Democrats' is toward the "Left," and the Republicans' is toward the "Right" of the abbreviated American political spectrum. This is clearly—if crudely—demonstrated in Figure 5-1, which shows the ideological make-up of the two parties during the postwar Congresses.

There is not much that the national

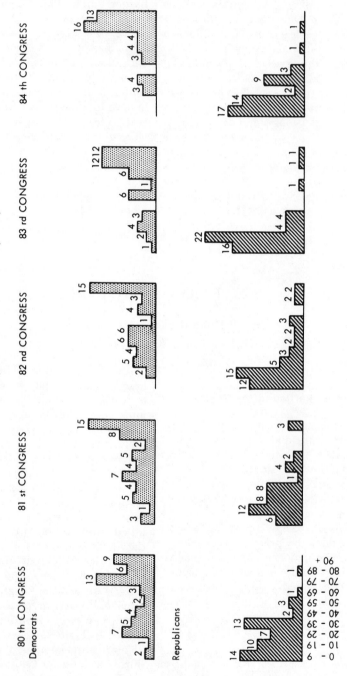

FIGURE 5-1.
Conservatism-Liberalism Scores, by Party.

leadership of the parties can do about this situation. With rare exceptions the senators are not beholden to the party leaders; they had little to do with the senators' nomination or election. The tradition of localism and popular reverence for legislative "independence" largely frustrate any efforts by the president, national chairman, or Senate leaders of a party to "purge" unfaithful members. As a result, the political parties in the Senate are, when compared with the parties in most parliamentary democracies and a number of American states, rather disunited organizations.

Look, for example, at Figure 5-2. The percentage of the time Democratic and Republican senators voted with a majority of their party on roll call votes, in which a majority of one party voted against a majority of the other, is presented in this figure for each Congress during the postwar decade. On the whole, the figures show that the "average" senator voted with his party about 75 or 80 per cent of the time on party-line roll calls. But notice also the wide range of party-unity scores to be found within both political parties. While the bulk of the senators seem to have been fairly regular party supporters, a few voted with the opposition more often than with their own party.

On the other hand, most senators do identify strongly with their party. They do want to be "good" Democrats or Republicans even though their definition of this state of grace does not always coincide with those of their colleagues. "None of us," one senator remarked, "likes to see the party split, openly and repeatedly." Another, whose voting record hardly indicates an addiction to party regularity, confessed with real emotion that "it's not pleasant to vote against a majority of your party." The Senate is organized in a way which reinforces and intensifies these feelings. After being in the Senate only briefly, one senator has written he saw.

How party spirit develops. The Republicans and Democrats sit on the floor of the Senate in separate groups, the Republicans on the right, the Democrats on the left. Most members eat their lunch in a small dining room 'For Senators Only,' and there the Republicans and Democrats eat separately. Republicans and Democrats even have separate lounges so that the contacts a freshman senator makes are largely with members of his own party. He loafs, he even takes a nap in this lounge, but it is a Republican—or Democratic—nap.

Moreover, the party leaders have a dominant influence—"control" would be too strong a word—over the legislative schedule and the utilization of the chamber's time. In a body faced with a permanent overload of work, this is especially significant. The importance of a senator's committee assignments to him and his political future can hardly be overestimated. This, too, is a party matter.

The division of the senators into two political parties is, therefore, a very significant feature of the chamber. Party "discipline" may be weak, but party "identification" is strong. Party affiliation, as we shall see in this and subsequent chapters, is a major influence on the senator's voting behavior. The parties provide the chamber with its members, have considerable influence on its procedure, and allocate members to fill its different positions. In the process, the parties help determine the distribution of power within the Senate.

FIGURE 5-2.

Party-Unity Scores, by Party.

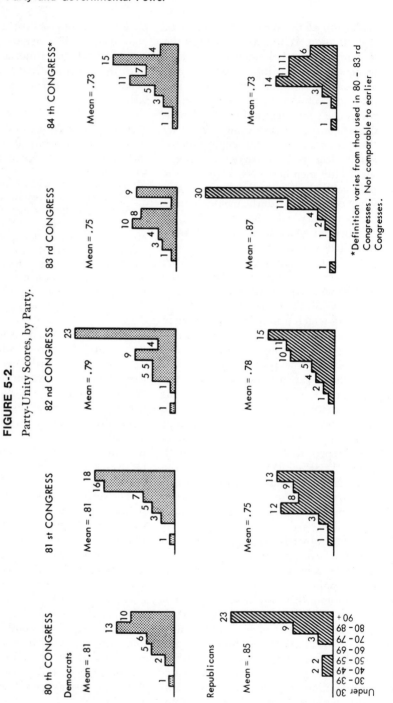

Party Organization: Democratic and Republican Contrasts

Both parties in the Senate are elaborately organized. The formal machinery, however, rarely operates in the manner one thinks, and the similar formal organizations of the Democrats and Republicans obscure the fact that the leadership of the two parties is quite different.

Democratic party leadership is highly personalized, informal, centralized in the hands of the floor leader. He may not be the most powerful Democrat in the chamber—indeed only Lyndon Johnson has come close to being so during the postwar era—but he, his staff, and his assistant (the whip) provide the party with whatever general and central leadership originates in the Senate itself. The Conference, a meeting of all Democratic senators, which officially serves as the supreme governing body of the party in the Senate, almost never meets. When a vacancy occurs in the leadership, it convenes to elect a successor who thenceforth directs the day-to-day tactics of the party as floor leader, appoints members to the important party committees and presides over the party as Conference chairman, directs the formulation of party strategy and the scheduling of bills for floor debate as chairman of the Policy Committee, and directs the appointment of Democrats to Senate committees as chairman of the Steering Committee.

The Conference (often, unofficially referred to by its earlier title of caucus) rarely meets again during the session. Moreover, policy is almost never discussed when it does meet, largely for fear of advertising the party's sharp internal divisions. "We hold few caucuses and they are almost always unsatisfactory," one senator explained. "While they are supposedly secret, an account of what happens always appears in Drew Pearson's column the next day." Debates on policy, furthermore, merely exacerbate personal relations and solidify the conflicting policy stances of different members of the party. Any effort to obtain a binding commitment from members is bound to fail ("Can't you see us trying to bind Eastland to the Democratic FEPC plank? *That* would be a fine day in Hell!") except where it is not needed anyway. To take an official party stand on this kind of issue would, in all likelihood, merely alienate like-minded Republicans. "Personally," one Democrat said, "I can't see any purpose in a caucus. You can't bind anyone. All you can do is talk. The same speakers would say the same things on the floor a little later on." Of course, the inactivity of the Conference serves to enhance the influence of the leader for "it's awfully hard to fight the party leadership when there are no caucuses." Since the leader appoints the members (and the staffs)of the Policy and Steering Committees and serves as their chairman, his wishes carry great weight in these agencies of party leadership as well.

The extent of the leader's influence varies, of course, from one leader to the next. Senator Barkley, who was Democratic leader during the Eightieth Congress before becoming vice-president, and Senator Johnson of Texas, widely recognized as the most technically proficient floor leader the Senate has seen in this generation, operated with very little guidance from the Policy Committee, the Conference, or any other formal organs of party governance. For all practical purposes, they were the Democratic party organization in the Senate. Senators Scott Lucas and Ernest McFarland, who served during the Eighty-first and Eighty-second Congresses, were both able enough leaders but neither possessed the prestige of a Barkley nor the manipulative skill of a Johnson. Both depended a great deal more on formal party agencies for advice, guidance, and the generation of support.

Even when compared with the Democratic party under a relatively weak leader, the Republican leadership is more formalized, institutionalized, and decentralized. In the first place, the elective jobs of floor leader, chairman of the Conference, chairman of the Policy Committee, and chairman of the Committee on Committees are held by different men. Even when separated, these positions bestow considerable influence: that of the floor leader flowing from his tactical control over procedure; and that of the chairman of the Conference from his ability to nominate members for party offices who are generally ratified by the Conference without controversy. The Republican Policy Committee, very large and characterized by a rapid turnover in personnel, is dominated by its chairman. He is, therefore, of considerable importance in determining party strategy and the legislative schedule. Only the Republican chairman of the Committee on Committees gains little influence from his party post because of the party's strict adherence to the seniority rule.

In the second place, the Republican Conference, while it suffers from many of the same debilities as that of the Democrats, is considerably more active and significant. During much of the Eisenhower administration, for example, weekly Conference luncheons were held at which the party leaders reported on their legislative discussions with the President. While no binding votes were attempted—indeed, veteran Republicans can never remember such a vote —some efforts were made, from time to time, to arrive at consensus.

Just as within the Democratic party, the actual pattern of Republican leadership depends in large measure upon the personalities, prestige, and skills of the men who hold the positions of leadership. There was, for example, a period during the postwar years when Senator Taft, first as chairman of the Policy Committee and later as floor leader, led his party as single-handedly as any Democratic leader. But most of the time, the leadership of the GOP is more nearly corporate than individual.

Party Leaders in Action

Senate party leaders generally conceive of their jobs not as creating an over-all party program of legislative action (this is generally supplied by the President) but as achieving as much party unity as possible on discreet pieces of legislation. Under modern conditions, the more ambitious role is no doubt beyond their power. Even the limited goals they set for themselves are very difficult to achieve. They have no control over the raw material they are expected to unify; new party members appear on the Hill and old members are defeated quite independently of the leaders' actions or desires. They have no major sanctions to employ against party dissidents. "I didn't," one former leader remarked, "have anything to threaten them with, and it wouldn't have worked even if I had tried . . . sure as hell, someone would have gotten up on the floor and accused me of trying to become a dictator." Moreover, as another senator said, "When the party division in the Senate is close (and the need for party discipline therefore greatest) the party leaders want every Democrat or every Republican they can get—no matter how irregular his voting record." Often, the leader has little control over the content of the measures on which he seeks party agreement. To do so, he must exert influence at the committee stage of the legislative process, and "committee chairmen are independent cusses, highly jealous of their prerogatives." Some leaders do not even try to exert influence until after the committee has made its report. "I always believed," the same former leader said, "that it wasn't the leader's job to try to influence committee decisions. The leader's job is to take bills which have already been reported out of committee and placed on the Calendar and try to obtain as much party backing for them as he can."

The party leader's principal weapon is his own persuasiveness. A major share of his time is devoted to lobbying —flattering, cajoling, appealing to the senators' sense of party loyalty, arguing the merits of legislative measures. The more effective leaders are, in fact, "conducting a continuous caucus on the floor, in the corridors and cloakrooms, over the telephone." If all efforts at persuading a straying party member fail, and they do with some senators on almost every vote in which the leadership takes an interest, the leaders seek to persuade the maverick to absent himself from the chamber during the vote, or to pair, or, at least, not to dramatize the party split by playing an active role in floor debate.

Much of this lobbying is done through emissaries. "The leader often sends a friend of mine around to see if he can change my mind. He drops in —not saying that the leader sent him, of course—and talks to me about the bill. But if I say that I have definitely made up my mind one way or the other, that's all there is to it." Some senators who are close both to the leader and to a group with which the leader has limited influence can develop a position of substantial power by playing the role well.

"Most of the time," one senator explained, "the leader is cast in the role of someone trying to help you with your problems." Does a senator want an office overlooking the Mall? Is he looking for an administrative assistant? Does he need to be out of town when an important roll call vote is likely to be taken? Does he desire a seat on the Foreign Relations Committee? Wish to make a four-hour speech next Thursday? Is he looking for a pair on the agriculture bill? Does he need to get his pet bill passed in order to stand a chance for re-election? Or does he want to know what S. 123 would *really* do to his constituents? The leader can be of at least some help, and often of very great assistance, in grappling with questions of this sort. As a result, the leader is in an excellent position to know every member's problems, ambitions, and idiosyncracies. If the leader makes a firm commitment to be of aid, a senator can count on his battling to keep his word—and reminding the senator of the favor if it should ever be necessary to do so!

Undoubtedly the biggest favor a party leader can do for a senator is to get him a desirable committee assignment. On initial assignments, the party leaders sometimes have a little maneuverability. Beyond this point, however, the leader's discretion is bound by the seniority rule; that is, once a senator is appointed to a committee he may serve on it as long as he desires and committee vacancies are given to the senator requesting them who has served longest in the chamber. The principal advantage of this system, of course, is that it almost automatically allocates the limited supply of desirable committees in an entirely "objective" way, thus minimizing intra-Senate conflict and logrolling. But it also largely eliminates a potential lever for the leaders to use against party irregulars.

The seniority system is not entirely automatic, since two or more party members with identical seniority may apply for the same vacancy. This dilemma is often solved by relatively weak leaders by ranking these men according to their previous political experience (former governors first, former representatives second, and so on), by resorting to the alphabet, or even by flipping a coin. Yet given the seniority system, a party leader can sometimes, within severely restricted limits, use his influence over committee assignments to punish friends and reward enemies. He can, for example, use his knowledge of the wants of his party's members to block the "promotion" of an uncooperative senator simply by persuading a man with greater seniority to apply for the committee assignment the recalcitrant senator desires. One rather independent Democrat applied three times for a seat on a major committee for which his seniority seemed more than sufficient. Each time he was beaten out by a surprise applicant with greater seniority. "I feel," the senator ruefully remarked, "that they are scouting around for men senior to me to put on that committee." Too much stress should not be placed on this point. If a committee assignment is really desirable a senior man will snap it up without any urging, but the party leaders can sometimes facilitate this process to serve their own ends.

Senator Johnson, as Democratic leader, has gone considerably further than this. By persuading many of the senior senators to give up one of their two desirable committees, he has been able to assure every senator, regardless of seniority, that he will quickly receive one important committee assignment. Here is no mean incentive to party regularity, although one which can be used only with relatively junior senators who have not yet achieved the committee assignments they prefer. It cannot affect the men who are already entrenched in good committee posts, and these tend to be the most powerful members in the Senate.

In addition to persuasion and the granting and withholding of favors, the party leaders have other methods of maximizing party unity. Their control over the parliamentary situation can be used for this purpose. "No Southern Senator—except perhaps the two from Alabama—", explained one member of a Democratic leader's staff, "can afford to vote for a public housing bill. The Northern Democrats can't afford to vote against one. You can't ask a senator to slit his own throat. So you bring up the bill in such a way that the Southerners can vote for it because it provides less housing than the alternative (or because it does not contain an FEPC provision) and the Northerners vote for it because it is better than nothing." Sometimes, the most petty floor maneuvers can make the difference between passage or defeat of a party measure. In a recent Congress, for example, Senator Johnson was positive that an important bill would pass if a certain Southern senator would vote for it, but according to a careful canvass of the situation the senator was still undecided. Abruptly, in the middle of floor debate, Johnson approached the wavering senator, announced that he had to leave the chamber for an hour or so and casually asked the potential dissenter to take over as floor manager of the bill. The senator hesitated and then agreed as Johnson left the floor. The undecided senator voted for the bill.

The party leaders can refuse to bring a bill to the floor if they are not satisfied that it will pass in a form acceptable to the party. Occasionally, they can even afford to ignore the bills of uncooperative members. "They don't dare do this often or they will have a revolt on their hands," but the threat of studied inaction can be potent even if rarely carried out.

Above all, the party leader must seek to anticipate intra-party controversy and "find a basis upon which the party can agree. This requires that he understand the problems of every member of his party and try to find a way of reconciling them." A good leader must be able to find "the bargaining point," the "common denominator of party accord."

32. PARTY DISCIPLINE IN THE HOUSE OF COMMONS —A COMMENT

Robert E. Dowse and Trevor Smith

. . . . .

The formal powers of persuasion and coercion available to the leadership are considerable, but by themselves they constitute only a partial explanation of party concord. Members of Parliament are a highly "political" group of people who would hardly submit meekly and continually to such pressures as are open to the leadership to use; nor is ideological allegiance sufficient to account for the maintenance of a united front and, given the volume of Parliamentary business, the extreme rarity of backbench revolt.

This striking fact of unanimity can best be understood, perhaps, by looking at the process of legislation (rather than simply emphasising the role of the Whips) and by looking in particular at the period of consultation with interested groups prior to the introduction of legislation.

The increase in the scope and range of government activity in the twentieth century has prompted governments to adopt the practice of discussing its legislative proposals with affected bodies. "Consultation generally takes place before bills are presented to Parliament." In many cases, consultation between government departments and relevant interest groups has become a continuous activity and an intricate machinery of consultation, sometimes formal but more often informal, has been developed. Pressure group officials have their opposite numbers in the ministries. Relationships of this sort are regarded as being of mutual advantage to both government departments and pressure groups, so much so that those pressure groups which can, prefer to exert their influ-

From Robert E. Dowse and Trevor Smith, "Party Discipline in the House of Commons—A Comment," *Parliamentary Affairs,* XVI, 2 (Spring, 1963), 159-64. By permission of the Hansard Society for Parliamentary Government.

ences at this level rather than through Parliament or on the general public. Such evidence that exists indicates that whereas in the past pressure groups tended to focus their attention on Parliament, nowadays they seem to prefer, wherever possible, to confine their lobbying to Whitehall. Thus, the completely successful group would be one which nobody had heard of, other than its own officials and the particular departmental committee with which it deals. In the very nature of things, such a group can only be a hypothetical model, though presumably it is one to which many groups seek to aspire. This "ideal" group would have no need to retain the services of an M.P., or group of M.P.s, to make representations on its behalf at Westminster since, *ex hypothesi*, its influence is maximised at departmental level; i.e., its views would have had the fullest consideration and satisfactory compromises would have been reached.

In practice, of course, total agreement between a department and a group on all issues is unattainable. Where there is a divergence of view the group is faced with the alternative of either letting the matter rest and accepting defeat or of seeking the assistance of friendly parliamentarians. Once an approach has been made, the individual M.P., or group of M.P.s, is in turn faced with a number of possible courses of action. He may decide to raise the issue at the appropriate backbench committee, or at a meeting of the parliamentary party; he may prefer to intercede directly with the Minister, or wait until the bill is introduced into the House before intervening when naturally, of course, his chances of securing any accommodation are substantially reduced. At any one of the stages prior to a bill's formal intro-

duction into the Commons the private member has an opportunity to present his case for an amendment *before* the Minister is publicly committed, and, therefore, less likely to accept changes.

Of course, the Minister can hardly be expected to reveal a great deal of the detail of proposed legislation, but, even so, the M.P. does have an opportunity, *in private*, to make his views known, and it would be a foolhardy minister who ignored informed backbench opinion. Indeed, Christopher Hollis, whilst arguing that it is "disgraceful" that M.P.s may say one thing in the privacy of a party meeting and vote another way in public, admits that they may compel a government to change its policy. Michael Foot, a constant opponent of Labor discipline as manifested in the standing orders of the Parliamentary Labor Party, makes a similar point when he states that the M.P. has his first opportunity to influence policy in "an earlier meeting of a specialised official group" and his second opportunity in "the secret conclave of the party meeting." During the very early 1960's when Labour was hardly functioning at all as an opposition, *The Times* political correspondent went even further, calling the Conservative backbench committees the real opposition. He also remarked: it is in such committees that "things are said and done that are more politically meaningful than a great deal that passes in the Chamber itself; and it would be easy to name four or five chairmen of backbench Conservative committees who by an inflexion of voice or a sour expression are nowadays able to do more to change the Government's mind in one private meeting with a Minister than all the Labour oratory." Committees, he went on to say, have developed "into one of the more important Conservative political instruments for the permeation of policy, for the meeting of minds that leaders and rank and file alike need, and for the discreet application of pressure out of earshot and eyeshot of the public."

A party backbench committee consists of all those M.P.s who happen to be interested in a particular problem or range of policy; for example, defense, foreign affairs, Commonwealth, Scotland, and agriculture, etc. In the Conservative Party Committees no vote is taken, no formal minutes recorded, the appropriate Minister is sometimes present, and a party whip attends all meetings. The Leader of the Conservative Party is also advised by the Business Committee "which consists of the principal officers of all the main 'functional' committees of the parliamentary party." Conservative Party Committees are usually more flexible, in terms of attending personnel, than are those of the Labor Party which tend to retain the same people. Perhaps the most important difference between the party committees is that "Ministers or shadow ministers are members of Labour Party Committees; in the Conservative Party, ministers attend only by invitation." Regular members of Labour Party Committees vote on the issues placed before them; normally (in opposition) a committee will consider an issue which is to come before Parliament, thrash out a draft resolution which will be placed before the Parliamentary Committee of the Parliamentary Labour Party (P.L.P.) which can modify the draft and place it before a full meeting of the P.L.P. In the form passed, if passed, by the P.L.P. the policy then becomes binding on the Parliamentary Committee; clearly the original functional committee is extremely well placed tactically. If a committee has done its homework

and has prepared a detailed brief in which the arguments for its proposals are set out, the chances of such proposals being accepted are much higher.

Certainly, it is obvious that a government M.P. is likely to be more effective in winning amendments, since, by definition, his support is more vital than is that of an opposition M.P. It is usually expected that an opposition will vote against a government, but that very fact is enough to account for the solidarity of H.M. Opposition since the range of choice open to it is limited: to vote for or against a government measure. Presumably the opposition M.P. will himself have consulted, or be a member of, the appropriate backbench committee in which those interested in a special geographical or functional area will be able to discuss and, probably, agree upon tactics and amendments during the public stages of a bill's progress. Hence, the general approach to Government business will have been thrashed out, the compromises reached, the amendments and arguments discussed amongst those who are most likely to be affected or interested. Naturally enough those M.P.s who are not interested in the particular aspect of government policy will take their lead from those in the same party who are. The average M.P., with a limited amount of time and having a limited number of interests can be presumed to be only too willing to follow the policy suggestions and discussions of the committees. Nigel Nicolson comments that if a matter was under discussion about which he knew nothing "it would not occur to me to take a stand against the party line . . . That is the explanation of sheep-like voting in the party's lobby. I do not find it shocking." It follows from this that the problem of discipline is really a problem of meeting the interests of M.P.s who are interested in a particular piece of legislation, and it can be surmised that such M.P.s are nearly always a minority. Politically, then, the government is presented with the task of retaining the support of the active minority, and it is obvious that in the greatest number of cases it has little difficulty in so doing. That the government of the day or the Opposition has little real difficulty in controlling its supporters, as is evidenced by the astonishingly small number of intra-party revolts, may be taken as evidence that the pre-introductory stages of a bill ensure that its more contentious elements have been eliminated. This is at least as reasonable a conclusion to draw from the virtual voting unanimity as any other, and is, on the face of it, more persuasive than the idea that M.P.s are merely a tribe whose emblem is servitude!

So far we have confined our attention to the effects which the major pressure groups—the "sectional/ spokesman groups" as they have been called—have on the behavior of M.P.s. What of the "groups that are primarily concerned with the propagation of attitudes?" These "cause groups," of which the Howard League for Penal Reform, the League Against Cruel Sports, and the various temperance societies are examples, are unable, generally speaking, to build up a close liaison with government departments and, as a consequence, they focus their activities on Parliament and on public opinion. This being so, it might be expected that M.P.s associated with such groups would give the Whips more trouble than those connected with the large "sectional/spokesman groups." However, this tends not to be

the case. Most "causes" cut across traditional party lines and the groups concerned try, wherever possible, to use the services of M.P.s from all parties. Because most causes fall outside the arena of party politics both front benches are usually—officially at least —indifferent towards them, and M.P.s can make their pleas unhampered by the Whips. . . .

That backbench M.P.s do consistently vote with their front bench is beyond doubt; why they do quite so consistently is not. We have attempted to demonstrate that the fact of persistent support need not be interpreted as stemming simply from pressure. As we remarked earlier, M.P.s are a highly "political" group—they are surely as capable of marshalling their forces as is the front bench. Nicely balanced coalitions, which is what British parties are, can hardly refuse to yield on every occasion to pressure from a substantial number of their supporters. Parties in the Commons are not monoliths. After a measure has been approved, or at least widely commented upon, by the extra governmental agencies likely to be effected, it is hardly to be wondered at that the average M. P. can find little in most bills to comment adversely upon. That most governmental measures are approved of is equally understandable; indeed, it is only after taking the prophylactic stage, the pre-introductory phase, into consideration that one is fully equipped to comprehend the effectiveness of whipping and blandishment. What more effective plea can a minister make to potentially hostile M.P.s than that the interests which are affected by a measure have been consulted and have given their approval?

Party and Ideology

33. ISSUE CONFLICT AND CONSENSUS AMONG PARTY LEADERS AND FOLLOWERS

Herbert McClosky, Paul J. Hoffmann, and Rosemary O'Hara

American political parties are often regarded as "brokerage" organizations, weak in principle, devoid of ideology, and inclined to differ chiefly over unimportant questions. In contrast to the "ideological" parties of Europe—which supposedly appeal to their followers through sharply defined, coherent, and logically related doctrines —the American parties are thought to fit their convictions to the changing demands of the political contest.

From Herbert McClosky, Paul J. Hoffmann, and Rosemary O'Hara, "Issue Conflict and Consensus among Party Leaders and Followers," *American Political Science Review*, LIV, 2 (June, 1960), 406-27, excerpts. By permission of the American Political Science Association.

According to this view, each set of American party leaders is satisfied to play Tweedledee to the other's Tweedledum.

Pressures Toward Uniformity and Cleavage

Although these "conclusions" are mainly derived from *a priori* analysis or from casual observations of "anecdotal" data (little systematic effort having been made so far to verify or refute them), they are often taken as confirmed—largely, one imagines, because they are compatible with certain conspicuous features of American politics. Among these features is the entrenchment of a two-party system which, by affording both parties a genuine opportunity to win elections, tempts them to appeal to as many diverse elements in the electorate as are needed to put together a majority. Since both parties want to attract support from the centrist and moderate segments of the electorate, their views on basic issues will, it is thought, tend to converge. Like giant business enterprises competing for the same market, they will be led to offer commodities that are in many respects identical. It is one thing for a small party in a multiparty system to preserve its ideological purity, quite another for a mass party in a two-party system to do so. The one has little hope of becoming a majority, and can most easily survive by remaining identified with the narrow audience from which it draws its chief supporters; the other can succeed only by accommodating the conflicting claims of many diverse groups—only, in short, by blunting ideological distinctions.

Constraints against enlarging intellectual differences also spring from the loosely confederated nature of the American party system, and from each national party's need to adjust its policies to the competing interests of the locality, the state, and the nation. Many party units are more concerned with local than with national elections, and prefer not to be handicapped by clear-cut national programs. Every ambitious politician, moreover, hopes to achieve a *modus vivendi* tailored to the particular and often idiosyncratic complex of forces prevailing in his constituency, an objective rarely compatible with doctrinal purity. Often, too, local politics are largely non-partisan or are partisan in ways that scarcely affect the

great national issues around which ideologies might be expected to form. The development and enforcement of a sharply delineated ideology is also hindered by the absence in either party of a firmly established, authoritative, and continuing organizational center empowered to decide questions of doctrine and discipline. Party affiliation is loosely defined, responsibility is weak or nonexistent, and organs for indoctrinating or communicating with party members are at best rudimentary.

Cultural and historical differences may also contribute to the weaker ideological emphasis among American, as compared with European, parties. Many of the great historical cleavages that have divided European nations for centuries—monarchism *vs.* republicanism; clericalism *vs.* anti-clericalism; democracy *vs.* autocracy, etc.—have never taken root in this country. Apart from the slavery (and subsequently the race) issue, the United States has not experienced the intense class or caste conflict often found abroad, and contests of the capitalism *vs.* socialism variety have never achieved an important role in American politics. In addition, never having known a titled nobility, we have largely been freed from the conflicts found elsewhere between the classes of inherited and acquired privilege.

Consider, too, the progress made in the United States toward neutralizing the forces which ordinarily lead to sharp social, and hence intellectual and political, differentiation. The class and status structure of American society has attained a rate of mobility equalling or exceeding that of any other long established society. Popular education, and other facilities for the creation of common attitudes, have been developed on a scale unequalled elsewhere.

Improvements in transportation and communication, and rapid shifts in population and industry have weakened even sectionalism as a source of political cleavage. Rural-urban differences continue to exist, of course, but they too have been diminishing in force and have become less salient for American politics than the differences prevailing, for example, between a French peasant proprietor and a Parisian *boulevardier*. In short, a great many Americans have been subjected in their public lives to identical stimuli—a condition unlikely to generate strong, competing ideologies.

The research reported here was designed not to refute these observations but to test the accuracy of the claim that they are sufficient to prevent differences in outlook from taking root in the American party system. We believed that the homogenizing tendencies referred to are strongly offset by contrary influences, and that voters are preponderantly led to support the party whose opinions they share. We further thought that the competition for office, though giving rise to similarites between the parties, also impels them to diverge from each other in order to sharpen their respective appeals. For this and other reasons, we expected to find that the leaders of the two parties, instead of ignoring differences alleged to exist within the electorate, would differ on issues more sharply than their followers would. We believed further that even in a brokerage system the parties would serve as independent reference groups, developing norms, values, and self-images to which their supporters could readily respond. Their influence, we felt, would frequently exceed that of ethnic, occupational, residential and other reference groups. In sum, we proceeded on the belief that the parties are not simply spokes-

men for other interest groups, but are in their own right agencies for formulating, transmitting, and anchoring political opinions, that they attract adherents who in general share those opinions, and that through a feedback process of mutual reinforcement between the organization and its typical supporters, the parties develop integrated and stable political tendencies. Other hypotheses will be specified as we present and analyze our findings. [Section describing research procedure omitted.]

Findings: Comparisons Between Leaders

No more conclusive findings emerge from our study of party issues than those growing out of the comparisons between the two sets of party leaders. Despite the brokerage tendency of the American parties, their active members are obviously separated by large and important differences. The differences, moreover, conform with the popular image in which the Democratic party is seen as the more "progressive" or "radical," the Republican as the more "moderate" or "conservative" of the two. In addition, the disagreements are remarkably consistent, a function not of chance but of systematic points of view, whereby the responses to any one of the issues could reasonably have been predicted from knowledge of the responses to the other issues.

Examination of Tables 5-5-A-E and 5-6 shows that the leaders differ significantly on twenty-three of the twenty-four issues listed and that they are separated on fifteen of these issues by .18 or more ratio points—in short, by differences that are in absolute magnitude very large. The two samples are furthest apart in their attitudes toward public ownership and are especially

Table 5-4

AVERAGE DIFFERENCES IN THE RATIO-OF-SUPPORT SCORES AMONG PARTY LEADERS AND FOLLOWERS FOR FIVE CATEGORIES OF ISSUES

Category of Issues	Democratic Leaders vs. Republican Leaders	Democratic Followers vs. Republican Followers	Democratic Leaders vs. Democratic Followers	Republican Leaders vs. Republican Followers	Democratic Leaders vs. Republican Followers	Republican Leaders vs. Democratic Followers
a. Public Ownership of Resources	.28	.04	.06	.18	.10	.22
b. Government Regulation of the Economy	.22	.06	.08	.10	.12	.16
c. Equalitarianism, Human Welfare	.22	.05	.08	.21	.06	.25
d. Tax Policy	.20	.06	.06	.20	.04	.26
e. Foreign Policy	.15	.02	.05	.08	.07	.10
Average Differences in Ratio Scores for all Categories	.21	.04	.07	.15	.08	.20

Sample Sizes: Democratic Leaders, 1,788; Republican Leaders, 1,232; Democratic Followers, 821; Republican Followers, 623.

Table 5-5-A

COMPARISON OF PARTY LEADERS AND FOLLOWERS ON "PUBLIC OWNERSHIP" ISSUES, BY PERCENTAGES AND RATIOS OF SUPPORT

Issues	Leaders		Followers	
	Dem. N=1,788	Repub. N=1,232	Dem. N=821	Repub. N=623
		(per cents down)		
Public Ownership of Natural Resources				
% favoring: Increase	57.5	12.9	35.3	31.1
Decrease	18.6	51.9	15.0	19.9
Same, n.c.*	23.8	35.2	49.7	49.0
Support Ratio	.69	.30	.60	.56
Public Control of Atomic Energy				
% favoring: Increase	73.2	45.0	64.2	59.4
Decrease	7.2	15.3	7.1	10.0
Same, n.c.	19.6	39.7	28.7	30.6
Support Ratio	.83	.65	.79	.75
Mean Support Ratios for the Public Ownership Category	.76	.48	.70	.66

* n.c. = no code.

divided on the question of government ownership of natural resources, the Democrats strongly favoring it, the Republicans just as strongly wanting it cut back. The difference of .39 in the ratio scores is the largest for any of the issues tested. In percentages, the differences are 58 per cent (D) *vs.* 13 per cent (R) in favor of increasing support, and 19 per cent (D) *vs.* 52 per cent (R) in favor of decreasing support. Both parties preponderantly support public control and development of atomic energy, but the Democrats do so more uniformly.

V. O. Key, among others, has observed that the Republican party is especially responsive to the "financial

Table 5-5-B

COMPARISON OF PARTY LEADERS AND FOLLOWERS ON "GOVERNMENT REGULATION OF THE ECONOMY" ISSUES, BY PERCENTAGES AND RATIOS OF SUPPORT

Issues	Leaders		Followers	
	Dem. N=1,788	Repub. N=1,232	Dem. N=821	Repub. N=623
	(per cents down)			
Level of Farm Price Supports				
% favoring: Increase	43.4	6.7	39.0	23.0
Decrease	28.1	67.4	27.6	40.3
Same, n.c.	28.5	25.8	33.4	36.7
Support Ratio	.58	.20	.56	.41
Government Regulation of Business				
% favoring: Increase	20.2	0.6	18.6	7.4
Decrease	38.5	84.1	33.4	46.2
Same, n.c.	41.3	15.3	48.0	46.4
Support Ratio	.41	.08	.43	.31
Regulation of Public Utilities				
% favoring: Increase	59.0	17.9	39.3	26.0
Decrease	6.4	17.6	11.1	12.0
Same, n.c.	34.6	64.5	49.6	62.0
Support Ratio	.76	.50	.64	.57
Enforcement of Anti-Monopoly Laws				
% favoring: Increase	78.0	44.9	53.2	51.0
Decrease	2.9	9.0	7.9	6.6
Same, n.c.	19.1	46.1	38.9	42.4
Support Ratio	.88	.68	.73	.72
Regulation of Trade Unions				
% favoring: Increase	59.3	86.4	46.6	57.8
Decrease	12.4	4.5	8.9	10.6
Same, n.c.	28.3	9.2	44.5	31.6
Support Ratio	.73	.91	.69	.74
Level of Tariffs				
% favoring: Increase	13.0	19.2	16.6	15.2
Decrease	43.0	26.3	25.3	21.3
Same, n.c.	43.9	54.5	58.1	63.4
Support Ratio	.35	.46	.46	.47
Restrictions on Credit				
% favoring: Increase	24.8	20.6	26.1	25.7
Decrease	39.3	20.6	22.2	23.8
Same, n.c.	35.9	58.8	51.8	50.5
Support Ratio	.43	.50	.52	.51
Mean Support Ratios for "Government Regulation of the Economy" Category	.59	.48	.58	.53

and manufacturing community," reflecting the view that government should intervene as little as possible to burden or restrain prevailing business interests. The validity of this observation is evident throughout all our data, and is most clearly seen in the responses to the issues listed under Government Regulation of the Economy, Equalitarianism and Human Welfare, Tax Policy. Democratic leaders are far more eager than Republican leaders to strengthen enforcement of anti-monopoly laws and to increase regulation of public utilities and business. Indeed, the solidarity of Republican opposition to

Table 5-5-C
COMPARISON OF PARTY LEADERS AND FOLLOWERS ON "EQUALITARIAN AND HUMAN WELFARE" ISSUES, BY PERCENTAGES AND RATIOS OF SUPPORT

Issues	Leaders		Followers	
	Dem. N=1,788	Repub. N=1,232	Dem. N=821	Repub. N=623
	(per cents down)			
Federal Aid to Education				
% favoring: Increase	66.2	22.3	74.9	64.8
Decrease	13.4	43.2	5.6	8.3
Same, n.c.	20.4	34.5	19.5	26.8
Support Ratio	.76	.40	.85	.78
Slum Clearance and Public Housing				
% favoring: Increase	78.4	40.1	79.5	72.5
Decrease	5.6	21.6	5.8	7.9
Same, n.c.	16.0	38.3	14.6	19.6
Support Ratio	.86	.59	.87	.82
Social Security Benefits				
% favoring: Increase	60.0	22.5	69.4	57.0
Decrease	3.9	13.1	3.0	3.8
Same, n.c.	36.1	64.4	27.5	39.2
Support Ratio	.78	.55	.83	.77
Minimum Wages				
% favoring: Increase	50.0	15.5	59.0	43.5
Decrease	4.7	12.5	2.9	5.0
Same, n.c.	45.2	72.0	38.1	51.5
Support Ratio	.73	.52	.78	.69
Enforcement of Integration				
% favoring: Increase	43.8	25.5	41.9	40.8
Decrease	26.6	31.7	27.4	23.6
Same, n.c.	29.5	42.8	30.7	35.6
Support Ratio	.59	.47	.57	.59
Immigration into United States				
% favoring: Increase	36.1	18.4	10.4	8.0
Decrease	27.0	29.9	52.0	44.6
Same, n.c.	36.9	51.7	37.6	47.4
Support Ratio	.54	.44	.29	.32
Mean Support Ratios for "Equalitarian and Human Welfare" Category	.71	.50	.70	.66

the regulation of business is rather overwhelming: 84 per cent want to decrease such regulation and fewer than .01 per cent say they want to increase it. Although the Democrats, on balance, also feel that government controls on business should not be expanded further, the differences between the two samples on this issue are nevertheless substantial.

The two sets of leaders are also far apart on the farm issue, the Democrats preferring slightly to increase farm supports, the Republicans, wanting strongly to reduce them. The Republican ratio score of .20 on this issue is among the lowest in the entire set of scores. The magnitude of these scores somewhat surprised us, for while opposition to agricultural subsidies is consistent with Republican dislike for state intervention, we had expected the leaders to conform more closely to the familiar image of the Republican as the more "rural" of the two parties. It appears, however, that the party's

Table 5-5-D

COMPARISON OF PARTY LEADERS AND FOLLOWERS ON "TAX POLICY" ISSUES, BY PERCENTAGES AND RATIOS OF SUPPORT

Issues	Leaders		Followers	
	Dem. N=1,788	Repub. N=1,232	Dem. N=821	Repub. N=623
		(per cents down)		
Corporate Income Tax				
% favoring: Increase	32.3	4.0	32.0	23.3
Decrease	23.3	61.5	20.5	25.7
Same, n.c.	44.4	34.5	47.5	51.0
Support Ratio	.54	.21	.56	.49
Tax on Large Incomes				
% favoring: Increase	27.0	5.4	46.6	34.7
Decrease	23.1	56.9	13.8	21.7
Same, n.c.	49.9	37.7	39.6	43.6
Support Ratio	.52	.24	.66	.56
Tax on Business				
% favoring: Increase	12.6	1.0	24.6	15.9
Decrease	38.3	71.1	24.1	32.6
Same, n.c.	49.1	27.8	51.3	51.5
Support Ratio	.37	.15	.50	.42
Tax on Middle Incomes				
% favoring: Increase	2.7	0.8	4.5	3.0
Decrease	50.2	63.9	49.3	44.3
Same, n.c.	47.1	35.3	46.2	52.6
Support Ratio	.26	.18	.28	.29
Tax on Small Incomes				
% favoring: Increase	1.4	2.9	1.6	2.1
Decrease	79.2	65.0	77.5	69.6
Same, n.c.	19.4	32.1	20.9	28.3
Support Ratio	.11	.19	.12	.16
Mean Support Ratios for "Tax Policy" Category	.36	.19	.42	.38

connection with business is far more compelling than its association with agriculture. The Republican desire to reduce government expenditures and to promote independence from "government handouts" prevails on the farm question as it does on other issues, while the Democratic preference for a more regulated economy in which government intervenes to reduce economic risk and to stabilize prosperity is equally evident on the other side. Party attitudes on this issue appear to be determined as much by ideological tendencies as by deliberate calculation of the political advantages to be gained by favoring or opposing subsidies to farmers. Comparison of our findings with Turner's earlier data on farm votes in Congress suggests, in addition, that the sharp party difference on the farm issue is neither a recent development nor a mere product of the personal philosophy of the present Secretary of Agriculture.

Having implied that agricultural policies partly result from principle, we must note that on three other issues in this category (trade unions, credit, and tariffs), principle seems to be overweighed by old-fashioned economic considerations. In spite of their distaste for government interference in economic affairs, the Republicans almost unanimously favor greater regulation of trade unions and they are

Table 5-5-E

COMPARISON OF PARTY LEADERS AND FOLLOWERS ON " FOREIGN POLICY " ISSUES, BY PERCENTAGES AND RATIOS OF SUPPORT

Issues	Leaders		Followers	
	Dem. N=1,788	Repub. N=1,232	Dem. N=821	Repub. N=623
	(per cents down)			
Reliance on the United Nations				
% favoring: Increase	48.9	24.4	34.7	33.4
Decrease	17.6	34.8	17.3	19.3
Same, n.c.	33.5	40.7	48.0	47.3
Support Ratio	.66	.45	.59	.57
American Participation in Military Alliances				
% favoring: Increase	41.5	22.7	39.1	32.3
Decrease	17.6	25.7	14.0	15.4
Same, n.c.	40.9	51.6	46.9	52.3
Support Ratio	.62	.48	.62	.58
Foreign Aid				
% favoring: Increase	17.8	7.6	10.1	10.1
Decrease	51.0	61.7	58.6	57.3
Same, n.c.	31.1	30.7	31.3	32.6
Support Ratio	.33	.23	.26	.26
Defense Spending				
% favoring: Increase	20.7	13.6	50.5	45.7
Decrease	34.4	33.6	16.4	15.4
Same, n.c.	44.8	52.8	33.0	38.8
Support Ratio	.43	.40	.67	.65
Mean Support Ratios for "Foreign Policy" Category (excl. Defense Spending)	.54	.39	.49	.47

more strongly disposed than the Democrats toward government intervention to restrict credit and to raise tariffs. Of course, party cleavages over the credit and tariff issues have a long history, which may by now have endowed them with ideological force beyond immediate economic considerations. The preponderant Democratic preference for greater regulation of trade unions is doubtless a response to recent "exposures" of corrupt labor practices, though it may also signify that the party's perspective toward the trade unions is shifting somewhat.

The closer Republican identification with business, free enterprise, and economic conservatism in general, and the friendlier Democratic attitude toward labor and toward government regulation of the economy, are easily observed in the data from other parts of our questionnaire. Republican leaders score very much higher than Democratic leaders on, for example, such scales as economic conservatism, independence of government, and business attitudes. On a question asking respondents to indicate the groups from which they would be most and least likely to take advice, 41 per cent of the Democratic leaders but only 3.8 per cent of the Republican leaders list trade unions as groups from which they would seek advice. Trade unions are scored in the "least likely" category by 25 per cent of the Democrats and 63 per cent of the Republicans. Similarly, more than 94 per cent of the Republican leaders, but 56 per cent of the Democratic leaders, name trade unions as groups that have "too much power." These differences, it should be noted, cannot be accounted for by reference to the greater number of trade union members among the Democratic party leadership, for in the 1956 conventions only 14 per cent of the Democrats belonged to trade unions, and while an even smaller percentage (4 per cent) of the Republicans were trade unionists, this disparity is hardly great enough to explain the large differences in outlook. The key to the explanation has to be sought in the symbolic and reference group identifications of the two parties, and in their underlying values.

Nowhere do we see this more clearly than in the responses to the Equalitarian and Human Welfare issues. The mean difference in the ratio scores for the category as a whole is .22, a very large difference and one that results from differences in the expected direction on all six issues that make up the category. On four of these issues—federal aid to education, slum clearance, and public housing, social security, and minimum wages— the leaders of the two parties are widely separated, the differences in their ratio scores ranging from .36 to .21. The percentages showing the proportions who favor increased support for these issues are even more striking. In every instance the Democratic percentages are considerably higher: 66 *vs.* 22 per cent (education); 78 *vs.* 40 per cent (slum clearance and housing); 60 *vs.* 23 per cent (social security); and 50 *vs.* 16 per cent (minimum wages). The Democratic leaders also are better disposed than the Republican leaders toward immigration: twice as many of them (36 per cent *vs.* 18 per cent) favor a change in policy to permit more immigrants to enter. The over-all inclination of both party elites, however, is to accept the present levels of immigration, the Democratic ratio score falling slightly above, and the Republican slightly below, the midpoint.

More surprising are the differences on the segregation issue, for, despite strong Southern influence, the Democratic leaders express significantly more support for enforcing integration than the Republicans do. Moreover, the difference between the two parties rises from .12 for the national samples as a whole to a difference of .18 when the Southern leaders are excluded. In his study of Congress, Turner found that the Republicans gave more support to Negro rights than the Democrats did. The reversal of this finding in our data does not necessarily mean that a change has occurred since Turner made his study, but only that the votes of the congressional parties do not always reflect the private feelings of the national party leadership. Then, too, Southern influence is disproportionately stronger in the Democratic congressional party than in the national Democratic organization as a whole, and disproportionately weaker in the Republican congressional party than in the Republican organization as a whole.

Examination of the actual magnitude of the ratio scores in this category reveals that the Republicans want not so much to abrogate existing social welfare or equalitarian measures as to keep them from being broadened. The Democrats, by comparison, are shown to be the party of social equality and reform, more willing than their opponents to employ legislation for the benefit of the underprivileged. Support for these inferences and for the greater liberalism of the Democrats can be found elsewhere in our data as well. Analysis of the scale results show Republican leaders scoring higher than Democratic leaders on such measures as chauvinism, elitism, conservatism, and right-wing values, and lower on tolerance, procedural rights, and faith in democracy. No differences worth noting, however, were found for ethnocentrism, faith in freedom, or the California F scale. The Democrats had a slightly higher average score on the left-wing scale, but the number of leaders in either party who scored high on this measure was fairly small.

The self-images and reference group identifications of the two parties also should be noted in this connection. For example, many more Democratic than Republican leaders call themselves liberal and state that they would be most likely to take advice from liberal reform organizations, the Farmers' Union, and (as we have seen) from the trade unions; only a small number consider themselves conservative or would seek advice from conservative reform organizations, the National Association of Manufacturers, or the Farm Bureau Federation. The Republicans have in almost all instances the reverse identifications: only a handful regard themselves as liberal or would seek counsel from liberal organizations, while more than 42 per cent call themselves conservative and would look to the NAM or to conservative reform organizations for advice. Almost two-thirds of the Republicans (compared with 29 per cent of the Democrats) regard the Chamber of Commerce as an important source of advice. Businessmen are listed as having "too much power" by 42 percent of the Democrats but by only 9 per cent of the Republicans. The Democrats are also significantly more inclined than the Republicans to consider Catholics, Jews, and the foreign born as having "too little power." While self-descriptions and reference group identifications often correspond poorly with actual beliefs—among the general population they scarcely correspond at all, in fact—we are dealing, in the case of the leaders, with a politically informed and highly articulate set of people who have little difficulty connecting the beliefs they hold and the groups that promote or obstruct those beliefs.

Our fourth category, Tax Policy, divides the parties almost as severely as do the other categories. The mean difference for the category as a whole is .20 and it would doubtless have been larger but for the universal unpopularity of proposals to increase taxes on small and middle income groups. Table 5-5-D shows that the differences between the parties on the tax issues follow the patterns previously observed and that tax policy is for the Democrats a device for redistributing income and promoting social equality. Neither party, however, is keen about raising taxes for *any* group: even the Democrats have little enthusiasm for new taxes on upper income groups or on business and corporate enterprises. The Republican leaders are overwhelmingly opposed to increased taxes for *any* group, rich *or* poor. This can be seen in their low ratio scores on the tax issues, which range from only .15 to .24. But while they are far more eager than the Democratic leaders to cut taxes on corporate and private wealth, they are less willing to reduce taxes on the lower income groups. These differences, it should be remarked, are not primarily a function of differences in the income of the two samples. Although there are more people with high incomes among the Republican leaders, the disproportion between the two samples is not nearly great enough to account for the dissimilarities in their tax views.

Of the five categories considered, Foreign Policy shows the smallest average difference, but even on these issues the divergence between Democratic and Republican leader attitudes is significant. Except for defense spending the Democrats turn out to be more internationalist than the Republicans, as evidenced in their greater commitment to the United Nations and to American participation in international military alliances like NATO. Twice as many Democrats as Republicans want the United States to rely more heavily upon such organizations, while many more Republicans want to reduce our international involvements. Both parties are predominantly in favor of cutting back foreign aid—a somewhat surprising finding in light of Democratic public pronouncements on this subject —but more Republicans feel strongly on the subject. Our data thus furnish little support for the claim that the parties hold the same views on foreign policy or that their seeming differences are merely a response to the demands of political competition.

Nevertheless, it would be incorrect to conclude that one party believes in internationalism and the other in isolationism. The differences are far too small to warrant any such inference. Traces of isolationism, to be sure, remain stronger in the Republican party than in the Democratic party— an observation buttressed by the finding that twice as many Republicans as Democrats score high on the isolationism scale. The pattern of Republican responses on both the issue and scale items signifies, however, that the leaders of that party generally accept the degree of "internationalism" now in effect, but shrink from extending it further. Consider too, the similarities in the leaders' scores on defense spending, for despite their greater leaning toward isolationism, the Republicans are no more inclined than the Democrats to leave the country defenseless.

In treating issues in the Elmira election study of 1948, Berelson, Lazarsfeld, and McPhee found it helpful to distinguish between "style" and "position" issues. "Style" issues principally yield symbolic, psychological, or subjective gratifications, and have relatively intangible consequences; "position" issues reflect direct, personal, and material interests, and have more objective consequences. According to the Elmira report, "position" issues (or what politicians might call "bread and butter" issues) divide voters more sharply than style issues. Most of the issues tested in the present study would have to be classified as "position" issues, but five of them—United Nations, international alliances, foreign aid, immigration, and segregation—could be classified as style issues. Four others—natural resources, atomic energy, education, and slum clearance—contain both symbolic and material elements and can best be described as "mixed."

Although the classification is crude, the findings it yields are generally consistent with the claims of the Elmira study. On the fourteen position issues—taxes, trade unions, tariffs, minimum wages, farm prices, social security, credit restrictions, and the regulation of business, public utilities, and monopolies—Democratic and Republican leaders show an average ratio score difference of .21. On the style issues the two parties differ by .13—a significantly smaller difference. Largest of all, however, are the differences for the "mixed" issues, which average more than .30. This result should occasion little surprise, for when ideology and interest are *both* at work, partisanship is likely to be intensified. Several considerations could account for the superiority of position over style issues as causes of political cleavage: they are "bread and butter" issues, and are thus more often subject to pressure by organized interest groups; they have immediate and tangible consequences, which may lead politicians to pay greater attention to them than they do to issues whose payoff is more uncertain; and, finally, they are not so likely bo be part of the common core of values upon which the community structure rests.

Comparison of the magnitude of the differences between groups can be seen in Table 5–6 where we have ranked the issues, high to low, according to the size of the difference between the groups being compared. By presenting a rank-order of differences for the two leader groups, for the two follower groups, and for the leaders and followers of each party, this table makes it possible to observe not only which issues most and least divide the several party groups, but whether they divide the leaders and followers in the same way.

Notice that the issues commonly thought to be most divisive do not always evoke the greatest cleavage between the parties. Immigration, tariffs, civil rights, monopoly control, and credit regulation fall toward the lower end of the rank order, while farm supports, federal aid to education, slum clearance, social security, minimum wages, public housing, and issues dealing with the regulation and taxation of business fall toward the upper end. Though by no means uniformly, the older, more traditional issues appear to have been superseded as sources of controversy by issues that have come into prominence chiefly during the New Deal and Fair Deal.

Comparisons Between Followers

So far we have addressed ourselves to the differences between Democratic and Republican *leaders*. In each of the tables presented, however, data are included from which the two sets of party *followers* may also be compared. The observation most clearly warranted from these data is that the rank and file members of the two parties are far less divided than their leaders. Not only do they diverge significantly on fewer issues—seven as compared with twenty-three for the leader samples—but the magnitudes of the differences in their ratio scores are substantially smaller for every one of the twenty-four issues. No difference is larger than .14, and on the majority of the issues the disparity is smaller than .05. Insofar as they differ at all, however, the followers tend to divide in a pattern similar to that shown by the leaders, the correlation between their rank orders being .72. All the issues on which the followers significantly disagree are of the "bread and butter" variety, the more symbolic issues being so remotely experienced and so vaguely grasped that rank and file voters are often unable to identify them with either party. Policies affecting farm prices, business regulation, taxes, or minimum wages, by contrast, are quickly felt by the groups to whom they are addressed and are therefore more capable of arousing partisan identifications. It should also be noted that while the average differences are small for all five categories, they are smallest of all for foreign policy—the most removed and least well understood group of issues in the entire array.

Democratic and Republican followers were also compared on a number of scales and reference group questions. The results, while generally consistent with the differences between the leaders, show the followers to be far more united than their leaders on these measures as well. Even on business attitudes, independence of government, and economic conservatism, the differences are small and barely significant. No differences were found on such scales as tolerance, faith in democracy, procedural rights, conservatism-liberalism (classical), the California F scale, and isolationism. The average Democrat is slightly more willing than the average Republican to label himself a liberal or to seek advice from liberal organizations; the contrary is true when it comes to adopting conservative identifications. Only in the differential trust they express toward business and labor are the two sets of followers widely separated.

These findings give little support to the claim that the "natural divisions" of the electorate are being smothered by party leaders. Not only do the leaders disagree more sharply than their respective followers, but the level of consensus among the electorate (with or without regard to party) is fairly high. Inspection of the "increase" and "decrease" percentage scores (Tables 5–5-A—E) shows that substantial differences of opinion exist among the electorate on only five of the twenty-four issues (credit restrictions, farm supports, segregation, and corporate and business taxes). Of course, voters may divide more sharply on issues at election time, since campaigns intensify party feeling

and may also intensify opinions on issues. Available data from election studies allow no unequivocal conclusion on this point, but even the party-linked differences found among voters during elections may largely be echoes of the opinions announced by the candidates—transient sentiments developed for the occasion and quickly forgotten.

Leader Conflict and Follower Consensus: Explanations

Considering the nature of the differences between the leader and follower samples, the interesting question is not why the parties fail to represent the "natural division" in the electorate (for that question rests on an unwarranted assumption) but why the party elites disagree at all, and why they divide so much more sharply than their followers?

Despite the great pressures toward uniformity we have noted in American society, many forces also divide the population culturally, economically, and politically. The United States is, after all, a miscellany of ethnic and religious strains set down in a geographically large and diverse country. Many of these groups brought old conflicts and ideologies with them, and some have tried to act out in the new world the hopes and frustrations nurtured in the old. Then, too, despite rapid social mobility, social classes have by no means been eliminated. No special political insight is needed to perceive that the two parties characteristically draw from different strata of the society, the Republicans from the managerial, proprietary, and to some extent professional classes, the Democrats from labor, minorities, low income groups, and a large proportion of the intellectuals. Partly because the leaders of the two parties tend to overrespond to the modal values of the groups with which they are principally identified, they gradually grow further apart on the key questions which separate their respective supporters. The Republican emphasis on business ideology is both a cause and a consequence of its managerial and proprietary support; the greater Democratic emphasis on social justice, and on economic and social levelling, is both the occasion and the product of the support the party enjoys among intellectuals and the lower strata. These interrelationships are strengthened, moreover, by the tendency for a party's dominant supporters to gain a disproportionate number of positions in its leadership ranks.

The differences which typically separate Democratic from Republican leaders seem also to reflect a deep-seated ideological cleavage often found among Western parties. One side of this cleavage is marked by a strong belief in the power of collective action to promote social justice, equality, humanitarianism, and economic planning, while preserving freedom; the other is distinguished by faith in the wisdom of the natural competitive process and in the supreme virtue of individualism, "character," self-reliance, frugality, and independence from government. To this cleavage is added another frequent source of political division, namely, a difference in attitude toward change between "radicals" and "moderates," between those who prefer to move quickly or slowly, to reform or to conserve. These differences in social philosophy and posture do not always coincide with the divisions in the social structure, and their elements do not, in all contexts, combine in the same way. But however crudely, the American parties do tend to embody these competing points of view and to serve as reference groups for those who hold them.

Party cleavage in America was no doubt intensified by the advent of the New Deal, and by its immense electoral and intellectual success. Not only did it weld into a firm alliance the diverse forces that were to be crucial to all subsequent Democratic majorities, but it also made explicit the doctrines of the "welfare state" with which the party was henceforth to be inseparably identified. Because of the novelty of its program and its apparently radical threat to the familiar patterns of American political and economic life, it probably deepened the fervor of its Republican adversaries and drove into the opposition the staunchest defenders of business ideology. The conflict was further sharpened by the decline of left-wing politics after the war, and by the transfer of loyalties of former and potential radicals to the Democratic party. Once launched, the cleavage has been sustained by the tendency for each party to attract into its active ranks a disproportionate number of voters who recognize and share its point of view.

Why, however, are the leaders so much more sharply divided than their followers? The reasons are not hard to understand and are consistent with several of the hypotheses that underlay the present study.

1. Consider, to begin with, that the leaders come from the more articulate segments of society and, on the average, are politically more aware than their followers and far better informed about issues. For them, political issues and opinions

are the everyday currency of party competition, not esoteric matters that surpass understanding. With their greater awareness and responsibility, and their greater need to defend their party's stands, they have more interest in developing a consistent set of attitudes—perhaps even an ideology. The followers of each party, often ignorant of the issues and their consequences, find it difficult to distinguish their beliefs from those of the opposition and have little reason to be concerned with the consistency of their attitudes. Furthermore, the American parties make only a feeble effort to educate the rank and file politically, and since no central source exists for the authoritative pronouncement of party policy, the followers often do not know what their leaders believe or on what issues the parties chiefly divide. In short, if we mean by ideology a coherent body of informed social doctrine, it is possessed mainly by the articulate leadership, rarely by the masses.

2. Differences in the degree of partisan involvement parallel the differences in knowledge and have similar consequences. The leaders, of course, have more party spirit than the followers and, as the election studies make plain, the stronger the partisanship, the larger the differences on issues. The leaders are more highly motivated not only to belong to a party appropriate to their beliefs, but to accept its doctrines and to learn how it differs from the opposition party. Since politics is more salient for leaders than for followers, they develop a greater stake in the outcome of the political contest and are more eager to discover the intellectual grounds by which they hope to make victory possible. Through a process of circular reinforcement,

those for whom politics is most important are likely to become the most zealous participants, suceeding to the posts that deal in the formation of opinion. Ideology serves the instrumental purpose, in addition, of justifying the heavy investment that party leaders make in political activity. While politics offers many rewards, it also makes great demands on the time, money, and energies of its practitioners—sacrifices which they can more easily justify if they believe they are serving worth while social goals. The followers, in contrast, are intellectually far less involved, have less personal stake in the outcome of the competition, have little need to be concerned with the "correctness" of their views on public questions, and have even less reason to learn in precisely what ways their opinions differ from their opponents'. Hence, the party elites recruit members from a population stratified in some measure by ideology, while the rank and file renews itself by more random recruitment and is thus more likely to mirror the opinions of a cross section of the population.

3. Part of the explanation for the greater consensus among followers than leaders resides in the nature and size of the two types of groups. Whereas the leader groups are comparatively small and selective, each of the follower groups number in the millions and, by their very size and unwieldiness, are predisposed to duplicate the characteristics of the population as a whole. Even if the Republicans draw disproportionately from the business-managerial classes and the Democrats from the trade union movement, neither interest group has enough influence to shape distinctively the aggregate opinions of so large a mass of supporters. Size

also affects the nature and frequency of interaction within the two types of groups. Because they comprise a smaller, more selectively chosen, organized, and articulate elite, the leaders are apt to associate with people of their own political persuasion more frequently and consistently than the followers do. They are not only less cross-pressured than the rank and file but they are also subjected to strong party group efforts to induce them to conform. Because their political values are continually renewed through frequent communication with people of like opinions, and because they acquire intense reference group identifications, they develop an extraordinary ability to resist the force of the opposition's arguments. While the followers, too, are thrown together and shielded to some extent, they are likely to mingle more freely with people of hostile political persuasions, to receive fewer partisan communications, and to hold views that are only intermittently and inconsistently reinforced. Since, by comparison with the leaders, they possess little interest in or information about politics, they can more easily embrace "deviant" attitudes without discomfort and without challenge from their associates. Nor are they likely to be strongly rewarded for troubling to have "correct" opinions. The followers, in short, are less often and less effectively indoctrinated than their leaders. The group processes described here would function even more powerfully in small, sectarian, tightly organized parties of the European type, but they are also present in the American party system, where they yield similar though less potent consequences.

4. Political competition itself operates to divide the leaders more than the followers. If the parties are impelled to present a common face to the electorate, they are also strongly influenced to distinguish themselves from each other. For one thing, they have a more heightened sense of the "national interest" than the followers do, even if they do not all conceive it in the same way. For another, they hope to improve their chances at the polls by offering the electorate a recognizable and attractive commodity. In addition, they seek emotional gratification in the heightened sense of brotherhood brought on by the struggle against an "out-group" whose claim to office seems always, somehow, to border upon usurpation. As with many ingroup-outgroup distinctions, the participants search for moral grounds to justify their antagonisms toward each other, and ideologies help to furnish such grounds. Among the followers, on the other hand, these needs exist, if at all, in much weaker form.

Leaders Versus Followers

In comparing each party elite with its own followers we were mainly interested in seeing how closely each body of supporters shared the point of view of its leaders, in order to test the hypothesis that party affiliation, even for the rank and file, is a function of ideological agreement. In predicting that the parties would tend to attract supporters who share their beliefs, we expected, of course, to find exceptions. We knew that many voters pay little attention to the ideological aspects of politics and that, in Gabriel Almond's phrase, a party's more "esoteric doctrines" are not always known to its followers. Nevertheless we were not prepared for the findings turned up by this phase of the inquiry, for the differences between leaders and followers—among the Republicans at

Table 5-6 RANK ORDER OF DIFFERENCES IN THE SUPPORT-RATIO SCORES OF PARTY LEADERS AND FOLLOWERS*

Democratic vs. Republican Leaders — Issues	Diff. between ratio scores***	Democratic vs. Republican Followers — Issues	Diff. between ratio scores	Democratic Leaders vs. Followers — Issues	Diff. between ratio scores	Republican Leaders vs. Followers — Issues	Diff. between ratio scores
1. Natural Resources	+.39	Farm Supports	+.14	Immigration	+.25	Fed. Aid to Edu.	−.39
2. Farm Supports	+.38	Gov't. Reg. of Business	+.12	Anti-Monopoly	+.15	Taxes-Large Income	−.32
3. Fed. Aid to Edu.	+.37	Taxes-Large Income	+.10	Taxes-Large Income	−.15	Taxes-Corp.	−.28
4. Taxes-Corp.	+.33	Minimum Wages	+.09	Taxes-Business	−.13	Taxes-Business	−.27
5. Reg.-Business	+.33	Taxes-Business	+.09	Reg. Pub. Util.	+.12	Natural Resources	−.25
6. Taxes-Large Inc.	+.28	Reg. Pub. Util.	+.07	Tariffs	−.11	Pub. Housing	−.23
7. Pub. Housing	+.27	Taxes-Corp.	+.07	Restrict. Credit	−.09	Reg. Business	−.22
8. Reg. Pub. Util.	+.26	Social Security	+.07	Natural Resources	+.09	Social Security	−.22
9. Social Security	+.23	Fed. Aid to Edu.	+.06	Fed. Aid to Edu.	−.08	Farm Supports	−.22
10. Taxes-Business	+.22	Reg. Trade Unions	−.05	Foreign Aid	+.08	Minimum Wages	−.18
11. Minimum Wages	+.21	Natural Resources	+.05	Reliance on U.N.	+.07	Reg. Trade Unions	+.17
12. Reliance on U.N.	+.21	Public Housing	+.05	Minimum Wages	−.05	Immigration	+.13
13. Anti-monopoly	+.20	Taxes-Small Income	−.04	Social Security	−.05	Reliance on U.N.	−.12
14. Atomic Energy Control	+.18	American Participation, NATO	+.04	Reg. Trade Unions	+.05	Enforce Integration	−.12
15. Reg. Trade Unions	−.18	Atomic Energy Control	+.04	Atomic Energy Control	+.04	Taxes-Middle Income	−.11
16. American Participation, NATO	+.13	Immigration	−.03	Farm Supports	+.02	Atomic Energy Control	−.10
17. Enforce Integration	+.12	Defense Spending	+.02	Reg. Business	−.02	American Participation, NATO	−.10
18. Tariffs	−.11	Taxes-Middle Income	−.02	Enforce Integration	+.01	Reg. Public Utilities	−.07
19. Foreign Aid	+.10	Reliance on U.N.	+.02	Taxes-Middle Income	+.02	Anti-Monopoly	−.04
20. Increase Immigration	+.10	Tariffs	−.01	Taxes-Corporation	−.01	Foreign Aid	−.03
21. Taxes-Small Income	−.08	Enforce Integration	−.01	Taxes-Small Income	−.1	Taxes-Small Income	+.03
22. Taxes-Middle Income	+.08	Restriction Credit	+.01	American Participation, NATO	−.01	Restriction Credit	−.01
23. Restriction Credit	−.07	Foreign Aid	−.01	Public Housing	.00	Tariffs	−.01
24. Defense Spending	+.03	Anti-Monopoly	.00	Defense Spending	**	Defense Spending	**

N's. Democratic Leaders: 1,788; Republican Leaders: 821; Democratic Followers: 1,232; Republican Followers: 623.

* The plus sign means that the first group listed in the heading is more favorable to the issue named than the second group; the minus sign means that the second group is the more favorable.

** Leaders and Followers cannot be compared on defense spending, for reasons given in footnote to Table 5-5E.

*** Size of difference required for differences to be significant at .01 level: Democratic Leaders vs. Republican—.048; Democratic Followers vs. Republican Followers—.063; Democratic Leaders vs. Democratic Followers—.054; Republican Leaders vs. Republican Followers—.068.

least—are beyond anything we had expected. Indeed, the conclusion is inescapable that the views of the Republican rank and file are, on the whole, much closer to those of the Democratic leaders than to those of the Republican leaders. Although conflicts in outlook also exist between Democratic leaders and followers, they are less frequent or severe.

If we turn once again to the table of rank order differences, we see that the Democratic followers differ significantly from their leaders on twelve of the twenty-three issues, and that the average difference in the ratio scores of the two samples is .07. Democratic leaders and Republican followers differ significantly on only eleven of the twenty-three issues, with an average difference between them of only .08. Notice, by contrast, that Republican leaders and followers diverge significantly on eighteen of the twenty-three issues, and show an average difference of .16. To complete the comparison, the Republican leaders and Democratic followers were in disagreement on nineteen of the twenty-three issues, their average difference being .20. As these comparisons make plain, there is substantial consensus on national issues between Democratic leaders and Democratic and Republican followers, while the Republican leaders are separated not only from the Democrats but from their own rank and file members as well.

Examination of the Democratic scores shows the leaders to be slightly more "progressive" than their followers on most of the issues on which differences appear. The leaders are, for example, more favorable to public ownership of natural resources, to regulation of monopolies and public utilities, to a reduction of tariffs, and

to a liberalized credit policy. They are more internationalist on the foreign aid and United Nations issues and substantially more sympathetic to the maintenance and expansion of immigration. The results showing the relative radicalism of the two samples are not unequivocal, however, for on several issues—federal aid to education, minimum wages, and taxes on business enterprise and large income—the followers take the more radical view. Nor are the differences significant on such issues as atomic energy, slum clearance, segregation, farm price supports, government control of business and trade unions, and taxes on middle and small income groups. In general, the followers turn out more radical chiefly on a few of the bread and butter issues—a reflection, no doubt, of their lower socio-economic status. When we control for occupation, the differences between Democratic leaders and followers on these issues largely disappear.

Consideration of the scores of Republican leaders and followers shows not only that they are widely separated in their outlooks but also that the leaders are uniformly more conservative than their followers. Only on the immigration issues is this trend reversed. The followers hold the more "radical" ideas on the two public ownership issues, on five of the six equalitarian and human welfare issues, on four of the seven regulation-of-the-economy issues, and on four of the five tax policy issues. They are also more willing to place greater reliance upon the U.N. and upon international military alliances. Observe that the largest differences occur on those issues which have most sharply separated New Deal-Fair Deal spokesmen from the hard core of the Republican opposition—federal aid to education, redistribution of wealth through taxes on business, corporations and the wealthy, public ownership of natural resources, public housing, regulation of business, social security, farm price supports, minimum wages, and trade union regulations.

In short, whereas Republican leaders hold to the tenets of business ideology and remain faithful to the spirit and intellectual mood of leaders like Robert A. Taft, the rank and file Republican supporters have embraced, along with their Democratic brethren, the regulatory and social reform measures of the Roosevelt and Truman administrations. This inference receives further support from the scores on our Party Ideology scale where, on a variety of attitudes and values which characteristically distinguish the leaders of the two parties, the Republican followers fall closer to the Democratic than to the Republican side of the continuum. Thus, in addition to being the preferred party of the more numerous classes, the Democrats also enjoy the advantages over their opponents of holding views that are more widely shared throughout the country.

Assuming the findings are valid, we were obviously wrong to expect that party differentiation among followers would depend heavily upon ideological considerations. Evidently, party attachment is so much a function of other factors (e.g. class and primary group memberships, religious affiliation, place of residence, mass media, etc.) that many voters can maintain their party loyalties comfortably even while holding views that contradict the beliefs of their own leaders.

Still, we are not entitled to conclude that issue outlook has no effect on the party affiliation of ordinary members. It is conceivable, for example, that the Republican party has come to be the minority party partly because the opinions of its spokesmen are uncongenial to a majority of the voters. We have no way of knowing from our data—collected at only a single point in time—how many "normally" Republican voters, if any, have defected to the Democrats or fled into independency because they disapprove of Republican beliefs. At the present stage of the analysis, we have no grounds for going beyond the proposition that political affiliation without conformity on issues is possible on a wide scale. In future analyses we shall attempt to learn more about the nature of the relationship between belief and party affiliation by stratifying voters according to the frequency with which they conform to the beliefs of their party leaders. We hope, in this way, to discover whether those who conform least are also less firm in their party loyalties.

The Homogeneity of Support for Leaders and Followers

So far we have only considered conflict and agreement *between* groups. We should now turn to the question of consensus *within* groups. To what extent is each of our samples united on fundamental issues?

In order to assess homogeneity of opinion within party groups, standard deviation scores were computed on each issue for each of the four samples. The higher the standard deviation, of course, the greater the disagreement. The range of possible sigma scores is from 0 (signifying that every member of the sample has selected the same response) to .500 (signifying that all responses are equally divided between the "increase" and "decrease" alternatives). If we assume that the three alternative responses had been randomly (and therefore equally) selected, the standard deviations for the four samples would fall by chance alone around .410. Scores at or above this level may be taken to denote extreme dispersion among the members of a sample while scores in the neighborhood of .300 or below suggest that unanimity within the sample is fairly high. By these somewhat arbitrary criteria we can observe immediately (Table 5–7) that consensus within groups is greater on most issues than we would expect by chance alone, but that it is extremely high in only a few instances. Although the Republican leaders appear on the average to be the most united and the Democratic leaders the least united of the four groups, the difference between their homogeneity scores (.340 vs. .310) is too small to be taken as conclusive. The grounds are somewhat better for rejecting the belief that leaders are more homogeneous in their outlooks than their followers, since the hypothesis holds only for one party and not for the other.

While generalizations about the relative unity of the four samples seem risky, we can speak more confidently about the rank order of agreement within samples. In Table 5–7 we have ranked the issues according to the degree of consensus exhibited toward them by the members of each of the four party groups. There we see that the leaders of the Republican party are most united on the issues that stem from its connections with business—government regulation of business, taxes (especially on business), regulation of trade unions, and mini-mum wages. The Democratic leaders are most united on those issues which bear upon the support the party receives from the lower and middle income groups—taxes on small and middle incomes, anti-monopoly, slum clearance, social security, and minimum wages. The Republican leaders divide most severely on federal aid to education, slum clearance, U.N. support, segregation, and public control of atomic energy and natural resources; the Democratic leaders are most divided on farm prices, segregation, credit restriction, immigration, and the natural resources issue. Among the followers the patterns of unity and division are very similar, as attested by the high correlation of .83 between the rank orders of their homogeneity scores. Both Republican and Democratic followers exhibit great cohesion, for example, on taxes on small and middle incomes, social security, slum clearance, and minimum wages. Both divide rather sharply on segregation, farm price supports, defense spending, U.N. support, and taxes on large incomes. The two sets of followers, in short, are alike not only in their opinions on issues but in the degree of unanimity they exhibit toward them.

Inspection of the homogeneity data furnishes additional evidence on the between-group comparisons made earlier. Whereas Democratic and Republican followers divide on issues in approximately the same way, the two sets of leaders differ from each other in this respect also (the correlation between their rank orders on homogeneity is only .28). Democratic leaders and followers tend to unite or divide on the same issues for the most part (r equals .77), but Republican leaders and followers are not parallel in this respect either (*r* equals .30). The pattern of homogeneity and dispersion among Republican followers is, in fact, much closer to that of the Democratic leaders (*r* equals .75).

In computing scores for homogeneity we were in part concerned to test the belief that political parties develop greatest internal solidarity on those questions which most separate them from their opponents. According to this hypothesis, external controversy has the effect of uniting the members further by confronting them with a common danger. Whether or not this hypothesis would be borne out in a study of small, sectarian parties we cannot say, but it receives no support from the present study of the American mass parties. Comparisons of the rank order data in Tables 5–6 and 5–7 show that there is no consistent connection between interparty conflict and intra-party cohesion. The correlations between the rank orders of difference and the rank orders of homogeneity are in every case insignificant.

Table 5-7
CONSENSUS WITHIN PARTY GROUPS: RANK ORDER OF
HOMOGENEITY OF SUPPORT ON TWENTY-FOUR ISSUES

Average Rank Order*	Issue	Democratic Leaders		Republican Leaders		Democratic Followers		Republican Followers	
		Rank Order	Sigma	Rank Order	Sigma	Rank Order	Sigma	Rank Order	Sigma
1	Tax on Small Incomes	1	.220	6	.270	1	.224	1	.250
2	Tax on Middle Incomes	3	.276	4	.248	6	.292	2	.278
3	Social Security Benefits	5	.282	8	.296	2	.266	3	.286
4	Minimum Wages	6	.292	5	.268	4	.276	4	.294
5	Enforcement of Anti-Monopoly	2	.246	13	.321	8	.324	7	.314
6	Regulation of Public Utilities	8	.307	10	.300	10	.336	5.5	.310
7	Slum Clearance	4	.276	23	.386	3	.274	5.5	.310
8	Regulation of Trade Unions	12	.356	3	.240	9	.331	15	.345
9	Government Regulation of Business	17	.376	1	.192	20	.363	8	.315
10	Tax on Business	9	.338	2	.236	19	.362	16	.348
11	Level of Tariffs	10	.350	16	.344	11	.338	9	.316
12	Public Control of Atomic Energy	7	.302	20	.362	7	.312	13	.340
13	Federal Aid to Education	13	.360	24	.394	5	.283	11	.322
14	Foreign Aid	19	.383	12	.317	12.5	.340	12	.340
15	Tax on Large Incomes	11	.356	9	.298	17	.358	22	.379
16	American Participation in Military Alliances, NATO	14	.370	18	.351	14	.350	14	.344
17	Immigration into U.S.	21	.399	17	.345	12.5	.340	10	.318
18	Corporate Income Tax	16	.375	7	.284	21	.371	17	.361
19	Restrictions on Credit	22	.400	14	.324	16	.358	18	.362
20	Defense Spending	15	.371	15	.334	22	.380	21	.366
21	Public Ownership of Natural Resources	20	.393	19	.354	15	.352	19	.362
22	Reliance on U.N.	18	.380	22	.384	18	.359	20	.365
23	Level of Farm Supports	24	.421	11	.306	23	.414	23	.397
24	Enforce Integration	23	.416	21	.382	24	.418	24	.399

* The range of sigma scores is from .192 to .421, out of a possible range of .000 (most united) to .500 (least united). Hence, the lower the rank order the greater the unity on the issue named.

Summary and Conclusions

The research described in this paper—an out-growth of a nationwide inquiry into the nature and sources of political affiliation, activity, and belief—was principally designed to test a number of hypotheses about the relation of ideology to party membership. Responses from large samples of Democratic and Republican leaders and followers were compared on twenty-four key issues and on a number of attitude questions and scales. Statistical operations were carried out to assess conflict and consensus among party groups and to estimate the size and significance of differences. From the data yielded by this inquiry, the following inferences seem most warranted:

1. Although it has received wide currency, especially among Europeans, the belief that the two American parties are identical in principle and doctrine has little foundation in fact. Examination of the opinions of Democratic and Republican leaders shows them to be distinct communities of co-believers who diverge sharply on many important issues. Their disagreements, furthermore, conform to an image familiar to many observers and are generally consistent with differences turned up by studies of Congressional roll calls. The unpopularity of many of the positions held by Republican leaders suggests also that the parties submit to the demands of their constituents less slavishly than is commonly supposed.

2. Republican and Democratic leaders stand furthest apart on the issues that grow out of their group identification and support—out of the managerial, proprietary, and high-status connections of the one, and the labor, minority, low-status, and intellectual connections of the other. The opinions of each party elite are linked less by chance than by membership in a common ideological domain. Democratic leaders typically display the stronger urge to elevate the lowborn, the uneducated, the deprived minorities, and the poor in general; they are also more disposed to employ the nation's collective power to advance humanitarian and social welfare goals (e.g., social security, immigration, racial integration, a higher minimum wage, and public education). They are more critical of wealth and big business and more eager to bring them under regulation. Theirs is the greater faith in the wisdom of using legislation for redistributing the national product and for furnishing social services on a wide scale. Of the two groups of leaders, the Democrats are the more "progressively" oriented toward social reform and experimentation. The Republican leaders, while not uniformly differentiated from their opponents, subscribe in greater measure to the symbols and practices of individualism, laissez-faire, and national independence. They prefer to overcome humanity's misfortunes by relying upon personal effort, private incentives, frugality, hard work, responsibility, self-denial (for both men and government), and the strengthening rather than the diminution of the economic and status distinctions that are the "natural" rewards of the differences in human character and fortunes. Were it not for the hackneyed nature of the designation and the danger of forcing traits into a mold they fit only imperfectly, we might be tempted to describe the Republicans as the chief upholders of what Max Weber has called the

"Protestant Ethic." Not that the Democrats are insensible to the "virtues" of the Protestant-capitalistic ethos, but they embrace them less firmly or uniformly. The differences between the two elites have probably been intensified by the rise of the New Deal and by the shift of former radicals into the Democratic party following the decline of socialist and other left-wing movements during and after the war.

3. Whereas the leaders of the two parties diverge strongly, their followers differ only moderately in their attitudes toward issues. The hypothesis that party beliefs unite adherents and bring them into the party ranks may hold for the more active members of a mass party but not for its rank and file supporters. Republican followers, in fact, disagree far more with their own leaders than with the leaders of the Democratic party. Little support was found for the belief that deep cleavages exist among the electorate but are ignored by the leaders. One might, indeed more accurately assert the contrary, to wit: that the natural cleavages between the leaders are largely ignored by the voters. However, we cannot presently conclude that ideology exerts no influence over the habits of party support, for the followers do differ significantly and in the predicted directions on some issues. Furthermore, we do not know how many followers may previously have been led by doctrinal considerations to shift their party allegiances.

4. Except for their desire to ingratiate themselves with as many voters as possible, the leaders of the two parties have more reason than their followers to hold sharply opposing views on the important political questions of the day. Compared with the great mass of supporters, they are articulate, in-formed, highly partisan, and involved; they comprise a smaller and more tightly knit group which is closer to the well-springs of party opinion, more accessible for indoctrination, more easily rewarded or punished for conformity or deviation, and far more affected, politically and psychologically, by engagement in the party struggle for office. If the leaders of the two parties are not always candid about their disagreements, the reason may well be that they sense the great measure of consensus to be found among the electorate.

5. Finding that party leaders hold contrary beliefs does not prove that they *act* upon those beliefs or that the two parties are, in practice, governed by different outlooks. In a subsequent paper we shall consider these questions more directly by comparing platform and other official party pronouncements with the private opinions revealed in this study. Until further inquiries are conducted, however, it seems reasonable to assume that the views held privately by party leaders can never be entirely suppressed but are bound to crop out in hundreds of large and small ways—in campaign speeches, discussions at party meetings, private communications to friends and sympathizers, statements to the press by party officials and candidates, legislative debates, and public discussions on innumerable national, state, and local questions. If, in other words, the opinions of party leaders are as we have described them, there is every chance that they are expressed and acted upon to some extent. Whether this makes our parties "ideological" depends, of course, on how narrowly we define that term. Some may prefer to reserve that designation for parties that are more obviously preoccupied

with doctrine, more intent upon the achievement of a systematic political program, and more willing to enforce a common set of beliefs upon their members and spokesmen.

6. The parties are internally united on some issues, divided on others. In general, Republican leaders achieve greatest homogeneity on issues that grow out of their party's identification with business, Democratic leaders on issues that reflect their connection with liberal and lower-income groups. We find no support for the hypothesis that the parties achieve greatest internal consensus on the issues which principally divide them from their opponents.

In a sequel to this paper we shall offer data on the demographic correlates of issue support, which show that most of the differences presented here exist independently of factors like education, occupation, age, religion, and sectionalism. Controlling for these influences furnishes much additional information and many new insights but does not upset our present conclusions in any important respect. Thus, the parties must be considered not merely as spokesmen for other interest groups but as reference groups in their own right, helping to formulate, to sustain, and to speak for a recognizable point of view.

34. SHOWING IDEOLOGY THE DOOR

Robert McKenzie

Tocqueville startled his European contemporaries one hundred thirty years ago by telling them to look to America, to the raucous democracy of Andrew Jackson, if they wished to understand the problems of the mass society which Europe too would face when eventually it entered the democratic age.

Never has the prescience of Tocqueville's views been more evident than in Britain in 1963. This has been the year of the Beatles, of consumer affluence and of trading stamps, of scandal in high political places, and, above all else, perhaps, of the discovery of mass education. All of these

From Robert McKenzie, "Showing Ideology the Door," *The Observer*, Dec. 8, 1963, p. 10. By permission of The Observer (London).

are "American" phenomena; or rather, they are symptoms of the kind of democratic mass society which America pioneered.

Equally striking is the "Americanization" of British politics which has occurred with staggering rapidity. Until yesterday it was fashionable to deplore the "style" of American politics; in Bagehot's phrase it was "displeasing to the cultivated mind of Europe."

But what aspects of American politics are we now in a position to deplore?

The length and tedium of their election campaigns? Officially ours still last for only three weeks; this was so much taken for granted that when the Attlee Government undertook the last full dress revision of electoral law in 1948 it gave no consideration whatever to extending the restrictions on election expenditure beyond the three week campaign period. But by 1959 the Conservatives, who alone among the parties had digested the conclusions of the psephologists, began their campaign eighteen months or more before polling day.

Now Labour has caught up and both parties had begun their massive election spending by mid-1963. If anything, the run-up to the British election of 1964 is going to prove longer (and perhaps more tedious) than the build-up for the American election of the same year.

Personality Cult

Or is it the excessive personalization of politics in America that we find repugnant? I doubt if the space taken up in Labour's advertisements by Mr. Wilson's picture is much less than that accorded by the American parties to their Presidential candidates. And the cult of personality is at least as highly developed on the Tory side.

The leadership issue swamped all else at this year's Tory conference as completely as it does an American convention. And Sir Alec's first move after forming his Government was to take to the TV cameras to tell the British public that it was his intention to take them fully into his confidence.

Although it can easily be exaggerated, there is something to the argument that we now have in Britain neither Cabinet nor parliamentary government but a quasi-Presidential system. There is therefore no ground for surprise if our election campaigns increasingly resemble the man to man contests, on the Kennedy-Nixon model, of an American Presidential year.

It was long fashionable to deplore the absence of ideology in American party controversy. The United States, it was said, had two political parties not because there were two sides to every question, but because there were two sides to every office: the inside and the outside. But British parties stood for something ("Socialism" vs. "Capitalism," for example). Since American parties were merely organized appetites for power, they shamelessly bid against each other for popular support by offering the public what the public thought it wanted.

In Britain, on the other hand, as recently as 1959 Aneurin Bevan could dismiss the idea that Labour should conduct an opinion survey designed to discover the social priorities preferred by the electors on the ground that this was an abdication of Socialist responsibility and that in any case "it would take the poetry out of politics." Now, however, both major parties are engaged in elaborate and expensive research into voter opinion and into the problems of their party image.

And day by day, as the Tories unhesitatingly match Labour's bid on higher education, or as Labor "clarifies its position" on the question of the immediate abolition of the British nuclear deterrent, the party electoral programs draw closer and closer together. We too now have full-blown "market politics." Indeed, if Senator Goldwater should prove to be the Republican nominee in 1964, it would certainly be arguable that the ideological gulf between the American party leaders would be wider than that which separates the electoral programs of the Conservative and Labour Parties.

By Senator Goldwater's standards, both British parties are campaigning on far-out New Frontier programs.

an American conservative the .ish Tories are committed to "me-tuoism" gone mad; the people, they would argue, "have no choice." And this was precisely the charge traditionally levelled by British observers of American politics against that country's party system.

Mass Society

In fact, our politics are for the first time coming fully to terms with mass society. Elitism in all its forms is being swept aside, whether it is the elitism of the "socialist vanguard" leading the workers into the New Social Order or that of the old aristocratic leadership appealing for support on the basis of its inherent qualifications to rule rather than by pandering to the public appetite for wordly goods and social services.

There is, perhaps, an added irony in the fact that this operation should be conducted on the Labor side by a man considered by many to be the first genuine "left-winger" to lead the party, and on the Tory side by the first aristocrat to leave the House of Lords to head the Conservative Party.

Is this, for better and for worse, the end of ideology? Certainly. Demos, speaking through the public opinion polls and ballot-box, is King, and market politics are, one suspects, here to stay.

35. AN AMERICAN LOOKS AT THE PARTY CONFERENCES

Malcolm Shaw

Last October I attended my first Labour and Conservative Party Conferences. This article consists of my reactions, as an American, to these meetings.

I was strongly impressed by three things: 1) the power of the party executives, 2) the class attitudes, and 3) the seriousness of the proceedings.

I

The power of the party executives left a strong impression on me, I

From Malcolm Shaw, "An American Looks at the Party Conferences," *Parliamentary Affairs,* XV, 2 (Spring, 1962). 203-12, excerpts. By permission of the Hansard Society for Parliamentary Government.

suppose, because the national executives of the major American political parties are weak by comparison. The Democratic and Republican parties are decentralized, undisciplined confederations of state parties. This is one of the consequences of federalism.

When the Democrats and Republicans hold their national conventions, they are indeed acting as national organizations. But this occurs only once every four years. Between conventions—and even to some extent during the presidential campaigns which follow conventions—the component state parties go their own ways. It is not surprising, therefore, that the national party executive does not dominate convention proceedings.

In Britain, on the other hand, the Conservative Central Office and Transport House exercise continuing control in a variety of ways over their respective constituency organizations. At annual conferences this control continues. By party executives I mean, of course, executives dominated by parliamentary leaders; I am not suggesting that faceless party bureaucrats or trade union leaders who do not hold public office are in control.

The physical arrangements at conferences and conventions illustrate in a striking way their basic differences.

At Blackpool and Brighton the executive leadership dominated the proceedings physically. The twenty-odd wise men (and women) sat in a line under spotlights on a high platform—radiating confidence, experience, and rank; there were no red or even yellow warning lights to impede their oratory, and the party chairmen who presided were in full control of the agenda. The delegates—remarkably orderly by American standards—looked on expectantly. Some of the delegates, at the discretion of the chairmen, were permitted to advance to a lower lectern to give five-or, occasionally, ten-minute speeches.

At American conventions (assuming that there is a contest for the presidential nomination) the powerful figures in the party are not necessarily on the platform at all; they are more usually on the convention floor or outside the convention hall. The British tendency to seek a lead from the platform is conspicuously absent. Governors tend to be more important than members of Congress, and the party chairman may be a minor figure. All speakers use the same rostrum and, thus, have the same chance of getting on television. TV commentators and cameramen, in point of fact, often ignore what is going on at the rostrum to buttonhole a delegation leader on (or off) the floor. The whole proceeding appears to be as decentralized as the party system itself. . . .

And so the Democratic and Republican platforms as approved in convention are not the result of floor debate. They are documents of compromise hammered out in private in hopes that they will not provoke a floor debate. As V.O. Key says, "When platform questions arise that are not susceptible of compromise the limits of action by the national convention have been reached. . . . Platforms are electioneering documents not blueprints for action."

The platforms are comparable to Labour and Conservative Manifestos. Manifestos, too, are electioneering documents drawn up in private—by the NEC and the Parliamentary Committee in the case of Labour and by the Conservative Leader.

Conference policy formulation, then, is different from platform-making. The former involves exchanges of ideas between the party leadership and tha rank and file. In these exchanges the point of view of the leadership nearly always prevailed at Blackpool and Brighton, but not always. This brings us to a much-discussed aspect of party organization in Britain—the power relationship between conference and leadership.

The Conservative situation is straight forward. The Leader is in charge of policy. Conference resolutions are advisory and are simply "conveyed" to him. The fact that conference does not have control over policy has led some to minimize the importance of the Conservative conference. Indeed the present Conservative chairman,

Ian Macleod, recently described the conference as "in many ways more of a rally than a conference." A leading authority, R. T. McKenzie, says: "Since 1945 all but three or four of the resolutions before each conference have been carried unanimously; and increasingly of late the conference has tended to serve primarily as a demonstration of party solidarity and of enthusiasm for its own leaders."

These comments notwithstanding, the Brighton Conference would seem to indicate that there's still life in the old conclave. Fifteen resolutions were taken up. The leadership was defeated on two of them—education and Schedule "A" taxation. On five others substantial divisions of opinion were indicated.

The health debate is an interesting case in point. The proposed resolution said:

That this Conference urges Her Majesty's Government to restrict free National Health services to those nationals whose countries offer reciprocal facilities to British subjects; namely Sweden, Norway, Denmark, and Yugoslavia.

The Minister of Health said he could not accept the resolution but gave partial assurances. Two votes were then taken, both showing the Conference to be evenly divided. The presiding officer was about to call for a third show of hands when the proposer agreed to withdraw his resolution. The official verbatim report of the conference says the resolution was not put to the Conference. This does not seem entirely in accordance with the facts. But it seems to show the importance that Conservative officials attach to conference voting.

As for the Labour Party, the power relationship between conference and the Parliamentary Labour Party has been widely discussed recently in the press and elsewhere. The basic issue that has been raised is: Can conference be the controlling source of policy in a party in a parliamentary democracy? The Labour Party Constitution, other Labour Party documents and prominent members of the Party suggest that it ought to be.

Superficially and to some extent actually, the verdict of Blackpool would seem to be in favor of the authority of the parliamentary party. After all, Gaitskell won; he got conference to reverse its defence decision of the previous year. But in another sense it should be kept in mind that Gaitskell felt it *necessary* to get that reversal in order to make his position tenable. Would a Conservative Leader feel the same need? McKenzie says "the annual conference plays a role in the affairs of the Labor Party which is very similar to that played by the conference of ... the Conservative Party." But is there not an all-important difference in degree involved? This is not a black-and-white matter. At the least it may be said that Labour's parliamentary leaders must be more sensitive to what conference does than their Conservative counterparts need be with respect to their conference.

II

Americans tend to be determinedly middle-class in their attitudes and politics, or at least they think they are which is the important thing. In view of this I could not help but be struck by the class attitudes at Blackpool and Brighton. ...

When one examines the resolutions and documents approved at the two conferences, one cannot say that vast differences of principle based on social class are generally revealed. The differences in policy which separate the two parties are, rather, differences of degree, as is normal in a two-party democracy. (I am referring, of course, to the differences which separate the dominant, i.e., moderate, wings of the two parties, not the differences which separate Lord Hinchingbrooke and Anthony Greenwood.)

At the same time, however, the underlying class attitudes are there. Professor Samuel Beer of Harvard attended the two conferences three years ago and was asked on television what struck him as the main difference between them. He said it was a class difference; at the Labour Conference they drank beer; at the Conservative Conference, whisky and soda. Put another way, at Blackpool the delegates went to political meetings in the evening; while at Brighton they put on tuxedos and went to parties.

The fact that trade unions are formally affiliated with the Labour Party is undoubtedly an important factor in all this. The presence of the unions hangs heavily over the Labour conference. They have five-sixths of the votes, twelve of the twenty-five elected seats on the NEC and more than half the delegates (if all attend). One can appreciate that in a class-conscious society some voters, even working-class voters, might find it difficult to support a party so closely identified with the working-class, whatever their sympathies regarding policy might be. Indeed Gaitskell heatedly asserted at Blackpool that "three out of every ten male trade unionists and four out of ten of their wives vote Tory."

The class factor also produces militant socialists whose doctrinaire speeches at Blackpool seemed to be so out of keeping with Gaitskell's. "Ever since I was born," one delegate declared, "I have lived under the crisis of capitalism. I have never known a minute's peace. and I am over fifty years of age." This brought a faint smile from Gaitskell. Concessions are made to this feeling. The delegates call one another "comrades," a term which has a special impact on anyone who lived in America during the McCarthy era. "The Red Flag" is sung; I must say I was delighted to find that the tune is one used by my college fraternity (a far from left-wing organization). There was a proletarian drabness at the Winter Gardens where the Conference was held, a Marxian sense of urgency, an underdog mood, a grim report on finances, an emotional earnestness. In a conversation with one delegate I was told briskly: "Don't talk to me about the American parties. They're both capitalist!" (Brooding over this later, I decided I should have replied: "So are yours.")

A persistent class feeling was in the air at Brighton, too, but it is harder to pin down. For one thing the Conservatives are free of a direct associational link of the trade union kind. Perhaps it was all the women in funny hats. Perhaps it was the painstaking listing of honors after names in the Program. Perhaps it was the patronizing attitude of the chairman who sometimes remarked, "That was a good speech," as though the delegate had just delivered a memorized talk at school. Perhaps it was the extravagant deference shown when the Prime Minister arrived at last on the scene "like Moses coming down with the tablets." Perhaps it was the exquisite planning, even to the Prime Minister's light-colored suit which set him off from his dark-suited ministerial colleagues. Perhaps it was the tendency of delegates to address the Conference as "My lords, ladies and gentlemen." Perhaps it was the delegate who imitated what he regarded as a working-class accent. Or the condescending tone of the speaker in the immigration debate who said: "You and I are keeping him and his wife and about six delightful little piccaninnies round his knees."

Some of these attitudes can be seen at American conventions but in muted and indigenous forms. The Democrats do not proclaim class war on the Republicans; the center in American politics is well to the Right of the Centre in Britain. The trade unions are friendlier to Democrats than to Republicans but are not institutionally connected with the Democratic Party. In some circles it is regarded as more respectable to be a Republican than a Democrat but not all that much more respectable. The Democratic Party has tended to be the majority party in America for more than a generation and consequently could hardly be classified as an underdog movement. The noncohesive character of American parties is another moderating factor. Also, a high percentage of American politicians are lawyers, which helps to give the whole political process a strongly middle-class flavor.

III

As one accustomed to the lively atmosphere of the American convention, I found the Labour and Conservative Conferences models of serious application to duty. This impression came right from the start when I arrived only ten minutes late for the first session at Blackpool and found the meeting already under way. At conventions it is considered remarkable if the chairman can "clear the aisles" in half an hour.

Then there was the unrelieved debate—weighty stuff most of it. At conventions there's quite a bit of hoopla to relieve the speech-making, including "demonstrations" of support for presidential candidates, i.e., parading down the aisles, shouting, singing, and waving posters. An American circus owner once conceded that the convention, not his circus, is the greatest show on earth. It is doubtful that Richard Crossman and Sir Douglas Glover saw their meetings in quite that light.

The convention calisthenics cannot be dismissed, however, merely as exhibitionism or amateur television entertainment. As Key sees it, "The pageantry and the demonstrations give the delegates something to do while their leaders are negotiating behind the scenes."

However you look at it the Labour Conference was another matter entirely. What went on on the floor itself was serious, demanding and arresting. A tremendous amount of information was exchanged by delegates with strongly-held views struggling through a far-ranging agenda. After a day's session was over the battle continued at the evening meetings. One day I wearily remarked that I might pass up a *Tribune* meeting that night; the delegate I was talking to became so alarmed at this possibility that in the end I promised I'd be there.

The contributions by George Brown, the Deputy Leader, struck me as the outstanding political achievement at Blackpool. His opening of the defense debate was a difficult assignment carried off brilliantly, and his wind up of the Common Market debate was also effective. The outstanding failure was a speech by Frank Cousins, the union leader, who failed to deliver a reasoned defence of the unilateralist position as was expected and conspicuously misjudged the mood of the Conference.

I could not help but be fascinated by the fact that Gaitskell and others on the platform wore dark glasses at some sessions (to protect their eyes from the floodlights). Because many Americans tend to regard politics as a sordid line of work few American politicians, particularly at the televised conventions, would dare lend support to this prejudice by hiding their eyes in this sinister way. The political career, for example, of Carmine DeSapio, former Democratic leader in New York City, was undoubtedly affected adversely by the fact that for medical reasons he wore dark glasses.

The Conservative Conference also was arresting and serious, if less demanding. The Tories are handicapped by the fact that everyone knows that their conference decisions are only advisory. But the party is willing to suffer a little dullness on occasion in exchange for what they regard as the proper relationship between the mass organization and the parliamentary party.

Still, the Brighton Conference was no rubber-stamp affair, as I have indicated. On the second day—when flogging and the Common Market were taken up—one saw as lively an exchange of views as one could hope for. The triumph of reason over emotion in the flogging debate was undoubtedly the highlight of the Conference although the intemperate tone of some of the speeches was depressing. To compensate for the delegate who suggested that Christ "took a whip and lashed" the money- changers out of the temple there was the admirable and adroit speech by the Home Secretary.

Mr. Butler's speech was interesting from two points of view. First, it was a skilful presentation by an experienced parliamentarian. Second, it was an occasion when, many believe, delegates were actually swung from one side to the other in the course of debate. . . .

PART SIX

The Future
of
American Parties

By its 1950 *Report*, The American Political Science Association's Committee on Political Parties brought to a head the controversy regarding the nature and desirability of change in the American party system. While the Committee recommended changes to develop disciplined parties within a modified presidential system, others argued for adoption of a modified parliamentary system, or that unless all the consequences of changes could be foreseen, no change should be made.

Since that time a number of proposals have been advanced, and some adopted. For example, the House of Representatives increased the power of the majority leadership by (a) expanding the size of the Rules Committee, (b) providing a way for bills to be brought out of Committee after twenty-one days, and (c) abolishing the requirement of unanimous consent for the appointment of conference committees. Presidential Commissions made basic and far-reaching recommendations regarding party finance and election procedures. Presidents Eisenhower and Johnson proposed to increase the terms of office of members of the House of Representatives so that all would be elected at the same time as the President. Both parties developed advisory councils as devices to articulate the feelings of party leaders outside Congress while the opposing party occupied the White House.

Important as these changes are, none except that dealing with the term of office of members of the House required any change in basic laws or the Constitution. Decisions regarding them were and are being made by politicians in a political context; they did not require broad popular support. Proposals to establish ideological parties with or without some type of parliamentary system require changes of an entirely different order of magnitude. They require Americans to develop new and different concepts of political parties, both as to their relationship with the electorate and their role in policy formulation and determination.

Certainly such changes in the American political culture would be most difficult to achieve; whether they would be desirable is far less certain. David Butler suggests that Montesquieu was not the last foreign observer of British politics and government to mistake what he saw for what he wanted to see. While Butler's article was written in 1954, the de-emphasis of clear-cut philosophical and policy differences between the Conservative and Labour Parties has been even more marked since that time. After Labour victories in 1964 and 1966 and after two years of Labour government—part of that time with a voting majority of 95—what once were described as policy differences can now be described only as different tendencies and inclinations. Neither has the passage of time compromised Butler's comments regarding internal democracy within the parties. Like Hugh Gaitskell's defiance of the 1962 Labour Annual Conference on the issue of unilateral disarmament, Harold Wilson's leadership of the Labour Government leaves no doubt of the monopoly the Parliamentary Labour Party has over the determination of government policy.

In a careful and restrained assessment of possible changes in the American party system, Paul T. David predicts that modifications will be the result of long-term secular trends. He particularly focused on the increasing competition between the parties on a national basis. This flows from population shifts and the spread of industrialization since early in World War II, and has been continuing rapidly.

36. AMERICAN MYTHS ABOUT BRITISH PARTIES

David Butler

Among British writers on British government there is a strain of complacency which would be hard to match even among the more chauvinistic American students of American government. Although there can be found British scholars who have indulged in stern self-criticism—Ramsay Muir and Harold Laski are the most outstanding—there are none who have looked across the Atlantic for examples of how government might be improved. In the United Stases, on the other hand, there has always been a school of critics which has seen in the British system of government a remedy for the weaknesses which to some seem all too obvious on the American scene. Woodrow Wilson and William Yandell Elliott are perhaps the best known of this school while E. E. Schattschneider and Thomas Finletter are the most recent.

Despairing at the roadblocks placed in the way of strong and efficient government—constitutionally by the separation of powers and the federal system, and politically by party confusion and party indiscipline—they have looked enviously to British arrangements and asked whether some at least of that apparently simple orderliness could not be imported. The idealized picture offered in British treatises is faithfully accepted;

British executive authority rests fully in the hands of a Cabinet drawn from, and loyally supported by, the party which has a majority in the House of Commons; untroubled by any traditional struggle between the legislative and executive branches, secure in its own unified authority, the Cabinet carries out the program on which the majority party won the last election; the Cabinet has complete power to act in the national interest, yet it is saved from the dangers of tyranny by the internal democracy of the party from which it is drawn by the miraculous device of the Parliamentary Question, by the British sense of fair play, and, most important of all, by the fear of the voters at the next general election. Such is the idyllic system, the example which has tempted some Americans to ask whether parts of it at least might not be copied. Would it not be possible to effect some fusion of the legislative and executive branches to reduce the wasteful and wearisome friction which is so customary between White House and Capitol Hill? Would it not be possible to develop a disciplined and responsible two-party system?

Even if the British system possessed all the virtues attributed to it, and even if the American people were willing to indulge in constitutional experimentation, it seems very doubtful whether any successful transplantation could be achieved. But, in any

From David Butler, "American Myths about British Parties," *Virginia Quarterly Review*, XXXI, 1 (Winter, 1955), 46–56.

event, the excellencies of the British system are misunderstood; the party system is especially misunderstood.

In 1950 a group of eminent American political scientists produced a report entitled "Towards a more responsible two-party system" which in effect pleaded for the development of parties democratically organized and differentiated in ideology; there could be no doubt that the British system was in the minds of many of the authors. It is the purpose of this article to show that the British parties are in fact much less differentiated and much less democratic than is often supposed, and that it is a good thing that this should be so.

II

There is a very deep-rooted assumption that Britain has two clearcut parties standing for clearly opposed philosophies of government. Since the eighteenth century and even more since the passage of the Great Reform Bill in 1832, the opposing parties have been seen as the stand-patters and the reformers, once the Tories and the Whigs, then the Conservatives and the Liberals, and now the Conservatives and the Labourites. When the socialist and working-class Labour party replaced the more moderate and middle-class Liberals as the standard-bearer of progress the contrast became all the sharper. In the 1930's it was perhaps to be seen at its peak. On the one side stood the Conservatives, ready to maintain or cautiously to improve upon the *status quo*—the capitalist economic system and the established social order. On the other side stood the Labour party, committed to a drastic program for the nationalization of industry, the redistribution of wealth,

and the transformation of many of the existing institutions of government. The two parties were well-disciplined and could be trusted to support their leaders in implementing these policies. At a British general election the voter knew what faced him; the program he voted for stood a good chance of being enacted if his party won. He had perhaps to choose the lesser of two evils, to select between misguided prescriptions for the nation's ills—but his choice was at least clear. The conscientious American citizen seeking, for example, to choose between a left-wing Republican and a right-wing Democrat or to estimate what chance rival presidential candidates would have of getting their respective programs through Congress, could envy the sharp distinctions which confronted the British voter. It is, of course, probable that if the Labour Party had in fact attained power in the 1930's its performance would have seemed decidedly less drastic than its mildly revolutionary promises. Nonetheless, the fact remains that twenty years ago there was thought to be, and to a large extent there was, a sharp cleavage between the parties. The public picture of government always lags behind reality. Too many people—and too many textbooks—still see the British party struggle in the terms of the 1930's. But it has changed profoundly.

The main revolution took place during the war: events began to effect a compromise between the parties. Full employment and much increased wage-rates went far to abolish extreme poverty while penal taxation went far to abolish extreme wealth. The Conservatives accepted as inevitable these equalizing consequences of the war. They went further; partly as a concession to their Labour partners in the coalition government, and partly as an expression of the reformist zeal which, at the climax of the war, swept over so many Western European countries, they accepted the principle of the Welfare State. Americans often forget that the characteristic institutions of the Welfare State in Britain, the National Health Service and the comprehensive system of social insurance, originated not from the postwar Socialist government but from the wartime coalition which was based on an overwhelming Conservative majority. By the end of the war the social grievances which had seemed to call for radical political action were on the way to being remedied—with the consent and approval of the Conservatives. At the same time the Labour leaders, with the chastening experience of five years in office, had learned to operate and respect the British governmental machine. They no longer believed that it would be necessary to reconstruct the machine before they could carry their program into action; and their program had, with the march of events and the modification of their own ideas, come to seem less radical.

This does not mean that the election of 1945 was not fought about real issues or that there was nothing to choose between the parties at that time; but in the fields of social and foreign policy they were far less divided than in the 1930's. The really big issue at stake in 1945, if personalities are ignored, was the nationalization of industry. In its manifesto the Labour party promised to take into public ownership the production of coal, domestic gas, electricity, and of iron and steel, as well as the main branches of public transport. The Labour victory in the election was followed in the next five years by the complete

fulfilment of these pledges, in the face of determined Conservative opposition. There has been no other question in postwar British politics on which the parties have been so unequivocally opposed. That is not to say that there were not many other issues on which there were major clashes during the life of the Labour government or that, nationalization apart, British politics would have been little different if the Conservatives had won in 1945. Unquestionably, the Labour government was in general more lavish with the taxpayers' money, more ready to control the detailed working of the national economy, and more hasty in yielding up sovereignty in India and the Colonial Empire than a Conservative government would have been. But since 1945 the parties have never clashed fundamentally on the principle of establishing the Welfare State and the levelling rates of taxation therein involved or on the basic issues of foreign and colonial policy. The general continuity in policy between the Labour government which left office in 1951 and the Conservative government which has ruled since then clearly underlines the narrowness of the gap between the parties.

In the last few years, moreover, the issue of nationalization, the one real policy issue at stake in 1945, has receded from the political scene. The Conservatives on coming into power reversed the nationalization of the Iron and Steel Industry—which had not proceeded very far—and they turned back to private ownership a large section of the Road Haulage Industry. The Labour party has promised that it will, at least in part, renationalize these two industries when it returns to power; this it was perhaps bound to say, if only to justify its past action. But the Labour party, it should be noted, has no definite plans to nationalize any other specific industry—except the largely municipalized one of water supply. In the several hundred resolutions sent in to the 1954 Labour party conference, only one explicitly asked for further drastic measures of nationalization. The truth is that British public opinion has come to feel that nationalization is neither a panacea nor a disaster. In none of the industries to which it has been applied has it failed spectacularly, but in none has it brought the full benefits for which its sponsors hoped. With the tacit consent of the Labour party, it has receded from the center of the political scene.

What, then, divides the parties today? If one judged them by their extremists—particularly the Labour Party—one would find an unbridgeable gulf between whole-hearted and sometimes almost fellow-traveling Socialists and high and dry orthodox Conservatives. But if one judges the parties by the words of their responsible leaders and, still more, by their performance in office, one finds that the gap is remarkably small. There will always be differences on day-to-day issues, the differences between the "ins" and the "outs," between those who, circumscribed by the hard facts of the situation, have to face the responsibility of action, and those who are living up to the traditional maxim of British politics, "The duty of the opposition is to oppose." There will always be differences between a Conservative party whose leadership is overwhelmingly recruited from the prosperous classes and a Labour party drawn from most sections of the community but primarily dependent upon the good will of the Trade Unions and the working-class. The instinctive reactions of Con-

servative and Labour politicians differ appreciably. Nonetheless, their politics remain astonishingly similar.

During the summer of 1954, Labour Members of Parliament have been rejoicing in Mr. Eden's performance and, in private at least, proclaiming that no Labour Foreign Secretary would have been so courageous in standing up against American policy. On the domestic scene a new work, "Butskellism," has been added to the political vocabulary by an article in The Economist entitled "Mr. Butskell's Dilemma," which explored the economic problems faced and the solutions likely to be found, by a British Chancellor of the Exchequer, be he the Conservative R. A. Butler or the Socialist Hugh Gaitskell. Most people in Britain would be surprised at the suggestion that there are no clear differences between the policies of the parties. But if one looks at realities and not at words, it is hard to see what they are. It seems reasonable to argue that the fate of Britain ten years hence will be far less affected by whether the Conservatives or the Labour Party win the next election, than the fate of the United States will be affected by the decision it will have to take in 1956 between a Republican and a Democrat. The choice may seem more confused in the United States, but it is more far-reaching. The parties in Britain may be distinct from each other, but they are not very different from each other.

III

More people have fallen into the trap of seeing the parties as clearly opposed rivals than into the trap of taking the parties' internal democratic machinery at its face value. Nonetheless, anyone who has escorted American political scientists to the British party conferences is forced to recognize a widespread confusion about the extent to which the British parties are, while democratic in form, oligarchic in fact. Facilities for the rank and file to participate in the decision-making process undoubtedly exist, but in practice they scarcely circumscribe the authority of the party leaders. American observers who go to local party meetings in Britain or to the annual conferences of the parties are usually much impressed by the serious purpose of the gathering, by the articulate and informed speeches of the men in the street who attend, by the devotion to questions of policy or principle to the exclusion of issues of personality, and by the absence of the jamboree atmosphere which sometimes characterises American political gatherings. The British example provokes speculation whether such earnestness could not be introduced into American parties, whether they too could not become educational and policy-formulating clubs instead of arenas for fights over patronage and the choice of candidates. To suggest this is to misconstrue first the nature of British parties and secondly the practical limits of the democratic process. It is a complete illusion to suppose, as some have done, that party democracy on the British model provides a workable substitute for direct democracy. The impracticability of Athenian democracy, of every citizen sharing in every decision, has long been realized; but, so runs the argument, even today it is still open to any citizen to join a party, to propose a resolution in the local branch, and, if it wins support there, to have it put forward at the annual

conference of the party; if the conference approves, it becomes an item in the national policy of the party, a policy that will be enacted when the party is next returned to power; anyone who wants to can take his share in choosing his candidate for parliament, in shaping his party's program, and in restraining or encouraging, in effect in selecting, its leaders. This is the idealized theory. What is the reality? How much say do the rank-and-file of the British parties actually have in the selection of their party's policy or its leaders?

It is proper to begin an examination of the extent of democracy in British parties by examining how many take any active share in it. At the 1951 election approximately fourteen million people voted for each of the major parties. But only three million people are even nominally subscribing members of the Conservative party and, despite the fact that five million Trade Unionists are formally affiliated to the Labour party, barely a million people have taken the trouble to join the party as individuals. Even party members, however, are for the most part totally passive. In very few constituencies do as much as ten per cent of them in either party play any active role. Even at an election only a few hundred thousand contribute any effort beyond going themselves to vote and, in between elections, when party policies are being hammered out, the number who participate in serious discussions can be at most fifty thousand; it is probably much less.

Do these few party zealots in the constituencies by their debates on national issues have much influence on the conduct of their leaders? It would seem not. In the Conservative party very much less policy discussion goes on than in the Labour party. The vast majority of Conservative Constituency Associations are characterized by loyalty to their leaders, by an unintellectual conviction that their leaders know best. The Conservative Annual Conference has virtually never made a decision of any importance. It is for all practical purposes a carefully managed pep-rally, a chance for the party workers and the party leaders to get together. It is true that should the leaders violently offend the susceptibilities of their followers, the machinery of revolt does exist. But it has long been idle, for the leaders of the Conservative party know their business. Within enormously broad limits they are free to shape the party's policy as seems best to them. They have to worry a lot about what the voters will think of them at the next election, but very little about what their party rank-and-file demand of them from day to day.

Is it the same with the Labour party? Its protagonists boast much about its democratic structure and its intellectual vitality. It is true that the constituency parties are constantly passing resolutions, asking their leaders for a change in policy. Of late years there has been a great deal in the newspapers about the struggle between the left and right wings of the party, between the Bevanites and the rest. But the dominant right wing of the party have been able to carry on in control, untroubled by the fact that a large majority of the active rank-and-file in the constituencies are Bevanites. The Bevanites are outnumbered by at least four to one both among the Labour Members of Parliament and on the National Executive Committee of the party,

and nothing in the foreseeable future seems likely to change this situation. The Bevanites may struggle to get resolutions for a more pacific foreign policy or a more revolutionary domestic policy passed by the Annual Conference of the Labour Party. But apart from the fact that the "block vote" of the Trade Unions is mainly right wing and can usually be trusted to defeat radical resolutions from the constituencies, such resolutions can also be lost or rendered meaningless by manipulating the complicated parliamentary procedure of a Labour Party Conference. Even if the Conference were to pass a resolution involving a change of policy, the National Executive would still have the right to decide when—if ever—and how the resolution should be implemented. People write of Mr. Bevan's "bid for power" and speak as though he had a serious chance of securing the leadership of the Labour Party in the near future. They forget that the Leader of the Labour Party is elected by the Labour Members of Parliament and that it is scarcely conceivable that he would ever command a majority among the present group of M.P.'s. The mortality of M.P.'s is low and the turnover is slow. It is a singular fact that, although many right-wing Labour M.P.'s represent constituencies in which the local Labour Party is Bevanite, there is not a single case where an M.P.'s views have or seem likely to cost him renomination. Even where vacancies have occurred, Bevanite local parties have far from always chosen a Bevanite. The local parties have the power to choose whom they will; but, in the case of incumbents, a natural loyalty to good and conscientious representatives and, in the case of vacancies, a desire to get the most appealing of the available candidates have prevented any drastic change in the proportion of Bevanite M.P.'s or candidates. Until the local Labour Parties start rigorously applying political tests, the present leadership of the Labour Party is secure.

All that has been said does not mean that there are not real and important struggles over policy going on throughout the Labour Party. But it would seem that, all things considered, the leaders of the Labour Party are as secure in power and have almost as free a hand in policy-making as their Conservative opposite numbers.

Those in America who envy the internal democracy of the British parties and imagine that the rank-and-file have a substantial share in settling party program, might well pause to examine whether in practice American party policies are not more effectively influenced by popular pressure than are British. Upon investigation the internal democracy of British parties appears to exist far more in form than in substance.

IV

To minimize the difference between, and the democracy within, the British parties is not to dispraise them. The British should be thankful that their parties have such similar policies and such untrammelled oligarchies.

The existence of deep divisions between the two parties which are alternately to be entrusted with full control of the machinery of state is not to be applauded. Lord Balfour achieved the classic summary of the situation when he wrote, "Our whole political machin-

ery presupposes a people so fundamentally at one that they can safely afford to bicker." The party differences being as small as they are, the course of British politics is likely to be an even one in the years to come; elections will not bring the risk of drastic and dislocating reversals in national policy. They will provide an opportunity for the voters to judge the performance of the governing party, to decide whether a change of men is desirable, to choose between different variants of basically similar policies; they will not open the way to drastic or irreversible decisions which might divide and endanger the nation.

The placing of excessive power in the hands of the militant rank-and-file of political parties would be equally to be deplored. This would be to place the destinies of the country at the mercy of a small, and not always very wise, minority of the people. If the determination of party policy were indeed to be left to the zealots in the constituencies, the gap between the parties would be widened to an extent unsuited to the smooth running of national affairs and repugnant to the more moderate, if more apathetic, bulk of British citizens. It is well that the party leaders, relatively immune from the danger of revolt by their active supporters, should be free to determine party policy, subject to the sure and certain checks of having to defend their views and actions in Parliament and, still more, of having in due course to present themselves for judgment before the British electorate.

Much may be wrong with American parties but those who have looked to the Britain system for remedies have surely erred in their analysis of its excellencies.

37. THE CHANGING POLITICAL PARTIES

Paul T. David

It is the general purpose of this essay to note some of the more important kinds of change existing and latent within the parties, and to explore their potential consequences.

Specifically, the objectives are as follows:

First, to discuss whether the American political parties are becoming more competitive with each other, and whether there is a rising level of competitive tension within the party system.

Second, to comment briefly on the relationships between competition, cohesion, and centralization in the party system, and to suggest some of the implications of these relationships.

Third, to consider the consequences of party competition for the organization of party leadership, the requirements of party finance, and the development of nationalizing tendencies in congressional politics.

A More Competitive Party System?

In a review of contemporary politics in 1961, it was my conclusion that "the party system as a whole now occupies what is probably the most highly competitive position it has ever reached in national politics." This conclusion was based on such factors as the following:

—the scale, scope, and nature of the national campaigns of 1960;

—the number of states in which the election was fought hard to a close outcome in presidential, congressional, and state elections;

—the speed with which the professionals and the party organizations in each party turned to preparations for the 1962 campaigns;

—the number of close votes in Congress on major items in the President's legislative program;

—the evident disposition of the administration to sharpen issues in Congress in preparation for future election campaigns;

—the aggressive character of the leadership that has come to the top in each of the national parties.

These signs, however, may be more persuasive than probative; and the future remains uncertain. We would like to know whether the 1960 elections were merely the highest point of a competitive tension that will recede until 1964 or 1968; and also whether the long-term drift toward a more competitive situation that has been evident for a generation will continue, despite the fluctuations that may be related to the circumstances of particular election years.

On the short-term side, there were indications early in 1962 that the Republican Party might do poorly in the 1962 elections, contrary to the historical experience in which the party out of power has usually gained seats

From Paul T. David, "The Changing Political Parties," *Continuing Crisis in American Politics,* ed., Marian D. Irish, (Englewood Cliffs, N. J.: Prentice-Hall, Inc., 1963), pp. 47–65, excerpts. By permission of the publisher.

in Congress in midterm elections. The Republican Party also has been engaged in an unusual amount of soul-searching over its internal problems; but the kind of ferment that is in process suggests that the Party will eventually recover strongly even if its competitive fortunes become worse before they become better.

The longer-term aspect of the problem of inter-party competition is obviously the more important for students of the party system; and an opinion that projects past trends into the future needs to be supported by some long-term interpretation of party history. Such a view could begin by noting the political events of 1896, when a Republican sweep elected William McKinley president.

The election of 1896 is generally credited with a restructuring of political affiliations that endured for more than a generation. The South became the solidly Democratic South. It is all too often forgotten that twenty northern states became so solidly Republican that they could reasonably have been called the "solid North." The period was the high point of a sectional political alignment, and the low point in the effectiveness of the competitive relationship between the Democratic and Republican parties, both nationally and in most states.

These relationships were changed by the realignments that occurred in 1928, 1932, and 1936. The Democratic Party replaced the Republican as the party with a majority following; and whereas the former Republican majority had been sectional, the Democratic majority was national. By 1940, the Republican Party had begun to recover, but a new cleavage line had been established between the parties. Though the South was still solid and still Democratic, in most of the nation, and

especially in the central urban and industrial areas from Massachusetts to California, the parties were again competitive in state-wide elections. The cleavage line within the electorate, moreover, essentially followed social and economic divisions in the states where the parties were competitive. . . .

In recent years, the partisan attachments of the electorate have been remarkably stable in most parts of the country. Throughout the Eisenhower period, apparently about 60 per cent of the voters continued to consider themselves Democrats. In a "normal" election, however, it has been computed that the Democratic share would be no more than 54 per cent, because many Democrats are habitual non-voters. This relatively narrow Democratic vote, moreover, consists of a lopsided majority in the South, and a 49 per cent *minority* outside the South.

It would be easier to predict that the two national parties will continue to become more competitive if some increase could be predicted in the Republican Party's share in the southern vote. On this, the Party's shortage of effective candidates is one of its most serious problems. As recently as 1960, it offered no candidate for Congress in 62 of the 106 congressional districts in the eleven one-time Confederate states. But in the more than forty districts where it offered candidates, it polled 26.5 per cent of the vote in 1948, 27.4 in 1952, 38.0 in 1956, and 37.8 in 1960. In recent years, seven of these districts sent Republican members to Congress. The Republican vote in many of the other districts is high enough to fall within striking range of a majority whenever the Party is again in a favorable position nationally in a presidential election.

Republican prospects in the South—

and the prospects for a two-party system in the southern region—were substantially improved by the Supreme Court's decision of March 26, 1962, in the Tennessee reapportionment case, *Baker v. Carr*. The new Republicans of the South have been concentrated in the most underrepresented urban and suburban areas. If given fair representation, they seem certain to expand their beachheads in southern state legislatures and in Congress. Attractive candidates developed through these opportunities could in turn do much to expand the Party's following throughout the South. On the other hand, liberal Democrats of the southern cities, also underrepresented in previous districting arrangements, will be able to increase their weight in southern Democratic Party affairs. Where this happens on a sufficient scale, conservative southern Democrats may find their inclination to shift to the Republican Party somewhat increased.

By a coincidence that is not entirely accidental, the effects of the Tennessee case are coming at the same time that major efforts to increase Negro registration and voting in the South are reaching fruition. If the increased Negro vote materializes, the new Negro voters may help to maintain Democratic Party majorities in presidential elections, while engaging in split-ticket voting locally on the basis of the characteristics of the candidates locally available. Obviously these are complex processes, but they seem more likely to increase competition between the parties in the end than to reduce it; and in time they will certainly change the nature of the Democratic Party in the South and in Congress.

In other parts of the country, substantial revisions of the political map are also in prospect as a result of the redistricting activity impelled by judi-

cial action. The rapidly growing suburban areas and smaller cities will be the major beneficiaries. The Republican Party will lose representation in some northern rural areas, but may achieve offsetting gains in big city suburbs. More important, however, opportunities for new political leadership may emerge in both parties from the new political units where population growth and economic activity are greatest.

In most of the states, neither party can any longer anticipate a permanent monopoly in the state-wide elections for governor, for senator, and for President. In these states, the long-term outlook continues to point toward a rising level of competitive tension. The readjustments resulting from *Baker v. Carr* and from other contemporary changes are likely to enhance the tension rather than to lessen it.

Competition, Cohesion, and Centralization

Politicians of both parties are undoubtedly like many businessmen in their preference for monopolistic situations in which benefits accrue with a minimum of risk and uncertainty. Situations of this kind have been so common that the normal thinking of party strategists seems often to run in terms of how to develop or maintain a monopoly, rather than in terms of how to be competitive if it is necessary to compete.

The logic of competitive success is different from the logic of monopolistic success. Monopolistic success usually turns on the exploitation of some built-in strategic advantage. Competitive success requires continuous attention to such factors as effective leadership, adequate campaign resources, and attractive programs and candidates. We can suppose, therefore, that if the competitive tension within the party system continues to rise during the years ahead, there will be a growing disposition to deal with the institutional problems that affect party leadership, campaign finance, the development of party programs, and the selection of party candidates. Conversely, if the tension sags and there is some kind of return to a less competitive party system, then the prospects for any form of innovative change in dealing with these problems would be poor.

The basic competition in politics today, however, is not between the Republican and Democratic Parties as such, but rather between the Republican Party and the majority wing of the Democratic Party, with a third force of southern Democrats who sometimes vote with one party, sometimes with the other, while generally also pursuing some special objectives of their own. The one-party Democrats will continue to be a confusing influence in Congress and elsewhere as long as they survive, but they are not likely to reduce materially the pressures of competition between the major parties in the states outside the South and in the nation as a whole.

If this is true, the theoretical relationships among competition, cohesion, and centralization in the party system may become increasingly important. Cohesion within the competing elements is a normal product of competition in any competitive system. Cohesion need not extend to a complete identity of points of view or objectives. What it does extend to generally is a program of cooperative action on whatever is deemed most essential for success in the competitive struggle. In the party system, those elements of each party the carry that burden of competition with the other party tend to become increasingly cohesive.

This applies not only in the case of campaign efforts, but also to the party task of governing when the party is in power—to the extent that party success in the activities of governing is deemed essential for party success in the next electoral competition.

Centralization is in turn a product of the cohesion that is induced by competition. For success in the competition, the executive functions of centralized communication, policy leadership, and strategical decision all take on an obvious importance. Under conditions of competition and cohesion, there is not much objection to a centralization of such executive functions and there may be a strong desire to achieve it. In such cases, centralization is not so much imposed from above, as supported from below. This is especially the case when institutions of majority rule make possible a choice among alternative sources of leadership; in this case, the chosen leadership can be instructed to maintain discipline and apply such sanctions as may be feasible in dealing with dissident minorities who are found to be trading with the enemy.

There are many areas of American politics in which we might conduct a search for the centralizing tendencies of party competition, examine their nature, and consider their effects. Within the limited scope of this essay, the search will be devoted to areas previously suggested: party leadership, party finance, and some aspects of congressional politics.

Leadership Problems: Ins Versus Outs

Within the last century, the President has been gaining stature in his own party. The solid base of the President's power is found in his position as the nation's leader in a dangerous world.

Often he must rise above party; but most students hold that it is not safe to rise too far—a capable President must continuously make certain that his partisan troops are still with him.

The evolution of the President's role as party leader has not been traced in adequate detail. Most scholars have given more attention to his role as leader of the legislature. Under modern conditions Congress cannot function effectively unless the President provides the legislative agenda. Even the Republican Party now accepts this; during the Eisenhower administration, many Republicans also came to feel rather strongly that when the President is functioning as legislative leader, he must also act visibly as the leader of his party if the basis is to be laid for partisan success in the congressional elections that are always just around the corner.

The President's connection with the party machinery and party functioning involves a series of problems on which there has been much controversy. It is also an area in which change in the norms of our political culture has come late and probably remains incomplete. Presidents had been renominated in national party conventions for a century before an incumbent President appeared in person to accept renomination, as Franklin Roosevelt did in 1936. It is generally accepted that the President may name the chairman of his national party committee, but this is not a responsibility of great antiquity. Presidential involvements in campaigns and elections have developed intermittently through a trial-and-error process, with every innovative precedent under attack but generally with some net increment of presidential influence when the dust had settled.

The President's combined role as party leader and legislative leader took on new importance on at least one occasion, however, with a minimum of fanfare. This was the meeting held at the White House on Monday morning, November 15, 1937; those present included President Roosevelt, Vice President Garner, Speaker Bankhead, Senate Majority Leader Barkley, and House Majority Leader Rayburn. This was not the first time this group had met, but it was the first time that they met with an intention to meet once a week, with a fixed membership constituted on an *ex officio* basis. This was the beginning of the regular weekly congressional leadership meetings at the White House—meetings that have continued through the successive administrations of Presidents Roosevelt, Truman, Eisenhower, and Kennedy. If those present had been formally designated "The Legislative Cabinet," and if the meetings had been initiated by an Act of Congress, they would have attracted immediate attention as a major innovation in American constitutional practice. As it was, even the White House press corps remained unaware for some years that the leadership meetings were different from the many other meetings at the White House that continued to involve members of Congress.

There is still much less than a full realization among political scientists that the American government now contains a collegial body, constituted on a partisan basis at the highest political level, that regularly concerns itself with the forward program of the party in power, with special reference to those program elements involving legislation, appropriations, and congressional action. Political scientists as eminent as Edward S. Corwin and Charles S. Hyneman, apparently unaware of what already existed, continued to advocate the creation of a presidential legislative council in books published long after 1937. The true importance of the leadership meetings was probably first noticed by the Committee on Political Parties in its report entitled *Toward a More Responsible Two-Party System*, published in 1950.

Out-party difficulties in developing a leadership that can compete for public attention have long been obvious, but only under the competitive pressures of recent years has there been any strong impulse to do something about it. Two leading precedents were provided by the Democrats while out of power between 1953 and 1961. One was Adlai Stevenson's demonstration of the potentialities inherent in the out-party titular leadership under modern conditions; his performance as Party spokesman and chief campaigner was especially noteworthy during the midterm campaign of 1954. The second precedent was the creation of the Democratic Advisory Council as an instrument of collective leadership for the presidential wing of the out-party between 1956 and 1960. Although the Council was boycotted by the congressional leaders, it provided an influential voice for majority elements in the Party. It also regularly brought together most of those who were most concerned over the succession in the Party nomination in 1960. By the end of 1959, all the Party's leading contenders for the presidential nomination of 1960 except Senate Majority Leader Lyndon Johnson had accepted membership on the Council.

Both precedents just mentioned were actively debated in the Republican Party as it went through its leadership crisis on leaving office in 1961. For a brief interval, it appeared that former Vice President Nixon would accept major responsibilities as the Party's new titular leader. Instead, he seems to have abandoned the role, apparently having concluded that he would be committed to a hopeless race in 1964 if he functioned actively in the titular leadership in the meantime.

Discussions of alternative patterns of collective leadership resulted in agreement that the Party's congressional leaders and the national Party chairman would hold weekly meetings (while Congress is in session), after which the leaders make their views public through a television show—the so-called Ev and Charlie show. Later, plans for an "All-Republican Conference" were developed, and six senators and six representatives were designated to draft a statement of Republican principles, with staff service provided by the Republican National Committee.

In all these efforts, the prize at stake is the opportunity to influence the development of the party image. The symbolism of program intentions can provide clues to whether the party is being merely defensive, or whether it is indeed actively developing alternatives to the programs advocated by the party in power. For much of this, the real payoff is the party's voting record in Congress. This is always likely to be more conservative than the party's next candidate for President might desire. Yet if leadership structures are devised in which the presidential wing of the out-party can be more effective, some influence may be exerted on the party's congressional leaders and on the party's legislative record. . . .

Nationalizing Tendencies in Congressional Politics

For some years, Professor E. E. Schattschneider has been saying in his various writings that Congress is increasingly involved in politics. He means, of course, an increasing involvement in the important varieties of politics: the politics of national issues, of nationally oriented interest groups, of the national parties, and of national campaigns and elections.

The evidence of increasing congressional involvement in presidential and vice-presidential nominations is especially clear. Senators have been gaining in strength as vice-presidential nominees and as potential presidential nominees; the successful nomination of Senator John F. Kennedy brings this progression to a realization. For about thirty years, congressional leaders have been dominant in both parties most of the time as the presiding officers at the national party conventions. This is a complete reversal of the nineteenth century practice under which convention leadership was almost completely divorced from congressional leadership.

For a century, there has been a slow increase in the proportion of senators who attend the party conventions as delegates; 64 of them did so in 1960. The patterns associated with this long-term tendency are highly revealing. Even in the late nineteenth century, when a state had one senator of each party—a prima facie case of active party competition—*both* senators were usually present at their respective party conventions as delegates. Conversely, in the states represented by two Republican senators, the integration between state and national politics has been so weak that the senators from these states still usually refrain from active participation in the conventions. The one-party Democratic states occupy an intermediate position in this form of political behavior: the senators from these states have usually attended the Democratic national conventions in recent years, presumably to defend sectional interests.

Members of the House of Representatives, less nationally oriented and less capable of securing prestige recognition from their state party organizations, have not served as convention delegates proportionately as often as senators. But even here there has been marked change; the number of members of the House of Representatives who served in convention delegations (as delegates or alternates) is as follows since 1948:

Year	Democrat	Republican
1948	32	20
1952	56	18
1956	80	39
1960	136	32

In view of the long-term data from the conventions, we can suppose that there may have been a similar long-term increase in the numbers of senators and representatives who have worked in national party campaigns outside the limits of their own states and districts. The data to test this tendency have never been accumulated, although possibly they could be secured from the archives of party speakers' bureaus or from newspaper files.

Campaigning by the candidates for President and Vice President has clearly become more national in scope, reaching the limits of the 50-state type of campaign in 1960. There is a general impression that the ticket-leaders are involved with the local candidates in more states than formerly as they progress from state to state. This is to be expected as more states become competitive, and the various candidates become more dependent on each other for marginal increments of strength in appealing to the voters.

The changing patterns of midterm

campaigning are even more striking and suggest marked change in the relationships of national party leaders to the congressional campaigns. For years, Woodrow Wilson was criticized for even his mild intervention in the 1918 campaign—an intervention that took the form of a brief press statement in which he expressed a hope for congressional majorities of his own party. But as the Roosevelt and Truman years wore on, there seemed to be increasing activity by the national party leaders in the midterm campaigns.

When President Eisenhower faced the issue for the first time, in 1954, his first inclination was one of withdrawal, following the doctrine of those who had criticized Woodrow Wilson. But after Adlai Stevenson had announced his intention to campaign actively from July to November, 1954, pressures from within the Republican Party brought President Eisenhower to a much more active performance than he had previously contemplated; Vice President Nixon was assigned the duty of campaigning in as many of the critical states as possible.

In 1962 President Kennedy kicked off the midterm campaign on January 20 at a $100-a-plate fund-raising dinner in Washington. Six thousand Democrats were present, including most Democratic members of Congress. He said:

What we are attempting to do tonight is to lay the groundwork for the Congressional campaigns of 1962, and we realize, I think, all the Members of the House and Senate, that history is not with us, that in this century only in 1934, during the periods of the great pre-eminence of the Democratic Party, did the Party in power ever win seats, let alone hold its own. But we believe in 1962 that the Democratic Party, both at home and abroad, is best fitted to lead this country

—and therefore we start tonight on the campaigns of 1962.

Later it was indicated that the President would undertake on-the-spot campaigning to assist members of his party in some instances, and that Vice President Lyndon Johnson would be available for active campaigning in at least a dozen states.

The dinner at which President Kennedy spoke was a sign of the new centralization of party fund-raising for congressional campaigns. For some years, the Republican National Finance Committee has been in charge of fund-raising for the Party's congressional campaign committees as well as for the National Committee. The Democrats came to this pattern in the spring of 1961 and seem likely to maintain it.

In the entire range of party affairs, centralization may come last and most slowly in the nomination of party candidates for Congress. Even here, however, one of the most respected students of the party system has suggested that "National party leaders in quest of a point of leverage to strengthen their party might well give thought to spending a few hundred thousand dollars a year in drumming up and supporting able House and Senate candidates for seats held by the opposition." Others have suggested that the Republican National Committee needs paid staff workers in every critical congressional district, presumably to perform functions somewhat similar to those of the British constituency agents who are paid from national party funds. So far, however, the national Party authorities seem mainly to have contented themselves with urging the local Party groups to work actively on candidate recruitment, so the Party may secure the kind of candidates for Congress that will enable it to compete more effectively.

The manner in which Richard Nixon was initially recruited to run for Congress in 1946 by a local group of Republican businessmen is well known. The activities of similar groups locally based but nationally oriented are probably becoming more important in the congressional nominating processes of both parties. Apparently they are a natural result of the club movement spreading in suburban politics. They also seem to be a natural result of the increasingly effective interventions of organized labor and of organized business in their political efforts to compete with each other.

From the Traditional to the Rational

In view of the data so far reviewed, the party system of this country may well be moving in some greater degree than formerly from the traditional to the rational. This is a process going on throughout the world in the underdeveloped countries. Most countries seem to be politically underdeveloped, and there are times when it is possible to suspect that even the United States belongs in this category.

In a rational world, political philosophers might suppose that political life would be primarily concerned with a politics of issues. That, at least, was the supposition of the Committee on Political Parties in its report of 1950, *Toward a More Responsible Two-Party System.* In the years since that report was published, the system seems to have moved at least slightly in the direction favored by the Committee; and the prospects for a further movement in

that direction now seem moderately favorable. If this is indeed the case, the workings of the competitive impulse in politics can be given most of the credit. Minority major parties that seriously seek to become competitive within the two-party system have found it expedient in state after state to develop a strong interest in issues—an interest that is practical and strategic, rather than doctrinaire, but one that nonetheless assists in the education of voter opinion, and that may eventually produce a marked increase in voter turn-out—especially in those states where turn-out has traditionally been low.

It has been assumed much too often in the one-party states and localities that it is necessary to join the dominant party in order to be politically effective. This may have been true thirty or forty years ago, but it does not seem to be true any longer. The situation has changed to the point where many of the greatest political opportunities of the future are probably now available in minority party situations where the smaller of the two major parties is still greatly outnumbered. The exploitation of these opportunities will require an eye for issues and a willingness to open them up for public debate. The process can be assisted by help from the central party headquarters when the central staffs are sufficiently vigorous and alert, but often it has proceeded even more fully on the strength of local impulses. The game of competitive politics can be initiated at any level, and it is a game in which any number can play. Fortunately it is a game in which all who participate can obtain some reward, and in which it is to the nation's interest for many to be engaged.